THE NAZI OLYMPICS

SPORT AND SOCIETY

Series Editors
Benjamin G. Rader
Randy Roberts

A list of books in the series appears at the end of this book.

The Nazi Olympics

Sport, Politics, and Appeasement in the 1930s

EDITED BY ARND KRÜGER AND
WILLIAM MURRAY

UNIVERSITY OF ILLINOIS PRESS
URBANA AND CHICAGO

© 2003 by the Board of Trustees
of the University of Illinois
All rights reserved
Manufactured in the United States of America
C 5 4 3 2 1

∞ This book is printed on acid-free paper.

Library of Congress Cataloging-in-Publication Data
The Nazi Olympics : sport, politics, and appeasement in the 1930s /
edited by Arnd Krüger and William Murray.
p.   cm. — (Sport and society)
ISBN 0-252-02815-5 (cloth : alk. paper)
1. Olympic Games (11th : 1936 : Berlin, Germany)
2. Olympics—Political aspects—Germany—History—1933–1945.
I. Krüger, Arnd. II. Murray, W. J. (William J.) III. Series.
GV7221936.N39   2003
796.48—dc21   2002011803
Revised

CONTENTS

PREFACE AND ACKNOWLEDGMENTS

Our original intention for this book was to cover all of the forty-nine nations that were represented at the Olympic Games in Germany in 1936, better known as the Nazi Olympics. This was overly ambitious, so we decided to concentrate on those countries that were most prominent at the 1936 Olympics, from a political as much as a sporting point of view. On both counts, these were the countries most deeply involved in the politics of compromising with the demands of the dictators, which has gone down in history as appeasement. Absent here as it was at the 1936 Olympics is the Soviet Union, ignored as much by the organizers of Olympic sport as it was by the leaders of the democracies in their relationships with the dictators.

These major countries are represented in the first six chapters: Germany and its preparation for a propaganda triumph; the United States and the crucial battle over its participation; Britain as the custodian of the amateur ideal; France as the birthplace of Coubertin and the Declaration of the Rights of Man; and Germany's two allies with whom it would form the Axis, Italy and Japan. Thereafter our choice fell on the Scandanavian countries, where sport and sports scholarship are highly advanced and whose people might have represented the Aryan ideal of the Nazis but whose social and political ideals were poles apart. These countries (and Finland) were also particularly involved in the Winter Olympics, which the Nazis used as a dress rehearsal for the main event in August. The absence of chapters on the Central and Eastern European powers of the 1930s, in particular Czechoslovakia, Hungary, and Poland, which were at the center of sporting and political affairs, is perhaps to be regretted. But this is in part a reflection of the level of sport scholarship in countries only recently released from the constraints of Communist conformity. Austria is also missing. Scholarship here has tended to ignore the Nazi Olympics, and it is only recently that scholars have been prepared to see Austria as a willing accomplice rather than a victim of the Anschluss of 1938. The Soviet Union, as the silent but ever-present observer of what was happening in the world of bourgeois sport, warrants inclusion, but its influence was felt mainly through its relations with the various international workers' sports organizations. The literature on this is extensive and is covered by the works of Krüger and Riordan referred to in the bibliographic essay at the end of the book.

The Iberian countries are not included here. Portugal was peripheral not only geographically but also in sport and politics. Spain, however, is of special interest in its attempt to organize a "popular" Workers Olympics in Barcelona as a "festival of fraternity," in contrast to the "fascist festival" in Berlin. The later Franco years have taken the interests of most recent sports historiography on Spain: 1936 has still to be explored more thoroughly.

Asia, Africa, and Latin America were all present in Germany in 1936, but apart from Japan we have not included specialist studies on particular countries from these vast geographical areas. Although the success of the Latin American countries was modest in 1936, they still warrant a book to themselves on the subject. In the 1930s most Asian and African countries related to Europe more by colonial connections than independent national activities. For the countries of the British Empire and Commonwealth, readers should refer to the works cited in the bibliographic essay.

Serious commentators on world affairs have often dismissed sport as a trivial pursuit. This may be so, but of all the trivialities in the world, today as yesterday, it is clearly the most important. Moreover, this very triviality provides an excellent measure of public opinion. The Olympic Games of 1936 were not the vast global enterprise they are today, but they were a world event that brought together the problems of the world in a single competition involving the countries that were to be the most important actors in the war to come. It is for this reason that the Nazi Olympics represent an inexhaustible source of interest, as much for the general historian as for the specialist in sports history.

* * *

It would have been impossible to fulfill the task of bringing this book to a conclusion without the help of many people. We would like to thank the Department of History at La Trobe University and the Institut für Sportwissenschaften at the Georg-August-Universität Göttingen for their institutional support and help. We would also like to thank Margrete Bartels, Nicole Beckedorf, Carol Curtis, Dr. Angela Daalmann, Brigitte Junge, John Horacek, Gwen Pache, Petra Prahl, Dr. Swantje Scharenberg, Heather Wilkie, Heidi Zogbaum, and the staff of the Borchardt Library at La Trobe University and the State and University Library of Göttingen, as well as our colleagues and students in Australia and Germany, who in classes and at international conferences have shared our enthusiasm for a topic we are so deeply involved in.

This book has taken longer to complete than we had anticipated. Contributions were written in more than ten languages other than English, some of which were translated into English by the authors, some were translated by Arnd

Krüger, and all were given their final form by William Murray. In this regard, we aimed at accuracy and readability without losing the flavor of the original. It is said that "translation is treason," but we hope we have been as faithful as possible to the original contributions. There was also the problem of the publisher, authors, and editors living on four different continents, and despite the globalized world we live in today, there still remain more problems in electronic and other forms of communication than we had anticipated. We have appreciated the cooperation and the patience of everyone involved with this project and would like to thank them for this.

THE NAZI OLYMPICS

INTRODUCTION

William Murray

The 1936 Olympic Games are invariably remembered as the Nazi Olympics, sponsored as they were by the Hitler regime, but even without the political odium that hung over them these Games would have been a landmark event in the history of sport. The Eleventh Olympiad of the modern era, awarded to the democratic Weimar Republic of Germany in 1931 and hosted by the dictatorship of the Third Reich in 1936 (the Winter Games in Garmisch-Partenkirchen in February and the Summer Games in Berlin with the sailing events in Kiel in August), came at a key moment in the development of international sporting competition. So great was the appeal of hosting a major sports event that even such renowned nonsports people as Hitler and Goebbels saw its potential. International sport did not play a major role in *Mein Kampf* or in Hitler's speeches, but as in other spheres he was happy to let his disciples outdo each other in interpreting what his wishes might be. In sport this allowed some of his more fanatical followers to preach a doctrine that would have brought an end to Olympic competition. Hitler himself had no wish to see proud "Aryans" competing with their racial inferiors, and as he later revealed to Albert Speer, in the Greater Germany of the future there would be only "Aryan Games," which would be held in Nürnberg under German rules. At the beginning of his dictatorship, however, Hitler had to establish his regime in the eyes of the world and the German people. It was only by overcoming his distaste for international competition without distinctions of race that Germany was allowed to retain the right to host the 1936 Olympics—yet the German organizers always kept open the option to stage purely German Games in case of a major international boycott.

Hitler was appointed chancellor of the already tottering Weimar Republic on January 30, 1933, and he wasted no time in finishing it off. Once in power, he immediately set about making a reality of the program from which he had hardly deviated in the past and to which he would continue to adhere in the future. In his domestic policies Hitler soon established his dictatorship and acted in accordance with his beliefs in regard to those races he regarded as subhuman, excluding Jews in particular from normal contact with fellow Germans, at work or on the sports fields. Among other indignities, Jews were not permitted to ride German horses, as this most German of all animals should not suffer from the contact, nor were Jews permitted to use public swimming pools—the water would have to be changed once somebody Jewish had been in it.

Abroad Hitler made no secret of his expansionist ambitions, which he was to carry out with contempt for the democracies. In sport, however, he had no clearly stated policy, although his racism had obvious implications for any nation hosting the Olympic Games. The worried members of the International Olympic Committee (IOC), however, soon had their fears put to rest when Hitler announced that he would hold the Games in accordance with IOC rules. Not only would he do so, but he would do so in a manner that befitted the "New Germany," sparing no expense to ensure that the best face of the Reich was put before the world when it visited Germany in 1936. The IOC was relieved, and the Nazis went on to make of the Games one of their greatest propaganda successes.

Even to individuals without a great interest in sport, it was clear in the 1930s that mass sport was part of the wave of the future, although it was the dictators who initially took advantage of this as a deliberate instrument of foreign and domestic policy. Boxing, cycling, and soccer were the three most popular sports at the time, and as a consequence their best representatives had turned professional and so could not take part in the Olympic Games. But even the Games themselves were expanding beyond the amateur ideals of the handful of aristocrats and millionaires who had guided their progress since they were revived by the baron de Coubertin in 1896. Coubertin had wanted the Games to be huge and splendid, to assure a prestige for the Olympics in modern times comparable to that which they had had in antiquity. The Games of 1936 were a further step in this direction, as the Summer Games were the first with over three million spectators, while the Los Angeles Games of 1932 had been the first with more than a million. In part, the Olympic Games were a victim of their own success, growing in size as they increased in popularity and thus becoming more interesting for politicians who looked for a stage for themselves and their politics. With technological developments in the 1930s, the Games had become a genuinely international event. By 1936 they were accessible to an audience of hitherto undreamed-of proportions. Three hundred million people followed the Berlin Games on the radio.

The 1930s represents one of the three major stages in the development of sport from its beginnings as a preindustrial village pastime to a global event of universal proportions. The earliest records of human behavior reveal that people have always shared a passion for physical contests. Between the industrialization of the late nineteenth century, which brought sport into the modern era, and the communications revolutions of the 1980s, which took sport into the postmodern era, the 1930s was the decade in which sport was poised between an older world of amateurism and elitism and the new world of commercialized mass sport.

Human beings, men more than women, have always exhibited a need to play, to compete, and to watch others do the same. They have run and jumped, thrown objects and maneuvered balls of various sorts with different parts of their bodies. At times this has been for personal amusement, often to show off, to win the esteem of peers, or to compete against them. The most skillful in such endeavors have won the admiration of their fellows and become the pride of their local region, gaining glory and prizes for their feats against rivals from other villages and regions. This constant in human behavior has been contained only by the technological restraints on its expression: the transportation of participants or spectators to the performance venue and the means to report the event to a wider public. Thus, in the days before rapid transportation and cheap newspapers, sport was restricted to village games and contests between locals, discussed mainly in proximity to the game and recalled in folk memory rather than written reports. By the late nineteenth century the introduction of steam-powered transportation and electrical illumination and communication meant that competitions could be held on a national basis or on a cross-town basis in the large urban conglomerates that were springing up in various parts of the industrialized world. At the same time that trains, trams, and, to a lesser degree, the internal combustion engine allowed cricket matches, race meetings, and football matches to be held on an ever-expanding basis, improvements in mass communication—the press, the telephone, and cable—allowed such events to be broadcast to a wide public within a few hours. In Britain and other regions of the English-speaking world, such developments were generally at least one generation in advance of the European continent and other industrialized areas.

By the 1920s, the technology that was in place to allow further expansion of sports was aided, as in the creation of the weekend in Britain from the 1880s, by the introduction of reduced hours of employment from 1919 in most European countries. It was in the 1930s, however, that sport as a mass phenomenon became widespread. In Europe, trains and trams linked nations and major cities, while coach travel allowed large groups to take advantage of the ever-improving road systems. Steam travel that allowed ships to cross the oceans had not changed much since the late nineteenth century, but the airplane, which had been a curiosity at the beginning of the century, was recognized as a force for the future. In 1928 a convention on warfare unsuccessfully tried to outlaw the use of poison gas being dropped from the air in any future conflict. The use of photos in newspapers and journals was becoming increasingly important, but it was in moving images and sound that the major technological revolutions were taking place.

Cinema made its debut in 1896, and by the 1920s it had become a major leisure pastime in most modern societies, while the addition of sound after 1927 prepared the way for the boom in the cinema industry in the 1930s. In the cinema, as in the press, images of sport were always sure to elicit the greatest public interest, along with sex and the thirties' equivalent of soaps. Radio was available to a privileged few in the early 1920s, but by the 1930s it was present in nearly every home in the Western world, an essential part of the furniture and a means of keeping in touch with current affairs, such as the progress of local sporting heroes: sports broadcasting did as much to further interest in sport as it did to seal the success of the revolutionary new medium. From 1927 the first hazy images of television were reproduced in laboratories, and in 1936 they were available to a public audience, albeit restricted and with images so poor that some contemporary critics dismissed it as a passing fancy. Others thought differently, but at the 1936 Olympics the greatest single medium in the transformation of sport was still a curiosity.

The commerce and politics that are ever-present in sports took on an added significance with the development of mass sport, as it provided an expanded market and a potential source of indoctrination. The new totalitarian dictatorships differed from their nineteenth-century counterparts in that they actively sought to involve the ordinary people. Leading the way was Mussolini and his Fascist glorification of adolescent values, which found a perfect outlet in sport. Stalin stood aloof from relations with Europe, but, faced by the improbable task of holding together his new multinational empire based on the principle if not the practice of international socialism, he found an ally in sports as a means of preparing for national defense and building a sense of ideological solidarity. Eclipsing both of these dictators in the political use of sports, Hitler's glorification of the body and delight in violent competition reached near perfection before arriving at its logical conclusion in the "Götterdämmerung" of 1945.

The democracies might have disdained the Fascist use of sport for political ends, but they allowed commerce to make its inevitable inroads into a market that was too obvious to be missed. With the exception of cycling, very little of this affected the sports themselves. Food and drink stalls inside or near stadiums, pubs, cafes, or restaurants in the locality, and the sale of favors to show support for a particular team or country were welcomed by the spectators; so, too, was the provision of transport to games, in coaches or special trains, or even tourist packages such as those that were arranged for the 1934 World Cup in Italy. These were a service to fans as much as a source of profit for the organizers. Advertising was not yet the eyesore it would become: some events were named after a sponsor, but not overintrusively, and while there were invocations to use particular products, sometimes proclaimed on stand roofs or other areas around the ground, these could easily be passed over. But the greatest link between sport and the people was the press, while the press and sport lived in a symbiotic relationship, as the one provided free publicity and the other a lucrative market. In the 1930s sporting journals like *The Referee* (1886), *La Gazzetta dello Sport* (1896), *L'Auto* (1900), and *Kicker* (1920) continued to thrive, with an increasing emphasis on photographs and illustrations. But now, as had been the case in the United States and Britain for decades, newspapers decided that sport could sell papers as successfully as a brutal murder or a sordid sex scandal. With improved graphic techniques, which made possible the rapid photographic transfer of sporting events from location to paper, sport could be presented as a drama, and accuracy and objectivity gave way to titillation, the personality of the athlete rather than his or her performance, and even the life of the athlete away from the public eye.

When Coubertin founded the IOC in 1894 it was the first international multisports federation. There had been world federations in particular sports before this, cycling and ice skating having held world championships a decade previously, but the IOC became the leading authority for sports not yet represented. By 1914 all major sports had their own international sports governing body, and these looked to the IOC for guidance. In France, for instance, the Comité National des Sports (CNS) was founded in May 1908 to supervise the increasing number of sports federations in the country, and in 1911 the French Olympic Committee was founded to work closely with the CNS. Similar developments took place in other countries, and the IOC, often instrumental in forming these federations, retained a close connection with them. By 1936, nineteen international sports federations were represented in Berlin, and the leading figures in the IOC were intimately involved with most of them. Count Henri de Baillet-Latour was not only president of the IOC but also of the International Committee for Modern Pentathlon; Sigfried Edström was IOC vice president at the same time as he was president of the International Amateur Athletics Federation (IAAF), the organization that ran international track and field; Dr. Karl Ritter von Halt, Germany's representative on the IOC and the president of the Organizing Committee for the Olympic Winter Games, was at the same time president of the International Team Handball Federation. By the 1930s the membership of the IOC was composed of two distinct groups: men with a title to nobility or who at least considered themselves to be "gentlemen," and others who shared their passion for sport but whose titles to nobility were more through money than blood and who took part in the world's elite amateur body as representatives of their own national federation in a particular sport, often as participants before becoming administrators. Coubertin was both a nobleman and someone who had served as secretary general of French university sports, but he preferred to think of himself as a nobleman rather than a secretary. Both qualifications would serve him well in his efforts to make a success of the first modern Olympics.

After World War I, the work of the IOC became a less strictly amateur pursuit. It had to adapt to the more bourgeois concern for efficiency as the sheer number of those taking part presented immense logistical problems. The ideals of the noble amateur were threatened by technocrats and nationalists whose goal was to win rather than to lose with grace and good humor. The Games, originally proclaimed to glorify the liberal aristocratic ideal that enshrined the primacy of the individual, were constantly beset by the nationalism that was so evident at the Athens Games and inexorably made its impact as individuals competed for the honor of their nation and the adulation of their compatriots. This was reflected in the burgeoning national federations, which often revealed themselves to be more interested in their own athletes than the disinterested pursuit of fraternal competition between the wealthy young men of the world. Women increasingly made their claims to join men in the pursuit of fame, and the desire on the part of the national federations to win and not only to make up the numbers meant that many national Olympic Committees encouraged women as well as men to win medals for their country, regardless of their social or financial station.

The American Avery Brundage, with his big business credentials, was one of the first outsiders to break into the charmed circles of the IOC. Driven by the frustration of seeing his own potentially brilliant international career cheated by the cancellation of the Berlin Games of 1916 and by a fanatical attachment to the amateur ideal, his dogged determination to defeat the rival federations and those outside the Olympic family who called for a boycott of the Nazi Olympics paved the way for his rapid rise to the highest sporting ranks. As president of the U.S. Amateur Athletic Union (AAU) and the American Olympic Committee (AOC) he defeated the boycott proposals within his own organizations and other sporting bodies that found the Nazi attitude to sport repugnant. As a result he was rewarded with membership in the IOC in 1936. The presidency came in 1952.

The main sporting organization in the United States after the AAU was the National Collegiate Athletic Association (NCAA), but the athletes from the U.S. college system were not represented internationally. In Europe, however, nearly all of the national student sport organizations were members of the Comité International des Etudiants (CIE), an international student sports federation that was founded in 1919 and held its first competition in that year. The World Student Games were hosted by Fascist Italy in 1927 (Summer Games, Rome) and again in 1928 (Winter Games, Cortina d'Ampezzo), at Darmstadt in Weimar Germany in 1930, before returning to Fascist Italy in 1933, the Winter Games in Bardonecchia in January and the Summer Games in Turin in September. This was a form of international competition denied the U.S. athletes, whose intercollegiate competitions prepared them for the world competition that came around every four years. These student organizations were generally considered a recruiting ground for the future world sports leaders; clearly they had no objection to fascism, and they would look on Hitler's Nazi variant with a similar benevolence.

The spread of sport after the First World War led many international sports federations to form European committees, and these often split off as independent European federations. They would go on to arrange European championships, and by 1936 track and field was one of the few sports that did not have a

European championship. The European organizers of sport were able to meet in international competition more often than was feasible for their American, Asian, or Australian counterparts. It also gave the athletes from the smaller countries a chance to perform in international competitions and helped prepare them to compete against the generally more dominant U.S. athletes.

In contrast to the United States, where most sports were under the authority of the AAU, in Europe a multitude of sports represented various political, religious, and even antireligious groups. Most of these bodies cooperated with the IOC through its various national Olympic Committees, although they retained the right to run their own national and international competitions. One of the biggest of these was the Fédération Internationale Catholique d'Éducation Physique (FICEP), a union of Catholic sports clubs founded in 1911, which became one of the most powerful sports organizations in Europe. Its strength came initially from Belgium and especially France, where the Federation of French Sporting and Gymnastic Patronages (Fédération Sportive et Gymnique des Patronages de France) was founded in 1903. In 1905 it had seventy-two clubs, which blossomed to 1,763 with 180,000 active members by 1914 and almost double this on the eve of the second European war, with 3,700 clubs and six hundred thousand members in 1938.

These Catholic sporting bodies were devoted to God and country, in that order, and to combat this clerical proselytizing, especially in France, where the clash between church and state was most divisive, teachers from the secular state system of education founded organizations to keep their young charges active beyond school hours with various leisure activities, including sport. These "Petites Amicales" were inspired by the anticlerical ideals of the Republic and a moral commitment to amateurism. In the late 1920s they were brought under the French Union of Secular Physical Education Societies (Union Française des Oeuvres Laïques d'Education Physique), which by 1939 controlled five thousand clubs with 310,000 members. The Catholic response to the threat posed by the godless Republic and the blandishments it offered to young Frenchmen in their leisure time was encouraged by Pope Pius X. In 1908 he gave his blessing to all attempts by Catholic sports clubs to ensure that this important part of youth education would not be left in laic hands. In Germany the Deutsche Jugendkraft (DJK) was founded in 1920, and by 1931 it had seven thousand members in Germany. The DJK clubs had to have the local priest on the Executive Board, the association boundaries were identical with the boundaries of the bishopric, and the church encouraged its members on city councils to invest in stadia. In the 1930s the FICEP had more than two million members.

Among Protestants who had been instrumental in popularizing "Muscular Christianity" from the mid-nineteenth century, the Young Men's Christian Association (YMCA) was started in England in 1844; it spread to the United States in 1851, where it made a particular impact. By the turn of the century, American YMCAs were sending directors and workers to countries around the world in reply to the many requests for their assistance. This "foreign work," as it was called, was the origin of the YMCA World Service. Competitive sport was high on the agenda, and one result was the invention of basketball and volleyball, the creations of James Naismith, the director of the YMCA at Springfield College in Massachusetts. Protestant sports groups in various countries collaborated closely under the roof of the YMCA. The German Eichenkreuz, a union of eleven previously independent Protestant sports organizations, formed in 1921 and had 225,000 members when the Nazis came to power.

The Jews had their own version of Muscular Christianity and through Jewish sports clubs sought refuge from the slights of endemic anti-Semitic bigotry. They also sought through these clubs to show the world that they were not the "water-shy weaklings" depicted by their enemies. At the second Zionist convention in Basle in 1898, Max Nordau called for the creation of a Muscular Judaism through which the derogatory term *Judenjungen* (Jew boys) would be converted into *junge Juden* (young Jews), and from this the Zionist movement in sport was born. Nordau's plea was followed by the formation of Jewish gymnastics and sporting clubs throughout Europe, the most famous of which was Hakoah ("Force" or "Strength"), founded in Vienna in 1909. Although it was not at first welcomed by the more liberal Jews of the Austrian capital who were opposed to Zionism and preferred not to draw attention to their religion, this changed with its success. Hakoah, with its blue and white jerseys sporting the star of David, was mainly famous for its soccer team, which went on with a calculated combination of physical confrontation and rare skills to win the first Austrian professional championship in 1924. It also produced famous swimmers and weightlifters, the latter happy to be present where their comrades were swimming and ready at the slightest anti-Semitic remark to throw the offender in the pool. At the Zionist World Convention in Carlsbad in 1921, the Maccabi world organization was founded, and in 1932 it staged the First Maccabiah, the Zionist equivalent to the Olympic Games, in Tel Aviv. When German sports clubs closed their doors to Jewish members after 1933, Jewish sports clubs in Germany were the only ones that did not fall under the Nazi policy of Gleichschaltung, or absorption into the unitary state, and as a result, for a short time at least, they had an unprecedented strength in membership.

The Maccabi included people from a mixture of languages, nationalities, social classes, and ethnic origins, all committed to the ideal of returning Jews to their biblical homeland. Two other major international sports organizations had similar political and nationalist ideals: the Pan-Slavic Sokol movement and the German Turner movement. The Sokol movement set out to use physical education and sport as a means of raising Slavic consciousness and bringing the Slavs of Europe and Asia together in a single Slavic union. Founded by Dr. Miroslav Tyrs in 1862, their inspiration was drawn from the battle of the White Mountain of 1620, which destroyed the existence of the Czechs as an independent people and threatened their culture with destruction in the Thirty Years

War. It was founded to prepare what they claimed to be a politically enslaved people for complete national and political freedom; this would be done through physical strength, discipline, and harmony, with each individual prepared to sacrifice his or her interests to the common cause. Membership of the Sokols, which included children and young people of both sexes as well as adults, was restricted to Slavs, and so included Czechs, Slovaks, Poles, Croats, Serbs, and the other Slavic people whose nationhood had been submerged under the rule of the Austrian, Prussian, and Russian empires. Sokols were also founded in Britain, France, the United States, and elsewhere, and the Czech Sokols in particular fought for their independence on the side of the Entente Powers in the First World War. With the breakup of the empires at the end of the war, some of these groups achieved national status, but the Sokol organization continued to flourish, especially in Czechoslovakia, where its insistence on developing the physical, mental, and moral strength of its members was to be the basis of the democracy of the new nation created by the Treaty of Versailles. By 1930 the Czech Sokol had 630,000 members, more than the Communist and Catholic (Orel/Eagle) sports organizations to which it was opposed and that of the Social Democrats. When the Pan-Slavic Svaz slovenského Sokolstva (SSS) staged its ninth Slavic Festival in Prague (where they had been held every six years) in 1932, there were over a hundred thousand participants. It lost nothing in fervor as the threat from its Nazi neighbor increased throughout the decade. Unlike most sports organizations—other than those of the socialists and the communists—the Sokols gave a prominent role to women in its sports and its administration from the earliest days.

German emigrants, whether following the repression of the 1848 revolutions or before, invariably took with them their peculiar form of gymnastics. These were all brought together by the Gau Ausland of the Deutsche Turnerschaft (DT), which combined German Turner clubs from all over the world. They had automatic voting rights inside the German Turner organization, which applied the principle that Germans were united by bonds of blood, and this remained unaffected by generations of continuous residence in the former German colonies in Africa or among the German communities of the Americas, Australia, and other countries, including Europe. This principle of blood bonds, used by the Nazis as well as the controllers of German citizenship today, was used to encourage Germans living abroad to come back to the Fatherland, with incentives such as free study in Germany. By 1932 the DT had 1,624,000 members, making it the largest single national sports governing body. But this did include Germans from twenty countries.

The German sports organizations generally preferred gymnastics to "British games," and the more nationalist organizations refused to compete with non-Germans. They had caused Coubertin some worries at the Athens Olympics, but the nonprofessional sports organizations most opposed to the Olympic Games were those organized by the leaders of the organized workers' movements who sought to engage in the class struggle through sport. Ironically, with their commitment to amateurism and their declared goal of sport as a means of cementing fraternal friendship, in principle and often in practice they were closer to the original ideals of the Olympic Games than most sports organizations. They were also the only groups to support unequivocally a boycott of the Nazi Olympics.

The largest workers' sports organizations were connected to the Social Democratic and Communist movements, the division coming after the Bolshevik Revolution of 1917. Before this the Socialist Worker Sport International (SWSI) had been founded in Gent, Belgium, in 1913, and refounded in Lucerne, Switzerland, in 1920. It was known as the Lucerne Sports International until it reverted to the SWSI in 1927. From 1921 it was confronted by a bitter rival in the Red Sports International, the body committed to the Communists and effectively directed from Moscow, although technically under the control of national organizations, especially the German Communists. This was a reflection of the split in the international socialist movement after the Bolsheviks came to power in Russia and set about establishing their Union of Soviet Republics and demanding that the workers of the world follow their example. The Comintern issued the Twenty-one Conditions that determined who could be members of the Communist International; those who accepted them became Communists, while those who refused to submit to Moscow domination called themselves socialists. Until 1934 and the policy of the Popular Front against fascism, these two groups in search of workers' souls were bitterly at war with each other, the Communists in particular doing all they could to win the workers in the socialist sports bodies away from their leaders, whom they denounced as bourgeois-reformist traitors. This Comintern policy lasted until Stalin realized that nazism was not a passing phase and Japanese aggression on his eastern border placed the Soviet Union between two deadly enemies.

The socialists had the most members, and by 1931 the SWSI had 2.6 million members in twenty-three countries. The largest national federation was in Germany, with 1.2 million members; the smallest was in the United States, with 697 members in twelve clubs. In some of the traditional workers' sports like weightlifting and wrestling the results of the worker sportsmen were as good as those of the "bourgeois" sports federations, but for talented working-class athletes the ban on competition with bourgeois federations was more likely to drive them out of the workers' organizations into others where their talent could be tested at the highest level. Since there was as yet no copyright on the word "Olympics," the socialists staged their own Olympic Games. The First Workers' Olympics took place in Frankfurt, Germany, in 1925, with more than 150,000 participants. Workers' sports, in contrast to the official Olympics, tried to involve as many as possible and not only the wealthy. Moreover, in deliberate defiance of the ban on Germany at the Olympic Games of 1920 and 1924, the SWSI was happy to stage their Games in Germany under the slogan "No More

War." The Second Workers' Olympics took place in Vienna in 1931 with more than a hundred thousand participants.

The Soviet-dominated RSI was formed in 1921, and although a Spartakiad had been organized in Prague a few weeks before the formation of the RSI, it was not until 1928 that the Soviet Union staged its first massive Spartakiad, the winter games held in Norway in February, the summer games in Moscow, a counterattraction to the socialist and bourgeois Olympics. The second Spartakiad planned for Berlin in 1931 was banned and had to be transferred to Moscow, and in 1934 the Moscow Spartakiad was replaced with a Rassemblement Sportif International (International Sporting Gathering) held in Paris as part of the attempts by the Soviet government to implement its Popular Front policy by bringing communist and socialist sports bodies together in one organization. While the union of socialist and communist worker sports was successful at the national level, at the international level the RSI and the SWSI never amalgamated. The Soviets did take part in the third Workers' Olympics held in Antwerp, Belgium, in 1937, however, where they displayed a fetish for competition and winning medals that previously they had dismissed as bourgeois egoism. Membership of the RSI is difficult to determine, as statistics coming out of the Soviet Union were never exact barometers of truth, but it is likely that there were slightly more than one million. However that may be, the monthly *Communist International* recognized in August 1937 that the communists had been tardy in trying to win the workers over to sport: it lamented that while an estimated fifty million workers were involved in sport in the capitalist countries, a mere half-million workers were involved in workers' sport.

While the socialists and communists did not encourage sporting competition with each other before 1934, they were equally adamant that their members completely shun all bourgeois sport. In practice, of course, talented workers were the backbone of professional or commercial sport, as the workers' sports leaders were eventually forced to admit. With the policies of the Popular Front, and while commercial or professional sport was still frowned upon, workers were encouraged to seek competition with the bourgeois federation, even stretching out a hand to the Catholics, a gesture that was not always welcomed. Coubertin, however, just as he was not as fanatical as Brundage in regard to amateurism, was not opposed to bringing the workers into his own Olympic family, even trying to win over at least the SWSI in what has been called a Second Crusade. Indeed, when Coubertin died just over a year after the Nazi Olympics, he was accorded some warm praise in the Communist press.

This was the ever-widening world of sport that awaited the organizers of the 1936 Olympic Games. Few of the problems regarding the Olympic Games in 1936 were new; what was different was their scale and intensity. Never before had an Olympic Games been subjected to such widespread media scrutiny, and never before had they been anticipated with so much popular fervor. Commerce, politics, and nationalism had all made their presence felt in Athens in 1896, but very little of this got beyond the borders of Greece except for short notices in the press of the more successful countries in that remarkably successful debut of the modern Olympics. They would reappear in increasing volume and in-trusiveness in subsequent Olympics, but sport still dominated the proceedings, despite the gloomy editorial in *The Times* of July 22, 1924, commenting on the recently completed Paris Olympics and claiming that the world was not yet ready for the brotherhood of nations that would form a "bulwark against the outbreak of all international animosities." The Amsterdam Olympics of 1928 passed with-out serious incident, while those of 1932 in California were held in the depths of a disastrous depression in a faraway country about which most Europeans knew little and cared even less. That was changing rapidly, as Hollywood began to flood the popular culture of the Western world, and the United States pre-pared for one of the few events in which it was prepared to present itself before the world beyond the Americas: the Olympic Games.

In 1930 the first World Cup in soccer was held in Uruguay, a major professional competition that would come to rival the Olympics, its popularity based on a game with a particular appeal to people regardless of their social standing. Be-fore the 1930s the spectators at the Olympic Games had been predominantly middle-class, and the Games themselves still retained the cachet that the followers of Coubertin hoped it would never lose, that of a competition for gentlemen of preferably European origins. The amateur principles of the Games kept the poor at bay, although competitors from unprivileged backgrounds were coming in-creasingly into prominence, and despite the male chauvinism of most of its members, the IOC reluctantly had to permit women to participate in more events at each succeeding Olympiad—and with increasing public approval. Some of the stars of 1936 were women, from Sonia Henie, the ice-skating film star, or Eleanor Holm, the glamorous swimmer who was expelled before the Games began for being too much of a woman, to those who participated in track and field, about whose actual gender the press liked to speculate. Press, radio, and film would be there not for the first time, but for the first time in numbers that reflected the worldwide interest in the event and, in the case of radio, providing direct com-mentaries beyond national boundaries. Most of this interest was sporting, but the politics could not be ignored, and for the first time a sports event was cov-ered by substantial numbers of political as well as sports reporters. The notion so cherished by the democracies that "sport and politics do not mix" was becom-ing increasingly hard to sustain and was challenged by movements in several countries calling for a boycott of the Games being organized by Nazi Germany. This challenge came mainly from liberal and left-wing groups and occasional voices of conscience from the Right—the workers' movement, in its various forms, conducted a sustained campaign against the "fascist festival."

This is the theme of the chapters that follow. We open with the host nation itself, aware of the odium it had brought on itself but anxious to convince the world that it would run the Games in the spirit in which they had been founded.

The biggest threat to the hosts was the United States, the world's largest democracy, a nation with a powerful Jewish minority and without whom the Games could not be considered a truly world event. Great Britain was still regarded in most sporting countries as the home of sport and the custodian of the amateur ideal; as such, its attitude to the 1936 Games was important, but more for moral approbation than for the performances of its athletes. Britain's former colonies, now part of the empire, could provide high-quality competition, but they were no longer under imperial control. Canada, Australia, New Zealand, and (white) South Africa decided for themselves whether or not to go to Berlin. Unlike France, which drew freely from its colonies to provide athletes of color to help it win medals, Britain made no effort to profit from its nonwhite subjects.

France, too, had a special place in the Olympic theater, as the birthplace of the baron de Coubertin, although it was one of the baron's lasting grievances that he was more admired outside France than he was by his own countrymen. France did not expect to do well in the 1936 Olympics, but more so even than Great Britain, its partner in the appeasement of the dictators, its political relations with an always difficult and once again threatening neighbor were vital.

The first chapters look at the organization of the Games by the host nation and the threats that might have been expected to come from the three most powerful democracies. It was in the year of the German Olympics that the Nazi government sealed its growing friendship with Italy and Japan, preparing the way for the much more spectacular international competition to follow. It was France and Britain's criticism of Mussolini's invasion of Ethiopia that helped drive him into the arms of the Führer, and British and U.S. objections to Japan's expansionist role in the Pacific encouraged Japan to seek an alliance with its fellow militarists in Europe, but regardless of their inevitability, all these high-powered political negotiations were aided by the cover of the Olympic Games.

Before the Games began, Italy and Japan made it clear that they stood firmly behind the Nazi organization, and much of the publicity surrounding preparations for the Games emphasized the friendly relations they had with each other and the respect in which they were held by the other competing nations. Indeed, the biggest potential conflict between them was whether Italy or Japan would be granted the 1940 Games, with Japan particularly anxious to stage these Games as they were to be held in the year in which it would celebrate the foundation of the empire twenty-six hundred years years before.

The other European countries reacted to the Games depending on their proximity to Germany and the politics of the regime. In the Scandinavian countries and the smaller democracies, trade and the threat posed by a more powerful neighbor clouded the purely sporting issue. In some ways this was further complicated when the most vigorous opposition to taking part in the Nazi Games came from the Communists and the trade unions, bigger threats to the moral order than the Nazis in some eyes. In all of these countries, however, as in the appeasing countries in general, strong voices of opposition were heard among the conservatives, and each country's reaction reflected its particular culture. By 1936 most of Southern, Central, and Eastern Europe was under some form of dictatorship, and few of these countries had moral objections to a regime that many of them admired. Latin America, Asia, and Africa sent representatives to Germany, and while this gave a genuinely global quality to the Games, these countries had little chance of influencing events in Europe. The one country that did have the power and numbers to affect the situation was the Soviet Union, but in 1936 Stalin was unprepared to put the reputation of his federation of socialist republics under the spotlight of international competition and refused to allow his sports bodies to join any bourgeois federations. Failure in sport would reflect badly on the great socialist experiment, but it is unlikely that he would have been issued an invitation to take part if he had shown a wish to do so. The democracies were no more willing to engage the Soviet Union in sporting events than they were to join it in a political pact to protect themselves against the Fascists.

The failure or unwillingness to take firm action against the aggressive expansion of the Fascist powers, particularly Italy and Germany, has come to be called appeasement, a contemporary expression that at first had no pejorative overtones. Since the betrayal of Czechoslovakia by Britain and France in September 1938 and the subsequent invasions of what remained of Czechoslovakia in March 1939 and Poland in September 1939, however, appeasement has become synonymous with weakness or even cowardice. The steps to appeasement in Europe can be marked in the failure to take strong action against Mussolini over Ethiopia in October 1935, the acceptance of the militarization of the Rhineland by Germany on March 7, 1936, in violation of the recently reconfirmed Locarno Treaty, failure to intervene in the Spanish Civil War (1936–39) despite the clear violation of the "nonintervention" agreement by Italy and Germany, recognition of the Anschluss between Germany and Austria in March 1938, and finally in surrendering to Hitler's demands in regard to Czechoslovakia in September 1938. While the often willful blindness of the leaders of the democracies is easy to blame, the bulk of the people at this time remembered too well the tragedies of the recent world war, lived in fear of another, and desperately hoped that such a catastrophe would never come again. Similar faults and human frailties can be found in the sports leaders and fans within the democracies. The genuine and wholehearted enthusiasm of the German people for the Olympic Games seemed to be an indicator that the people of Germany wanted to live in peace and friendship with the rest of the world and that even its leaders had not completely abandoned the comity of civilized nations. For the three months of the "Olympic pause," when the darker aspects of the regime were cast into the background, ordinary Germans could regain their common humanity and meet and converse with foreigners regardless of their ethnic or religious background. For some Jews, the temporary relief brought a modicum of joy into an otherwise bleak existence. The most optimistic could believe that Germany was playing by the rules and that another holocaust of young lives as had blighted Europe in the most inappropriately named "Great War" would never be repeated. Nevertheless, and whatever the motives, the willingness of the rest of the world to play games with Germany in 1936 was an act of appeasement, even if the full evil of the regime was still to unfold. However that may be, the attitudes of the countries that took part in the Nazi Olympics is a powerful indicator of the state of public opinion on the eve of one of the world's greatest tragedies.

CHAPTER 1

Germany:
The Propaganda Machine

Arnd Krüger

The Olympic Games of 1936 are best known as the Nazi Olympics, yet many of the features that distinguished these Games were well established at that time and would become even more familiar in the future. Long before the Nazis came to power in Germany in January 1933, Germans had been used to their government involving itself in areas that elsewhere were the province of the private sphere. This Sonderweg, the way in which Germany took a radically different course from other European countries, could be seen in the German interpretation of Social Darwinism: while countries like Great Britain and the United States saw this as survival of the fittest individual,[1] in Germany it was interpreted as the survival of the fittest race.

The German state also determined the form of physical education that would apply in Germany. Through the Prussian army and the Prussian school system, this was taken up directly by the Prussian Parliament. German Turnen won the day in 1863 against Swedish gymnastics, and thus physical education, Turnen, and sport were taught in the context of national education, not health education as in other Central European countries.[2]

Germany had taken part in each Olympics since 1896, and when Berlin was awarded the 1916 Games, the national government undertook not only the financial guarantees to underwrite the cost of the event, as was done in other countries, but went even further and paid for the selection and preparation of the athletes, a path the United States would not take until 1978.

The intervention of the state was wholeheartedly approved by two individuals who became prominent as organizers of the 1936 Olympics: Theodor Lewald and Carl Diem. Lewald, the government official responsible to the minister of the interior in Parliament, persuaded the government to take an active interest in the preparations for the Berlin Games of 1916, urging that in spite of its intrusion on state rights, the greater interest of the nation as a whole to be properly represented internationally was at stake. He showed that international sport ought to be treated like a world trade exhibition and thus should be heavily subsidized by the Reich. National coaches were hired, including a prominent track and field coach from the United States. Selection trials were held and intensive training camps were organized to prepare the best athletes under the best coaches to present the best possible image of the regime. The young Carl Diem was the press secretary of the national Olympic Committee at the time. A high school dropout who was trained in commerce, he became the full-time administrator in charge of the preparation of the athletes and later of the Olympic Games of 1916.[3] Twenty years later the team of Lewald and Diem was again in charge.

The First World War put an end to the preparation of the athletes, but the ground rules were in place for a government-sponsored elite sport system. The Swedes invented the state amateur when they called their able-bodied athletes into national service, thus staying within the rules and giving their athletes a chance to prepare full-time for the Games. Germany followed that example.[4]

Setting the Stage

Germany was awarded the Olympic Games of 1936 in a showdown vote against Barcelona in 1931. Lewald had duly impressed the IOC when it had met in Berlin in 1930 and had used his far-reaching connections to influence IOC members. Even Diem, who was not known to be modest when it came to claiming his own glory, had to confess that it was Lewald and Lewald alone who had brought the Games to Germany. In fact, Diem had advised not to apply for the Games yet, as Germany had been excluded from the Olympic family after World War I and was permitted to participate for the first time after the war in 1928. Lewald knew better. One year after becoming an IOC member, he was elected to the executive board.[5] From this inside position he applied and won.[6]

The German Olympic movement was firmly in the hands of representatives of the bourgeois sports movement at that time, most notably Lewald and Diem. Lewald—who was undersecretary of state when he retired from government service in 1921[7]—became the president of the German Sports Federation and the national Olympic Committee, and from 1926 onward he was a member of the IOC,[8] while Carl Diem was the full-time administrator and acting director of the German Academy of Physical Education (with an honorary doctorate in medicine). There were others: men like Karl Ritter von Halt,[9] a member of the IOC and the president of the German Track and Field Federation, a former Olympian and a banker by profession. There was no separate Nazi sport organization. Although the Nazis used sport for their paramilitary storm troopers to get them fit,[10] no Nazi had built himself up as a "natural" choice as a national sports leader. Physical education and sport seemed to serve too many conflicting purposes.[11] There were, however, separate Catholic, Jewish, Protestant, Social-Democratic, and Communist sport movements.[12] As the Nazi newspaper *Völkischer Beobachter* carried the news services of the Deutscher Turnerbund, an anti-Semitic Turner organization that had left the mainstream Turner movement, the impression was created that the Nazis were following that organization, one that was firmly opposed to competitive sport and resented athletic meets with "non-Aryans." During the 1932 Olympics, the IOC executive board asked Ritter von Halt to inquire from Hitler whether the Olympic Games could properly take place should the Nazis be in power by 1936. Von Halt, who was close to some of Hitler's best friends and later became a high-ranking Nazi himself,[13] talked to the Nazi leader and got Hitler's approval that if he was in power by then he would not interfere with the Olympic Games or take action against Negro or Jewish competitors on other teams.

This was a hypothetical question in the summer of 1932, as the Nazis, while by far the largest party in the Reichstag, were well short of a majority; this changed dramatically by the end of the year when, on January 30, 1933, Hitler was appointed chancellor of a Nazi-conservative coalition government. Lewald, a Protestant of Jewish decent on his father's side, was worried, however, that the Nazis might soon win complete power. As a smart lawyer he formed an Organizing Committee (OC) for the 1936 Olympics as a separate nonprofit society three days before Hitler's appointment by the president of the Republic, Hindenburg. Although the registration of such a nonprofit organization would normally take six weeks, Lewald was well-enough connected to achieve this in an hour. He created this independent entity with personal members so that if the Nazis won the elections, he and Diem might be dismissed from other elective sports functions but not from their "private" organizing committee. He registered the new society immediately in the belief that any new government would respect the German legal system, as had happened in the German Revolution of 1918, in which Lewald had been at the center. He had personally written the declaration of abdication of the last imperial government and handled the transaction from an imperial to a democratic government.[14] As it turned out, Lewald had been correct in his assumptions.

That no one really knew the Nazi position in sports is best exemplified by the interviews published in *Forum*, the journal of the students of the Berlin Physical Education Academy, in the winter of 1932–33.[15] They asked several prominent sport leaders what they expected for 1933. Many foresaw a Nazi government, but everyone expected a different sport system. Carl Krümmel,[16] Ritter von Halt, and others close to the old Munich ranks of the Nazi party expected a Nazi government to follow the lead of the Italian Fascists with their strong state support for sport, centralized and geared toward successful international competition to show not only pride and commitment to the Fatherland but also fitness and ability. The surprising success of the Italian athletes at the Los Angeles Olympics, coming second, with Germany seventh, led to them being called "Mussolini's Boys" by the American press.[17] The Turner leadership expected to have a powerful role under a Nazi government and so backed them in their bid for power, but the Nazis wanted a strong organization that stayed away from the old quarrels between the physical exercise systems.[18]

One of the first acts of the Nazis was to install for the first time a Minister for Volksaufklärung und Propaganda, (popular enlightenment and propaganda) better known as Promi,[19] and later a national sports leader, the Reichssportführer, to guarantee the influence of the Nazi state. Krümmel, who became responsible for school and university sport within the new government, was proven correct: the Nazis at first followed the Italian model in sport, cooperating with the international sports organization. Augusto Turati, the general secretary of the Fascist party of Italy and an ardent fencer, had even been a member of the IOC. Hans von Tschammer und Osten, a brutal regional leader in the Brown Shirts, better known as the SA (Sturmabteilung) and an elected member of Parliament for the central German district of Anhalt, whose storm troopers had killed several workers' sportsmen and children, was made responsible for all sports in the newly created office of Reichssportführer. At the same time he was made a government official in the Ministry of the Interior—where elite sport was traditionally located in Germany. He eventually rose to become undersecretary of state.[20]

Joseph Goebbels, a Ph.D. in German studies, had only been minister of the Promi for five days when he received Theodor Lewald, who explained to him the propaganda potential of the Olympic Games. The seventy-three-year-old had influential friends in all ministries, as he had been responsible for the selection and training of most of the young lawyers in government service for a ten-year period, and as a result he was admitted to the new ministry—although Goebbels seemed to have more pressing things to do than to look after a sport meet.[21] Lewald convinced Goebbels that the Olympic Games should have first priority in his young and growing ministry.[22] This was surprising, as neither Goebbels nor Hitler were known to be interested in sports, in contrast to Mussolini, their idol, who was a true all-round athlete.[23]

But Goebbels understood well that having power was only half of the problem: you also had to win the heart of the people. Sport was one way to achieve this, and eventually his ministry had eleven sections dealing with sport.[24] In assuring Nazi hegemony, a culture of consent[25] was reached to offset the more brutal and coercive elements of the regime: a growing movie industry,[26] cheap holidays,[27] successful sports for national pride, and other forms of popular entertainment. But the Nazis also manipulated language, resorting to euphemism to conceal harsh realities. The law to expel all Jews (and those who were married to Jews and refused to get a divorce) from government service was called the "Law to Re-establish Professionalism in the Civil Service." In the context of the Olympic Games it was obvious that the Olympic Village for men consisted partially of existing army barracks and partially of new ones: these became the northern section of the Olympic Village.[28] Goebbels set about controlling the thinking of the people, insisting on mass participation in actions that under-scored the power of the new system.[29] Sport played a key role in his attempt to secure hegemony: it provided a sense of self-sacrifice, of courage, while display-ing the elitism of a natural order according to physical traits. Sport in this way was a secular cult of physical strength and endurance.[30] For the French sociolo-gist Jean-Marie Brohm, the Olympic elite sport system contains so many proto-fascist elements that the Olympic Games of 1936 were not perverted by the Nazis—they merely built on the inherent elements of the Olympic Games.[31] The cult of the winner and the contempt for weakness and the loser are inherent in the celebration of elite sports and much of Fascist ideology.[32]

From the start, the Nazis developed two main strategies in conjunction with the Olympic Games: to assure propaganda within Germany and to break the cultural isolation of the Reich's government by propaganda abroad. To achieve these functions a Propaganda Committee was formed under the chairmanship of a Promi official called Haegert. He had easy access to Goebbels and kept his boss informed of all matters related to the Olympic Games.[33] This committee functioned as part of the Organizing Committee that was chaired by Lewald and for which Diem as secretary general took central responsibility. In the OC, the city of Berlin, the German Railway Office, and all other official German insti-tutions that might be affected by the Olympics were represented. The Propa-ganda Committee of the OC, chaired by Haegert, became most influential in the struggle for the soul of the German people at home and the image of nazism abroad. It was this concerted propaganda effort that made the Olympic Games of Berlin the first truly modern Games. The Games also broke all spectator records. While the Olympic Games in Los Angeles in 1932 were the first to have more than one million spectators, Berlin attracted over 3.7 million. The open-ing ceremony of the Olympic Winter Games in Garmisch-Partenkirchen in 1936 had more spectators than those attending the entire Winter Games at Lake Placid in 1932.[34]

The Promi was not against Nazi terror, but it had to make it palatable at home and abroad. The Nazi government wasted no time in showing that its hatred of Jews was not merely an abstract theory, and following some brutal outrages the IOC feared that it would threaten the holding of the Games in Germany. This was therefore a matter of extreme importance at the annual meeting of the IOC in Vienna in May 1933. Choosing the site of the Winter Games was normally a formality for the host nation, but the IOC could veto this: it could thus have indicated its dislike of Nazi racial theories and apparent practices. As Germany was still represented by Lewald, von Halt, and von Mecklemburg as IOC mem-bers, with Carl Diem as their secretary, it was relatively easy for them to con-vince the IOC that everything in Germany was normal. Although they had given up their offices in the sport federations—with the exception of von Halt, who was still a Nazi and president of the Track and Field Federation—they were still the core of the OC. They readily reached a deal with the IOC that was in their mutual interest: the IOC demanded that its German members and friends maintain responsibility for the Olympics and that the Olympic rules be upheld. This included the acceptance of Jews and "Negroes" on foreign teams. In exchange the IOC guaranteed that the Olympics would not be moved from Germany and that the Winter Games would be staged in Garmisch-Partenkirchen. In this way the IOC strengthened the position of its German members.

This deal would have satisfied everybody had it not been for General Charles H. Sherrill, an IOC member for the United States, the former American ambassador to Turkey, Italy, and Argentina, and a former Ivy League sprint champion from Yale who was one of the inventors of the crouch start.[35] Although from his publications—such as his biographies of Mussolini and Atatürk—one can safely assume that he favored many elements of fascism,[36] this New York Republican insisted that "in principle German Jews *are* part of the German team" (italics added). This demand was unheard of, as it clearly interfered with the rights of a national Olympic Committee to be represented by whom it pleased. No one had demanded previously that African Americans be allowed to qualify for the American team, and those from the South had to travel to the North at their own expense to be permitted to compete in the Olympic selection meets in 1936. Lewald was so hard-pressed from both sides that he accepted this demand, and after some negotiations he came up with a statement by the undersecretary of state, Pfundtner, who was in charge of national representation through sport on a governmental level. As Lewald had held the same post until ten years before, many important officials—including Lammers, Hitler's chief of the chancellery office—were still on friendly terms with him and helped him to get a cleverly worded paper that insisted "that in principle German Jews *could be* part of the German team" (italics added). This paper was celebrated in the United States as an American success, but it was not published by the state-controlled German press. Many German government officials, including Hitler, were therefore unaware that such a paper existed.[37]

With this threat removed, the plans for the Games progressed according to schedule. Then Hitler investigated the development of the building sites and on October 5, 1933, personally changed the entire arrangement. Diem and Lewald had presented a balanced budget that they asked to have prefinanced by the government between 1933 and 1936, while income would be accrued mainly from ticket sales in 1936. They anticipated using existing facilities and enlarging the spectator space with some provisional stands to ensure that the Olympic Games would not cause a financial burden on the weak German economy. To their surprise, Hitler placed the full resources of the state behind the Olympic preparations, the first head of state to do so.[38] In this, however, he was no different from the German Parliament, which decided in 1914 that the state would fund the staging of the Olympic Games of 1916 and pay for the preparation of the athletes.

Hitler's reasoning was simple: if you have the whole world as your guests, you should present your country at its best. If you convert the stadium, you should do so permanently with natural rock in the grandiose style of the new system. Goebbels, as local party leader in Berlin and government minister, also agreed, as there was as yet no suitable space in the city for true mass demonstrations; the Olympic Stadium would fill that function.[39] In their third assumption they were wrong, however. They assumed that most of the workers would be low-skilled and could be employed under the new scheme to get the unemployed back into the workforce. The new stadium, however, the most modern in the world at the time, required a large number of highly skilled workers to meet the deadline, and so the Olympic Stadium complex turned out far more expensive than anticipated. But despite costing more than thirty times the original estimate, Hitler never backed down. After the death of Hindenburg, the German president, on August 2, 1934, Hitler became the official patron of the Games the following November.[40]

The sports organizers wasted no time in taking advantage of the situation. Carl Diem, as secretary general of the OC, increased his own salary by 300 percent for the four years in charge of the Games. The OC went on to defend the Olympics in Berlin and Garmisch-Partenkirchen against all onslaughts from abroad.[41] As von Halt's secretary said, from the time Hitler took charge in October 1933, money did not matter any more.[42]

The Nazis went on to strengthen the sport system: they introduced daily physical education in the schools, and a good basis was laid for the sports clubs. The workers' sport federations, which contained about 20 percent of the athletes in Germany, were closed down, although their members were allowed to join the normal bourgeois clubs provided they dispersed sufficiently and provided two sworn statements that they were not active "Marxists."[43] Other clubs had to abandon their religious orientation but could otherwise maintain their identity.[44] Jews were excluded from all sports clubs, which at first strengthened the Jewish sport federations, but with the increasing incidence of pogroms and political pressure, emigration figures rose, thus weakening the Jewish organizations, including those of Turnen and sport.[45]

The German Turners presented one of the major problems faced by von Tschammer and the new "coordinated" sports federation. They had a strong national tradition, which made them reluctant to compete against anybody other than Germans and their allies in the First World War. The Turners had only officially participated in the Olympic Games once, in 1904, when the St. Louis Turnverein was the organizer. By coordinating the sports movement the separatism of the Turners was forcefully ended, and they were reduced to just another sports federation.[46] All sports clubs were reorganized according to the Führer principle, which meant that their presidents were no longer freely elected by the membership but appointed from above.[47] In many cases the president in office became the new Führer, as the bourgeois sports movement on the whole was conservative, with a long tradition of selecting as representative of the club someone of the same political orientation as the local government, so that he could easily negotiate on behalf of the club. Some clubs and federations resented the appointed Führer, but they could have him replaced only by another Nazi.[48] Jews in Germany were set apart for public humiliation, but Jews from abroad were to be treated like any other guests. The Nazis did not have a monolithic structure, but this was achieved by a number of competing organizations all struggling for Hitler's approval. The sport movement was no different in that respect.

Propaganda within Germany

As the German news media were fully controlled by the Nazis, propaganda within Germany was dominated by the Promi.[49] At national press conferences, through the national news service, and in special pieces of "advice" the German newspapers were instructed what to report and how to report it. They seldom received orders to use specific wording, which assured that in the Nazi sense of the term there was still a free press.[50] The national daily press conference was the main instrument to coordinate the German press. If a news editor did not go along with the orders, he lost his job and could not get another in the culture and information business.[51]

The Promi was vexed by the contradictory nature of the Nazi regime and the Olympic ideals. The Nazis stood for German racial supremacy and militant nationalism, while the Olympics stood for international friendship and the brotherhood of nations;[52] Jews in Germany were told they were undesirables, while Jews from abroad were to be welcomed as guests. The press was ordered not to mention the Jewish origins of the athletes.[53] African Americans were little more than animals to the Nazis, who thought that they gave the American team an unfair advantage, but as with the Jews, they had to be welcomed as guests.[54] The only way the Germans could criticize the race of the U.S. visitors was to quote directly from those U.S. papers, and there were enough of them, especially in the South, who were as racist as the Nazis.[55] The first problems for the propagandists came at the Winter Games in Garmisch-Partenkirchen in Bavaria in February 1936, but the racist slurs greeting visitors were soon acted on. The Reich's minister of the interior issued the following orders to the Bavarian minister responsible for the police: "It is the explicit desire of the Führer that all signs, banners, and similar placards relating to the Jewish question are to disappear along the railway line and the road from Munich to Garmisch-Partenkirchen because of the upcoming Olympic Winter Games. This order relates also to the exhibits of *Der Stürmer*. You are requested to complete this action by January 1, 1936."[56] The SS had to make sure that these orders were respected, including the temporary and locally restricted suppression of its favorite paper.

The open intimidation of Jews in Germany was suspended, so the beating of Jews, previously reported to make the Jews look criminal and to justify their lynching, was outlawed. The order for the national press was explicit: "With respect to the upcoming Olympic Winter Games and until further notice, it is strictly prohibited to report disputes with foreigners in Germany or actual controversies with Jews. Even in local reporting such incidents are not to be mentioned under any circumstances, to avoid giving foreigners propaganda to use against Germany."[57]

The "pause" on Jew-baiting in the press remained through the Summer Games, forcing the yellow press to overlook stories of the rigorous application of the Nuremberg Laws that previously it had assiduously dwelt on. During the Summer Games a Jew was executed for alleged kidnapping, in accordance with the law, but the press could do no more than publish the story in small print and without comment.[58] The "pause" also applied to African Americans, and as late as 1937 Jesse Owens was still accorded the race-free adulation he had won in August 1936. When the leading Nazi paper *Der Angriff* went against the orders and called Owens and the other black athletes "black American auxiliaries," a phrase that was repeated in the U.S. press, it was immediately cautioned.[59] There was no such "pause" for the six hundred gypsies ("Sinti" and "Roma") in Berlin. They were deported to a camp close to the city limits to be out of sight of the tourists. This new camp was maintained until the spring of 1943, when the Berlin gypsies were deported to Auschwitz and murdered.[60] The discrimination against gypsies in German sport is a historical event that has only recently drawn the attention of researchers.[61]

Other newspapers that did not follow official instructions were promptly punished. A special issue of *Die Sonne* on the Olympics was reprimanded for quoting a lengthy section from L. Tirala's racist book on sport; it had been intended that the publication of extracts from Tirala's *Sport und Rasse* be delayed until the foreign visitors had returned home. Newspapers were not even allowed to mention the anti-Nazi exhibition being held in Amsterdam, "The Olympic Games under Dictatorship." Newspapers that performed the way the Promi wanted were selected for praise and shown as examples of the way events should be reported.[62] A prize was even offered for the best reporting of the Games, according to the Promi guidelines,[63] and individuals were presented with specially created civil honors.

The "Olympic pause," however, brought little comfort to the Christian churches, and newspapers that failed to report critically on the sexual misdemeanors on the part of some Catholic priests were hauled over the coals. Protestant opponents of the regime within the Evangelische Kirche, which generally went along with the regime, were left alone. They were even allowed to have a special tent church at the time of the Berlin Olympics. Martin Niemöller,[64] one of their most prominent pastors, pointed out in his preaching the sudden Olympic tolerance and the way in which the churches normally suffered in the daily life of the nation. The secret police carefully took note of all this but permitted the pastor to continue. It seemed less dangerous for the Nazi system to give a show of liberty than to prohibit the tent church.[65] When the weekly *Die Stimme* published a polemical commentary against the actions of the Protestant churchmen, it was confiscated within twenty-four hours and closed down for four months.

The orders given at the national press conference or sent out by cable to the newspapers were very precise: for instance, a press conference on February 19, 1936, decreed: "Helene Mayer, the well-known German fencer, has arrived today in Germany from the United States. The press is asked not to report her arrival. The only exceptions are permissible in the newspapers of Hamburg, Bremen, and Offenbach, which may carry the news because of special local interest. Commentaries about her 'non-Aryan' descent and her chances for an Olympic gold medal are undesirable."[66]

It is apparent from the orders of this body that the officials remained doubtful about their success in breaking out of Germany's cultural isolation. For this reason the option of converting the Games into an all-German competition was kept open until the last moment, at least until it was certain that the U.S. team would turn up.[67]

Similar anxieties can be seen in the way the foreign press was carefully monitored: favorable reports might have been selected for publication in the German press, while references to boycott movements were suppressed. Foreign ambassadors were left in no doubt that reports of the Games appearing in their country were carefully scrutinized, and pressure was brought to bear on them to take action against journalists in their country. Most important, the errors made at the Winter Games were carefully recorded so they could be avoided in the Summer Games. The propaganda within Germany and the propaganda abroad can be seen as a feedback system.[68] When the Berlin Games got under way and the success of the organization surrounding the Games and the athletes on the field became obvious, the German press was actually ordered to downplay German success to avoid offending the foreign guests. In the beginning, medal tables were published that showed the German superiority, but when the IOC protested, as it had banned such tables (although other countries had published them), the Nazis gave a full demonstration of their restricted press by immediately prohibiting them. Nothing, however, could conceal the fact that Germany had done better than ever before and beaten the United States in the unofficial medal count. Germany had teams and athletes in all sports, while the Americans had left out many and dominated only track and field and swimming. When the Games were over, medal tables were permitted again, and the way medals ought to be counted was explained to the editors.[69]

The German press followed a rigid public relations pattern that left little space for improvisation. Only German photographers were permitted inside the sports arenas. This had already been the case at the Amsterdam Olympics. It had been argued that the Organizing Committee had photo rights, and their photos were rigorously selected before the national and international press had a chance to take their pick. At the competition in the swim stadium, for example, Hitler had been approached and kissed by a female American fan. The German press was not sufficiently flexible to use this for public relations purposes.[70] Perhaps it was undesirable for security reasons, as it showed up an otherwise tight security system: plainclothes policeman were everywhere,[71] the foreign athletes and officials in the Olympic Village were subject to mail censorship, and there were daily police conferences to ensure close cooperation between the OC and the secret police. If these conferences were representative of the problems of police-OC interaction, then their main problem was prostitution. During the Olympic period, Berlin prostitutes were not permitted in the inner city. Many took to the woods and solicited their services to foreign Olympic officials and athletes at the fence of the Olympic Village, keen on fit bodies and/or foreign currency. For some in the daily security meetings this was a public relations problem to be watched at low key, while for others it was an ugly case of Rassenschande (racial dishonor) when "non-Aryan" Olympians used the services of the Berlin ("Aryan") prostitutes.[72]

The entire press went to great lengths to show their fellow Germans how much the foreign visitors were impressed with the new Germany. Their presence was frequently reported, except when there was a hint of anything seditious.[73] In this respect, however, the biggest trouble came from overenthusiastic Sudeten Germans, whose calls for absorption into the Reich would have to wait for a couple of years.[74] For the moment, their crude protests were overlooked. Nevertheless, the press took every opportunity to show how many of the foreign athletes were of German descent, insisting that on all occasions they be referred to by their German name: the Italian from the German-speaking area of Southern Tyrol, Giorgio Oberweger, for instance, who came in third in the discus, had to be called Georg Oberweger. Editors were solemnly warned about the crime of Entdeutschungen, the creation of un-German words.[75]

The Games were also used as a test for the implementation of a full range of audio-visual propaganda; the first live television coverage of any sports meet was in Berlin at the time of the Olympics. More important, since television was little more than a novelty at the time, was the use of the new short-wave radio transmitters. Specially established so that the German speakers in South America could tune in to the Games,[76] they could later be used for specifically political propaganda. Film was, with radio, the most immediately accessible of the mass media, and while Leni Riefenstahl's classic, *Olympia*,[77] would take two years to reach the general public, previews were readily available in newsreel and other shorts.

Inside Germany the Olympic Games of 1936 can be considered one of the emotional highlights of the Nazi period. At this time more than any other the Nazi slogan *Ein Volk, Ein Reich, Ein Führer* (one folk, one empire, one leader) was a living reality. There was almost complete approval. The German people liked their Olympic Games. This was the way Germans liked to see themselves: open to the world, tolerant, splendid hosts, perfect organizers. It was a complete sell-out.[78] The interior propaganda was so successful that until the early 1970s very little criticism was voiced against these Games inside Germany. On the sixtieth anniversary of the Winter Olympics, the mayor of Garmisch-Partenkirchen applauded them as nothing but a sporting triumph.[79]

The Olympic Games also acted as a cover to tighten sporting organizations in Germany. The Deutsche Turnerschaft, the oldest and largest German association for physical activity, was finally dissolved.[80] Old forms of greetings within the various sports organizations became a unified *Sieg Heil*. All reference to other officials had to be as *Kamerad* (comrade), and all letters had to be signed with *Heil Hitler*.[81] This helped to undermine the traditions of the various sports and helped to increase the coordinated unity of the sports organization. By 1938 all sports organizations finally became subsections of the Nazi party.[82]

On the first day of the Summer Games, all German youth organizations outside the Hitler Youth (HJ) were dissolved. This meant that sports clubs lost all members between ten and eighteen years of age. As competitive sport was run almost entirely as club sports and not as part of the educational system, the physically active youth could no longer avoid being indoctrinated by the Nazi party if they wanted to continue to participate in competitions. Although the young athletes continued to practice their sports at the club grounds, the HJ selected the coaches and youth leaders. If a coach was not sufficiently in line with nazism, he or she did not get their (often part-time) contract renewed. The club seldom objected, as the coaches were now financed by the HJ, which helped ease the financial burden of the sports clubs. But it meant that Nazi party loyalty became as important as technical skill. In the context of the Olympic Games, this total indoctrination was to be celebrated in the German press as victory of the Olympic spirit.[83]

German Propaganda Abroad

Prior to the Olympic Games, Nazi propaganda abroad had been directed at Germans in Austria, particularly with the attack on Dollfuss and the near farce following the Austrian chancellor's assassination by Austrian Nazis encouraged from Germany, and more successfully at the Saarland, which voted overwhelmingly to return to the Reich in January 1935.[84] Reaching a foreign audience beyond nearby German-speaking neighbors was a much more difficult task. There were also economic reasons to encourage as many visitors as possible.

At first it was also assumed that the Games would attract enough foreign currency to make it an economic success, but the Nazis found out that they had to invest so much in food imports to show off German well-being that more hard currency had to be spent than the tourists would actually bring into the country.[85] Specially designed public relations campaigns directed at economic leaders were cancelled, as it was assumed that they would be favorably impressed by the Games themselves.[86] They were, however, invited to a special opera evening, where they were treated as VIPs.[87]

In their glorification of the host nation, and in many other respects, the Nazis were merely continuing an established tradition at the Olympic Games. The French press in particular had blasted the 1932 Games in Los Angeles as a sustained advertisement for California and cynically looked to 1940 as a glorification of Nippon enterprise. Coubertin himself welcomed the Nazi Olympics as fulfilling his ideals and was delighted that Tokyo was to host the 1940 Games. Coubertin supported the Nazis in their effort to stage the Games—although he did not support their inhumane ideas—in an international radio address in his native French language exactly one year prior to the opening of the Berlin Games.[88] In the German translation of Coubertin's address, the founder of the modern Olympic Games sounded far more pro-Nazi than in the original.[89] It all revolved around one's opinion of the host nation, and Coubertin was either unaware or unconcerned about what the Nazis were doing in Germany.[90]

Coubertin's views were backed up by contemporary journalists like the American John Kieran[91] and historians like Otto Meyer, as well as the IOC itself.[92] Later historians have been less impressed: the German historians Hajo Bernett,[93] Hans Joachim Teichler[94] and Klaus Ullrich[95] believe that anything an evil government does is evil in itself. Nevertheless, several aspects of the 1936 Olympics have become essential parts of future Games, such as the torch relay, the Olympic bell (with the swastika) alongside the Olympic rings—a harbinger of corporate sponsorship[96]—and Hitler's invitation to "the youth of the world."

Unlike the democracies or the capitalist countries[97] the Nazis barely distinguished between advertising, persuasion, and propaganda.[98] The German press did little to emphasize the importance of the athletes initially, since they were expected to finish behind the United States, but this changed as Germany placed seventh behind Norway in the Winter Games, eight places up from the Lake Placid Games, and then went on to "win" the Summer Games, having come seventh in Los Angeles.[99]

More important, so far as upholding the rules of the Games is concerned, was the IOC stipulation that they be run by the national Olympic Committee, not the government. Lewald had a key role to play here, trying to convince the IOC that he was in charge. In fact Lewald was soon brought to order whenever he went against von Tschammer,[100] and while he might have been the link with the IOC, in Germany the national Olympic Committee was under the direct control of the Reichssportführer. No one objected when the Nazis assumed full financial responsibility for the Games.[101] To avoid criticism from the regime's many enemies abroad, Lewald was to continue to represent the Organizing Committee, "but inside Germany he had the national, moral, and legal obligation to follow the Reichssportführer."[102] Although they knew better, Lewald and Diem told their friends abroad that they were still acting according to their own free will.

The main propaganda struggle took place in the United States, as the American team had been by far the strongest in all previous Olympic Games and was neutral toward Germany. The German IOC members directed most of their declarations to the American press. Although the U.S. government was well aware of the situation in Germany and the importance of the Olympic Games, it neither interfered nor passed its knowledge along.[103] So the warning of the American consul general in Berlin that Lewald was "no longer a free agent" and did not resign but instead preferred to hoodwink his foreign friends went unnoticed.[104] Lewald, who was fluent in English and French and had lived two years in the United States when he was in charge of the German pavilions at the World Exhibitions in Chicago 1893 and St. Louis in 1904, kept in constant touch with events in North America.

The situation of the Jews in Germany was a major stumbling block, for despite the protestations of Diem and Lewald to the contrary, it was obvious that the Jews were not competing on a level playing field. Two "alibi" Jews were allowed to take part: the ice hockey player Rudi Ball at the Winter Games and the fencer Helene Mayer[105] at the Summer Games. As they were—by the Nazi definition—50 percent Jewish, as was Lewald himself, they were still permitted to represent Germany at that time. By Jewish definition, neither of them was Jewish, as only the children of Jewish women are considered Jewish. Helene Mayer was studying in California in 1936, where she had won the U.S. fencing championships. She had been an Olympic champion in 1928, placed fifth in 1932, and was generally considered one of the best foil fencers in the world. Ball left Germany to play hockey first in Switzerland, then in Italy. Both countries had rich "amateur" hockey teams for which Ball could make more money than at home—and he could stay out of the potential trouble in his Berlin home.

The real test case was Gretel Bergmann, a Stuttgart high jumper. Fully Jewish and a member of a Jewish sports club, she was nevertheless permitted to receive expert coaching at all of the training camps of the German Track and Field Federation from 1934 through 1936. She had gone to school in England and won several meets there, and she probably benefited from the pressure on the Germans to include Jewish athletes in the German team. In 1936 she won the regional championships in Württemberg with 1.60 meters (5 feet, 3 inches), a height that would have given her a medal six weeks later in the Games had she been allowed to compete, and had she repeated that performance under the pressure of the Olympic Games and a hundred thousand spectators. She was not permitted to take part in the German championships because the Jewish club to which she belonged—like all Jewish clubs—could not be part of the German Track and Field Federation. All the way to the final selection she was led to believe that she would be part of the team.[106] Von Tschammer knew better, however, and although Helene Mayer made the team, Gretel Bergmann did not. The third slot on the German team in women's high jump was kept vacant instead. As compensation she received a formal but friendly letter telling her that she had not qualified for lack of form and was offered free tickets (standing room only) for the Games. The letter was sent to her only after the American team had already left New York for Berlin, in case there were any adverse reactions.

Her coach and club officials were locked away for the duration of the Games to avoid negative press; she later emigrated to the United States while she still could.

Sherrill's efforts to get a Jew on the German team had been shown to be mere eyewash. Hitler's true feelings were revealed a year earlier, on August 24, 1935, when he insisted that he would rather replace the international Olympic Games with "purely German Olympics" than permit foreign nations to decide who should be on the German team.[107] He would not interfere with the selection process in other countries, so the IOC should not interfere in German matters.[108] Sherrill was shocked, as this contradicted the Vienna Accord. He immediately sent an urgent letter to the IOC president, Count Henri de Baillet-Latour:[109] "I am of course entirely willing to tell you everything said by the Führer on the subject, but cannot risk putting it in a letter [sent from Germany]. Entirely confidentially, and not to be repeated by you to any of our colleagues (especially not the Germans!), I urge you to talk personally with the Führer, and show him the Ministerium des Inneren June 1933 letter you received in Vienna from Berlin about exclusion of German Jews from the German 1936 team. You are in for the greatest shock of your entire life! It will be a trying test for even your remarkable tact and savoir faire; and the sooner you meet the situation, the better the hope for your success, instead of a destructive explosion."[110]

Meanwhile, Hitler was assured that the apparent concessions to Jews were only to placate foreign public opinion: the Reichssportführer would select the teams according to the best "physical and moral standards," thus banning Jews from competition. Sherrill was soon reassured and won over when he was invited to the Nuremberg Nazi Party Rally, where he was treated like an active rather than a retired diplomat. He saw Helene Mayer in training, but he died before he got the chance to see her perform in the Summer Games. Sherrill and the international press were only too willing to accept what the Nazis told them.

It was not only the Jewish sports organizations that were banned when the Nazis came to power. Workers' sports federations were also brought under the single control of sport, but while a worker could conceal his political opinions, a Jew could not conceal his or her "race": indeed, the fourth place in the main wrestling event went to the prominent German Communist Werner Seelenbinder. Had he won a medal, he had pledged to use the occasion to protest against the regime; the punishment that this would inevitably have brought was thus delayed—it was not until 1944 that he was executed after languishing for some time in prison.[111]

The Official Olympic Propaganda

The propaganda for the Games started in late 1933 with the publication of the Olympic bulletins in five languages. This was the only edition of that publication that was not fully controlled by the Promi, as it came out three weeks before the propaganda committee was officially founded. From then onward, the

Promi was fully in control. This created an international press service to reach as many newspapers and press agencies around the world as possible in German, English, French, Spanish, and Italian. It began with thirty-four hundred addresses, mainly supplied by the OC of the 1932 Los Angeles Games, but soon reached an increasing number of outlets on a monthly basis. By October 1934 it was providing twenty-four thousand copies worldwide to 2,030 German and 5,120 foreign addresses. This included 615 German and 3,075 foreign newspapers and journals.[112] In February 1935 the travel offices of German Railways abroad started to advertise the Olympic Games as the best place for a holiday in 1936. In April 1935, the press service was enlarged and was now translated and printed in fourteen languages (Dutch, Danish, Norwegian, Swedish, Finnish, Polish, Hungarian, Czech, and Portuguese, in addition to the original five). In total, thirty-three of these press-service bulletins were printed.[113] In June 1935 Olympic placards were distributed, complete with logo, in nineteen languages and a total press run of 156,000 copies. The Olympic rings and the Olympic bell with Hitler's appeal to the youth of the world established the sponsor's name. In September 1935, leaflets were distributed in fourteen languages and a press run of 2.4 million. Photographs of superb quality were sent out worldwide. The ten days of the torch run from Olympia to Berlin[114] received the full attention of every aspect of the German media. As well as spreading the good word, the committee countered the bad.[115] Press conferences stressed the peace message of the Games to which the host nation fully adhered.

Since 1928 an Olympic flame has been lit in the Olympic Stadium. Diem now proposed a torch relay—having made use of drawings on ancient vases—to bring the fire to the Olympic Stadium. This was done for the first time in Berlin (as mountain passes as high as five thousand feet had to be crossed, it was not feasible to have this run for the Winter Games). Haegert's committee developed all the details for this propaganda stunt and had a crew drive from Olympia to Berlin in 1935. This gimmick of the Nazi Games has been maintained as part of the invented tradition of the Games ever since.[116] Von Tschammer went to Olympia beforehand and used the meetings with sport leaders on the future way of the torch to advertise himself as the major European sports leader.[117] He also convinced Hitler that the Third Reich ought to sponsor the excavations of the ancient Olympic sites in Olympia.[118]

The purpose of the relay that ended in the Olympic Stadium at the opening ceremony was to turn world attention to the Olympic events. This was the first time such a relay was proposed. Coubertin was enthusiastic about it and wrote a message of support. For him, it was a symbol that his modern Olympic Games were in the tradition of the ancient Games, and thus the "eternal Hellenism" that assured the combination of intellectual, artistic, and physical skills were brought to light.[119] In the relay many elements came together. There is a German tradition of long distance relays since the late nineteenth century that Diem—himself a co-organizer of the Potsdam-Berlin (25 kilometer) annual relay—could rely upon. Organizing 3,075 torch runners from five different countries, covering one kilometer (1,100 yards) each, was far less of a logistical feat than the 120,000 relay runners that had brought messages from all over Germany to Hitler in Koblenz in the Saartreuestaffel in 1934.[120] The logistics of such a relay were, however, nonetheless difficult, as it went through five different countries before it entered Germany. The organizers made use of the opportunity to put the "new" Germany into the ancient tradition. The Krupp Company, Germany's largest armament producer, created and sponsored the torches, which were to burn for ten minutes. The first torch manufactured was used to ignite a new high furnace for the production of extra-strong steel used in the construction of long-range Krupp canons. The Nazi anthem, "Horst-Wessel-Lied," was played in ancient Olympia when the fire was lit. Altars were set-up along the way for semireligious ceremonies in the tradition of the ancient fire cults, which had been prevalent in ancient Greece, as in ancient Germany.[121]

The ceremony in Vienna was used by the Austrian Nazis as a demonstration of their strength. It suggested that the Anschluss two years later was enthusiastically welcomed by many—if not all—in the Austrian capital. The ceremony in Prague, however, ended in street fighting between the Sudetendeutschen, the German minority at the rim of Czechoslovakia, and the Czechs. The torch run was broadcast live by a German radio team, which reported only on the friendly sights and sounds[122] and gave the image that everybody was happy about the coming Olympic Games in Berlin.[123] As the torch relay was under German rather than IOC jurisdiction, the ceremonies could be used for unabashed Nazi ceremonies.

Each Olympic team received carefully selected bilingual student helpers who had the task of giving full reports on the attitude of the foreign teams. Spying on the teams was not difficult, as the young Germans soon gained the confidence of the officials of the foreign teams.[124] At Garmisch-Partenkirchen there was no Olympic Village, but the athletes and officials were all privately housed. In this situation it would have been difficult to supervise the foreigners had it not been for the student helpers. They had to report back immediately and write a lengthy report afterward, which went together with a systematic press review done by the foreign section of the party.

One of the major results of this analysis was to avoid the use of uniforms. Westwood Pegler in the *Washington Post* was only one prominent writer who complained about the military character of the Games; the presence of so many people in uniforms worried athletes, officials, and press alike.[125] Because of unpredictable snow conditions, the German Organizing Committee for the Winter Games had brought together six thousand men from the Reichsarbeitsdienst, voluntary uniformed workers who had joined a paramilitary work service, often with little choice. To the uninformed these all appeared to be soldiers. Ritter von Halt needed them, as during the Games there was at first not enough snow and later there was too much. Most of the officials showed up in uniform so that when Hitler opened the Games he was one of the few in civilian clothes. This was completely changed for Berlin. While the friendly applause the French team had received in Garmisch-Partenkirchen served Hitler in the Reichstag to explain his peaceful intentions—he was soon to send troops into the demilitarized Rhineland—the friendliness and nonmilitary atmosphere had to become visible for the foreign guests. So everybody was ordered to leave their uniforms at home. There were more helpers from the various military or paramilitary groups attending the Games in Berlin than in Garmisch-Partenkirchen, yet the Promi was far more efficient in controlling the public image of the Games.

Only German photographers were permitted at the Winter Games.[126] Forty six were accredited, while forty-nine radio reporters worked from Garmisch-Partenkirchen, along with 403 journalists. On the whole these 498 accredited journalists represented twenty-nine different countries.[127] These were the first Winter Olympic Games to be transmitted live on international radio. Relatively little was done to influence the journalists, and they were impressed by the large numbers of enthusiastic spectators and the technical possibilities at their disposal.[128] In Berlin there were even more journalists covering the event; not even the OC knew the exact number. The Summer Games issued passes to 593 foreign publishers and had personal data on more than seven hundred foreign journalists. It was assumed that the 225 German publishers present had close to a thousand journalists, and fifteen wire services were present with 150 journalists. Fifty-five German-speaking journalists came from abroad; within a couple of years many of them would no longer be "foreigners." And finally there were thirty freelance writers covering the Games.[129]

Victor Boin, the Belgian president of the international sports writers organization, assumed that there were twelve hundred foreign journalists in Berlin and that radio coverage from Berlin reached three hundred million listeners, making it by far the largest international media event in history.[130] These were the Olympic Games with the first live global radio coverage: forty-one radio corporations from forty-one different countries broadcast in fifty languages and dialects on medium (AM) and short waves in over three thousand different transmissions. More than one hundred stations in the United States alone covered the Summer Games regularly on the CBS and NBC networks,[131] 450 radio technicians from all of Germany were brought together in Berlin to help their foreign colleagues and thus to give a positive impression about German technical skill.[132]

Again, only German photographers were permitted inside the stadium. Of the 15,950 photos they delivered, only those that coincided with what they considered the spirit and the image of the Games were distributed. Such was the profusion of pictures available that journalists could, if they wished, find evidence of Nazi symbols—but overall it was the nonpolitical atmosphere that was presented.

Despite their constant protestations of peaceful intentions, the Nazis used the cover of the Olympic excitement to carry out the normal and more questionable affairs of state. The breach of the Versailles Treaty, with the remilitarization of the Rhineland on March 7, 1936, came fast on the heels of the Winter Olympics,[133] and while an obviously enthusiastic Hitler could be seen every day watching the events of the Summer Olympics, behind the scenes he was conducting the negotiations that would help ensure Franco's victory in the Spanish Civil War.[134] The Games were hardly concluded when Hitler doubled the time for the compulsory military service, which he had reintroduced in March of the previous year in defiance of the Versailles Treaty. The Nuremberg Rally of September 1936 brought the Germans back more closely to the real nature of the regime.

Conclusion

George Messersmith, the American ambassador in Vienna who would later become the assistant secretary of state, reported from Austria prior to the Berlin Olympics: "There are many wise and well informed observers in Europe who believe that the holding or non-holding of the Olympic Games in Berlin will play an important part in determining political developments in Europe. I believe that this view of the importance of the Olympic Games being held in Berlin 1936 is not exaggerated."[135]

Messersmith was certainly right. The 1936 Olympics consolidated Hitler's popularity at home and with German-speaking people abroad. The absence of any serious boycott and a virtually incident-free running of the Games led Germans to believe that their new regime was universally admired, and as the party that accompanied the Olympic pause continued, so more quietly were the concentration camps filled. Before the Games the Saar had already become part of the new Germany, the Rhineland was remilitarized between the Winter and Summer Games, and Austria and the German-speaking parts of Czechoslovakia would soon become part of the Greater German Reich.

The success of the Games according to foreign opinion is more doubtful: the foreign press admired the organization, but opinions held before the Games tended to be confirmed one way or the other.[136] The IOC showed itself a bounteous admirer of the regime. In 1939, even after the invasion of the rump of Czechoslovakia left over from the depredations of Munich the previous year, it awarded the 1940 Winter Games to Garmisch-Partenkirchen. Admittedly Sapporo, Oslo, and St. Moritz, for varying reasons, had refused the offer, but the invitation to a country even then so obviously bent on aggressive war was made without a single objection. This would prove to be a valuable bargaining tool for German officials after the war when they tried to regain their reputations as decent sportsmen.[137]

Nowhere is the image of the Nazi Olympics better encapsulated than in the classic film of the event by Leni Riefenstahl. Here we can see the most perfect sport in a most perfect setting, sport in the tradition of the ancient Greeks.[138] But this was no longer the Greece of Athens, the cradle of democracy; it was the

Greece of Sparta, driven by the most barbarous of ideologies and armed with the might of modern technology.[139]

Notes

1. R. Hofstadter, "Darwinism and Western Thought," in *Darwin, Marx, and Wagner*, ed. H. L. Plaine (Columbus: Ohio State University Press, 1962), 53–55. For the same in a cultural context, see A. Krüger, "Zwischen Sex and Zuchtwahl: Nudismus and Naturismus in Deutschland und Amerika," in *Liberalitas: Festschrift für Erich Angermann*, ed. N. Finzsch and H. Wellenreuther (Stuttgart: Steiner, 1992), 342–65. For a history of the Sonderweg in sports, see A. Krüger, "The German 'Sonderweg' in Turnen and Sport, 1870–1914: What's So German about the Germans?" in *International Perspectives and Results of Historical Research on Physical Education and Sport*, ed. Committee for the Commemoration of Prof. Dr. J. Narita (Tokyo: Tsukuba University Press, 1996), 585–607.

2. A. Krüger, "Geschichte der Bewegungstherapie," in *Naturheilverfahren und unkonventionelle medizinische Richtungen: Lose Blatt Sammlung. 8. Nachlieferung*, ed. M. Bühring and F. M. Kemper (Heidelberg: Springer, 1995), 1–20.

3. H. Bernett, "Carl Diem und sein Werk als Gegenstand der sportgeschichtlichen Forschung," *Sozial-und Zeitgeschichte des Sports* 1 (1987): 7–41. When streets, gymnasia, and stadia named after Carl Diem were asked to be renamed in the political sphere, H. J. Teichler recommended that they should not. See H. J. Teichler, "Die Rolle Carl Diems in der Zeit und im zeitlichen Umfeld des NS-Regimes," *Sozial-und Zeitgeschichte des Sports* 10.3 (1996): 56–74. The position of the German Sports Federation was similar; see "DSB-Präsidium: Stellungnahme der Expertenkommission zu Werk und Person von Carl Diem (1882–1962)," *Sozial-und Zeitgeschichte des Sports* 10.3 (1996): 75–79. A critical review of this in H. Dwertmann, "Die Rolle Carl Diems im nationalsozialistischen Regime: Zum Gutachten H. J. Teichlers und zur Stellungnahme der Expertenkommission," *Sozial-und Zeitgeschichte des Sports* 11.2 (1997): 7–47.

4. A. Krüger, " 'The Olympic Spirit of the Modern World Has Given Us a Symbol of World War': Sport and the National Representation at the Eve of World War I," in *Sport et relations internationales*, ed. P. Arnaud and A. Wahl (Centre de Recherche d'Histoire et Civilisation de l'Université de Metz, vol. 19, Metz: Université, 1994), 47–64.

5. W. Lynberg, *Fabulous 100 Years of the IOC: Facts, Figures, and Much More* (Lausanne: IOC, 1996), 85.

6. C. Diem, *Ein Leben für den Sport* (Düsseldorf: Henn, 1974), 115.

7. He continued as chief negotiator for the Reich concerning the German-Polish border disputes.

8. A. Krüger, *Dr. Theodor Lewald: Sportführer ins Dritte Reich* (Berlin: Bartels and Wernitz, 1975); R. Pfeiffer and A. Krüger, "Theodor Lewald: Eine Karriere im Dienste des Vaterlands oder die vergebliche Suche nach der jüdischen Identität eines Halbjuden," in *Menora: Jahrbuch für deutsch-jüdische Geschichte 1995* (München: Piper, 1995), 233–65.

9. P. Heimerzheim, *Karl Ritter von Halt—Leben zwischen Sport und Politik* (St. Augustin: Academia, 1999).

10. According to H. Bernett, " 'Wehrsport—ein Pseudosport," *Sportwissenschaft* 11.1 (1981): 295–308, it is questionable whether their activities should actually be called "sport."

11. A. Krüger, "Breeding, Rearing, and Preparing the Aryan Body: Creating the Complete Superman the Nazi Way," *International Journal of the History of Sport* 16.2 (1999): 42–68.

12. A. Krüger, *Sport und Politik: Vom Turnvater Jahn zum Staatsamateur* (Hannover: Fackelträger, 1975).

13. W. Joch, "Kontinuität und Wandel, Elend und Würde: Karl Ritter von Halt (1891 bis 1964)," in *Umbruch und Kontinuität im Sport—Reflexionen im Umfeld der Sportgeschichte: Festschrift für Horst Ueberhorst*, ed. A. Luh and E. Beckers (Bochum: Brockmeyer, 1991), 442–56.

14. A. Krüger, *Die Olympischen Spiele 1936 und die Weltmeinung* (Berlin: Bartels and Wernitz, 1972), 29ff.

15. A. Krüger, "'Heute gehört uns Deutschland und morgen . . . ?': Das Ringen um den Sinn der Gleichschaltung im Sport in der ersten Jahreshälfte 1933," in *Sportgeschichte: Traditionspflege und Wertewandel,* ed. W. Buss and A. Krüger (Duderstadt: Mecke, 1985), 175–96.

16. H. Ueberhorst, *Carl Krümmel und die nationalsozialistische Leibeserziehung* (Berlin: Bartels and Wernitz, 1976).

17. R. Bianda, G. Leone, et al., *Atleti in camicia nera: Lo sport nell' Italia di Mussolini* (Rome: Voepe, 1983); F. Fabrizio, *Sport e fascismo: La politica sportiva del regime, 1924–1936* (Rimini: Guaraldi, 1976); A. Krüger, "The Influence of the State Sport of Fascist Italy on Nazi Germany, 1928–1936," in *Sport, Culture, Society,* ed. J. A. Mangan and R. Small (London: Spon, 1986), 145–65; A. Krüger, "Der Einfluß des faschistischen Sportmodells Italiens auf den national-sozialistischen Sport," in *Sport und Politik, 1918–1939/40,* ed. M. A. Olsen (Oslo: Universitetsforlaget, 1986), 226–32; A. Krüger, "Sport im faschistischen Italien (1922–1933)," in *Sport zwischen Eigenständigkeit und Fremdbestimmung,* ed. G. Spitzer and D. Schmidt (Bonn: P. Wegener, 1986), 213–26; A. Krüger, "Fasci e croci uncinate," *Lancillotto e Nausica: Critica e storia dello sport* 8.12 (1991): 88–101.

18. H. Ueberhorst, "Ferdinand Goetz und Edmund Neuendorff—Wirkungsgeschichte zweier Sportführer," in *Sportgeschichte,* ed. W. Buss and A. Krüger, 147–60.

19. For its structure see G. M. Müller, *Das Reichsministerium für Volksaufklärung und Propaganda* (Berlin: Junker and Dünnhaupt, 1940).

20. K. Pätzold and K. Weissbecker, *Hakenkreuz und Totenkopf: Die Partei des Verbrechens* (Berlin: Deutscher Verlag der Wissenschaften, 1982), 210–11.

21. See A. Grosser, *La presse et la naissance d' une dictature* (Paris: Colon, 1972).

22. For the theoretical discussion about what actually constitutes propaganda in a discursive context, see T. Smith III, ed., *Propaganda: A Pluralistic Perspective* (New York: Praeger, 1989); A. Pratkanis and E. Aronson, *Age of Propaganda: The Use and Abuse of Persuasion* (New York: Freeman, 1991); G. S. Jowett and V. O'Donnell, *Propaganda and Persuasion* (London: Sage, 1992); D. Welch, *The Third Reich: Politics and Propaganda* (London: Routledge, 1993). For a broader theoretical background, see N. Stevenson, *Culture: Understanding Media* (London: Sage, 1995).

23. For the connections between the Fascist sport systems, see A. Krüger, "Strength through Joy: The Culture of Consent under Fascism, Nazism, and Francoism," in *The International Politics of Sport in the Twentieth Century,* ed. J. Riordan and A. Krüger (London: Spon, 1999), 67–89.

24. H. J. Teichler, "Berlin 1936—Ein Sieg der NS Propaganda?" *Stadion* 2 (1976): 265–306.

25. For the Italian model, see V. de Grazia, *The Culture of Consent: Mass Organization of Leisure in Fascist Italy* (Cambridge: University Press, 1981); and chapter 5 in this volume.

26. E. Leiser, *"Deutschland Erwache!": Propaganda im Film des Dritten Reiches* (Reinbek: Rowohlt, 1968).

27. H. Bernett, "Nationalsozialistischer Volkssport bei 'Kraft durch Freude,'" *Stadion* 5.1 (1979): 98–146.

28. H. Bohrmann, ed., *NS-Presseanweisungen der Vorkriegszeit,* vol. 4 (München: Saur, 1993), 782.

29. J. Martin-Barbero, *Communication, Culture, and Hegemony* (London: Sage), 1993; T. J. Jackson Lears, "The Concept of Cultural Hegemony: Problems and Possibilities," *American Historical Review* 90.3 (1985): 567–93. For a debate over the usefulness of this concept, see *Journal of American History* 75.1 (1988): 115–57; and L. Haywood, "Hegemony: Another Blind Alley for the Study of Sport?" in Mangan and Small, *Sport, Culture, Society,* 234–39.

30. For the connection between sport and religion, see O. Korsgaard, "Sport as a Practice of Religion: The Record as Ritual," in *Ritual and Record,* ed. J. M. Carter and A. Krüger (Westport, Conn.: Greenwood, 1990), 135–52; and C. S. Prebish, ed., *Religion and Sport: The Meeting of Sacred and Profane* (Westport, Conn.: Greenwood, 1993).

31. J. M. Brohm, "Zum Verhältnis von Olympismus und Nationalsozialismus," in *Olympia-Berlin: Gewalt und Mythos in den Olympischen Spielen von Berlin 1936,* ed. G. Gebauer (Berlin: Freie

Universität Berlin, 1986), 190–205. For a broader and less radical analysis that is influenced by Brohm, see T. Alkemeyer, *Körper, Kult und Politik: Von der "Muskelreligion" Pierre de Coubertins zur Inszenierung von Macht in den Olympischen Spielen 1936* (Frankfurt/M.: Campus, 1996).

32. T. Tannsjö, "Is It Fascistoid to Admire Sports Heroes?" in *Values in Sport: Elitism, Nationalism, Gender Equality, and the Scientific Manufacture of Winners,* ed. T. Tannsjö and C. Tamburrini (London: Spon, 2000), 9–23.

33. Goebbels kept himself well informed about the discussions at the AAU conference to debate U.S. participation in the Olympic Games (see E. Fröhlich, ed., *Die Tagebücher des Joseph Goebbels: Fragmente,* vol. 2 [München: Saur, 1987], 594). For the work of the propaganda committee of the OC, see Organisationskomitee für die XI. Olympischen Sommerspiele, ed., *Amtlicher Bericht,* 2 vols. (Berlin: Limpert, 1937).

34. A. Krüger, "Deutschland und die Olympische Bewegung (1918–1945)," in *Geschichte der Leibesübungen,* vol. 3, pt. 2, ed. H. Ueberhorst (Berlin: Bartels and Wernitz, 1982), 1026–47.

35. George H. Shuster described Sherrill as follows: "the general is not a huge windbag of illustrious Brundage type, but an upright citizen" (*Commonweal,* Nov. 8, 1835, 40).

36. "I wish to God, he [Mussolini] would come over here and have a chance to do the same thing" (Sherrill, in a speech to the Chamber of Commerce of New York, quoted in *The Nation,* Dec. 11, 1935, 666).

37. Krüger, *Die Olympischen Spiele 1936,* 53ff.

38. It could be argued that the Swedish government was the first to do this in 1912, but it organized a national lottery to pay for the building of the new Olympic Stadium and did not pay for it directly out of taxes. See J. Lindroth, *Idrottens väg till folkrörelse: Studier i svensk idrottsrörelse till 1915* (Uppsala: Acta Universitatis, 1974).

39. For the details of the stadium, see V. Kluge, *Olympiastadion Berlin: Steine beginnen zu reden* (Berlin: Parthas, 1999). Werner March (1894–1976), the architect and the son of the builder of the Olympic Stadium of 1916, insisted on a "modern" stadium with concrete and glass. Hitler's chief architect, Albert Speer, redrew the plans in one night, dropping the glass and covering the concrete with travertin, the natural rock Hitler preferred The stadium today is as it was in 1936. See J. Titel, "Die Vorbereitung der Olympischen Spiele in Berlin 1936: Organisation und Politik," in *Berlin in Geschichte und Gegenwart: Jahrbuch des Landesarchivs Berlin* 12 (1993), 113–71; and T. Schmidt, "Werner March und seine Planungen zum ehemaligen Reichssportfeld, errichtet anlässlich der Olympiade 1936," *Berlin Forschungen,* vol. 2, ed. W. Ribbe, (Berlin: Colloquium, 1987), 235–62, esp. 252–57.

40. Krüger, *Die Olympischen Spiele 1936,* 216ff.

41. Diem's salary increased to 1,500 RM from 500. See Bundesarchiv, Berlin, R18 Rep. 320 Nr. 608, Haushaltsplan.

42. Personal interview with the author, Feb. 1996, during celebrations for the sixty-year anniversary of the Olympics in Garmisch-Partenkirchen.

43. A. Krüger, "The German Way of Worker Sports," in *The Story of Worker Sport,* ed. A. Krüger and J. Riordan (Champaign, Ill.: Human Kinetics, 1996), 1–27.

44. H. E. Rösch, *Sport um der Menschen willen: 75 Jahre D.J.K.-Sportverband, Deutsche Jugendkraft, 1920–1995* (Aachen: Meyer and Meyer, 1995), 29ff.

45. A. Krüger, "'Wenn die Olympiade vorbei, schlagen wir die Juden zu Brei': Das Verhältnis der Juden zu den Olympischen Spielen von 1936," in *Menora 5: Jahrbuch für deutsch-jüdische Geschichte 1994* (München: Piper, 1994), 331–48; A. Krüger, "'Once the Olympics Are Through, We'll Beat Up the Jew': German Jewish Sport 1898–1938 and the Anti-Semitic Discourse," *Journal of Sport History* 26.2 (1999): 353–75.

46. For the attempts to make all sports subsections of the Turners, see H. Ueberhorst, *Edmund Neuendorff: Turnführer ins Dritte Reich* (Berlin: Bartels and Wernitz, 1970).

47. H. Bernett, *Der Weg des Sports in die nationalsozialistische Diktatur* (Schorndorf: Hofmann, 1983).

48. For the example of the National Cycling Federation, see Krüger, "Heute gehört uns Deutschland."

49. R. Rohrbach, ed., ". . . *bis zum letzten Atemzuge": Propaganda in der NS-Zeit* (Göttingen: Goltze, 1995).

50. Bohrmann, *NS-Presseanweisungen*. In a major research effort, these press orders are now being reconstructed to determine their results. Some eighty thousand orders are still available in all fields put together, but, of course, only a small number of these relate to sport or the Olympic Games. The project started in 1984 and is still not finished. Most of the material is from the Federal Achives in Koblenz and from the German Newspaper Archive in Dortmund.

51. G. Toepser Ziegert, "NS-Presseanweisungen der Vorkriegszeit," in Bohrmann, *NS-Presseanweisungen*, vol. 1, 17–60.

52. I. Kershaw, *The Nazi Dictatorship: Problems and Perspectives of Interpretation* (London: Arnold, 1993); J. Noakes and G. Pridham, eds., *Nazism: A History in Documents and Eyewitness Accounts, 1919–1945*, 2 vols. (New York: Schocken, 1984).

53. Bohrmann, *NS-Presseanweisungen*, vol. 3, 865–66.

54. M. Dodd, *Through Embassy Eyes* (New York: Harcourt, Brace and Co., 1939). Although Goebbels personally resented the success of the African Americans, his propaganda scheme overrode his personal interests. See Fröhlich, ed., *Die Tagebücher des Joseph Goebbels*: "We Germans won one gold medal, the Americans three, two by negroes. What a shame. The white part of the American team ought to be embarrassed. But what does this matter in this country without any decent civilization [Kultur]" (vol. 2, pt. 1, 655).

55. Bohrmann, *NS-Presseanweisungen*, vol. 4, pt. 2, 853.

56. Federal Archives, Koblenz, NS 19/1641, Mar. 12, 1935.

57. Bohrmann, *NS-Presseanweisungen*, vol. 4, pt. 1, 85.

58. L. Gruchmann, "'Blutschutzgesetz' und Justiz: Zur Entstehung und Auswirkung des Nürnberger Gesetzes vom 15. September 1935," *Vierteljahreshefte für Zeitgeschichte* 31 (1983): 418–42.

59. Bohrmann, *NS-Presseanweisungen*, vol. 4, pt. 2, 875.

60. W. Wippermann and U. Brucker-Boroujerdi, "Nationalsozialistische Zwangslager in Berlin: Das 'Zigeunerlager' Marzahn," in Ribbe, *Berlin Forschungen*, vol 2, 189–201, esp. 190–94.

61. See C. Grote, "Johann Wilhelm Trollmann, gen. Rukelie, gen. Gipsy: Eine Außenseiterbiographie im deutschen Boxsport," in *Aus Biographien Sportgeschichte lernen*, ed. A. Krüger and B. Wedemeyer (Hoya: NISH, 2000), 177–99.

62. See chapter 2 in this volume. As so much effort was made to please the Americans, the peculiarities of other nations were covered with less care, and this often hurt the feelings of those nations. Before the Games even started, the Chinese had complained twice, and the press was warned to handle foreign customs with more care. See Bohrmann, *NS-Presseanweisungen*, vol. 4, 795.

63. Bohrmann, *NS-Presseanweisungen*, vol. 4, 732.

64. J. Bently, *Martin Niemöller* (Oxford: Oxford University Press, 1984).

65. V. Barnett, *For the Soul of the People: Protestant Protest against Hitler* (Oxford: Oxford University Press, 1992).

66. Bohrmann, *NS-Presseanweisungen*, vol. 4, pt. 1, 189.

67. A. Krüger, "'Dann veranstalten wir eben deutsche Olympische Spiele': Die Olympischen Spiele 1936 als deutsches Nationalfest," in *Schwimmsport und Sportgeschichte: Zwischen Politik und Wissenschaft*, ed. H. Breuer and R. Naul (St. Augustin: Academia, 1994), 127–49.

68. H. Bernett, "Sportpublizistik im totalitären Staat, 1933–1945," *Stadion* 11 (1985): 263–95; J. Bellers, ed., *Die Olympiade Berlin 1936 im Spiegel der ausländischen Presse* (Münster: Lit., 1986); *Außenpolitische Rundschau* 13 (1936).

69. Bohrmann, *NS-Presseanweisungen*, vol. 4, pt. 2, 887.

70. Promi to OC, Aug. 19, 1936, Bundesarchiv, Berlin, R43 II/731. The woman who approached Hitler was a Californian from Artesia; see *Pathfinder*, Aug. 29, 1936, 6.

71. The Security Service (SD) had received three hundred transferable all-access passes to all of the Berlin Sporting facilities and seventy seats inside the Olympic Stadium; the Gestapo (secret police) had received fifty all-access passes and demanded twenty more tickets that were not identifiable. This shows that the German authorities anticipated more problems with foreigners to be dealt with by the SD than with Germans used to their Gestapo. See Titel, "Die Vorbereitung der Olympischen Spiele," 147n.164.

72. Krüger, *Die Olympischen Spiele 1936*, 171, 194. The organizers had learned from the Winter Games when Konrad Henlein, the Sudeten Führer, who was also president of the Sudeten Turner Organization, had been given too much attention, and this was criticized by the international press.

73. See, for instance, the meeting of the Swedes in Bohrmann, *NS-Presseanweisungen*, vol. 4, pt. 2, 847.

74. On the Sudetendeutsche with the explicit order that news of the VDA (the Nazi propaganda organization directed toward people of German origin) should not be printed until further notice, see ibid., 878. For the role of the Sudeten Germans in the internal sports struggle in Czechoslovakia, see M. Waic, "Die Beteiligung der Tschechoslowakei an den Olympischen Spielen im Jahre 1936 und die Sudeten-Deutschen in der tschecholowakischen Repräsentation," *Sozial-und Zeitgeschichte des Sports* 10.2 (1996): 35–45.

75. Bohrmann, *NS-Presseanweisungen*, vol. 4, pt. 2, 843. The *Amtlicher Bericht*, however, called him by his Italian name (Olympischen Sommerspiele, *Amtlicher Bericht*, vol. 2, 676). Similar advice had already been given in the case of the Winter Games. See Bohrmann, *NS-Presseanweisungen*, vol. 4, part 1, 131.

76. Krüger, *Die Olympischen Spiele 1936*, 201.

77. C. C. Graham, *Leni Riefenstahl and Olympia* (Metuchen, N.J.: Scarecrow, 1986); T. Wiener, "Good Sports," *American Films* 9.9 (1984): 66–69. For Riefenstahl's connections with the regime, see H. Bernett, "Leni Riefenstahls Dokumentarfilm von den Olympischen Spielen in Berlin 1936," in *Untersuchungen zur Zeitgeschichte des Sports*, ed. H. Bernett (Schorndorf: Hofmann, 1973), 115–40. Richard D. Mandell's *Nazi Olympics* (Rpt., Urbana: University of Illinois Press, 1987) is still one of the best analyses. On the special charms of Fascist sport movies, see H. Hoffmann, *Mythos Olympia: Autonomie und Unterwerfung von Sport und Kultur* (Berlin: Aufbau Verlag, 1993); Leiser, *"Deutschland Erwache!"*

78. The German press was told to publicize the ready availability of housing in Berlin for short stays and at inexpensive rates. They were also told to deemphasize track and field in their reporting, as Germans would be successful in other sports as well. See Bohrmann, *NS-Presseanweisungen*, vol. 4, pt. 2, 830, 836. The Olympic Stadium was sold out, although there were still seats available at some of the other sports.

79. Garmisch-Partenkirchen celebrated the sixtieth anniversary of their Games in exactly the same spirit. See "Das andere Gesicht der Winterspiele '36," *Garmisch Partenkirchener Tageblatt*, Jan. 27, 1996. For the Nazi atrocities in Garmisch-Partenkirchen, see A. Schwarzmüller, "'Juden sind hier nicht erwünscht': Aus der Geschichte der jüdischen Bürger in Garmisch-Partenkirchen von 1933–1945," in *Mohr, Löwe, Raute: Beiträge aus der Geschichte des Landkreises Garmisch Partenkirchen* 3 (1995), 184–232.

80. Had the Olympic Games been boycotted, the Turners would have been necessary for the organization of National Olympic Games. See Krüger, "'Dann veranstalten wir eben.'"

81. *DRL-Pressedienst*, vol. 1, *Mitteilungen*, Oct. 3, 1936.

82. Bernett, *Der Weg des Sports*, 93ff.

83. Bohrmann, *NS-Presseanweisungen*, vol. 4, pt. 2, 804. According to the *DRL-Pressedienst* (vol. 1, *Mitteilungen*, Sept. 29, 1936), there were an estimated 710,000 youths enrolled in sport organizations.

84. Z. A. B. Zeman, *Nazi Propaganda* (London: Oxford University Press, 1964), 104ff.

85. Krüger, *Die Olympischen Spiele 1936*, 228–29.

86. German business concentrated so much on the booming German market that little time

and thought was spent on regaining the international ones. See D. Petzina, *Autarkiepolitik im Dritten Reich* (Stuttgart: DVA, 1968), 18–19.

87. The Deutsche Opernhaus in Berlin had a special Wagner Festival at the time of the Olympic Games (Aug. 3 to 16, 1936). For the special invitations (preferably to business leaders of "Aryan descent"), see correspondence in the Political Archives of the German Foreign Ministry, Bonn. P.A., Referat Deutschland, Olympiade 1936, Wirtschaftsführer, Az. 86–26 W. Their special opera evening was in the splendor of the Berlin Schloss.

88. P. de Coubertin, "Les assises philosophiques de l'olympisme moderne," in *Pax Olympika: Weltsendung des Reichssenders Berlin am Sonntag, dem 4. August 1935 mittags*, ed. Organisationskomitee für die XI. Olympiade (Berlin: OK, 1935), 8–18 (French), 117–26 (German). See also *Le Sport Suisse* 31 (Aug. 7, 1935): 1.

89. See the introduction in my retranslation of P. de Coubertin's "Die philosophischen Grundlagen des modernen Olympismus," trans. A. Krüger, *Leistungssport* 2.4 (1972): 239–41.

90. B. Murray, "France, de Coubertin, and the Berlin Olympics: The Response," *Olympika* 1 (1992): 46–69. See also chapter 4 in this volume.

91. J. Kieran and A. Daley, *The Story of the Olympic Games* (Philadelphia: Lippinkot, 1965), 153–81.

92. O. Meyer, *A travers les anneaux olympiques* (Geneva: Caillet, 1960).

93. H. Bernett, *Sportpolitik im 3. Reich* (Schorndorf: Hofmann, 1971).

94. H. J. Teichler, "Coubertin und das Dritte Reich," *Sportwissenschaft* 12.1 (1982): 18–55; H. J. Teichler, *Internationale Sportpolitik im Dritten Reich* (Schorndorf: Hofmann, 1991).

95. K. Ullrich, *Olympia—geliebt und gehasst* (Berlin: Sportverlag, 1987).

96. For the early connections between the IOC and the sales value of the Games, see A. Krüger, "'The Masses Are Much More Sensitive to the Perfection of the Whole Than to Any Separate Details': The Influence of John Ruskin's Political Economy on Pierre de Coubertin," *Olympika* 5 (1996): 25–44. All Games since have not just used the five rings but a special logo created for each particular Olympic Games.

97. In this context I do not want to go into the problems of totalitarianism and start comparing the 1936 and the 1980 Olympics.

98. Coca-Cola, an Olympic sponsor since 1928, was also present in Berlin. See R. Rürup, *1936: Die Olympischen Spiele und der Nationalsozialismus* (Berlin: Stiftung Topographie des Terrors), 82.

99. This changed after the Berlin Games, when Germany staged seminars for international athletes and coaches to learn about the German way of training.

100. For the importance of the uniformity of monumental art for the corporate identity of nazism, see O. Thomae, *Die Propaganda-Maschinerie: Bildende Kunst und Öffentlichkeitsarbeit im Dritten Reich* (Berlin: Gebr. Mann, 1978).

101. Bundesarchiv, Koblenz, Aktenvermerk (von Lex) betr. Verhältnis OK, DOA, RMI, Oct 15, 1934, R18, Rep. 320, Nr. 611.

102. Olympiaarchiv quoted in Krüger, *Theodor Lewald*, 45. See A. Krüger, "The Olympic Games Berlin," in *The Modern Olympics*, 2d ed., ed. H. Ueberhorst and P. Graham (Cornwall: Leisure Press, 1979), 172–86.

103. A. Krüger, "'Fair Play for American Athletes': A Study in Anti-Semitism," *Canadian Journal of the History of Sport and Physical Education* 9.1 (1978): 42–57; S. R. Wenn, "A Suitable Policy of Neutrality? FDR and the Question of American Participation in the 1936 Olympics," *International Journal of the History of Sport* 8.3 (1991): 319–35.

104. The American consul general in Berlin, George Messersmith, reported extensively about the German preparation for the Olympic Games, first from Berlin later from Vienna. For the quote, see National Archives, Washington, D.C., RG 59, General Records of the Department of State, 862–4063/Olympic Games/1, after an interview with Lewald, Nov 28, 1933.

105. For a short biography of her, see G. Pfister and T. Niewerth, "Jewish Women in Gymnastics and Sport in Germany, 1898–1938," *Journal of Sport History* 26.2 (1999): 287–325.

106. Bohrmann, *NS-Presseanweisungen,* vol. 4, pt. 2, 735. Margret ("Gretel") Bergmann married Dr. Bruno Lambert, a German, and so went to New York as Mrs. Lambert. See A. Guttmann, "'The Nazi Olympics' and the American Boycott Controversy," in *Sport and International Politics: The Impact of Fascism and Communism on Sport,* ed. P. Arnaud and J. Riordan (London: Spon, 1998), 31–50. Guttmann mistakes Gretel Bergmann and Margret Lambert for two different people and thus doubles the German injustice (43).

107. There had been a long tradition of national Olympics in Germany that was particularly strong in the Turner movement but also nationally during the time when Germany was excluded from the Games (1920–28). See Krüger, "'Dann veranstalten wir eben.'"

108. There are two records from this interview: one by the interpreter (Schmidt), in Political Archives of the German Foreign Minister, PA Olympiade 36, AZ 86–26, vol. 1; and one by Hitler's personal advisor (Meissner), in Bundesarchiv, Koblenz, R43, II/729 (Reichskanzlei/betr. Olympiade 1936).

109. For Baillet-Latour's difficult situation, see K. Lennartz, "Difficult Times: Baillet-Latour and Germany, 1931–1942," *Olympika* 3 (1994): 99–106.

110. Handwritten letter by Sherrill to Baillet-Latour (August 30, 1935), IOC Archives, Lausanne, Jeux Olympiques 1936, Question juive.

111. See W. Radetz, *Der Stärkere: Ein Buch über Werner Seelenbinder* (Berlin: Sportverlag, 1982).

112. Olympischen Sommerspiele, ed., *Amtlicher Bericht,* vol. 1, 92.

113. Ibid., vol. 1, 304.

114. All data are from the Olympischen Sommerspiele, ed., *Amtlicher Bericht,* vol. 1, 40ff.

115. In any case, the Promi knew beforehand what was to be in the papers, as it provided the *Mercedes Schreibdienst,* a speedy typewriter service: "You dictate—we typewrite, without expenses." See Organisationskomitee für die IV. Olympischen Winterspiele, ed., *Amtlicher Bericht* (Berlin: Limpert, 1936), 164.

116. W. Borgers, *Olympic Torch Relay* (Kassel: Agon, 1996).

117. D. Hart-Davis, "The Torch Run" in *Hitler's Games: The 1936 Olympics* (London: Century Hutchinson, 1986), 132–37.

118. The Third Reich sponsored the excavations of the athletic sites with RM 300,000 (about $75,000).

119. P. de Coubertin, "Aux coureurs d'Olympie-Berlin," *Le Sport Suisse* 32 (July 22, 1936): 1, reprinted in Pierre de Coubertin, *Textes choisis,* vol. 2, *Olympisme,* ed. N. Müller (Zürich: Weidmann, 1986), 430–34.

120. H. Bernett, "Zur Geschichte der Fern-und Großstaffelläufe," in *Leichtathletik im geschichtlichen Wandel* (Schorndorf: Hofmann, 1987), 222–29.

121. H. Eichberg, *Massenspiele: NS-Thingspiel, Arbeiterweihespiel und olympisches Zeremoniell* (Bad Cannstatt: Frommann-Holzboog, 1977).

122. When the public reaction was unfriendly, the team simply improvised but reported this to the Berlin police authorities. See J. Titel, "Die Vorbereitung der Olympischen Spiele."

123. H. Bernett, M. Funck, and H. Woggon, "Der olympische Fackellauf 1936 oder die Disharmonie der Völker," *Sozial-und Zeitgeschichte des Sports* 10.2 (1996): 15–34.

124. Report of the Deutsches Studentenwerk (NS national student organization), Munich Division, to Le Fort, secretary general of the Winter Games (Apr. 16, 1936). Krüger, *Die Olympischen Spiele 1936,* 175–76.

125. *Washington Post,* Feb. 14, 1936, 7, Feb. 18, 1936, 9, Feb. 20, 1936, 9.

126. The first to claim exclusive photo rights to an Olympic Games were the Dutch in 1928.

127. V. Kluge, *Winter Olympia Kompakt: Daten, Fakten, Hintergründe der Olympischen Winterspiele von 1924–1992* (Berlin: Sportverlag, 1992), 68.

128. Two hundred fifty German radio transmissions from Garmisch-Partenkirchen (604 hours on the air) plus 201 foreign radio transmissions of an unknown duration. Organisationskomitee für die IV. Olympischen Winterspiele, ed., *Amtlicher Bericht* 176.

129. Olympischen Sommerspiele, ed., *Amtlicher Bericht,* vol. 1, 311.

130. Bohrmann, *NS-Presseanweisungen,* vol. 4, pt. 2, 854.

131. *Newsweek,* July 18, 1936, 31; *Literary Digest,* June 6, 1936, 47; July 4, 1936, 33. In 1932, the Los Angeles organizers had not made any effort to provide worldwide coverage. See A. Rhodes, *Propaganda: The Art of Persuasion, World War II* (London: Angus and Robertson, 1976), 30.

132. *New York Times,* May 21, 1936, 28. For the media theory at the time, see S. A. Lowery and M. L. Defleur, *Milestones in Mass Communication Research: Media Effects* (New York: Longman, 1988).

133. Adolf Hitler, *Des Führers Kampf um den Weltfrieden: Reichstagsrede vom 7. März 1936* (München: Eher, 1936), 21.

134. Ibid., 937ff. In his diaries, Goebbels called this "the perfect timing of the Führer." See Fröhlich, ed., *Die Tagebücher des Joseph Goebbels,* vol. 2, 666 (Aug. 25, 1936).

135. Messersmith's letter to Cordell Hull (Nov. 15, 1935), National Archives, Washington, D.C., Dept. of State, RG 59, 862.4063, Olympic Games, no. 57.

136. Great Britain was shocked about the poor showing of British athletes in Berlin, placing only seventh internationally, their poorest result ever. It was therefore recommended that they follow German physical-training schemes for the benefit of the army and elite sports. See M. Grant, *Propaganda and the Role of the State in Inter-War Britain* (Oxford: Clarendon, 1994), 168–69; *The Times,* August 17, 1939; *Hansard,* July 14, 1936, 314.

137. Krüger, "Deutschland und die Olympische Bewegung," 104ff.

138. For the myth of the Berlin Olympics, see Hoffmann, *Mythos Olympia.*

139. A. Krüger and D. Ramba, "Sparta or Athens? The Reception of Greek Antiquity in Nazi Germany," in *The Olympic Games through the Ages: Greek Antiquity and Its Impact on Modern Sport,* ed. R. Renson et al. (Athens: Hellenic Sports Research Institute 1991), 345–56.

CHAPTER 2

United States of America: The Crucial Battle

Arnd Krüger

Since the first modern Olympics in Athens in 1896, the United States had played a dominant role. As a host in the Depression Games at Los Angeles in 1932 it virtually swept the field, with forty-four of the 125 gold medals, well ahead of Italy, which placed second.[1] Competition in Berlin four years later looked like it would be tougher, especially as the Italians would be joined by the Germans of the new Reich who were eager to prove the superiority of their political and social systems. The press in the United States played its part as it prepared public opinion for the ensuing competition: "Common interests, common loyalties, common enthusiasms—those are the great integrating factors in any culture. In America sports have provided this common denominator in as great a degree as any other single factor."[2]

* * *

For the Nazis, as seen in the previous chapter, the participation of the United States was vital. At a time when Hitler played on the iniquities of the Diktat of Versailles, Germany was equally anxious to point to the moderating role of the United States in the postwar period and later as a friendly trading partner. But while Nazi propaganda was directed with special intensity from a single source, public opinion in the United States, then coming under the scrutiny of the new Gallup polls,[3] was formed and maintained through a host of competing media outlets.

The role of the United States in the 1936 Olympics, particularly the boycott campaign, has frequently been retold,[4] but the issues raised in the press by the two sides have still to be exhausted. Arthur Morse, in *While Six Million Died*, claims that American apathy led directly to the abyss of the Second World War.[5] This is an unprovable claim, and, as was shown in the debate over whether or not the United States should send a team to Nazi Germany for the 1936 Olympic Games, many Americans were far from apathetic, but the way the American Olympic Committee (AOC) handled the matter played into the hands of the Nazis. That Americans took their sport seriously was never in doubt, as *The Nation* pointed out in 1935: "[Sports] are unimportant to you? Perhaps, but remember that to millions and millions of your fellow citizens, who first turn to the sports pages when they open a newspaper, they are the breath of life. . . . The World Court? Unemployment? Rising taxes? Yeah, but what about the Babe, izzy gonna play next year or not? Yes, these are our gods, more important than Father Coughlin, and more important than Roosevelt himself."[6]

And, as was noted in the previous chapter, the U.S. ambassador in Vienna, George Messersmith, later to become the assistant secretary of state, insisted that the importance of the political developments emerging out of the boycott debate in the United States "could not be exaggerated."[7]

Most Americans cared little about sport outside North America, and there was not a single sports reporter in Europe in the 1930s on the staff of an American paper. Golf and tennis had some international appeal, but these were minority sports, while boxing was professional. It was only with the Olympic Games that the U.S. sporting public as a whole became interested in international competition. In 1936 there was the added ingredient of politics, keenly felt in a nation with an influential Jewish minority and whose major athletes included a small but significant number of blacks, consigned like the Jews by the regime in Germany to subhuman status. For a nation that had no guilty conscience in spite of its own discrimination against Jews and blacks, U.S. reporters were faced with a ticklish problem. In Europe the fight against the Nazi Olympics was conducted mainly by socialists, communists, and left-wing intellectuals as well as Jews and other victims of the Nazis. Politically committed workers' organizations were comparatively small in the United States,[8] and the debate was essentially conducted through divisions within what in Europe were called bourgeois sports organizations.

Vienna 1933

Not surprisingly, it was a Jewish newspaper that first raised the issue of a boycott in the United States. This was in April 1933 when the *Baltimore Jewish Times* asked Avery Brundage, the president of the AOC, about the American reaction to the German boycott of Jewish shops and the pogroms after the Nazi takeover in Germany. The idea was taken up the next day by the *New York Times* with the headline: "1936 Olympic Games May Be Cancelled Due to Germany's Campaign against Jews."[9] According to Brundage, there were three possibilities: the Games could be transferred to a different country, as Rome and Tokyo had been interested in staging the Games; they might be totally cancelled, as in 1916; or the Games could take place in Berlin but be boycotted by so many countries, since

Germany did not respect the Olympic spirit of racial, religious, and political tolerance, that the Games would have no propaganda value for the organizer.

Brundage went on to dismiss these criticisms and pointed out that the issue would be dealt with in June at the annual meeting of the IOC in Vienna. The U.S. press already sensed a good story, however, and in its own way went on to make an issue of it. Shortly after the *Baltimore Jewish Times* article, the *New York Times* published an interview with Carl Diem in which he expressed a "mixture of shock and incredulity" that the Americans were thinking of a boycott or the possibility that the Games might be relocated.[10] Diem insisted that there was not the slightest hint of discrimination in Germany, but the *New York Times* was not to be put off and followed the interview with its own pointed political comments. These would not be its last.

Indeed, it was in the political rather than the sporting columns of the U.S. press that the issue was pursued.[11] Political commentators were not restrained by some of the sporting realities, such as the logistics of running a major sports event, precisely the same mentality that led President Jimmy Carter four decades later to assume that the venue for the Games could be shifted on short notice.[12]

Under pressure for his attitude in regard to the upcoming IOC meeting in Vienna, particularly from organs of Jewish opinion, Brundage assured all who wanted to know that he would not allow the Games to be held in a country that violated Olympic rules. Theodor Lewald, as we have seen, was already hard at work using his deep knowledge of American sport to influence Brundage, assuring him that "there will not be the slightest discrimination."[13]

The precise nature of the "Olympic rules" was widely discussed in the American press, and while it was agreed that the Germans would be good hosts and would not interfere in the selection of the athletes in visiting teams, the issue of Jews in Germany could not so easily be dismissed. In an Associated Press interview, the newly appointed Reichssportführer protested that this was an internal German affair. "German sports are for Aryans. . . . German youth leadership is for Aryans and not for Jews."[14] Besides, to be part of the German team contenders did not only have to show a decent "performance" but "their general and moral fitness for representing Germany."[15] The Jewish tennis star Dr. Prenn had been excluded from the German Davis Cup team at this time, which was to become a cause célèbre in the British press.[16] Many German sports organizations had taken over the rules of the Deutsche Turnerbund, which required a test of "Aryan" descent and of *völkisch* knowledge as a prerequisite for participation.

It was thought that the IOC would make the right decision in Vienna when it met at its annual conference. No one was arguing that the decision was too important to leave to a sporting body. Formally, the IOC does not have members of particular countries but members who represent the IOC in particular countries. The three American members were Colonel William May Garland (1866–1948), a Los Angeles businessman and president of the Organizing Committee of the Olympic Games of 1932,[17] Commodore Ernest Lee Jahncke (1877–1960), a former assistant secretary for the navy under President Hoover,[18] and Brigadier General Charles H. Sherrill (1867–1936), a former ambassador of the United States in Argentina and Turkey. In sporting circles Sherrill had the best reputation, as he had a lifelong involvement in sports, first as a top class sprinter for Yale, many times an Ivy League champion and one of the inventors of the crouch start. Before going to Vienna, Sherrill telegraphed the Jewish Congress that had lobbied against Olympic Games in Berlin: "Rest assured that I will stoutly maintain the American principle that all citizens are equal under all laws."[19]

On June 5, 1933, the Olympic Games in Berlin made the front-page headlines of the *New York Times* for the first time. What was discussed mainly on the sports pages and in some of the specialist press had reached the scope of a potential sensation: "Sherrill Demands Equality for Jews in the Olympics."[20] It was noted that the IOC was possibly the first international body to react forcibly to the oppression of the Jews in Germany: the first signs of the cultural ostracization of Germany were appearing, especially when the next day it was reported that Arturo Toscanini refused to conduct the symphony orchestra at the annual Bayreuth Opera Festival.[21] That same day a leading article in the *New York Herald Tribune* claimed that arrangements for the Games could not wait for a change of heart, and so the Germans should relinquish them.[22]

The press speculated widely about what was going on behind closed doors at the Vienna meeting, assuming that members would vote according to the politics of the country they represented. The member for pro-Fascist Hungary was quoted as saying, "if the Germans declare at the Congress that they will abide by all the principles that govern Olympic participation and guarantee not to disturb the conduct of the festival, we are not in favor of transferring it elsewhere."[23] On June 7, to set the stage for the IOC Congress, the *New York Times* published a declaration by the new German Turner leader Edmund Neuendorff[24] on its editorial page without any further commentary: "Many . . . misunderstandings have arisen out of my recent decision in 'Aryanizing' the Turner organizations that an exception should be made of Jews who have fought at the front [in the War], sons and daughters of Jews who fell in battle and fathers and mothers of sons who died. I therefore cancel the above exceptions and hereby decree that male and female Turners of Jewish descent as far back as grandparents must be separated from our organization. This decision is to be put into effect at the very latest by the time of the next national Turner festival [in seven weeks]."[25]

In the correspondence between members prior to the Vienna meeting, the IOC president, Count Henri de Baillet-Latour, told German members that he was against "German Games,"[26] and even the pro-Nazi president of the International Amateur Athletics Federation (IAAF) and the vice president of the IOC, Sigfrid Edström,[27] came to the conclusion in a letter to Baillet-Latour: "Now Mr. Hitler can make up his mind whether he wants the Olympic Games or not."[28] For Baillet-Latour it was not important where the Olympic Games of 1936 took place so long as they did take place. For this reason he wanted to take a decision for a different city than Berlin if the German chancellor or one of his ministers did not come up with a declaration to assure all members that the principles of the Olympics be honored.[29]

As discussed in the previous chapter, the Vienna meeting came up with a face-saving device that pleased Sherrill. The Germans still had to produce an unambiguously worded communiqué about the nonexclusion of German Jews, but Sherrill celebrated what he saw as a victory, and this was how it was reported in the front pages of the press: "Reich Keeps Games—Giving Way on Jews,"[30] "Germany Keeps Olympics by Pledging Equality to Jews."[31]

Sherrill gave lengthy interviews about his role in the negotiations, saying of his German colleagues: "I do not know how they did it—but they did it."[32] The *New York Times* celebrated the victory as a "great surprise . . . and the opinion has been expressed that a real blow had been struck in the cause of racial freedom at least in the realm of sports."[33] In a leading article, the *New York Times* followed it up the next day: "Nazi leaders are always speaking of the necessity of combating a world propaganda directed against them. Let them be assured that there is no more effective way of combating anti-Hitler propaganda then the avowal of error and the promise of amendment as in the Olympic case."[34]

The *Literary Digest* summarized the situation appropriately: "Practically universal approval is given General Sherrill and those who took their stand with him."[35] It was not quite so simple, however. Some newspapers criticized what they saw as interference in another nation's affairs, while the *New York Evening Post* reported sarcastically that if Germany wanted to handicap itself by barring Jews then it should be allowed to do so.[36] On the whole, however, the Americans congratulated themselves that an American had forced Germany to adopt a more civilized position, and for the next five months the issue virtually disappeared from the political columns of the press. It would reappear with explosive impact following the meeting of the American Athletic Union's (AAU) annual convention in 1933.

The 1933 Annual Convention of the AAU

The AAU convention of 1933 was the forty-fifth annual meeting of that body, but never before had it been attended with such publicity. A few individual sports people had expressed their concern about the 1936 Olympics,[37] but no one was prepared for the furor that unfolded at the meeting in Pittsburgh. Although Arthur Daley[38] wrote a preview of it over five columns in the *New York Times*,[39] he only mentioned in passing that there might be a resolution dealing with the situation in Germany. Gustavus Kirby, the former president and now treasurer of the AAU, proposed the resolution that eventually passed with only three abstentions.

This made the headlines in the East Coast press, as no U.S. organization with so many members had taken such a strong position against Nazi Germany.[40] The only opposition had come from the German-American wrestling chairman

Dietrich Wortmann of New York,[41] who pointed out that the standard required from Germany in that resolution would not be met by the United States itself because of its blatant racial discrimination against African Americans. Only recently had the American track and field championships been moved from New Orleans to Lincoln, Nebraska, and the boxing championships from Baltimore to Boston to assure that African Americans were allowed to participate.[42]

The AAU resolved that it would not certify any American Olympic athletes for the Games in Nazi Germany, "until and unless the position of the German Olympic Committee . . . is so changed in fact as well as in theory as to permit and encourage German athletes of Jewish faith or heritage to train, prepare for, and participate in the Olympic Games of 1936."[43]

Without the endorsement of the AAU, no athlete belonging to that body could go to Berlin. The AAU was only one of the bodies represented on the AOC, but it was by far the strongest, and its delegates were instructed to make their position known at the AOC. This was a threat the Germans could not treat lightly.

The first comment on the situation came from Bill Henry in the *Los Angeles Times*. He was also a member of the AOC, but while he did not share the East Coast hard-line attitude, he cautioned: "The International Olympic Committee is located in Europe . . . it is in a position to definitely KNOW what is going on in Germany. This country would be a lot better off if it left the decision regarding the fitness of Germany to hold the Games to the international body. They'll eventually decide anyway."[44]

The reaction in Germany was reported at length on the front page of the *New York Times* with the headline: "Vote of American A.A.U. to Shun Olympic Games Falls Like a Bomb in Berlin."[45] The Berlin Organizing Committee immediately sent a telegram to the AAU convention stressing that after Vienna everything had been done to honor its pledge. The telegram was read at the convention and tabled.[46] The day after the AAU convention, many of the delegates stayed on for the AOC convention. The resolution was presented there, and it was now General Sherrill who spoke against it and had it amended "so as to be a protest and not a threat."[47] He believed in the honesty of the German pledge in Vienna that he had brokered, unlike the AAU delegates, who were reluctant to accept that anything had changed in Germany for the better. The *New York Times* summarized the situation in its next headline: "U.S. Olympic Body Takes More Temperate Stand Than A.A.U. on Racial Issue."[48]

Hitler was well informed about the American position and discussed it with Lewald on December 14. Lewald pointed out to Hitler that he was sure the situation would calm down as soon as the Reichssportführer included some Jewish athletes in the national training camps to prepare for the Olympics.[49] In a letter to the subminister of the interior, Hans Pfundtner, who was responsible for sport on behalf of the government, Lewald sounded worried: "If the American Olympic Committee follows the decision of their sport federation [AAU], an American participation in the Olympic Winter and Summer Games will be impossible. After discussion with my colleagues [v. Halt and v. Mecklemburg] we are convinced that the IOC will follow the American Olympic Committee. If at the next IOC convention in Athens the Americans declare that they will not participate in Germany, we are sure that the IOC will choose a different city—and that all the more as Italy and Japan have declared that they are still ready to take over the Games."[50]

The Americans delighted in the anxiety of the Germans. A commentator in the *New York Herald Tribune* wrote, "it is my feeling the Eleventh Olympic Games will not be held in Berlin."[51] *Amateur Athlete*, the monthly magazine of the AAU, printed the Kirby resolution in full and reprinted the coverage of the *New York Times* and the *New York Herald Tribune*, refraining from a commentary of its own.[52] *The Nation*, which seldom dealt with sport, reprinted the full Kirby resolution on the inside front cover and commented: "Do Nazis still believe that opposition abroad to their anti-Jewish policy is fomented by, or limited to, Jews and Marxian elements? "[53] Joe Williams in the *New York World Telegraph* put the question in simple language: "Germany has made it plain that the native Jew has lost his birth-right. That should be reason enough for this country and all other competing countries to insist that the Games be moved elsewhere without qualifying provisions."[54]

Neither the delegates nor the press, however, were aware of the extent to which the situation had been staged by Avery Brundage and the IOC. Brundage, who was the chairman of the AAU and had an ardent desire to be elected onto the IOC, had asked Baillet-Latour confidentially for advice before the convention, "since I do not want to embarrass the IOC."[55] Baillet-Latour answered: "It would be unwise to believe all that is said by the other side. I am not personally fond of Jews and of the Jewish influence but I will not have them molested in any way whatsoever." He therefore recommended a strongly worded resolution by the AAU, as "this would strengthen enormously my personal position."[56] While the president of the IOC was "not very fond of Jews," his vice president expressed a hearty hatred. Sigfrid Edström claimed that the IOC should stand more firmly behind their German colleagues in face of the "international Jews" who "embarrassed their preparations."[57] Others found the matter rather tiresome. Lord Aberdare, Britain's IOC member and one of the nine members of the IOC executive board, claimed: "The whole thing turns upon the one sentence 'the true spirit of the Olympic movement.' . . . I feel a certain definite uneasiness which only Germany herself can remove."[58] Lewald wrote a letter to the IOC president in confidence: "I hope that in Athens, Sherrill or Garland will not bring up the question any more."[59]

Athens 1934

The 1934 meeting of the IOC was held in Athens, Greece, between May 15 and 19. The fortieth anniversary of the IOC was celebrated, but the meeting was attended by only twenty-three IOC members. The Executive Committee had met in Brussels just prior to this session and hoped that they had buried the Jewish issue there. Aberdare had pointed out that at Los Angeles only one of the seventy-four British athletes had been Jewish, while Sherrill gave the figure of five Jews out of four hundred for the U.S. contingent. Lewald then pointed out that since the war, only three German athletes out of 412 had been Jewish.[60] Nevertheless, Aberdare promised to stand by the Americans should they boycott on the grounds of violation of Olympic principle,[61] while the Germans blustered that they might not be able to find a single Jewish athlete and that this should not be construed as proof that all Jews had been banned. There had been comparatively few Jews of Olympic caliber, mainly because their preferences often were for non-Olympic sports,[62] but what no one tried to explain was the relevance of numbers to ethics.

The main topic for discussion at Athens was the German plans for the Winter and Summer Olympics, including issues such as the proposed torch relay from Olympia and the organization of the banquets. Only three people raised the issue of the situation in Germany. Garland was the most explicit when he said that he was not sure whether he would actually get enough votes together to send an American team. Lewald and von Halt promised that they would honor their pledge in Vienna "loyally" and pointed out that they had started to include the Jewish clubs in their campaign to find the unknown sportsman, as they were really concerned to find one for the benefit of the German team.[63] The Reichssportführer actually did improve on the conditions of the Jewish sports clubs, which reached the high point in their development in 1934.[64] The American press found little of this to be of great public interest.

The next meeting of the AOC was held on June 4, 1934, and to the surprise of some, resentment against participation in Germany was still strong. The AOC decided to send its president, Avery Brundage, on a fact-finding tour, on the result of which it would base its decision. The *Christian Science Monitor* called this committee of one a "rather large assignment."[65] But the sports world trusted Avery Brundage, the self-made Chicago conservative millionaire who had been a successful engineer in the construction business after a brilliant athletic career that included participating in the 1912 Olympics.[66] He had been reelected five times already as president of the AAU. *Amateur Athlete* praised him: "It is a tremendous burden that is placed upon the shoulders of one man, but happily enough that stalwart Chicagoan is eminently fitted for the task that has been imposed upon him. He has keen insight, strength of purpose and moral courage to do what is right and just."[67] Brundage combined his trip with a visit to the International Amateur Athletics Federation, to which he had been previously committed. On the way to Germany he wrote an article for the *American Olympic News,* the organ of the AOC, which showed that he had already made up his mind on the issue. He claimed that the Games in Germany would lead to "better international understanding . . . a better human race through the influence of the Olympics."[68] This went down badly with the American public. Congressman Emanuel Celler went straight to the point: "The American public demands that you at least withhold your judgement until you know all the facts."[69]

Brundage soon found the facts he was after in a six-day tour organized by his old drinking friend, Ritter von Halt. With little understanding of German he had to rely on von Halt, and when he interviewed the leading Jewish sports leaders in the Hotel Kaiserhof in Berlin it was in the presence of Arno Breitmeyer, the deputy Reichssportführer, complete with SS uniform and cavalry boots. He was at pains to point out that in the United States his club in Chicago barred Jews: Americans believed in equal but separate development. This did not infringe upon Olympic rules.[70]

None of this was conveyed by Brundage to the American press, and at the next meeting of the Executive Committee of the AOC it was unanimously decided to accept the invitation to go to Germany.[71] In Germany the decision was greeted as a "turning-point in the campaign of hate against Germany,"[72] but in the United States it led to a resurgence of the boycott debate. At the Miami conference of the AAU in December 1934 it was decided to delay a decision on the vote until the following year. Both sides were happy with this; those in favor of a boycott because it would give them more time to organize, Brundage and his followers because they knew it would be difficult to pull the plug on the eve of the Winter Olympics. A new figure entered the proboycott forces when Jeremiah T. Mahoney, a judge on the New York Supreme Court and a member of the New York Athletic Club who was also former high-jump champion and associated with the Democratic party, replaced Brundage as president of the AAU. Brundage concentrated on the presidency of the AOC and cleared the way to get himself elected to the IOC.

The Summer of 1935

In the first months of 1935 the German propaganda machine got under way to accompany the release of tickets for sale. The issue had subsided from the press, but it was raised in the first of the Gallup polls that were being conducted for the first time. Although these polls normally related to politics, the issue of the Olympics was raised in March 1935. A representative sample of adult Americans was asked: "Should America refuse to participate in the Olympic Games which are to be held in Germany next year?" Forty-three percent answered "Yes" and 57 percent "No."[73] This poll shows the high esteem of the traditional value of fair play, as the result was far higher than comparative questions relating to a trade boycott of Germany. It should be noted, however, that in a *Fortune* survey published at the same time, 17.3 percent of the population considered Germany the most disliked of foreign nations, followed by Japan (11.2 percent) and Russia (6.7 percent).[74]

It was at this time that Brundage set about raising the money to send the U.S. team to Germany. His task was made more difficult by the U.S. government, which insisted that they go on an American ship despite the fact that a German ship would have been much cheaper, heavy discounts being offered in order to attract foreign currency.[75] Congress resolved, however, that athletes in the military forces could train while on duty and use their horses for the Olympic Games at no charge to the AOC.[76] His biggest problem, however, was that the usually generous donations that could have been expected from Jewish sources were not forthcoming. This policy was fully backed by Samuel Untermyer, the president of the Non-Sectarian Anti-Nazi League. "All propaganda to the contrary notwithstanding, the major sports among the Nazis continued to be street-brawling, hooligan mob assaults, the goose-step of the barracks and the lock step of the 'concentration camp.'"[77] Brundage had to seek other sources, although the bulk of the funds were to come from gate money at the Olympic trials. Nevertheless, the words of Untermyer expressed an irritating reality: "The question of American participation in the 1936 Olympics will not be closed without a desperate struggle to prevent such a body blow to sport, fair play and world liberalism regardless of race or creed."[78]

In the second half of 1935 the boycott debate reached its peak, fueled by events in Germany, where the Nuremberg Laws, the closure of independent church sports organizations, and the expansionist ambitions of Germany gave any right-thinking person reason for pause. The *Bremen* incident had nothing to do with sport, but it showed the extent to which feeling against Germany was building up in the United States. American sailors had hauled down the Nazi flag on the German liner *Bremen* in New York harbor. The sailors were taken to court and were not sentenced as Judge Brodsky called the swastika, which was not yet the official flag of the Reich, a pirate's flag that was not protected by American law.[79]

The stage was set for the biggest boycott ever in the history of sport. The trigger was the outlawing of the Deutsche Jugendkraft, the federation of Catholic sport in Germany. An editorial in *Commonweal,* the influential Catholic journal, took up all the issues that until then had been put by the Jewish organizations and their supporters: "We summoned each and every organization identified with the Church to make it clear to its members that participation in the approaching games means endorsement of willful and violent persecution. And we respectfully petition the hierarchy to warn the faithful concerning the issues involved, so that no Catholic young man or his friends unwittingly give to enemies of the faith opportunity to question the sacred solidarity of the Christian belief. . . . Let there be no compromise. . . . A German Government which does not respect a covenant solemnly arrived at with the Holy See will probably not bother a great deal about what it says to Mr. Brundage. There is nothing to add. It is inconceivable that Catholic America should not rise to the occasion. It will rise to it."[80]

Prior to publication, the editorial was released to the daily press,[81] which took up the issue with relish. *Commonweal* continued to maintain its stand over subsequent issues and was joined in its campaign by the *Christian Century,* a liberal Protestant journal,[82] and *The Nation.*[83] The latter two journals drew extensively from daily events in Germany to back up their call for a boycott.

There were no further Gallop polls on the Olympics after March 1935, but later in the year the *American Israelite* and the *Cincinnati Post* published the results of their own surveys. The *American Israelite,* the oldest Jewish paper in the United States, conducted its survey in cooperation with a paper in a predominantly German area with the oldest German Turnverein.[84] As such it can be regarded as reasonably objective. The survey was carried out in towns with more than a hundred thousand inhabitants. The thirty editors and fifty-five sport editors surveyed represented a newspaper circulation of 6.2 million, reaching 22.2 million inhabitants. They were asked: "Do you believe that the 1936 Olympic Games should be held in Germany?" Thirty sports editors said "Yes," twenty-five said "No." Of the political editors it was the other way around: twenty-three said "No," and only six said "Yes." Their second question was: "Do you believe that the United States athletes should participate in the 1936 Olympics Games, if the Games are not moved from Germany?" Thirty-five sports editors said "Yes," twenty said "No." Of the political editors, twelve said "Yes," eighteen said "No."[85] The United Press News Agency conducted a survey among thirty sports editors who were chosen randomly by a lottery. Thirteen of them were in favor of sending an American Olympic team to Germany, eleven were against it, and six were still undecided.[86]

While the endorsement of newspapers may be important in the political arena, it is less so in the field of sport. The *American Hebrew* published a list of the newspapers and organizations that had supported the boycott by November 1935 and gave the impression that everybody in any position of importance was against sending the team.[87] Their list contained 232 newspapers with a circulation of 15 million, reaching 36.2 million people.[88] An inspection of the list, however, reveals that some newspapers that should have been on it, such as the Communist *Daily Worker,* were omitted, while others were included that should not have been there, such as the *Los Angeles Times* and the *New York Herald Tribune.*

The real test would come with the annual meetings of the AAU and the AOC, both in December. Brundage was well prepared, as he could expect a tough fight from Mahoney. Although Brundage had the backing of such powerful forces as the IOC and the AOC as well as relevant powers in Germany, he still had to win the vote of the AAU. To accomplish this he revealed the cunning that would keep him in the fore in Olympic politics over the next decades. According to IOC rules, the application of an athlete to participate in the Games required three signatures: that of the athlete, that of his sport governing body (for most sports the AAU) and of the national Olympic Committee (the AOC). Brundage convinced the IAAF president Edström[89] and the IOC president Baillet-Latour that his signature for the AOC would suffice under these extraordinary circumstances to certify that the athlete was an amateur in good standing.[90]

Although this move helped Brundage to outmaneuver the AAU, he tried to win its vote nevertheless. For this he prepared a sixteen-page pamphlet, *Fair Play for American Athletes,* ten thousand copies of which were printed; half of these were distributed by October 1935. It contained the sixty-two names of the members of the AOC, of which fifty-eight had agreed to publish the pamphlet in a secret ballot.[91] The pamphlet made the point that sports-minded people should consider America first and should not risk the "birthright"[92] of the American athletes for the benefit of one or two Jews on the German team. The pamphlet associated the Jewish position with communism and appealed to the "loyal, red-blooded citizen of the United States, who has the true welfare of amateur sport at heart," and asked for support—including financial—"in this patriotic enterprise."[93]

Leading the opposition, Judge Mahoney gained support for his campaign for a boycott from an unusual quarter when he was joined by Ernest Lee Jahncke, the third American member of the IOC. Jahncke had said nothing on the issue before and had never attended an IOC meeting outside North America.[94] His reward was to be ousted at the 1936 session of the IOC, held during the Games, and replaced by Brundage.[95]

The boycott coalition—which had organized itself as the Committee for Fair Play in Sports—reacted fast and published its own pamphlet protesting Brundage's pamphlet and placing their demand to preserve the Olympic ideal before President Roosevelt.[96] The sixty-four-page pamphlet was mainly based on newspaper editorials showing the wide support for the Olympic boycott and rebutting the arguments of *Fair Play for American Athletes.* It included many pictures portraying the reality of daily life in Nazi Germany, with the assumption that by going to the Olympics in that country the athletes would be supporting such abuses.[97] Olympic years are also election years in the United States, and domestic politics could not fail to become mixed in the discussion. While Brundage was a conservative Republican, supporting isolationism and a policy of "America first," and as such was seen to stand for "middle America," those on the Committee for Fair Play in Sports were seen to be liberal Democrats, supported by internationalists such as Jews and Catholics and the world represented by New York. Brundage has often been called an anti-Semite, but this label does not really fit his complex personality. Brundage was so deeply involved in sports culture that he blatantly disregarded the political consequences of his actions. He had a number of Jewish personal friends, yet he leased his ground to a golf club that did not permit Jewish members.

In a country where it was estimated that a third of its voters depended for their opinions on what was said by a political columnist,[98] three of the most popular of these pundits were in favor of a boycott: Arthor Brisbane, Westbrook Pegler, and Heywood Broun. For Brisbane, who supported the boycott by the trade unions, it was clear that "a country in which the principle 'game' seems to be persecuting Jews and Catholics hardly needs any additional games."[99] Pegler, who was also critical of the treatment of African Americans in the American South, was equally outspoken: "The plans of the Nazis . . . would make use of the athletes of 48 nations to exalt everything that Adolf Hitler represents, including the kicking and the beating of women by mobs in the streets and the assassination of thought, freedom and human beings."[100]

Other columnists took up the issue, and rallies were organized in New York,[101] but the crucial test would come with the meeting of the AAU.[102] Brundage complained of the money at the disposal of his opponents, while he did not even know where he was going to get the money to send the team to Berlin,[103] but he would easily make up for this in the back rooms of power. The U.S. government itself refused to be drawn into the dispute. As the secretary of state, Cordell Hull, explained in a letter to Senator Augustine Lonnergan (Connecticut): "The question of participation, of course, does not fall within the competence of any agency of this government but is a matter exclusively for determination by the private organizations directly concerned."[104]

It was at this time that the issue of Helene Mayer was raised, to the advantage of the antiboycott forces, although their opponents answered:[105] "she could not reject the invitation, knowing very well what might happen to her family and friends in Germany in case she demurred."[106] From her statements at the German consulate in San Francisco[107] and the knowledge of one of her best friends,[108] it is more likely that she was extremely ambitious and simply wanted to regain her Olympic title. If she had not competed for the German squad, she would have tried to qualify for the American team.[109]

The other personality to play a role at this time was Sherrill, who was still enjoying the reflected glory of his role in Vienna two years earlier and who did not allow reality to cloud his support for participation thereafter. Not all of his dealings with the Germans were known, and so he was held in some trust by both sides, while in New York, although a Republican, he was popular as a commander in the New York Home Guard during World War I. His support was sought by the proboycott forces, and when he spoke out against the boycott his opinion made the front pages of the New York Times.[110] This was the first time that the paper had placed an antiboycott opinion on its front page.[111] For the Daily Worker the situation was clear: "The trouble with General Sherrill is that the speeches he heard at the Nazi Congress in Nuremberg, where he spent four days as Hitler's guest, are still ringing so loudly in his ears, that every time he opens his mouth, all he can emit is an echo."[112]

The 1935 AAU Convention

The AAU convention took place between December 6 and 8, 1935, in the Hotel Commodore in New York. Brundage considered the location "the worst possible place under the present conditions," as the atmosphere in New York favored a boycott.[113] Mahoney did all he could to bring pressure his way and found himself at odds with Paul Gallico, America's leading sportswriter, who attacked the convention for having nothing to do with sport: "The truth of the matter is that the agitation on this side of the water is nothing but political attention-calling."[114]

On the evening before the meeting the AAU Executive Committee decided in a ten-to-five vote to bring the matter to the delegates without any recommendation.[115] This could be seen as a small victory for Brundage, as Mahoney had tried to get a majority for a resolution that solemnly called upon American athletes to refuse to participate.[116] The Executive Committee agreed, however, that both sides should get two hours to present their case.

The next morning Brundage made a smart move, testing his strength. He had one of his followers apply to vote on the issue without any discussion. The complicated voting procedure resulted in a $60^{11}/_{20}$ to $55^{7}/_{60}$ majority for Brundage. Every AAU district had three votes, no matter how many delegates were present. If more than three were present the vote was to be divided so that everyone in a district had the same vote—unless that district had previously voted to cast its three votes in a particular way. The sport federations that were associated to the AAU (such as the Jewish Welfare Board or the YMCA) each had one vote. It became obvious in this first voting that Mahoney had the majority of the AAU districts. It looked as if Mahoney had simply overlooked the possibility of recruiting a large vote in the associated sports federations, while Brundage confessed that he had brought in his support the previous evening.[117] With amendments added, the discussion was finally started, and it lasted all day. The New York Sunday papers reported the tight voting on the front page and set the scene for the decisive showdown vote.[118]

The discussion failed to produce a compromise: the team to participate in the Olympic Winter Games had to leave for Europe soon, and there was no chance for further postponement of the decision. Eventually the boycott was avoided by a vote of $58^{1}/_{4}$ to $55^{3}/_{4}$. The AAU districts had voted $54^{1}/_{2}$ to $41^{1}/_{2}$ in favor of the boycott, the past presidents and secretaries had voted 1.75 to .25 against the boycott, and the associated organizations voted 15 to 1 against the boycott. Brundage knew the rules better than his opponents, so he made sure that many federations that had little to do with the Olympics but were members with voting rights were present to vote. In the end, he had won the day with the help of a German spy (the German Athletic Union), a rabid anti-Semite (the American Turnerbund) and the representative of a professional organization (the National Cycling Association). But he won.[119] A lukewarm declaration that American participation did not mean the support of Nazi politics was passed by acclamation, so the conference could end on a friendly tone. Mahoney did not seek re-election, as he saw himself outmaneuvered by Brundage's move to bring in extra representatives of the associated organizations, more than had ever attended. So it was that Brundage was elected president of the AAU for another year.[120]

The AAU vote did not change the opinion of the press, but once the decision was made, it had to be accepted. This was perhaps best summed up in a cartoon in the *New York Journal* in which a smiling American athlete exclaimed, "All right,

Let's go!"[121] *The Nation*[122] and the *New Republic*[123] said that they would continue the struggle, while *Opinion,* the voice of Jewish America, found the AAU vote "pivotal to the entire world controversy that ranges around the Nazi problem."[124]

The African American position was quite difficult. Although race relations had been improving in the United States, African Americans were still discriminated against in sport as much as in other walks of life.[125] The large majority of the African American newspapers expressed the feeling that a special boycott on the part of black athletes was naive and foolish.[126] Of course, African Americans could use such a boycott to protest racial discrimination, but why should the African American stars suffer? Only thirty years later the situation had sufficiently changed to the extent that Harry Edwards could show that a threat of boycott against discrimination in American sport does have some effects.[127] In 1935, the majority of the African American newspapers assumed that the ideal way to combat the notion of Aryan supremacy would be to go to Berlin and defeat the Nazi youth. Many African American newspapers also pointed to the hypocrisy in America, where whites complained about racial discrimination in Germany while African Americans were denied equal rights and equal opportunity in the United States. The argument against Germany could have also been used against the United States in their bid for the 1932 Olympics in Los Angeles. At that time there were no African Americans in the white organized professional leagues nor in any college sport in the South.[128]

The IOC and the German committee were relieved that the Americans had finally agreed to come. The German committee was, however, extremely careful not to aggravate the situation in Germany, which was still seen as shaky by Brundage. Brundage then asked his friend, the Chicago journalist Clarence A. Bush, who was the AOC secretary and had served as Brundage's ghostwriter on his *Fair Play* pamphlet, to write to Carl Diem about the situation: "It seems that each time Mr. Brundage has made a bold stroke for participation, this has evoked a story from Germany capitalizing on it for the benefit of Nazi propaganda. This has given the Anti-Nazi forces in this country the chance to say 'I told you so' which has been embarrassing for Mr. Brundage and our entire campaign. . . . Cannot some care be used to prevent relating Nazi propaganda to our participation battle, either by coincidence of timing, or by similarity of subject matter?"[129]

From then onward, Nazi propaganda and the efforts of Avery Brundage were better coordinated. The main battle ahead was to ensure the financing of the team and to avoid falling into any trap on the way to Garmisch-Partenkirchen or Berlin.

The Olympic Games in Germany

Brundage had every reason to be worried about the traps that lay in Germany, but the Germans were learning quickly. While the debate raged in New York, most of the U.S. team was participating in the winter sports in Europe. For them the

Olympic Games were only one event, albeit the biggest, of their winter sports activities. By the time they got to Garmisch-Partenkirchen, the insulting anti-Jewish signs that formerly greeted visitors had been taken down. Baillet-Latour is usually credited with this, but in fact Sherrill had warned the secretary of the Winter Sports, Le Fort, "that those anti-Jewish signs in Garmisch-Partenkirchen park etc. be taken down before the American team arrives. If not, there is a serious risk that many of the American team will leave and then Berlin will lose out."[130]

The opening ceremony of the Winter Olympics attracted a larger crowd than that for the entire Lake Placid Games in 1932. This was somewhat spoiled by the preponderance of uniforms, and Westbrook Pegler, the only major American columnist who made the trip to Garmisch, poked fun at this in his column, "Fair Enough?" When told that some of those in uniform were cobblers, he replied that it was strange that they chose to walk in columns of four.[131] Most reports to appear in the United States praised the welcome and the strict adherence to rules and procedures. The Winter Games were not a popular topic, however, and they were covered by correspondents already in Europe. This meant that they wrote more about the political aspects, taking the sporting stories from the German or the international press services. It is obvious that the Games did not change the attitude of the papers. Pegler, who pointed out that "at home we have never thought it necessary to mobilize an army for a sport event,"[132] was relatively friendly to Hitler, who "gave autographs to a hundred or more as willingly as Babe Ruth."[133] But with his relative naiveté concerning sport, he raised the suspicion of Bill Henry, who had been responsible for the press at the 1932 Olympic Games in Los Angeles: "It is a shame to have sports written by those who have no understanding."[134] But then, of course, the question was and still is whether this was a mere sporting event. Richard Vidmer concluded in the *New York Herald Tribune*: "There is nothing really the matter with the Olympic Games. They're alright, it is just that their original premise makes them look bad. Because there is some sort of idea that the object of the Games is to promote international amity. The arguments and protests . . . make it seem as though the Games are a failure."[135]

The reaction of the American team in Germany was effectively spied upon by the student helpers who reported the mood and every single move.[136] The German press reports of the Nazi party's Foreign Office were quite accurate[137] and showed a shift from a somewhat negative prejudice to a friendly neutrality, particularly for those journalists who normally reported in other European countries. The relatively positive reporting by the people at the site of the Games in the *New York Times*, for example, had been broken up and "distorted" by the editors in New York. It was obvious to the Nazi party that "International Jewry" had not given up yet but rather saw the boycott of the Berlin Games as just one more aspect of their general campaign of hatred against Germany.

Brundage's main problem between Garmisch and Berlin was raising the funds for the athletes' expenses: in contrast to many other nations, the Americans received no help from the government.[138] The government's insistence on the team traveling on an American ship, however, raised the cost to an estimated fifty thousand dollars. Brundage's problem could have been solved if he used the solutions of a later age, but his rigid adherence to the principles of amateurism led him to refuse an offer of a hundred thousand dollars from a breakfast-food manufacturer for the exclusive rights to claim that theirs was the "breakfast food of champions."[139] The athletes had to pay their own way to the trials and had further to raise funds at meets after the Games; while the athletes got little from this, the AOC raised enough to ensure its own operating costs over the next four years.[140]

Sherrill, who saw nothing of the Winter Games, nevertheless claimed on over forty-two stations of the NBC chain that he had been there and saw nothing to complain about the way people were treated.[141] Lewald, an early supporter of dirigibles, was keen to visit the United States on the *Hindenburg*'s maiden flight in order to publicize the Games, but much to his chagrin this was refused.[142] It was thought better to keep the sight and sound of things Nazi hidden away. Baillet-Latour did not fare much better: Brundage asked him to lie low while passing through Chicago on a trip to Tokyo to inspect conditions for the 1940 Games.[143] When Edström came to Chicago his trip was kept quiet.[144] The spirit of the 1932 Olympics did not carry over to Berlin, and when Garland asked the Los Angeles City Council for two thousand dollars to take the IOC flag from one site to the next, the millionaire was told that it would be cheaper to send it by mail and was offered $1.50 instead. Garland then agreed to take it at his own expense.[145]

Untermyer continued to discourage people from going to Berlin, sending out five hundred thousand brochures detailing what life was really like in Germany and asking that tourists boycott that country and discouraging them from contributing to the expenses of sending athletes to Berlin.[146] The boycott forces asked President Roosevelt, whose name as honorary president of the AOC was on their letterhead in soliciting donations, to express his disapproval or even withdraw from the campaign.[147] He did not, but neither did he give the customary farewell address to the departing athletes, although this could have been because he had also been asked to speak to the workers departing for the Workers' Olympics in Barcelona and preferred to bestow his presence on neither.[148] New York's mayor Fiorello La Guardia, who had supported a boycott, sensed the last-minute support for the Olympic effort and in a complete turnaround addressed the departing team.[149] While one Jewish American athlete had gone to Garmisch, six were on the U.S. squad to Berlin in spite of all of the boycott campaigns.[150]

As in most countries, however, the papers aimed at the broad populace carried the day in their support for the Games. Grantland Rice ridiculed as "bunk" the notion that international sport contributed to international goodwill, but the *Sportsman* (Boston) was closer to the public pulse: "If we are going to send a team to Berlin, let's foot the bill like the great big grown-up tax payers that we are, and stop crying about it."[151]

Once in Berlin, the press was full of admiration for the greetings extended to the visitors: "The Germans are acting as if the Americans were the whole show. . . . The rest of the world ought to get a little jealous. Even the Nazi organ *Der Angriff* is full of enthusiasm for America and things American."[152] Brundage had brought things back to normal when he suspended Eleanor Holm Jarrett, the defending Olympic swim champion in the 100 meter backstroke, for breaking team rules on the boat. The attractive swimmer was caught twice drinking too much at night. As she had been drinking with journalists and was very popular with the press, she did not return to the United States as ordered by Brundage but stayed on as a correspondent for the Hearst press in Berlin.[153]

The first negative reporting came with the news that Jahncke had been dropped from the IOC, prompting even the Republican papers that favored participation into making some critical comments.[154] The easygoing Americans found the atmosphere to be on the sinister side, and even the Fascist-leaning Hearst press remarked on how its correspondents in Berlin "seemed to see only the dark shadow of dictatorship and approaching war over the Olympic scene. Why, we don't know. Couldn't possibly know at this distance, perhaps it is inescapable."[155] On the whole, the Olympic Games were treated for what they were, a gigantic propaganda show: "past masters of kidding the public, the Nazis are now concentrating on kidding a few thousand athletes and officials."[156]

The American press was impressed by the opening ceremony in Berlin but was not won over to the spectacle as a whole. The Americans were really only interested in the events of the first week, the swimming and the track and field, so when these were over they declared themselves the winners and ignored most of what remained of the Games. Jesse Owens was the darling of the German crowd, but readers of the *Atlanta Constitution* and other newspapers of the white American South did not see any picture of him, while most of the German press celebrated him as much as warranted a four-time gold medal winner and hero of the Games.

One of the affairs most publicized at the time of the Games and since was the question of whether or not Hitler shook Owens's hand. On the first day of the track competition Hitler welcomed the medal winners of the first three track and field events to his VIP box after the victory celebration. These included the Germans Hans Woelke, the surprise winner in the shot put, and Karl Hein, who won the gold medal in hammer throw, and the three Finns who had won a clean sweep in the 10 kilometer race. The last event of the evening was the high jump, which was won by the African American Cornelius Johnson. Hitler watched his final attempt (2.08 meters), which took place in semidarkness, much later than anticipated, and left before the victory ceremony. That way, he seemed to discriminate in public against the black American athletes. The next day, the IOC protested Hitler's behavior and asked that he greet all or none of the victors in public. As it would have been impossible for him to welcome all, he met from then on only the German medal winners in the VIP lounge below the grandstand, unseen by the public. The voice of the *New York Evening Journal* can stand for the typical American reaction: "Chancellor Hitler, who has yet to pay homage to any of the Negroes whose spectacular performance has done more than any other single factor to make these the greatest Olympics in history, left the stadium immediately after the conclusion of [Owens's] race."[157]

As Hitler had welcomed many of the lesser stars of the Berlin Olympics, the public waited for a gesture toward the towering Jesse Owens. Owens later claimed that Hitler had waved at him, but there is no evidence for that in the American press reports, and Hitler certainly never shook his hand. Jesse Owens has always been the darling of the Germans, however—more so than of the American public.[158]

Owens was inadvertently involved in a more serious controversy when the head track coach, Lawson Robertson, changed the American sprint relay one day before the heats and dropped the two Jewish sprinters, Marty Glickman[159] and Sam Stoller, to bring in his best two sprinters, Jesse Owens and Ralph Metcalfe. In hindsight and even with the expectations of the times this move was unnecessary, as the U.S. team won easily by 1.3 seconds over Italy; with the two Jewish sprinters the team would have run slower but still won. It is open to speculation why the University of Southern California coach withdrew the Jewish sprinters. Was he really afraid that the Germans had some super sprinters who were not entered in the individual sprints? Was he pressured by American anti-Semites not to race them?[160] Was he afraid that the Jewish sprinters would not be able to handle the stress of Olympic competition in an environment not exactly friendly to Jews? Did he want to do Owens and the American track and field scene a favor? After all, his decision assured Jesse Owens the number-one spot in the Olympics with four gold medals, while otherwise two German gymnasts and a Dutch swimmer would have won the same number of gold and more overall medals than Owens. Outside the United States Robertson's decision was not noticed, as it appeared quite natural to run the first four of your national champions and keep the fifth and sixth finishers as reserves, but in the tradition of the American track supremacy they should have been raced.[161]

The fact that Hitler spent so much time at the Games was commented on favorably, with Grantland Rice writing enthusiastically: "Hitler was rooting for the Germans like a Yale sophomore at a Harvard game . . . you would almost hear him saying, 'Block that Kick! Hold 'em Yale!'"[162]

The journalists in Berlin reported unfavorably about an article in Streicher's *Der Stürmer* that had complained that the Americans had used African American athletes. Even the usually pro-German Hearst press, like the *New York Evening Journal*, quoted *Der Stürmer* at length under the headline: "Nazi Newspaper Scorns U.S. Use of Negro Auxiliaries."[163]

The journalists who stayed on into the second week were amused and then annoyed at the way the Germans invented scoring systems that were to their own benefit.[164] And those who were critical before the Games justified their position during them: "All the evidence accumulating at Berlin emphasizes what this newspaper, along with many others, pointed out many months ago—that the Hitler government is twisting the entire tradition of the Olympic Games to serve the purposes of the Nazi dictatorship. It is apparent that despite the spectacular American successes we are going to be increasingly sorry for American participation."[165]

Another American sporting legend, John Lardner, claimed that the Balkan War was a honeymoon compared to the Berlin Games,[166] but the *Los Angeles Times* showed that its support for participation was well justified: "Thousands will sigh, as they did in Los Angeles, when the great flame fades, wishing that the Games with their exaltation of friendliness in international rivalry could go on indefinitely."[167] Among the rare papers that were softened by the Games was the *New York Times*. It came to the conclusion that the visitors would take home from Berlin "a highly favorable impression and that this was partially so because of the German propaganda but again there was goodwill behind it."[168] It argued, "however much one may deplore or detest some of the excesses of the Hitler regime, the Games make it clear beyond question the amazing new energy and determination that has come to the German people."[169]

In their final commentaries the American press was duly impressed, but they varied in how they interpreted this. They congratulated the Berlin organization for its thoroughness, its technical proficiency, and especially for its knowledge of social psychology. The Eleventh Olympiad was truly the greatest publicity stunt in history.[170] The *Herald Tribune* called it "the most stupendous, most colossal, the greatest show yet fashioned under the aegis of the five interlocking circles." But it also warned that "there was a definite absence of warmth of feeling in the atmosphere of the Games. Germany has no affinity for sport for sport's sake. . . . The Olympics were a festival of Germanism. . . . Whatever else may be said about the Olympic Games of 1936, it is certain that they achieved a world wide interest beyond any Olympics that have preceded them."[171]

In the final analysis it is clear that German propaganda had little effect in the United States. Had there been more purely sporting journalists covering the events perhaps there would have been less criticism, but on the whole the Americans were not the sort of people to be won over by the heavy-handed propaganda that Goebbels was able to wield with such apparent effect in Germany. Some Americans were angered by Goebbels's lecture to eight hundred journalists on the eve of the Games, while more made fun of it: "Reichsminister Dr. Goebbels, in charge of propaganda, threw a party for about 800 journalists the other night, and the boys accepted the situation in the right spirit. That is to say they consumed about 1,500 bottles of wine and after-dinner liquors in acquiring a frame of mind in which to applaud enthusiastically a very fine welcome speech by Dr. Goebbels . . . if the propaganda was as good as the food and the wine, we know that Dr. Goebbels must have done a fine job."[172]

Brundage won his antiboycott battle without any real help from Germany. But he won it, and so far as the German people were concerned the Americans were happy to visit the new Germany: thus the German propaganda machine was able to show that Germany was not culturally ostracized. The Americans neither won nor lost from their visit; Hitler gained a great deal. And when the searchlights died on the closing ceremony, and the athletes and visitors packed up and went back home, the grimmer realities of life had to be faced by those Germans who had at least for the time of the Olympic pause been allowed to enjoy the warmth of normal human relations. But it was no more than a pause, and as the fanatics of the SA put it bluntly, now that the Olympics were over, they could get back to "beating the crap out of Jews":[173] "Wenn die Olympiade vorbei, Schlagen wir die Juden zu Brei!"

Notes

1. E. Kamper, *Enzyklopädie des Olympischen Spiele* (Dortmund: Harenberg, 1972). For the reasons for their success, see M. Dryreson, "Marketing National Identity: The Olympic Games of 1936 and American Culture," *Olympika* 4 (1995): 23–48.

2. W. Cozens and F. S. Stumpf, *Sports in American Life* (Chicago: University of Chicago Press, 1953), 299.

3. H. Gallup and S. F. Rae, *The Pulse of Democracy: The Public Opinion Poll and How It Works* (New York: Greenwood, 1968); P. Lazerfeld, "Magazines in 90 Cities: Who Reads What?" *Public Opinion Quarterly* 1.4 (1937): 29–40.

4. See A. Krüger, *Die Olympischen Spiele 1936 und die Weltmeinung* (Berlin: Bartels and Wernitz, 1972); G. Moshe, "The American Controversy over the Olympic Games," *American Jewish Historical Quarterly* 67 (1972): 181–213; D. K. Wiggins, "The 1936 Olympic Games: The Response of America's Black Press," *Research Quarterly for Exercise and Sport* 54 (1983): 279–82; D. A. Kass, "The Issue of Racism at the 1936 Olympics," *Journal of Sports History* 3.3 (1976): 223–35; S. R. Wenn, "A Tale of Two Diplomats: George S. Messersmith and Charles H. Sherrill on Proposed American Participation in the 1936 Olympics," *Journal of Sports History* 16.1 (1989): 27–43; A. Krüger, "'Fair Play for American Athletes': A Study in Anti-Semitism," *Canadian Journal of the History of Sport and Physical Education* 9.1 (1978): 43–57; S. R. Wenn, "Hotel Commodore Revisited: An Analysis of the 1935 A.A.U. Convention," in *Proceedings: Sixth Canadian Symposium on the History of Sport and Physical Education*, ed. D. Morrow (London, Ont.: Western, 1989), 188–201; R. D. Mandell, *The Nazi Olympics* (Rpt., Urbana: University of Illinois Press, 1987); A. Guttmann, *The Games Must Go On: Avery Brundage and the Olympic Movement* (New York: Columbia University Press, 1984); A. Guttmann, "The Nazi Olympics and the American Boycott Controversy," in *Sport and International Politics: The Impact of Fascism and Communism on Sport*, ed. P. Arnaud and J. Riordan (London: Spon, 1998), 31–50.

5. A. Morse, *While Six Million Died: A Chronicle of American Apathy* (New York: Random House, 1968).

6. Leftwing, "Men Who Make American Gods," *The Nation*, Feb. 27, 1935, 245.

7. Messersmith's Letter to the Department of State, National Archives, Washington D.C., Dept. of State (hereafter cited as National Archives), RG 59 862.4063, Olympic Games, no. 57.

8. A. Krüger and J. Riordan, eds., *The Story of Worker Sport* (Champaign, Ill.: Human Kinetics, 1996).

9. *New York Times*, Apr. 18, 1933, 18 (by Arthur Daley, one of the main sports editors). For the role of Jewish sport in the United States, see S. A. Riess, ed., *Sports and the American Jew* (Syracuse, N.Y.: Syracuse Universty Press, 1998); and G. Eisen, "Jews and Sport: A Century in Retrospect," *Journal of Sport History* 26.2 (1999): 225–39.

10. *New York Times*, Apr. 19, 1933, 21.

11. *New York Times,* Apr. 20, 1933, 16 (the first editorial on the subject).

12. M. B. Vinokur, *More Than a Game: Sport and Politics* (Westport, Conn.: Greenwood, 1988); D. L. Hulme Jr., *The Political Olympics: Moscow, Afghanistan, and the 1980 U.S. Boycott* (New York: Praeger, 1990); J. Hoberman, *The Olympic Crisis: Sport, Politics, and the Moral Order* (New Rochelle, N.Y.: Cratzas, 1986).

13. *New York Times,* May 17, 1933, 21.

14. *New York Times,* May 9, 1933, 24.

15. *New York Times,* May 29, 1933, 11.

16. *The Times* (London), Apr. 18, 1933, 10.

17. See J. A. Lucas, "Prelude to the Games of the Tenth Olympiad in Los Angeles 1932," *Southern California Quarterly* 64 (1982): 313–17.

18. J. A. Lucas, "Ernest Lee Jahncke: The Expelling of an IOC Member," *Stadion* 17 (1991): 53–78.

19. *New York Times,* June 2, 1933, 24.

20. *New York Times,* June 5, 1933, 1.

21. *New York Times,* June 6, 1933, 1 and 15.

22. *New York Herald Tribune,* June 6, 1933, 22.

23. *New York Times,* June 7, 1933, 10.

24. See H. Ueberhorst, *Dr. Edmund Neuendorff: Turnführer ins Dritte Reich* (Berlin: Bartels and Wernitz, 1976).

25. *New York Times,* June 7, 1933, 20 (the translation is accurate).

26. Baillet-Latour in a letter to Ritter von Halt (May 26, 1933), IOC Archives, Lausanne, Jeux Olympiques de 1936 et la question juive (hereafter cited as IOCA).

27. See Krüger, "'Fair Play for American Athletes.'"

28. Edström in a letter to Baillet-Latour (May 8, 1933), IOCA.

29. Baillet-Latour in a letter to the German IOC member Count von Mecklemburg (May 21, 1933), IOCA.

30. *New York Times,* June 8, 1933, 1.

31. *New York Herald Tribune,* June 8, 1933, 1.

32. Ibid.

33. *New York Times,* June 8, 1933, 1, 8.

34. *New York Times,* June 9, 1933, 16.

35. *Literary Digest,* June 24, 1933, 28.

36. Quoted in *Literary Digest,* June 24, 1933, 28.

37. *New York Times,* Nov. 1, 1933, 26; *New York Times,* Nov. 17, 1933, 25.

38. For the importance of Arthur Daley, see J. Zuite, ed., *Sport of The Times: The Arthur Daley Years* (New York: New York Times Book, 1975).

39. *New York Times,* Nov. 19, 1933, 11.

40. *New York Times,* Nov. 21, 1933, 1; *New York Herald Tribune,* Nov. 21, 1933, 1; *New Yorker Staatszeitung und Herald,* Nov. 21, 1933, 1; *Los Angeles Times,* Nov. 21, 1933, 9.

41. W. Gray, "A Question of Loyalty: New York German-Americans and Their Influence on Proposed Participation in the 1936 Olympic Games," in *Proceedings: Sixth Canadian Symposium on the History of Sport,* 173–87.

42. *New York Times,* Nov. 21, 1933, 1, 25.

43. Ibid.

44. *Los Angeles Times,* Nov. 21, 1933, 9.

45. *New York Times,* Nov. 22, 1933, 25.

46. Ibid.

47. *New York Herald Tribune,* Nov. 23, 1933, 1.

48. *New York Times,* Nov. 23, 1933, 26.

49. Lewald's minutes of the meeting, in the Archives of the Olympic Winter Games, City Archives, Garmisch-Partenkirchen.

50. Lewald in a letter to Pfundtner, Federal Archives, Koblenz (Nov. 21, 1933), R18, Rep. 320, Nr.614.

51. *New York Herald Tribune,* Nov. 26, 1933, 4.

52. *Amateur Athlete* 4 (Dec. 1933), 10ff.

53. *The Nation,* Nov. 29, 1933, 607.

54. Quoted in *American Hebrew,* Nov. 24, 1933, 26.

55. Confidential, Brundage to Baillet-Latour (Oct. 27, 1933), IOCA.

56. Confidential, Baillet-Latour to Brundage (Nov. 3, 1933), IOCA.

57. Confidential, Edström to Baillet-Latour (Dec. 6, 1933), IOCA.

58. Unpublished newspaper article (Dec. 1933), IOCA.

59. Lewald to Baillet-Latour (Dec. 2, 1933), IOCA.

60. *New York Times,* May 9, 1934.

61. Copy of letter from Aberdare to Lewald, private and confidential (Feb. 5, 1934), IOCA.

62. B. R. S. Silverman, ed., *The Jewish Athletes Hall of Fame* (New York: Shapolsky 1989); P. Y. Mayer, "Deutsche Juden im Sport: Ihre Leistungen—ihr Schicksal," in *Menora 5: Jahrbuch für deutsch-jüdische Geschichte* (Munich: Piper, 1994), 287–312.

63. *IOC Bulletin,* English version (Oct. 1934), 8.

64. A. Krüger, "'Wenn die Olympiade vorbei, schlagen wir die Juden zu Brei': Das Verhältnis der Juden zu den Olympischen Spielen von 1936," in *Menora 5,* 331–48; A. Krüger, "'Once the Olympics Are Through, We'll Beat up the Jew': German Jewish Sport 1898–1938 and the Anti-Semitic Discourse," *Journal of Sport History* 26.2 (1999): 353–75.

65. *Christian Science Monitor,* June 5, 1934, 6.

66. Guttmann, *The Games Must Go On;* A. Engelbrecht, *Avery Brundage, "The All-American Boy": Die amerikanische Antwort auf die Olympische Frage* (Göttingen: Cuvillier, 1997).

67. *Amateur Athlete* 5 (June 1934): 15.

68. "For Honor of Country and Glory of Sport," *American Olympic News* (Aug. 1934), quoted in *Olympic Games News Service* (Aug. 30, 1934), 6–7.

69. *New York Times,* Aug. 26, 1934, 2.

70. R. Atlasz, "Der jüdische Sport in Deutschland vor und nach 1933," in *Vor der Katastrophe,* ed. K.-J. Ball-Kaduri (Tel Aviv: Europäische Verlagsanstalt, 1963), 76; R. Atlasz, "Eine historische Sitzung im Kaiserhof," in *Bar Kochba: Makkabi Deutschland, 1898–1938,* ed. R. Atlasz (Tel Aviv: Bar Kochba-Hakoah, 1977), 141–42; "Brundages Reiseeindrücke in Deutschland," *Reichssportblatt,* Sept. 30, 1934, 917. S. Edström participated silently in the meeting.

71. *New York Times,* Sept. 27, 1934, 28.

72. *New York Times,* Sept. 30, 1934, 9.

73. H. Cantril, ed., *Public Opinion, 1935–1946* (Princeton, N.J.: Princeton University Press, 1951), 810–11.

74. Quoted in D. Day, "American Opinion of German National Socialism, 1933–1937" (Ph.D. diss., University of California at Los Angeles, 1958), 4.

75. *Congressional Records,* 74th Congress, vol. 79, pt. 8, S. ad. 1803, HR 5721 (May 29, 1935), p. 8365.

76. Ibid., pt. 7, S. ad. 1803 (May 27, 1935), p. 7744; see also *U.S. Statutes at Large,* vol. 49, pt. 1, 292.

77. *American Hebrew,* June 7, 1935, 78.

78. Ibid.

79. *New York Times,* Aug. 9, 1936, 10, points out the parallels between the *Bremen* incident and the Olympic boycott.

80. *Commonweal,* Aug. 9, 1935, 535ff.

81. *New York Times,* July 31, 1935, 3.

82. "Move the Olympics," *Christian Century,* Aug. 7, 1935, 1007–8.

83. "Boycott the Olympics," *The Nation,* Aug. 21, 1935, 201.

84. H. Ueberhorst, *Turner unterm Sternenbanner* (Munich: Moos, 1978); H. Metzner, *History of the American Turners* (Rochester: National Council of American Turners, 1974); A. R. Hofmann, *Aufstieg und Niedergang des deutschen Turnens in den USA* (Schorndorf: Hofmann, 2001).

85. *American Israelite,* Sept. 12, 1935.

86. United Press quoted by the *Los Angeles Times,* Aug. 7, 1935, 19.

87. *American Hebrew,* Nov. 15, 1935, 54ff.

88. Their main sports writer, Bill Henry, a personal friend of Carl Diem, was very active against a boycott, and their editor in chief was quoted as saying that "two wrongs do not make one right." See *Los Angeles Times,* Aug. 9, 1935, 4.

89. Brundage to Edström (Sept. 12, 1935), Avery Brundage Collection, Archives of the University of Illinois at Urbana-Champaign (hereafter cited as Brundage Collection), box 42 (Edström).

90. Brundage to Baillet-Latour (Nov. 17, 1935), Brundage Collection, box 42 (Baillet-Latour).

91. Brundage to Kirby, Rubien, and Raycroft (Nov. 1, 1935), Brundage Collection, box 35 (Individuals Rubien).

92. General Sherrill brought the question of the birthright into the discussion. See *Commonweal,* Nov. 11, 1935, 40.

93. American Olympic Committee, ed., *Fair Play for American Athletes,* (Chicago: n.p., 1935), 9. For its latent anti-Semitism, see Krüger, "'Fair Play for American Athletes.'"

94. Lucas, "Ernest Lee Jahncke."

95. A. Krüger, "Deutschland und die Olympische Bewegung, 1918–1945," in *Geschichte der Leibesübungen,* vol. 3, pt. 2, ed. H. Ueberhorst (Berlin: Bartels and Wernitz, 1982), 1041.

96. National Archives, Olympic Games, nos. 55 and 58.

97. Committee on Fair Play in Sports, ed., *Preserve the Olympic Ideal* (New York: CFP, 1936).

98. Cantril, *Public Opinion,* 514.

99. Committee on Fair Play in Sports, ed., *Preserve the Olympic Ideal,* 40.

100. The full text of the *Washington Post* coverage was sent by the German embassy in Washington back to Berlin. See Political Archive of the German Foreign Office, Bonn, Olympic Games 1936, vol. 1.

101. Of particular interest in showing how helpless these resolutions were is the one passed by the State Assembly of Massachusetts that advised citizens of that state not to travel to Germany as participants or spectators of the Olympic Games (*New York Times,* Aug. 25, 1935, 3). The American Federation of Labor resolved that its members should not participate in the Olympic Games. See American Federation of Labor, ed., *Report of the Proceedings of the 55th Annual Convention Held in Atlantic City, N.J.* (Washington: AFL, 1936), 186, 559–60, 801. There were many similar resolutions from chapters of the American Legion and from church groups.

102. New Jersey and South Atlantic delegates were bound, Metropolitan (i.e. mainly New York City) delegates could freely decide. See *New York Times,* Oct. 8, 1935, 12; Sept. 17, 1935, 14; Oct. 9, 1935, 25.

103. Committee on Fair Play in Sports, ed., *Fair Play for American Athletes,* 2.

104. National Archives, Dec. 9 and 12, 1935, Olympic Games, no. 59.

105. *American Hebrew,* Oct. 25, 1935; *New York Times,* Sept. 27, 1935, 23; Sept. 30, 1935, 9; Oct. 19, 1935, 1; Oct. 26, 1935, 7.

106. *American Hebrew,* Nov. 1, 1935, 3.

107. Ponschab to Luther (Nov. 18, 1935), Political Archive of the German Foreign Office, Bonn, Olympic Games 1936, vol. 6.

108. A. Krüger, "Der Fahnenträger: Hans Fritsch (1911–1987)," in *Aus Biographien Sportgeschichte lernen: Festschrift zum 90. Geburtstag von Prof. Dr. Wilhelm Henze,* ed. A. Krüger and B. Wedemeyer (Hoya: NISH, 2000), 252–71.

109. Her mother even claimed that Helene was the offspring of a relationship out of wedlock with an "Aryan" lover to improve the chances of the "*blonde He*" to compete. For this she was despised by the German-Jewish community. See Atlasz, Eine historische Sitzung," 142.

110. *New York Times,* Oct. 22, 1935, 1.

111. *New York Times,* July 27, 1935, 1; Aug. 12, 1935, 1; Oct. 18, 1935, 1; Oct. 19, 1935, 1; Oct. 21, 1935, 1 were all proboycott.

112. *Daily Worker,* Oct. 25, 1935, 6.

113. Brundage to Edström (Aug. 29, 1935), IOCA.

114. *Life,* Dec. 1935, 32–33.

115. *New York Times,* Dec. 7, 1935, 1.

116. AAU., ed., *Minutes of the Annual Meeting 1935* (New York: AAU, 1936), 124.

117. German General Consulate, New York, to German Foreign Office (Dec. 11, 1935), Political Archive of the German Foreign Office, Bonn, Olympic Games 1936, vol. 3.

118. *New York Times,* Dec. 8, 1935, 1; *New York Herald Tribune,* Dec. 8, 1935, 1.

119. AAU, ed., *Minutes of the Annual Meeting,* 129–215.

120. Ibid., 213.

121. *New York Journal,* Dec. 9, 1935, 21.

122. *The Nation,* Dec. 18, 1935, 698.

123. *New Republic,* Dec. 18, 1935, 155.

124. *Opinion* 5 (Dec. 1935): 7.

125. For more details, see D. K. Wiggins, "The 1936 Olympic Games in Berlin."

126. For example, see *Philadelphia Tribune,* Dec. 19, 1935; and *Baltimore Afro-American,* Dec. 24, 1935.

127. H. Edwards, *The Revolt of the Black Athlete* (New York: Free Press, 1969). But during those thirty years the proportion of African Americans on the U.S. Olympic team had increased tremendously.

128. P. M. Hoose, *Necessities: Racial Barriers in American Sports* (New York: Random House, 1989).

129. Bush to Diem (Dec. 26, 1935), Brundage Collection, box 155 (Clarence Bush).

130. Olympic Archives, Potsdam, 33/39/G-122 (Dec. 30, 1935).

131. *Washington Post,* Feb. 20, 1936, 9.

132. *Washington Post,* Feb. 18, 1936, 9.

133. *Washington Post,* Feb. 21, 1936, 9.

134. *Los Angeles Times,* Feb. 17, 1936, 9.

135. *New York Herald Tribune,* Feb. 14, 1936, 22.

136. For the reports, see Studentenwerk to Le Fort (Apr. 16, 1936), Olympic Archives, Potsdam, 33/31/G-64.

137. *Presseberichte des Aussenpolitischen Amtes der NSDAP,* Reichsleitung, no. 13 (March 1936), Federal Archives, Koblenz, BA, NSD 15.

138. A. Krüger, "'Buying Victories Is Positively Degrading': The European Origins of Government Pursuit of National Prestige through Sports," *International Journal of the History of Sport* 12.2 (1995): 201–18.

139. *New York Times,* Apr. 6, 1936, 25; July 17, 1936, 12.

140. *New York Times,* Feb. 18, 1936, 28.

141. Ambassador Luther to Lammers (Apr. 21, 1936), Political Archive of the German Foreign Office, Bonn, Olympic Games 1936, Presseberichte.

142. Hinrichs (German Foreign Office) to Lewald (May 4, 1936), with reference to letter by Ambassador Luther (Apr. 23, 1936), Federal Archives, Koblenz, BA, R43 II/730.

143. *New York Times,* Feb. 28, 1936, 25.

144. *New York Times,* Mar. 13, 1936, 31.

145. *Los Angeles Daily News,* July 10, 1936.

146. See Krüger, "'Fair Play for American Athletes.'" It is difficult to judge the success of the campaign, but I assume that it failed. In the month of August, 7,791 American citizens spent a total of 52,015 nights in Berlin hotels, the largest contingent of any nation. Czechs (including the Sudetendeutsche, with Czech passports) were the largest group with 12,215 but with shorter stays, 51,771 nights in total. Sweden was third with 6,764 people staying 46,113 nights; Great Britain was fourth with 5,159 tourists spending 29,032 nights. These figures neither include the Olympic ath-

letes and registered team officials nor the participants in the international youth camp. See R.
Rürup, ed., *1936: Die Olympischen Spiele und der Nationalsozialismus* (Berlin: Topographie des
Terrors, 1996), 108.

147. For example, it was used by William Dalton, president of the N.Y. Athletic Club (*Winged
Foot* 47 [May 1936]: 19). However, it was also used by Dietrich Wortmann's German American
Olympic Fund Committee, which recommended that visitors should come back from Germany
"as apostles of truth and justice for the promotion of friendship between our great nations." Few
Americans cared about German-style "truth and justice." See *Circular German American Olympic Fund Committee*, National Archives, Olympic Games, no. 78, as attachment to letter by Hoff-
man to F. D. Roosevelt (Apr. 15, 1936). The first to recommend that Roosevelt should give up the
honorary presidency of the American Olympic Association had been the *Jewish Examiner* (as early
as Oct. 26, 1934). See National Archives, 811/American Olympic Assciation/3.

148. National Archives, Olympic Games 1936 (July 2, 1936) 108; (July 8, 1936), 112.

149. *New York Times,* July 16, 1936, 1; *New York Herald Tribune,* Aug. 7, 1936, 18.

150. S. A. Riess, "Sports and the American Jew: An Introduction," in Riess, *Sports and the American Jew,* 32–33.

151. *Sportsman* 10 (Aug. 1936): 13.

152. *New York Times,* July 23, 1936, 17.

153. A. Guttmann, *The Olympics: A History of the Modern Games,* 2d ed. (Urbana: University of
Illinois Press, 2002), 64.

154. See, for example, *New York Herald Tribune,* Aug. 1, 1936, 10.

155. *New York Journal,* July 28, 1936, 19.

156. *New Masses,* July 28, 1936, 4.

157. *New York Evening Journal,* Aug. 3, 1936, 1.

158. W. J. Baker, *Jesse Owens: An American Life* (New York: Free Press, 1986); J. Owens, *Black-
think: My Life as Black Man and White Man* (New York: William Morrow, 1970). While white
Americans virtually forgot him for almost a generation until he was needed by the American government to help fight the cold war—and because of his Jim Crow position he never was a hero
for the young African Americans of the 1960s either—the Germans named several roads after him
and invited him many times to Germany after the war.

159. M. Glickman and S. Isaacs, *The Fastest Kid on the Block: The Marty Glickman Story* (Syracuse, N.Y.: Syracuse University Press, 1996); P. Levine, "'My Father and I, We Didn't Get Our
Medals': Marty Glickman's American Jewish Odyssey," *American Jewish History* 79 (1989): 399–
424.

160. Riess, "Sports and the American Jew."

161. I have quite thoroughly checked newspapers of many countries for reference to this incident, and it was only discussed in the American press.

162. *Los Angeles Times,* Aug. 4, 1936, 13.

163. *New York Evening Journal,* Aug. 5, 1936, 28.

164. See, for example, *Literary Digest,* Aug. 29, 1936, 33.

165. *Cincinnati Enquirer,* Aug. 11, 1936, 4.

166. *Atlanta Constitution,* Aug. 9, 1936, B3.

167. *Los Angeles Times,* Aug. 4, 1936, 4.

168. *New York Times,* Aug. 16, 1936, 4.

169. *New York Times,* Aug. 18, 1936, 18.

170. *Opinion* 6 (Oct. 1936): 10–11.

171. *New York Herald Tribune,* Dec. 27, 1936, 7.

172. *St. Louis Post Despatch,* Aug. 13, 1936, B1.

173. *Neues Tagebuch* (Paris), May 2, 1936, 431.

CHAPTER 3

Great Britain:
The Amateur Tradition

Richard Holt

The British occupied a special place in world sport between the wars. As the inventors of modern sport, Britain's influence was out of proportion to its increasingly modest athletic performance. The British claim to sport was not only a matter of origins; they saw it as a question of values summed up by a single word: "amateurism." This meant not only an absolutely clear distinction between paid and unpaid athletes but also clearly implied the rule of private voluntary associations run by largely unpaid officials and independent of the state. Of course, Britain had a large professional spectator sport "industry," but even this was subject to amateur regulation. Modern track and field athletics was almost an entirely amateur preserve, originating in the public schools but enjoying particular prominence at Oxford and Cambridge, which supplied the founders of the Amateur Athletic Association (AAA) and led the attack on professional running, or "pedestrianism."[1]

This ethos strongly influenced Coubertin's conception of sport and his aspirations for the modern Olympic Games. Britain supported the baron's brainchild with certain reservations; this ambivalence was partly to do with French dominance of the new structure and partly came from a long-standing belief that some nations did not really conform to British conceptions of amateurism—an issue that was to come sharply into focus in the Olympic Games of 1936. Fears for amateurism as much as fear of nazism caused British concern at Berlin.[2]

Any kind of formal state involvement ran strongly against the British code. Sport and politics were genuinely, if naively, seen to be antithetical. No British politician had any direct control over sport, and even state education left the playing of sport up to local authorities and individual schools. If sport was not political, however, it was obviously in a wider sense ideological, and especially imperial. Cricket played an important part in cultural relations within the empire, especially in Australia. On the rare occasion that sporting differences threatened imperial harmony—as in the case of the Bodyline tour of 1932–33— both governments quietly took the protagonists aside.[3] But even this gentle and reluctant intervention was exceptional. The Empire Games, an athletic festival begun in Canada in 1930, was not really a state initiative, and the Foreign Office confined itself to refusing the odd visa to Soviet sportsmen. The Foreign Office, for example, had not taken a direct part in banning the Germans and their allies from the Antwerp Olympics in 1920—this came from the sporting bodies themselves, many of whose leaders had lost family or friends in the war.[4]

And so it continued. As a Foreign Office official observed in 1935, a sports event "is a private affair between private individuals and it is not for the government to interfere."[5] This was a view with which the bulk of the British people appeared to agree. No British political party was officially linked to a sports movement, as was the case in Germany both before and after the rise of Hitler. Nor did British churches manipulate sport politically as they did in France. Germany had a vast Social Democratic sports and gymnastic structure under Weimar, but the sporting efforts of British organized labor were puny by comparison. At heart, the Left distrusted popular culture.[6]

While the British Left failed to influence mass participation, they did begin to engage ideologically with sport between the wars. This arose mainly in response to Hitler's rise to power in Germany in 1933 and the consequent persecution of political opponents, notably trade unionists and communists, and of Jews. It was not so much fascism as nazism that galvanized the British Left.[7] Mussolini had been able to suppress or forcibly incorporate rival sporting bodies into his new Dopolavoro structure without much comment. The Italians were former allies of a sort, and Fascist bellicosity seemed more like posturing than anything else. It was the arrogance of the Italians in claiming superiority to the English in football that caught the public imagination, not the nature of the regime. Far from refusing to play against the Italians because they were Fascists, the English were particularly keen to teach them a lesson. This was rather brutally administered at the "Battle of Highbury" in November 1934.[8] Just as the British were trying to construct a common front to contain Hitler, of which Italy was to be a vital member, sport had become a source of popular resentment between the two countries. The last thing the British government wanted was an ill-tempered confrontation on the football field. Yet the Foreign Office did not try to intervene or "manage" the event to promote good relations. They even failed to see that the Italians had enough tickets. Sport was sport, politics was politics, and the Foreign Office, unlike Mussolini, appeared to show no signs of getting them confused.

This remained the attitude when sporting contacts with Hitler's Germany became a public issue late in 1935. There was no sudden change in the "official mind." The Foreign Office simply wanted to carry on as before. The problem was that this was no longer possible or, at least, no longer so easy. The outrage provoked by nazism among an articulate minority, mainly on the Left but including some influential conservative anti-appeasers, forced the issue. The open politicization of sport and the ruthless "integration" of alternative structures into the New Germany, where all opposition was crushed, led to more vehement protests. Britain was urged to refuse to have sporting contacts with Germany by influential papers like the *Manchester Guardian.*[9] Jewish groups agitated sporadically for action against Germany, including the cutting of sporting contacts; the Trade Union Council (TUC) protested mass persecution, and its leader, Walter Citrine, went out of his way to denounce German sport in the name of British "fair play."[10]

Such agitation placed the government in a tricky position. Several senior figures in the Foreign Office, including Sir Robert Vansittart, the permanent secretary, and Orme Sargeant, who handled German relations, were deeply suspicious of Germany. However, they were also disinclined to use sport as a weapon in the struggle. It went against the grain of their own public school traditions and was generally unpopular in Parliament and in the press. It was also in conflict with government policy toward Germany, which was split into two parts: the first was to begin rearmament on a modest scale while putting together a broad alliance of friendly powers to enforce the Treaty of Locarno against "flagrant aggression"; the second concerned the advantages of a bilateral understanding with Germany, such as the Anglo-German Naval Agreement of June 1935, which limited naval strengths but antagonized other friendly powers, especially France. Such a policy of making deals with Germany when it suited the British was bolstered by seeking German goodwill, if necessary by a process of peaceful renegotiation of historic grievances, which came to be known as "appeasement." This dual policy of containment and concession gradually turned into a more full-blooded effort to conciliate Germany at all costs from 1937 onward when Neville Chamberlain became prime minister.[11]

The arrangement of a football match between England and Germany in London in early December 1935 proved to be a dress rehearsal for the debate over Olympic participation. The Football Association had set up the match without consulting the government—an independence of action that was inconceivable for their opponents—as part of an effort to widen the circle of England's international fixtures. The venue chosen was White Hart Lane, the home ground of Tottenham Hotspurs, which ironically had significant Jewish support from the surrounding East End of London. Left activists saw the opportunity to protest against nazism through sport, especially since a story was circulating that a Jew had recently been beaten to death by Nazis at a German football match. Of particular concern was the German proposal to bring up to ten thousand "supporters" to the game. How would such a vast number get to the ground? Would they not wish to march through the streets, provocatively close to Jewish areas, waving Nazi flags amid choruses of "Sieg Heil" and the Horst Wessel song? The

TUC demanded that the game be called off, which led to the first ministerial meeting in British history on the politics of sport.[12]

This brought the vexed relationship of sport and politics into the public arena. With the exception of the *Daily Herald* and the *Manchester Guardian,* the national press were uniformly hostile to pressure being brought on the Football Association to withdraw from the match or a ban being imposed to avoid public disorder. The strength of feeling against interference in the quality and in the popular press was extremely strong, with the *News Chronicle* complaining of a "detestable poisoning of the springs of human fellowship" and *The Times* concluding that a ban would be "abhorrent to the English spirit."[13] The fact that it was the Germans and not the British who had politicized sport, as Citrine and others said repeatedly, had little effect. Such a view was either brushed aside as malicious exaggeration or accepted with the proviso that as the self-appointed moral guardians of sport, Britain should set a good example.

The authorities were faced with both the danger of public disorder and the manifest unpopularity of getting involved. The mandarins maneuvered behind the scenes. At the Home Office there were genuine concerns about the maintenance of public order. They tested out the Foreign Office to see if a reason could be found for calling off the match, but the Foreign Office was not going to be compromised in this way. Although it might have been better if the game had not been arranged in the first place, it would be "difficult to cancel without causing an incident for certain, although there may be worse incidents still if there is an unchecked Nazi influx."[14] Such was the view of Vansittart, who counted on the home secretary and the police to see that the event passed off peacefully. It was not a matter of pleasing Germany by encouraging sporting contacts. It was rather that they did not want to cause problems with Germany for no obvious advantage to Britain. Refusing sporting contacts with Germany would not bring down Hitler, whatever a few antifascists might think. It would be presented to the German people by Goebbels and the propaganda machine as yet another example of the conspiracy against the German people and the hypocrisy of those who claimed to stand for fair play. So the Foreign Office passed the matter back to the Home Office, advising that this was an internal question of public order. Assurances were obtained from the Germans concerning the behavior of their supporters, and the police made appropriate arrangements to avoid trouble.

In fact, the Left had misunderstood the Nazi purpose, which was not to provoke or make a show of strength but something altogether more insidious. The German football team announced it was coming "in homage" to the inventors of the game. This was done to encourage good sporting relations with England with the upcoming Winter and Summer Olympic Games in mind. As the *Manchester Guardian* remarked of Hitler a few days before the match, "it is known that he is getting anxious lest anything be done to prevent the Olympic Games being held in Germany next year."[15] The Nazis were mindful of the dangers of a boycott, as an examination of the top-secret *Presseberichte des Aussen-politischen Amtes der NSDAP* reveals.[16] The Germans were extremely concerned that the kind of boycott movement that had arisen in the United States, where an opinion poll in March 1935 had shown 43 percent against participation, should not spread.[17] Despite the desperate efforts of Avery Brundage, there was only a slim majority in favor of going. As a sardonic memo from the British ambassador in Berlin made clear, there was "considerable anxiety and relief . . . when it was heard that the American team had actually arrived in Garmisch-Partenkirchen for the Winter Games."[18] When later "news of dissatisfaction in the American camp" leaked out, "a high ranking official was sent down to pacify the Americans, possibly assuming the role of a cheerleader on the American model."[19] Comic German earnestness and pampered American egotism were among the cherished stereotypes of the British amateur.

Wider Nazi foreign policy aims and the specific Olympic agenda were combined in the British case. The Americans were the dominant athletic power, but the British, as the originators of sport, had a position of prestige rivaled only by France as the founder of the modern Games; if either the United States or the United Kingdom pulled out, the French might follow suit, and the Games would be ruined. As long as the British were on board, the Games could go on. No wonder Hitler was prepared to sanction the exceptional expenditure of sending ten thousand members of the "Kraft durch Freude" movement to watch a game that the Germans announced in advance they expected to lose. This fitted nicely with Nazi foreign policy, which claimed to be seeking an accord with Great Britain. After all, in Nazi eyes the British were an anticommunist and racially acceptable power that had merely been weakened by liberal democracy. Hitler was said to admire the British Empire. Sporting contacts can partly be seen as a charm offensive against the British. This had already produced the naval agreement brokered by von Ribbentrop, the future German ambassador in London, who would attempt to use the Berlin Olympics to neutralize British objections to the Nazi regime.[20]

The German team and supporters were instructed to behave impeccably and honor the "mother of sport" from whom there was much to learn. The game passed off without a hitch. The Germans duly lost, and the crowd appreciated the "underdog" and applauded the efforts of an outclassed German side. "The experts must decide whether it was good football, it was certainly good fun," noted the *Manchester Guardian;* "the game itself was amazingly clean . . . and the amount of handshaking was almost comical . . . everybody was saying during the game and as they laboriously left the ground, 'How different from the Italian match!'"[21] A dinner was held afterward to celebrate the game, at which the Reich's commissioner for sport, von Tschammer und Osten, and the chairman of the German Olympic Committee, Theodor Lewald, were present. All had come "as apprentices to the masters who taught them."[22] The following night the pro-Nazi Anglo-German Fellowship was founded at a dinner at the same hotel with the same German dignitaries. Lewald's presence at a professional sporting event with no obvious Olympic connection was especially significant. The Germans knew that if they could win this battle the chances of a successful boycott of the Berlin Games would be remote.

They were right. Sporting ostracism of Nazi Germany had been floated and had failed to find support. This, of course, did not stop some from urging an Olympic ban immediately after the match. The *Manchester Guardian*'s athletics correspondent produced a lengthy two-part account of the state in sport in Germany, leaving readers in no doubt that the Nazis had flouted Olympic principles "because Jews are now incapable of competing on an equal footing with other athletes"; undertakings given to the IOC president, the Belgian Count de Baillet-Latour, were "valueless." The article concluded, "evidently the IOC is not equal to dealing with the situation."[23] The next day a long letter appeared from Philip Noel-Baker, who had been captain of the British team at Antwerp in 1920 and was a rising figure in the Labour party. He advocated complete withdrawal because the Nazis had "injected politics into sport" and trampled on the basic principle "of the equality of all competitors."[24] Another letter from Vienna pointed out that a reluctant and belated Nazi invitation to two female German Jewish athletes, Gretel Bergmann and Helene Mayer, was no more than "calculated humbug." "A few Jews being invited pro forma, the 'Jews not admitted' placards are being removed for a few days—all in order to tempt the visitors to come."[25] The editor gave a ringing endorsement to these protests. The 1936 German Games were "spiritually dead. How can this country approve and confirm this perversion of a noble principle by joining in?"[26]

But these were lone voices. With the Winter Games imminent, the British Olympic Committee (BOC) went on the offensive. Sir Noel Curtis-Bennett, a member of the BOC, inveighed against "a lot of well meaning busybodies who try to mix sport and politics."[27] In an editorial entitled "More Power to Busybodies," the *Manchester Guardian* demanded to know, "Who thrust politics into sport? Did the busybodies invent this or did the Nazis do it?"[28] The Germans kept a close eye on international press reaction, noting the exposé of the temporary removal of anti-Jewish posters to placate the Belgian president of the IOC and the Americans. The Nazi official, Dr. Alfred Mischke, who carried out this confidential press survey, reassured his masters that apart from the *Jewish Chronicle* and one or two other liberal or socialist papers, there was no strong line against the Games. "The mass of Englishmen do not have the kind of mentality that listens to, or acts upon, complex arguments," he observed.[29]

The opening of the Winter Games, however, brought the issue of a summer boycott back into public debate, at least in elite circles. The Oxford student magazine *Isis* insisted, "we must lift sport out of the mire into which Dr. Goebbels has thrown it."[30] Given the importance of Oxbridge in the amateur athletic establishment, this was more significant than it might at first appear. Lord Aberdare replied immediately in the *Oxford Magazine* for the BOC, stressing the firm assurances the IOC had received that "Jews of all nations will be welcome," adding with a crassness rare even among the peerage, "Germany will be represented by more Jews than has ever before been the case."[31] Despite continuing muted protests and letters to the press, a boycott movement similar to that which had arisen in 1935 in the United States did not gain momentum in Britain. There was no powerful Jewish lobby with a clear agenda; nor were there black athletes to consider. British involvement in the Winter Games went ahead without much protest or publicity. The opening ceremony was reported in the major papers, with *The Times* citing without comment Dr. Ritter von Halt's assertion in his opening address that "Germany has spared no efforts . . . to make a reality of these festivals which symbolize peace and a sincere understanding between all nations."[32] The British public was not very interested in skating, ice hockey, or skiing. The real importance of the Winter Games was that the Olympic process was under way. As long as no major incident intervened, success at Garmisch would make it all the harder to vote for a boycott of Berlin.

So it transpired, though not everything at Garmisch was sweetness and light. The leader of the British team, Arnold Lunn, the "father of alpine ski racing" and a British public school amateur to the core, was a conservative Catholic who disliked the "professionalism" of National Socialist sport. However, his loyalty to the Olympic movement, which had included skiing for the first time at an official event in 1936, was stronger than his hostility to German fanaticism. "In Nazi Germany sport is a branch of politics," he observed; he refused to go to the official receptions, complaining that "in modern Europe a great athletic contest is a political and social, no less than a sporting event."[33] This touched on a profound difference between the British and the European understandings of the term "amateur." The Germans seemed to think an amateur was a non-commercial athlete in the service of the state. Lunn's disgust for the way the Germans flouted British ideals of amateurism was strengthened by the knowledge that his team had been allocated only a few hundred pounds to prepare for the entire event. His chief weapon was ridicule, but he was too marginal and idiosyncratic to carry real weight. When asked by German broadcasters for his opinion of the Games, he remarked, "'Let me tell you a little secret. There are still some people who ski for fun'"; on another occasion a Nazi official asked him if he had seen Jews smuggling jewelry in toilet paper in the train lavatory, to which he replied, "'Such is my love of solitude that I never share a train lavatory with anybody.'"[34]

Lunn's repartee was more likely to amuse a dinner party than damage the Nazi sports movement. It was the Left, in the form of the National Workers Sports Federation, that took the lead in pressing for a boycott of the Summer Games, backed by the Labour *Daily Herald* and the *Manchester Guardian*. A motion was duly put to the annual meeting of the AAA in late March. Two objections to a boycott were raised: the first was that the Winter Games had already taken place, so it would be illogical to refuse to go to Berlin in the summer; the second was more directly political: "this is a moment for behaving with particular tact towards Germany and not increasing the bitterness."[35] The German military reoccupation of the Rhineland had concentrated the public mind wonderfully, making the danger of Germany more obvious and the risk of antagonizing her all the greater. Harold Abrahams, who had a special influence as a famous Jewish athlete and British Olympian, spoke out against a boycott, thinking British involvement could only "be an influence for the good."[36] A decision was deferred to a special meeting in May, which eventually voted overwhelmingly against a boycott by two hundred to eight.

Only ten days after Hitler remilitarized the Rhineland, the BOC, true to its tradition of private finance, made a public appeal in *The Times* for funding for the British delegation to the Summer Games. "The Olympic Games have always stood for the ideal of harmony and reconciliation between nations, and it would be nothing short of a calamity if, at this very critical stage in world affairs, this country, to whom the world so often looks for a lead, were not fully represented," wrote Lord Portal, Lord Aberdare, Lord Burghley, and Sir Noel Curtis-Bennett, collectively.[37] They assured the public that there was no question of any race prejudice in selecting a British team and that firm assurances had been given that there would be no discrimination during the Games. This seems to have been enough to take the athletic establishment and most of the country with them. Britain didn't want a fight, not with the IOC and certainly not with Germany—at least not until Hitler's expansionist mania was proved beyond doubt in the spring of 1939. Up to that point the mainstream British position was that Nazi Germany was an unpleasant regime but one they had to live with, especially when air power now made "our frontier on the Rhine," as Baldwin starkly put it. It would no doubt have been better if the Games had not been promised to Germany in the first place; but this was a fait accompli, and refusing to participate made it appear that it was the British who were bringing sport into politics and a sour note into international relations.

This seems to have been the public view, and it was certainly the view of the press. If we stopped playing with all the regimes we disliked, where would we draw the line? Within the Foreign Office, where an awareness of the danger of Nazi expansionism was greater than elsewhere in the country or in Whitehall, top officials like Vansittart and his deputy, Orme Sargeant, were aware of the power of a boycott "for Herr Hitler's prestige and for German finances."[38] The issue arose just as the Foreign Office was trying to prevent an incident over the England-Germany game, and on reflection they doubted it would work or do anything for the Jews in Germany. However, they were equally determined that the government should not be maneuvered into the position of official support for the British team. Hence their skepticism and fastidiousness about any official contacts with either the British or the German organizers in the first half of 1936. When the BOC invited the prime minister to an Olympic dinner, the Foreign Office temporized. "I do not see that there could be any F.O. objection. On the other hand there is no reason why we should advise the P.M. to attend."[39] The dinner invitation for the following May came just before the German remilitarization of the Rhineland on March 7, and the diplomats decided to wait "until the present crisis resolves itself."[40] Meanwhile, inquiries were made about who would be there and what, in particular, would be the nature of German representation. Could we be sure this was a purely British matter? Having been reassured on these points and with the immediate threat of military action past, approval went ahead on the understanding that it be "made clear" that attendance implied "no connection with, and no responsibility for, the Committee and its works."[41]

The question of government involvement was made even more concrete by the invitation to send a warship to Kiel for naval celebrations and races during the Games that came at around the same time. The Admiralty consulted the Foreign Office, who passed the matter back to the Admiralty, suggesting delay. It was agreed to in May by the secretary of state, but problems about the disposition of ships brought the matter up again in June. Official indecision is instructive, and it deepened when a Foreign Office memo suggested reversing the decision to send a ship because, over the preceding six weeks, "the German government's attitude has not been positively such as to give evidence either of any particular anxiety for our goodwill or any particular amenability to minor courtesies."[42] The cruiser *Neptune* was sent with the gift of a bell from the battleship *Hindenburg*, which had been scuttled in Scapa Flow in 1919. Was this a subtle reminder of British naval power, a morbid military ritual of the sort relished by the Nazis, or just diplomatic routine? The Canadians had returned some of the wreckage of von Richthofen's plane as a token of goodwill for the Games, and perhaps the British thought some similar gesture to loyal foes was appropriate.

While the British government was willing to show "minor courtesies," it was apparently adamant about official nonintervention. In May 1936, in response to a query from the Spanish ambassador, the Foreign Office stated unequivocally that "the question of British participation is left entirely in the hands of the B.O.C., a private organization with whom H.M.G. have no connection, and there is no question of any official patronage or assistance (financial or otherwise) being given."[43] This was true so far as it went; but as usual what was unsaid was more revealing. For, during the first half of the year, the British government had been actively involved in persuading the BOC to withdraw a bid for the 1940 Olympics in order to avoid problems with Japan, "for reasons of high policy and contrary to the normal rule of non-intervention."[44] This "normal rule" was broken again when a "very confidential" telegram was received from the British ambassador in Berlin on May 16, 1936, reporting that, according to the French ambassador, "left parties are putting pressure on the French Government to refuse to send French candidates to the Olympic Games." "This," warned Phipps, who was Vansittart's brother-in-law, "would mean the end of any hope of agreement between France and Germany. . . . His Excellency feels sure Soviets are behind this as they have of course not been invited to the Games."[45] The British reaction is instructive. The desk officer took the standard line, merely noting, "this sort of thing leads one to believe H.M.G. are right to have no official connection whatever with the Olympic Games"; but Vansittart, in a note in his own hand, intervened immediately, "advising the French Ambassador against this foolishness."[46]

It was hardly surprising that the head of the Foreign Office, despite his anti-German reputation, did not favor a boycott of the Berlin Games in 1936. However, Vansittart's quick reaction to rumors of French opposition rather weakens the case made by Duff Hart-Davis for "Van" as the anti-Nazi hero of the Berlin drama.[47] Vansittart's role in the Olympics was ambiguous. He opposed a French boycott because he thought it "could do no possible good," not because of any sympathy for the Germans.[48] Unlike government ministers, he went to Berlin and was courted by the Germans, who thought they could win him over, with Hitler chatting amiably to Lady Vansittart, who recounted the conversation to Hart-Davis "with astonishing precision" at the age of ninety-five.[49] No doubt Vansittart used the event as a way of informally sounding out Nazi opinion. But his presence and formal civility were initially misinterpreted by Goebbels and Ribbentrop as admiration for what had been achieved in the New Germany.

These apparently minor diplomatic exchanges are more important than they might appear. They make it clear that intervention in the politics of sport was an option when important British interests were thought to be at stake. The foreign secretary, Anthony Eden, had even jokingly offered to run in the mile himself if the award of the 1940 Olympics would help British relations with Japan.[50] Similarly, British officials seem to have wanted the Games to go on even if they did not wish to be formally associated with them. The last thing they were looking for was a new problem with Germany, although they were not willing to seek German friendship as openly as Chamberlain was to do. Phipps, Vansittart, and Eden—the three main diplomatic actors in the Berlin Games on the British side—all later resigned or were replaced by Chamberlain.

Why, then, did the British fail to take seriously the possibility of weakening Hitler by refusing to go to Berlin? This was not only a question of the amateur ethic of nonintervention, nor was it due to ignorance of the Nazi danger. It was partly a matter of strategic reality. The relatively minor matter of Olympic participation has to be seen in the wider context of "overcommitment." Faced with Italy in the Mediterranean, Japan in East Asia, and Germany in the North Sea, the defense of the Home Islands, let alone the empire, was becoming a potential nightmare; to make matters worse, air power made Britain newly vulnerable, and fear of mass bombing was widespread. This combined with a certain feeling—strengthened no doubt by the need to rationalize Britain's actual weaknesses—that Germany had been unfairly treated at Versailles.[51] Perhaps most important of all was sheer war-weariness, which unfortunately was not shared by most Germans. Hence the government simply stonewalled awkward questions from the Right and the Left about Britain's role in the Berlin Games. When an MP asked if Britain had received "any assurance from the German Government that they do not propose to make use of the occasion of the Olympic Games for the purposes of political propaganda," the minister of state, Viscount Cranborne, replied "No"; a blunt reply repeated by the foreign secretary himself a week later in response to the same question.[52] The official line was that the British government was not responsible for the decision to send a British team, and it was not their business to seek such assurances.

There is no doubt that the scale of the Berlin Games, the rituals, the sums spent, and the sheer thoroughness of it all made a big impression on the British. Press reports, radio, and newsreels brought to Britain not only the sports themselves but the wider German world with all its efficiency, fanaticism, and mass ritual. As Vansittart starkly pointed out, "these people are the most formidable proposition that has ever been formulated; they are in strict training now, not for the Olympic Games, but for breaking some other and emphatically unsporting world records, and perhaps the world as well."[53] How much of this filtered through to the general public is difficult to say. As the diplomatic report to the foreign secretary noted afterward, "it is difficult for anyone in England to understand the importance attached to the Games in Germany. No trouble or expense was spared to make them an advertisement for the National Socialist regime."[54] The opening ceremony was widely reported. *The Times* called the Olympic Youth Pageant on the opening evening a "flood lit masterpiece," and the *Manchester Guardian,* which had thundered about "a wild nationalistic race" and "an athletic war," confessed to "moments of beauty and significance which one will remember."[55] Much attention was paid to the opening ceremony, especially the march of the athletes and the possible confusion between the Olympic and Nazi salute. The British decision, like the Americans', to avoid any misunderstanding by giving an "eyes right" salute was less popular with the crowd than the French raised-arm salute, but it was deemed more appropriate. It is perhaps worth stressing the point. If the BOC had wished to please the Germans at all costs, nothing would have been simpler than to give the raised-arm salute, as Chamberlain's replacement for Phipps, Sir Neville Henderson, notoriously advised the visiting English football team to do in 1938.

It is easy for scholars to exaggerate interest in the opening ceremony. What the British public wanted was British victories, especially on the track, which carried far greater prestige than other events. The BBC, true to their cheerful amateur traditions, managed to send along a commentator who knew no German and could not understand the opening speeches. But as soon as the events began, coverage quickly switched from the political to the athletic. Not that there was much to cheer about. From the British point of view the Games were a disappointment, with only four gold, seven silver, and three bronze medals, compared to totals of thirty-three, twenty-six, and thirty, respectively, for the Germans, which were, however, happily not won on the track. Here the Americans reigned supreme. Godfrey Brown, the Cambridge University athletics captain, was just beaten in the 400 meter final, but the British team won a marvelous 4 × 400 meters relay. The British made a virtue of their lack of preparation. Godfrey Rampling, who ran a superb second leg, later recalled saying, "'Look here, chaps, we really ought to practice some baton changing.' But we soon got bored and packed it in."[56] Less flamboyantly but in the same vein, Harold Whitlock, a London motor mechanic, who won the 50 kilometer walk, was held to represent the honest British tradition of private individual endeavor. In fact, he'd been given time off from his job tuning Bentleys at Brooklands to train while Rampling, like so many of the Germans, was a serving army officer. The British, with their reputation for hypocrisy, had to be careful here. In British eyes it was a question of the right sort of amateur attitude rather than a strict matter of occupation. Germans performed for the regime with the expectation of official advancement; the British ran for their club and their country without crude inducements from the state. After all, a man like Albert Hill, the postwar hero from the trenches who had won the 800 and 1,500 meters in Antwerp in 1920, had stayed a railwayman and newspaper packer. Amateur sport was not supposed to change your life.

The real British hero of Berlin was not in fact British but an inconspicuous New Zealander named Jack Lovelock. The advantage of having an empire, especially one in which there were "White Dominions," composed largely of former British emigrants, was that Britain could claim part of the credit for their achievements. Lovelock, who had come to Oxford to study medicine and was living in London, carried off the 1,500 meters with a brilliant finish. Harold Abrahams, whom the BBC had sent out as a broadcaster, hailed the victory, yelling the New Zealander's name triumphantly down the microphone. The fact that Jack Lovelock had been beaten not long before in the AAA mile by Sydney Wooderson, the great British middle distance runner who was ruled out of Berlin by a foot injury, no doubt made Lovelock's victory even more satisfying.[57]

Apart from such moments of national feeling, it was the performances of Jesse Owens that had the greatest impact in Britain as elsewhere. The idea that black athletes were more naturally gifted than whites at certain athletic events was not a form of racial stereotype that the British, with their tradition of manly sports and imperial rule, were likely to adopt. Owens was taken at face value as a splendid individual athlete. The question of confounding or confirming Nazi theories of the "master race" did not occupy the public to any great extent, though it was widely believed that Hitler had snubbed Owens in an unsporting way. The British certainly did not draw the conclusion of some French commentators that they should use their empire to find black athletes to win medals for them. The imperial British amateur was too racially arrogant and too genuinely "sporting" for such a thing.

The British women did not excel at Berlin—a fact that reinforced their second-class status within British sport and left the way open for juicy stories about

Eleanor Holm Jarret, the gorgeous swimmer who was banned from the American team for her wild antics on the ship coming over. Helen Stephens, the phenomenal young American sprinter, also caught the British eye. But predictably it was in "human interest" stories where women were featured most prominently. Take the case of Madame de Vries, the Norwegian wife of a Dutchman living in California, who dodged bodyguards and kissed Hitler; this incident was more widely reported than most of the female athletics. Hitler apparently "smiled, blushed and looked at his feet, while the crowd laughed delightedly."[58] Here was an angle that would appeal to the nonsporting female reader while offering a reassuringly unthreatening image of the Führer. Francina (Fanny) Koen appeared as an eighteen-year-old in Berlin, but nobody noticed this Dutch girl who came in sixth in the high jump. It was not until after the war that Fanny Blankers-Koen, married and the mother of two, would really capture the British imagination with four sprint gold medals in the 1948 Olympics.

When the Games ended and the time came for taking stock, it was amateurism as much as nazism that seemed to be important. Predictably, the Official Olympic Report of the BOC, which was edited by Harold Abrahams, "was remarkable for its utter lack of political discussion."[59] *The Times*, which avoided overt political comment and dwelt at length on the British way of sport, was concerned with how world sport was leaving "the originator and teacher" in the wake of the Americans and Germans with their belief in "long, scientific and intensive training."[60] In a letter to the editor, Lord Decies was a bit more forthcoming, claiming, "some of the competitors have been in Berlin for two months. How do they afford it? Have they no profession?" to which he added an ominous closing observation: "I left Berlin with the impression of a new race of energetic, virile young people . . . ready to go anywhere under the orders of the Führer—a nation fully armed, equipped with the best war material, and an air force second to none."[61] Decies even suggested it would be more honest to open the Games to professionals.

The British typically consoled themselves with the idea that they were the moral victors—"amateurs in the truest sense" was the favorite term. Voices from abroad were produced to bolster this notion; Lucien Dubech, writing in the French extreme-right-wing *Candide*, was cited in *The Times* to the effect that Britain had eschewed vulgar chauvinism in sport, which "for her is a pleasure, a self-imposed discipline, one of the essential elements of moral education. . . . Great Britain is the only nation to show a truly sporting spirit."[62] The headmaster of Hulme Grammar School wrote in a similar vein to the *Manchester Guardian* criticizing the elitism of the Games and stressing that "what a boy needs from games is exercise, education in social virtues, and recreation; in all his sport there should be the feeling that games should not be taken in the wrong sort of serious spirit or their whole value is lost."[63]

Keeping a sense of proportion and a sense of humor was seen as authentically British. The example of a Boys Brigade contingent at the Berlin Olympic

Youth Camp was quoted approvingly. Apparently these lads had refused to rise at half past six for mass gymnastics with their hearty German hosts, whom they had further baffled by singing "What Shall We Do with the Drunken Sailor?" rather than "Land of Hope and Glory" or "God Save the King."[64] This small triumph of British common sense, which was quite widely reported, sat nicely alongside the more general criticism that "the Games had been organized into immobility," whereas the White City athletics afterward were "handled much more amateurishly but also much faster."[65]

For all this, and despite the reassuring knowledge that the Germans had failed on the track, there was undoubtedly a sense of foreboding about the sheer scale of the German athletic effort. Significantly, the British took up an invitation to send a physical education delegation to Germany later in the year, which in due course reported on how the benefits of the German system could be incorporated into the British curriculum.[66] Despite ministerial denials, there can be little doubt that the massive funding and priority given to physical culture under nazism, as symbolized by the Berlin Olympics, helped bring forward the Physical Education Act of 1937. The government claimed it was simply responding to the needs of physical educators and the demand from the public for better facilities—and to an extent that is true—but the context of Berlin and the Nazi appropriation of youth and sport was never far away. Yet the British did not slavishly copy German methods. They retained their broadly decentralized and noncompulsory approach, and the new act had a relatively modest budget of two million pounds over three years. Sport was not made obligatory in state schools until 1944. If anything, there was a stiffening of official resistance to being "drawn into this hornets' nest," as the Foreign Office described Olympic politics in 1938.[67] Berlin had not really changed the face of British sport.

Despite a growing awareness of sporting success as a cheap way of projecting a positive national image, the British government remained wary of getting involved in international sport. In practice, as Peter Beck has pointed out, government activity was mainly "ad hoc" and aimed at "damage limitation," intervening to ensure nonintervention.[68] British sporting associations guarded their financial and political autonomy from the state with a fierce determination. The government had no powers to compel the BOC to comply with official requests, though "a word in the ear" from one gentleman to another could be very effective. This was the case when the government stepped in to support Japan's application to host the Olympic Games in 1940. This, however, was a rare exception to the "laissez-faire" tradition that left sporting bodies remarkably free to run their own affairs.

Notes

I wish to thank Paul Spencer of La Trobe University for access to extensive typed extracts from articles on the Berlin Olympics appearing in *The Times* and the *Manchester Guardian*. Home Office (HO) and Foreign Office (FO) documents are deposited at the Public Record Office, Kew, London.

1. For a general survey of amateur dominance, see R. Holt, *Sport and the British* (Oxford: Oxford University Press, 1989), pt. 2. For relations between Great Britain and Europe in Association Football in the interwar period, see Peter J. Beck, *Scoring for Britain: International Football and International Politics, 1900–1939* (London: Frank Cass, 1999).

2. There is no satisfactory history of British Olympic participation. Richard Mandell, *The Nazi Olympics* (Rpt., Urbana: University of Illinois Press, 1987), has little on Britain. However, the British reaction is well handled by Duff Hart-Davis, *Hitler's Games: The 1936 Olympics* (New York: Harper and Row, 1986). For an assessment of this work and a review of other literature, see Bill Murray, "Berlin in 1936: Old and New Work on the Nazi Olympics," *International Journal of the History of Sport* 9.1 (Apr. 1992): 32–34.

3. See, for example, R. Mason, *Ashes in the Mouth: The Story of the Body-line Tour of 1932–33* (London: Penguin, 1984); and R. Sissons and B. Stoddart, *Cricket and Empire* (London: Allen and Unwin, 1984).

4. R. Renson, *Les Jeux Réssuscités: La VIIe Olympiade, Anvers 1920* (Brussels: Comité Olympique Interfédérale Belge, 1994): 26–27. The key role in demanding a ban on the Germans and their allies was taken by Sir Theodore Cook, a British member of the IOC but not a member of the British government.

5. FO 371 18884/C7757.

6. S. G. Jones, *Sport, Politics and the Working Class* (Manchester: Manchester University Press, 1988), chap. 1.

7. Ibid., chap. 7. See also the important article by B. Stoddart, "Sport, Cultural Politics, and International Relations: England versus Germany, 1935," in *Sport History: The Olympic Scientific Congress*, ed. N. Müller and J. K. Rühl (Niederhausern: Schors, 1985).

8. R. Holt and T. Mason, "Le football, le fascisme et la politique étrangère britannique," in *Sports et Relations Internationales*, ed. P. Arnaud and A. Wahl (Metz: Université de Metz, 1994), 76–80.

9. *Manchester Guardian*, Dec. 7, 1935.

10. Walter Citrine, *Under the Heel of Hitler: The Dictatorship over Sport in Germany* (London: N.p., 1936).

11. The literature of appeasement is vast. Among the most useful recent general works are R. J. Q. Adams, *British Politics and Foreign Policy in the Age of Appeasement, 1935–39* (Stanford, Calif.: Stanford University Press, 1993); and R. A. C. Parker, *Chamberlain and Appeasement: British Policy and the Coming of the Second World War* (London: Macmillan, 1993).

12. HO 45/16425: "Notes on the Deputation from the Trades Union Congress to the Home Secretary" (Dec. 2, 1935). For a fuller discussion of the politics of the match, see R. Holt, "The Foreign Office and the Football Association: British Sport and Appeasement, 1935–1938," in *Sport and International Politics, 1900–1941*, ed. P. Arnaud and J. Riordan (London: Spon, 1998), 51–66. For a good account, see Beck, *Scoring for Britain*, 173–212.

13. *News Chronicle*, Nov. 28, 1935; *The Times*, Dec. 3, 1935.

14. FO 371 18884/C77757.

15. *Manchester Guardian*, Nov. 30, 1935.

16. I am grateful to Arnd Krüger for supplying a copy of this document, pp. 9–13 of which deal with Britain.

17. A. Guttmann, *The Olympics: A History of the Modern Games*, 2d ed. (Urbana: University of Illinois Press, 2002), 60.

18. FO 371/19940/C3930.

19. Ibid.

20. Hart-Davis, *Hitler's Games*, describes Ribbentrop as "rich and well-connected" and as "an ass" (25).

21. *Manchester Guardian*, Dec. 5, 1935, 9.

22. Hart-Davis, *Hitler's Games*, 89.

23. *Manchester Guardian,* Dec. 6, 1935, 11.

24. *Manchester Guardian,* Dec. 7, 1935, 8.

25. Ibid.

26. Ibid., 12.

27. Hart-Davis, *Hitler's Games,* 106.

28. *Manchester Guardian,* Jan. 15, 1936, 8.

29. *Presseberichte des Aussenpolitischen Amtes der NSDAP,* 13.

30. Hart-Davis, *Hitler's Games,* 107.

31. Ibid., 99. For a fuller discussion of Lunn, see R. Holt, "An Englishman in the Alps: Arnold Lunn, Amateurism, and the Invention of Alpine Ski Racing," *International Journal of the History of Sport* 9.3 (Dec. 1992): 421–32.

32. *The Times,* Feb. 7, 1936, 5.

33. A. Lunn, *Come What May* (N.p.: Eyre and Spottiswood, 1940), 268.

34. A. Lunn, *The Kandahar Story* (London: Allen and Unwin, 1969), 45, 49.

35. *Manchester Guardian,* Mar. 23, 1936, 10.

36. Hart-Davis, *Hitler's Games,* 111.

37. *The Times,* Mar. 7, 1936.

38. FO 371/18863/C7600.

39. FO 371/19940/C1346.

40. Ibid.

41. Ibid.

42. FO 371/19940/C4511.

43. FO 371/19940/C3137.

44. M. Polley, "Olympic Diplomacy: The British Government and the Projected 1940 Olympic Games," *International Journal of the History of Sport* 9.2 (Aug. 1992): 182.

45. FO 371/19940/C3697.

46. Ibid.

47. Hart-Davis, *Hitler's Games,* esp. 179–82.

48. FO 371/19940/C3697.

49. Hart-Davis, *Hitler's Games,* 6, 209–10.

50. Polley, "Olympic Diplomacy," 176.

51. This "revisionist" view of appeasement has yielded an extensive monograph literature based on case studies using official papers. For a short introduction, see Adams, *British Politics and Foreign Policy;* and Parker, *Chamberlain and Appeasement.*

52. *Hansard,* July 16 and 22, 1936.

53. Hart-Davis, *Hitler's Games,* 227.

54. FO 371/19940/C5983.

55. *The Times,* Aug. 3, 1936, 11; and *Manchester Guardian* Aug. 3, 1936, 9.

56. N. Duncanson and P. Collins, *Tales of Gold* (London: Queen Anne-Macdonald, 1992), 33.

57. N. McWhirter, *The Olympics, 1896–1972: In Support of the British Olympic Appeal* (London: Esso, 1972), 47. See also Hart-Davis, *Hitler's Games,* 193–95. Mandell claims that he trained "for three years in his native New Zealand for this minute" (*Nazi Olympics,* 162). In fact, he was a medical student in London at the time and had been at Oxford prior to that.

58. *The Times,* Aug. 17, 1936, 9.

59. Mandell, *Nazi Olympics,* 297n.28.

60. *The Times,* Aug. 17, 1936, 11.

61. *The Times,* Aug. 21, 1936, 11.

62. *The Times,* Sept. 2, 1936, 6.

63. *Manchester Guardian,* Aug. 24, 1936, 16.

64. *Manchester Guardian,* Aug. 17, 1936, 8.

65. Ibid.

66. H. Bernett, "National Socialist Physical Education Policy as Reflected in British Appease-ment Policy," *International Journal of the History of Sport* 5.2 (Sept. 1988): 161–84.

67. FO L370/551/7826 provides a brief survey of Foreign Office interventions in the Olympics from 1936–38, before which it was "our policy to refrain from any form of official intervention."

68. Beck, *Scoring for Britain*, 276.

CHAPTER 4

France:
Liberty, Equality, and the
Pursuit of Fraternity

William Murray

Although France is better known for its intellectual culture than the feats of its athletes, it nevertheless occupies a special place in the history of sport. It was the birthplace of the baron de Coubertin, whose patriotic horror at the defeat of France by Prussia in the war of 1870–71 led him to found the modern Olympics. For this he has been honored in the special place given to France and the French language in the conduct and administration of the governing body of the Olympic movement, the International Olympic Committee. France was also the birthplace of Western liberal democracy, and as the country that gave the world the Declaration of the Rights of Man and Citizen in 1789, it has stood for traditions in politics that were the antithesis of nazism. France thus might have been expected to have more strenuous objections to playing games with an aggressive neighbor that saw sport as a tool for propaganda and preparation for war.

In addition to theoretical discussions about the uses of sport, at the grassroots level there were many people in France in 1936 who could still remember the two invasions of their country that had wrought terrible devastation; after the catastrophic defeat of the Franco-Prussian War, France had a savage and humiliating peace treaty imposed on her by the newly created Second Reich, proclaimed in the palace of Versailles in January 1871 before an impotent French nation. In 1914 France was again invaded by Germany in a war that lasted for four years and laid waste to whole areas of the northeastern regions of the country. With the peace treaties of 1919, it was France's turn to impose retribution, which it saw as justice, although the Germans saw it as infamy.

The spirit of enmity carried over into sporting relations, with Germany banished to the international sporting wilderness for several years after 1918,[1] while the attempts to ease tensions between the two peoples with Gustav Stresemann and the Locarno Treaty of 1925 ended when Hitler came to power in Germany in 1933. Now France was faced by a revitalized Germany whose leader had a deep hatred for the country he believed had humiliated Germany in the peace treaties imposed after World War I. Many Germans, and not only the followers of Hitler, also rejoiced in their francophobia. Prominent among these was Kurt Münch, a member of the Board of the German Gymnastics Federation, which was responsible for Turner culture (and later indoctrination). Münch wrote a manual for schools in which France was depicted as a nation obsessed by fear of Germany's powerful popular forces and that claimed that while Slavs and southern Latins had to be mistrusted because of their racial contamination, "the title of 'hereditary enemy' belongs above all to the French." For such ideas he was promoted and made responsible for the indoctrination not only of the Turners but all of German sports. Bruno Malitz, a writer and sports ideologist who enjoyed the favor of Himmler and the SS, included the French along with "Belgians, Pollacks, [and] Jew-Niggers" as people who had fouled German sports fields and swimming pools.[2] Despite such clearly expressed opinions, the IOC had its reasons to overlook the Nazi attitude to international sporting competition; the French would find their own.

In addition to its association through Coubertin with the modern Olympic Games, France was also the creator of many other great sporting tournaments. It was in France in 1904 that the world body for governing association football (FIFA) was founded, and it was the Frenchman Jules Rimet who created what was to become the only other global sports tournament that could rival the Olympic Games, the World Cup in soccer. First held in Uruguay in 1930 and thereafter played every four years in tandem with the Olympics (except 1942 and 1946), the World Cup was open to professionals from the beginning and had a particular appeal to the poorest sections of society and not only the aficionados of elite amateur sport. France is also home to the Tour de France, arguably the most grueling of sporting competitions, with its four weeks of sustained cycling through the mountains and plains of the French (and now neighboring) countryside. By the 1930s, however, cycling had lost the aura that surrounded it at the turn of the century, when it was a sport with a wide international appeal. At the time of the 1936 Olympics, while indoor cycling enjoyed some popularity in several European countries, the only nations to rival France in road cycling were Italy and Belgium. In motor sports, France had been a leader with Le Mans, and in the 1920s France enjoyed international success in professional boxing and tennis. Despite France's contributions to sport (and despite the recent successes of the French national soccer team), some people still associate France only with its cultural achievements, which has tended to hide the passion most French people have for their sports at all levels.

France shared in the expansion of mass sport in the 1930s,[3] with the professional sports of boxing and cycling providing the national heroes, while football, which was professional from 1932, drew the largest number of spectators. In international competition, France's sporting prowess was in eclipse. In the late 1920s it had dominated tennis with its "Four Musketeers"—René Lacoste, Henri Cochet, Jean Borotra,[4] and Jacques Brugnon—while Suzanne Lenglen was the undisputed female champion of that era.[5] In boxing, Georges Carpentier, the world light-heavyweight champion and unsuccessful challenger for the heavyweight title against Jack Dempsey in 1921, had retired, and while Marcel Thil was also a world champion (middleweight), he never achieved the fame of Carpentier. Tennis was no longer an Olympic sport, while boxing and cycling at the Olympic level were essentially a step on the way to the professional circuits. After the turmoil surrounding the adoption of professionalism, France did not send a soccer team to Berlin. Of the Olympic sports, interest in track and field in France plummeted after the disqualification of Jules Ladoumègue on the eve of the 1932 Olympics. A silver medallist in the 1,500 meters in Amsterdam in 1928, Ladoumègue was a champion in the class of Olympic medallists like Jean Bouin (silver, 5,000 meters, in 1912), Joseph Guillemot (gold, 5,000 meters, and silver, 10,000 meters, in 1920), and the Algerian El Ouafi Boughera[6] (gold, marathon, in 1928), as well as Georges André (champion in many sports between 1908 and 1924 who twice narrowly failed to gain an Olympic medal). Ladoumègue surpassed all of these athletes in popularity.[7] France's best hopes in the blue riband events of the 1936 Summer Games were placed in the swimmer Jean Taris, the holder of three world records and silver-medal winner at Los Angeles in the 400 meter freestyle, but he failed to place in Berlin.[8] France's young cyclists, and to a lesser degree its boxers, did well, but their eyes were less on Olympic gold than entry into the world of professionalism. France did comparatively well in the less prestigious sports, with gold in weightlifting, wrestling, boxing (two medals), and cycling (three medals). French fencers disappointed, gaining two silver and one bronze. In total France gained seven gold, six silver, and six bronze—placing sixth, three places down from Los Angeles in 1932.

There were some who claimed on the eve of the 1936 Olympics that France was the only country not smitten by Olympic fever, but this was belied by the large crowds who came to see the athletes off at the Gare du Nord on the evening of July 29, likened by one observer to the crowds usually associated with "savants and film stars."[9] Despite the controversies that preceded their departure, the French delegation of 215 athletes and twenty-five officials left for Berlin with the best wishes of the French sporting public, even those who had advocated a boycott, behind them. The media were behind them, too, and the press prepared a saturation coverage that had never before been given to any sporting event except, perhaps, the Tour de France.

* * *

In *L'Auto* France had the oldest European sports daily. Founded in 1900, four years after Italy's *Gazzetta dello Sport*, which did not, however, become a daily until 1912, it emerged out of a political rivalry with France's first sporting daily, *Le Vélo,* and its success came with the creation and sponsorship of the Tour de France in 1903. Its yellow pages are still commemorated in the yellow jersey worn by the leader of that race. The founder of *L'Auto,* Henri Desgrange, a pioneer in international sport because of his passion for cycling and the organization of innovative competitions, also invented the Le Mans twenty-four-hour auto race and was involved in the purchase and control of several sporting venues, all of whose events he publicized to the exclusion of those of his rivals. The spirit of honest competition lauded in the sports columns was not echoed in the commercial rivalry of a press that was notorious for its corruption. Among *L'Auto*'s rivals were *Sporting* and *Echo des Sports,* while some of the major information papers had a sporting offshoot: *Match* was the weekly sports journal for *L'Intransigeant, Miroir des Sports* for the *Petit Parisien.*

By the 1930s the popular interest in sport was such that biographical dictionaries that excluded sports stars in the 1920s included them in the 1930s, and so great was the upsurge in interest that some believed a generation gap had been created between parents who knew nothing about sport and children who were obsessed by it—it was, however, a gap that the novelist Jean-Michel Renaitour, writing in 1934, believed was being rapidly overcome. He tells the story of Robert Pajol, who runs away from home, and when his distraught mother seeks a means of finding him she inserts a notice in *L'Auto,* knowing that it is the only paper her son reads each day from cover to cover.[10] The French dramatist and actor-manager André Obey, whose plays enjoyed some success after 1931 and who recorded his conversion to the joys of sport in *L'orgue du stade* (1924), tells of students going to school with a copy of the ancient classics in one hand, *L'Auto* in the other, as enchanted by stories from Homer's *Illiad* as they were by a stage in the Tour de France.[11]

The most significant development in sports reporting in the 1930s, however, was the way in which it was taken up by the information press when it discovered that the exploits of the new popular heroes could sell papers as well as a good crime or a sex scandal. Most dailies presented sport as a news item, with Sunday and Monday editions usually devoting part of the front page and a special section to sport. The leader in this was Gaston Bénac, whose treatment of sport as drama, backed up by spectacular photographs and striking graphics, helped take sales of the evening daily *Paris-Soir* to over one million, occasionally reaching two million.[12] In a country as politically aware as France, with a wide variety of political opinions and newspapers to propagate them, the French press of the 1930s, with all its contradictions and despite its sensationalism, is a particularly rich source for judging the climate of public opinion. The right-wing newspapers, from royalist and nationalist to anti-Semitic and near-fascist, were quicker to embrace sport, but even the more politically committed papers of the Left, like *Humanité* (Communist), *Populaire* (Socialist), and *Oeuvre* (Radical), had a sports section and specialist sports writers. Despite the notorious lack of interest in sport among the leaders of the workers' movements,[13] the amalgamation of the bitterly divided Communist and Socialist parties into the antifascist Popular Front came about as a result of sporting contacts between the Communist workers' sport organization (FST) and the Socialist workers' sport organization (USSGT), which merged to become the Workers' Sport and Gymnastic Federation (FSGT) in December 1934. This breathed new life into the Communist weekly sports journal, simply called *Sport*, which enjoyed its heyday in the years before and just after the 1936 Olympics. The FSGT and *Sport* both played an important role in the election of the Popular Front government in May 1936.[14]

In many ways the 1930s were the heyday of the press: television was still a remote novelty, cinema was a source of escapism and relaxation, while radio, despite its boom in popularity and the fears of some in the press that it would make them redundant, worked alongside rather in competition with the written word. Cinema was the most popular leisure pursuit, in France as elsewhere, and from the flickering images invented by the Lumière brothers in 1896 through the talkies of the late 1920s into the 1930s it was a regular part of life for most French people. The newsreels that accompanied the main features always included some sports event, and cinemas like Cinéac showed nothing but newsreels: during the Games it had permanent sessions featuring Olympic events, showing daily from ten o'clock in the morning to midnight, with seats costing two to four francs (at five francs for a U.S. dollar).[15] Radio was the most rapidly improving popular medium of communication in the 1930s, and for those who could not afford a private set there was the pleasant alternative of gathering with friends in the local café. No café was complete without a large and luxurious version of the latest multivalve wireless. Radio thrived on sport and gave regular broadcasts of the Games, while athletes were frequently interviewed on the air.

It was the press, however, that was the main media outlet, taking full advantage of the Nazi propaganda services to present their readers with spectacular photographs of the Games and regale them with stories of the events surrounding them. The importance of the press in publicizing the Olympic Games was recognized by the German Press Bureau, which monitored reports on the Games from all major countries but paid particular attention to how they were covered in France.[16] It was especially concerned about the boycott movements that started to come into prominence during 1935.

The press of the Popular Front were the main organs backing a boycott of the Nazi Olympics,[17] but since this opposition was as much political as sporting, it could be dismissed by the German Press Bureau. And even among these committed antifascists, it was not until well into 1935, with the boycott debate raging in the United States and the passing of the Nuremberg Decrees on September 15, 1935, that anything approaching a campaign against holding the Games in Hitler's Germany got under way in France. Acting under the mistaken belief that the United States had decided to boycott, *Sport* ran an editorial in its

August 7, 1935, issue under the slogan, "Pas un sportif à Berlin" ("No athletes for Berlin"). On September 25 it proclaimed, "The Olympic Games must not take place in Berlin," pointing out how the Olympic Charter was being violated in Germany. It supported what it claimed to be the growing boycott movement in Europe and said, somewhat optimistically, that Baillet-Latour would soon arrange for their transfer from Germany.

Two weeks later, on November 6, *Sport* pointed to the "wave of protests" against the "Hitlerian Olympic Games" and followed with another editorial headed by what became a regular slogan: "Pas un sou, pas un homme pour Berlin" ("Not a penny, not a man for Berlin").[18] It continued to give examples of the persecution of Jews in Germany and reported the dissolution of Catholic and Protestant associations, borrowing freely from papers like *Intransigeant* and *Echo des Sports*, especially when they criticized the Nazis. This included one lengthy quote from *Sporting*, which allegedly argued, "The Olympic Games must not be held in a country stained with blood," although *Sporting*, having no wish to be associated with a Communist paper, later denied it supported a boycott.[19] A group called the Friends of Sport, made up of three hundred former athletes, formed a Committee against the Hitlerian Games, and on December 7, 1935, an International Anti-Fascist Conference in Paris gave birth to the International Committee for the Defence of the Olympic Idea. In the French Parliament on December 17, the Socialist deputy, Jean Longuet, unsuccessfully moved that since the regime of Hitler no longer had anything to do with the homeland of Goethe and Schiller, Beethoven and Kant, Marx and Liebknecht, it could no longer be seen as a worthy neighbor; the French government, therefore, should withdraw its promise of a subsidy for the athletes going to Berlin.[20] Throughout 1936, the FSGT and *Sport* continued to advocate the removal of the Games from Berlin, but they were also caught up in the election campaign to secure the victory of the three major left-wing parties, Radical, Socialist, and Communist, who were seriously divided among themselves but united in their opposition to fascism and pledged to work together in a Popular Front government. A major issue in the campaign was the call for the government to introduce a "New Deal for French Youth"[21] to bring about reforms that would make the poor and underprivileged of the towns and countryside fitter, healthier, and happier. It was also expected that a Popular Front government would support those fighting for a boycott of the Nazi Olympics.

Sport's optimism that public opinion in France was moving toward support for a boycott turned out to be misplaced. The German Press Bureau detected a hostile view of Germany in *L'Auto* and *Intransigeant*, which in its warped way it put down to the "Jew Wertheimer" on *L'Auto* and Louis Lazarus, the director of *Intransigeant*.[22] The reality was different, for while both these papers would launch attacks on the Nazi Games, neither was a constant critic. No newspapers other than those supporting the Popular Front maintained a consistent opposition to holding the Games in Nazi Germany.

Although the Winter Games were completed before the election campaign got under way in April and May 1936, even before then, and despite some isolated criticism from moderate and right-wing sources, France's participation in the Winter Olympics was never under threat. In August 1935, Gaston Bénac was taken on a tour of the Olympic Village that was being constructed for the Summer Games and made no bones about its ultimately military purpose. He concluded his impressions of the elaborate preparations with a warning that the village being built was no mere temporary structure but would be turned over to the military on its completion. As a result, Bénac concluded, "a Saint-Cyr in the latest fashion will arise at the gates of Berlin on the occasion of the Olympic Games."[23] Thereafter he retained a cynical note in his reporting. In *L'Auto,* Jacques Goddet wrote a mildly critical article on the eve of the Winter Games in the guise of comments from Coubertin, the gist of which he would take up at the close of the Games in a much more vitriolic fashion: he criticized the enormous amounts of money spent bolstering a political regime in the same way as Los Angeles had used the Games as propaganda for a tourist resort.[24] The German Press Bureau was not amused, but *L'Auto* reported at the end of the Winter Games that von Tschammer und Osten, the chief of German sport and president of the German Olympic Committee as well as an accomplished linguist, had read every issue and could find nothing but praise for its coverage.[25] Bénac would continue to offer criticism, and as the Games got under way he led the criticism in the press, but like *L'Auto* he was never a serious opponent of holding the Games in Germany. These two leading sports writers reserved their most stinging criticisms for the hypocrisy of the amateur oath, with *L'Auto* in particular campaigning for an "open" Olympics. But its main editor, Henri Desgrange, although no lover of Germany, was a tight-fisted entrepreneur who would never pass up the opportunity to make more money[26]—and in France the coming Olympic Games promised to be an even bigger money-maker than the Tour de France.

* * *

The Winter Olympics served as a dress rehearsal for the Summer Games, with the Nazis anxious to clean up their act and present a positive image of the "New Germany" to the anticipated hordes of foreign reporters, the advance guard of which came to "Ga-Pa" in February. The stories they sent back to their home country left the Nazi organizers with plenty to think over, but by and large the reports by the French observers were favorable, even rapturous at times, as their vocabulary was stretched to think of variations on words like "colossal" and "grandiose" to describe the (always "methodical") preparation. Their vocabulary would be stretched even further in August. Minor complaints came in the constant "Heils!" and the sight of swastikas everywhere, but the French reporters were most concerned about the extent to which its athletes had fallen behind other nations, leading to calls for the government to take a more active interest in the health of its subjects—a topic that had long been of major concern in the left-wing papers. In Lake Placid at the 1932 Games, France had placed seventh; in 1936 it was tenth, with only one bronze medal.

The role of the government would be even more forcibly brought into question as a result of the poor performances in Berlin, but the biggest minor furore of the Berlin Games was also prefigured at the Winter Games with the rapturous reception given to France when its delegation seemed to give the Hitler salute at the opening ceremony; in fact, it gave the rather similar Olympic salute. Also in anticipation of Berlin was the delirium that invariably accompanied the appearance of Hitler, causing Georges Briquet to claim that this and the fervor of the crowd infused a renewed dynamism in the German athletes.[27] Briquet also noted the silence that befell the success of non-German athletes, unless they were (in order) Austrian, French, or Hungarian. Robert de Thomassin in *Match* praised the way nothing was overlooked, and in that same paper Jean de Lascoumettes, discounting the doubters, claimed that the applause for France was too spontaneous to have been "on command": on the contrary, it was for the very faults of the French, who lost with a smile, were friendly to their opponents, and generally disported themselves in a frolicsome "frondeur" spirit.[28] This same spirit of "désinvolture" would be attributed to France's failures in Berlin, part in praise, but also with a sense of urgency that without a more serious approach to sport France would fall behind its neighbors in other matters as well. Marcel Berger, a respected right-wing intellectual writing in the ultranationalist *Flambeau*,[29] raised a "Cry of Alarm" in which he showed how physical fitness in Britain, the United States, and Scandinavia was a normal part of their civilization, while in Italy, Germany, and the Soviet Union it had become a religion of state. Despite this and the alarming figures on health in France, "sport continues to be ignored, if not scoffed at, by the Councils of our Governments." Also ignored in most press reports was the absence from the French team of the Jewish bobsled riders Jean Rheims and Philippe de Rothschild.

The greatest controversy to emerge from the Winter Games, however, erupted a couple of weeks after they were completed, when Hitler sent soldiers into the demilitarized zone of the Rhineland on March 7, 1936, in violation of the recently reconfirmed Locarno Pact. The controversy came with an open letter from one of France's leading social commentators and a prominent member of the French Academy, Claude Farrère, who claimed that the Winter Olympics had been in part used as a cover for Germany to breach its international obligations. Farrère's letter was spread across the front page of the *Intransigeant* on March 12, under the heading, "Should We Go to Berlin for the Olympic Games?" Farrère agreed that sport should be above politics, although he admitted it could do more good than much of the twaddle talked at Geneva. But he was above all concerned that France learn the lessons of Garmisch-Partenkirchen. Like the Winter Games, the Summer Games would be well run, France might even win a medal, and it would be well applauded. But herein lay the problem. The Winter Games had been too well organized for the tumultuous reception for the French not to have been an accident. Indeed, they were organized by an "acclamation brigade" ("brigade d'acclamation") acting "on orders." Why then should France expose itself to further painful and humiliating episodes in five months' time—unless, of course, something more dreadful intervened in the meantime? The acclamation brigade had been there at the Rhineland, and if the Winter Games acted as a cover for this maneuver, might not the cheering at the Berlin games indicate something more ominous?

The article provoked the desired response, as *Intransigeant* canvassed opinion from a wide range of sports leaders in national and international bodies as well as former athletes and the spokespersons for various sports federations. These opinions varied from the inevitable "sport and politics do not mix" to the equally predictable comment from Jules Rimet, the president of FIFA as well as the French National Sports Committee, who urged that France "wait and see." Jules Codenat (international rugby) said that there might be some ratbags in Germany, but none of them were to be found among its sportsmen. The former French athletic champion Joseph Guillemot was one of the few to agree with Farrère, but not for the same reasons—France did not have any athletes worth sending, and it was hardly worth going just to hold the jackets. Baillet-Latour, speaking as the official voice of the IOC, was quoted as saying that only a war could stop the Games from going ahead.[30]

There was no support for a boycott, with most commentators urging concern but no action. Thoumazeau in *Le Jour* claimed enigmatically that to send athletes to Berlin when the state's finances were in a parlous situation was more than an ambition—it was a duty, and if France's athletes did as poorly as expected, at least they should go there to learn something.[31] In *Match* René Lehmann quoted from Kurt Münch's education manual expressing his hatred for France, but merely commented resignedly: "These are the people who are organizing the Olympic Games in Berlin this year!"[32] Roger Malher in the *Petit Parisien* presented two sides of the argument, quoting the marquis de Polignac of the French Olympic Committee, who emphasized that it was not Germany but the IOC that was running the Games and pointed to the participation of Rudi Ball and Helene Mayer as proof of how the IOC had forced Germany to include Jewish participants.[33] He saw no reason why the athletes should be punished or France should be the only country to withdraw and reminded his readers of the wonderful welcome extended to France at Garmisch-Partenkirchen. But he concluded that whatever the decision, "a vast plan for the organization of the physical life of our youth must soon be brought into being." Roland-Lennad claimed that it would be naive to think that Berlin would be punished by France's absence, for "we would be punishing only ourselves."[34] France's great swimming hope, Jean Taris, proclaimed that he would take part in the Games even if he was the only Frenchman to go.[35] An ironical account by Clément Vautel pointed out how the cry of the warmongers in 1914—"To Berlin! To Berlin!"—had now been taken over by the pacifists, for it was the friends of Germany who wanted to go and its enemies who wanted to stay away.[36] And not because of Hitler's reorganization of the army, or for having sent his troops across the bridges of the Rhine toward France, but because they did not like his political, social, and racial theories. Vautel admitted that Hitler applied some of these theories rather crudely, but this was no reason for the French to get upset. His main concern was that if France went, it would be merely to "pick up the caps," but in keeping with the eternal hope that lies in the heart of all true sports fans, he added that the glorious incertitude of sport was such that perhaps there could be some surprises.

One of the best arguments in favor of going to Berlin came from the left-leaning *Marianne,* a newspaper that had quoted freely from Malitz's anti-French diatribe when it came out in 1934.[37] This time Pierre Bost headed an article "To Berlin?" opening with the controversy that had been aroused by the regime's attitude to Jews and Negroes: "It is also true that Germany will take advantage of the Olympic Games to spread throughout the world a politico-moral propaganda that knows no limits. The Winter Games in Garmisch gave us a rather unpleasant foretaste of this. It is regrettable, but there is nothing we can do about it. Such advertising is quite in order. Moreover its efficacy will depend on our own press. . . . One might not like the German regime; one might detest its racist doctrines, or better, find them ridiculous. One can consider that the organization of sport in Germany is based on frightful principles; that the stadiums there are too redolent of military parade grounds; one can wax indignant at the way Jews are excluded from the big clubs so that that most fundamental law of sport, the same rules for all, is not respected. All that is valid, all that is only too true."[38]

Bost went on to claim that he did not believe in the moral but only the physical values of sport and that the making of military men had nothing to do with making sportsmen. After all, "Peasants don't play any sport." He well understood why certain individuals, like Rothschild or a Communist, might not want to go, and their reasons had to be accepted, even honored. But these had to be individual refusals. Not only had the leaders of the Olympic movement no right to make such a decision, they had no right even to pose the question. A boycott would be useless, as the sanctions against Italy had shown. France had to go to Berlin, and each athlete would have their own reasons for doing so—however sad the occasion might turn out, there were a few hours of happiness to be stolen from it. The French could be sure that they would be acclaimed "as usual," but that would not mean anything—any more than its opposite would. The French could be even more sure that their athletes would not do well, but that would be the last reason not to go. It was too late: "We must go to Berlin."

In Germany the observers of events in France were disturbed by Farrère's letter, especially Theodor Lewald. On March 31 he sent a letter to Coubertin enclosing a copy of Farrère's article, "in case he had missed it," and asked that he write an article in response pointing out its falsehoods: he was sure that *Intransigeant* would be happy to print it. He also sent a copy of "our friend" Polignac's article that had appeared in *Le Journal* contradicting what Farrère had said. Farrère himself wrote to Coubertin as well, pointing to what he saw as the danger of France being outclassed by German athletes "notoriously superior to ours." He added that Germany had never respected anything but force and that if the German public saw France's inferiority in the sport field, it could be persuaded that France was "equally our inferior in artillery, aviation and poison gas—to say nothing of our navy, which is nothing, and theirs which is formidable."[39]

Like other ambassadors in Berlin, the French ambassador, François Poncet, had no illusions about the nature of the Nazi regime nor of the importance it placed on sport as a means of inculcating Nazi values in German youth and the propaganda value of the Games to be held in Berlin. But he did not suggest that France refuse to participate. If the French had replied with immediate action when German soldiers entered the Rhineland, this would have been understood in Germany, but to reply with a pinprick when the chance to land a major blow had been withheld would be seen as a pointless insult. In a letter of June 22 he pointed out that despite rumors in the foreign press, Germany would not embark on any "new adventures" before the Olympic Games: it was too well aware that if the Games did not take place, for whatever reason, "the public disappointment would be immense." Moves into Danzig, Czechoslovakia, or Austria were thus not on the immediate agenda.[40] But nor were they removed, and in a curious reversal of Poncet's prediction, it would be Austria, Czechoslovakia, and Danzig that succumbed to Nazi expansionism before the attack on Poland showed that there were few limits to Hitler's horizon.

Hitler's decision to send troops into the Rhineland was probably the greatest bluff of his career. It violated a treaty that he had freely ratified and so gave France a casus belli, his generals were against the move, which came at a time when France was superior to Germany in military terms, and even Hitler had ordered his officers to retreat if they met opposition from the French. His bluff was not called, his stocks rose in the eyes of the generals, and to the German people it was another stain removed from German honor so ignominiously betrayed in the signing of the Versailles Treaty. It only needed a successful Olympic Games for Hitler to seal his rapidly advancing reputation as a genius.

* * *

For most of April and May 1936, France was in election fever, and at the time of the Rhineland crisis the government saw itself in a caretaker role. The refusal to recognize the German threat, however, was a reflection of the chronically divided nature of French society, still suffering from the attempted right-wing coup that had threatened to topple the republican government on February 6, 1934, accompanied and followed by riots and demonstrations that resulted in many deaths. This led some on the Left to the realization that the Fascist threat was real and that they would have to overcome their own differences if it was to be met. The apparent triumph of the three major left-wing parties in the elections of 1936 (the Radicals later joined the Communists and Socialists) soon led to disillusionment. As soon as the Popular Front came to power, the new government, headed by the Socialist Léon Blum, was faced with a wave of sit-in strikes that eventually encompassed more than a million workers. The government was forced to introduce much-needed reforms of the workplace and working conditions, most of which would be lost by inflation and other factors, but one of which, the granting of two weeks' paid holidays, the workers would never relinquish in peacetime. In view of this and other problems, the promise of a million francs ($200,000) for the French delegation to Berlin was hardly a grave issue, but it nonetheless occasioned several agitated editorials, letters to the editor, and articles of opinion, mostly urging that the new government not go back on the promise of its predecessors. To add to the agitation, in late May Spain's Popular Front government, elected the previous February, offered Barcelona, with its magnificent new Montjuic Stadium, as the site for a Popular Olympics to open on July 19 for those who did not want to take part in the "fascist festival" in Berlin.[41]

Blum appointed the young and enthusiastic deputy from the north, Léo Lagrange, to the newly created post of undersecretary for sport and leisure. Lagrange, a politician of rare integrity whose name is commemorated in swimming pools and state-run leisure facilities throughout France (in part because of his heroic death at the front in 1940), was ideologically committed to the notion of sport for all, the provision of basic facilities for the masses rather than elite facilities for champions. Swimming pools were to be provided to prevent the scandalous number of deaths from drowning each year rather than to train potential medal winners at the Olympics.[42]

Not surprisingly, the friends of sport and glory whipped themselves into an apoplexy about whether he would withdraw the promised subsidy. They need not have worried. On June 19 the Blum cabinet agreed to set aside one million francs for the Berlin delegation and six hundred thousand for those going to Barcelona. The Communists denounced the treachery of the Socialists, while the French Olympic Committee bewailed the reduced subsidy, which it said would force them to cut back on their representation.[43] The Right in general denounced what it saw as a gratuitous political gift; *Sporting* pointed out that Catholics who went to their games in Vienna and Jews who had gone to the Maccabi Games in Tel Aviv had attracted neither protests nor subsidies, yet those of the "red religion" were paid for an event in which sport was only a secondary consideration.[44] After three weeks of heated debate the issue was finally put to a vote in Parliament on July 9, with the Communist deputy Florimonde Bonte, constantly interrupted by the Right, denouncing the subsidy for Berlin as making France an accomplice with hangmen.[45] It was the Communists who were out of step, however, or perhaps ahead of their time. The French public was committed to sending a delegation to Berlin, and by and large they could not see why the athletes should foot the bill for the politicians. Nor could they see why athletes who had trained for years for their big moment should forgo their chance of a lifetime. This was ultimately recognized by those who had been urging a boycott, and when the athletes left for Berlin in late July the FSGT wished them well and asked only that they not associate themselves with the regime that was running the Games.[46] As for the Barcelona Olympics, they were ended before they had begun, when the Civil War, launched two days earlier, reached Barcelona early on the morning of the opening ceremony.

The Left's opposition to the Nazi Olympics was clear-cut; for the Right, however, support for the Nazis posed some intriguing dilemmas. They shared the same enemies—liberalism and popular democracy in general, trade unions and Bolsheviks in particular, with a significant minority venomous in their hatred for Jews—and in their nationalism they could appreciate the Nazis' contempt for international peace. But they could not overlook the humiliations inflicted on France by their unfriendly neighbor and the renewed threat of German aggression inherent in Hitler's expansionist ambitions. For some this fear was overcome by taking comfort in Hitler's clearly stated intentions to move eastward, and the Right held to the comforting belief that Hitler stood as a bulwark against bolshevism. As much as those on the Right might dislike the Nazis, they hated the Left even more—one of their slogans for the 1936 elections was "Sooner Hitler than [the Jew] Blum." Such tensions were clearly stated in the *Echo de Paris, Figaro,* and, before it was bought out by the Nazi cause, by *Le Jour.*

On July 22 an article in *Le Jour*'s political columns pointed out that for Germany the Olympics were not only a matter of sport but also a gigantic publicity stunt for its economy. On the eve of the departure of the French athletes, it headed a front-page article in its issue of July 29: "It Is No Longer Berlin / It Is a Film Set / Eve of Battle in the Capital of the Olympic Games." The Germans, claimed *Le Jour,* were falling all over themselves to welcome foreigners, learning new languages through Berlitz School courses and even allowing some barely "Aryan" faces to be seen in the streets. Aware of its isolated position in world opinion, the German capital was recapturing some of the spirit of the Weimar period. But the stamp of the Third Reich and the influence of Hitler were clearly to be seen in the forest of masts, flags, and swastikas. Foreign editors had been inundated with statistics about the preparations, and those dealing with the Olympic Village alone provided enough information to take up more than four times the space given to the Civil War in Spain. As much as in the press, opinion in the cinema and radio were "finely orchestrated by the incomparable Dr. Goebbels." Such effort and such expenditure would be wasted were it merely in the cause of sport, and never before had any country tied together so closely the organization of the Games and national propaganda. Success was no mere matter of "amour propre" for Germany, which was out to impress its guests among the great nations and show that it was worthy of being accepted back into their company. To this end it was prepared to paint over a few cracks and conceal a few nasty realities.

There were other forces at work on *Le Jour* as it headed down the road to complete collaboration, a path already marked out in its reporting of the Olympics. Overlooking the realities of recent history, it explained the applause for France at the opening ceremony as being due to "the glorious evocation of our history, the tradition of heroism that our flag recalls,"[47] and intertwined with a description of the sporting festival, it claimed that the Reich wanted nothing more than to stay at peace with France. Only the Bolsheviks could upset such peaceful intentions, and should they threaten to take over in France, only then would the Reich respond to "the most tragic of necessities."[48] The racism more zealously propagated in newspapers like *Action Française, Je suis partout, Gringoire,* and *Candide* made its appearance in the paper: when Cornelius Johnson was interrupted by von Tschammer's speech during his high jump attempt, *Le Jour* claimed that "superstitious like all blacks, he thought he heard the voice of Jupiter thundering out,"[49] and in another aside it reported the disgust of a German who thought that Paris had a colony of fifty thousand Senegalese who interbred freely with the locals. Their sports reporter, Thoumazeau, claimed that the superiority of the blacks in athletics was merely because they were closer to nature.[50]

Figaro was an elitist paper then as today, its readership reflected in advertisements aimed at the more affluent sections of society, while in sports reporting it favored amateurism and gave more space to motor sports, tennis, and golf than the more popular papers. It revealed the usual hypocrisies of the amateur position, constantly breaking up the text or captions in photos with the commercial intrusions that are the blight of modern sport. For instance, it was always happy to point out that this or that athlete appreciated a drink of "PERRIER WATER" after their endeavors. Nevertheless, it showed an acute awareness of the reality behind the Nazi Olympics. Having given a rosy picture of the arrival of the French athletes and the conditions at the Olympic Village and expressing the wish that all petty personal interests and the inevitable problems of sport be submerged by the greater spectacle, the political editor, Wladimir d'Ormesson, published a front-page article on August 2 revealing the darker side of the Nazi Games.

No country, he opened, understands propaganda better than Germany, and none more than Hitler's Germany, where Goebbels was only too ready to seize the gift of the Olympic Games to add to Nazi glory. With more than a little exaggeration, he claimed that seven million had come to Paris for the 1924 Olympics, while many more were expected in Berlin. (In fact, as we have seen, Los Angeles was the first Games to attract more than a million visitors, and more than three million would come to Berlin). Without wishing to detract from the sporting aspects of the Games, d'Ormesson pointed out that it would be stupid not to take into account the other benefits, political as well as financial, accruing to Germany: the profits to be gained from the foreign money pouring in to help staunch some of Dr. Schacht's financial wounds, and the dignitaries who would be wooed and won over by the sheer glory of Hitler's triumphs, persuaded to overlook the remilitarization of the Rhineland and its condemnation by the League of Nations. Forgotten, too, would be the murders of June 30 (the "Night of the Long Knives") and the treaties trampled underfoot, for the dictatorial terror of the regime that bore down on the locals would not be felt by the foreigners. They would also be oblivious to the smoke from the war factories working day and night in the Ruhr and Silesia, getting ready for what? The visitors would see only a wild, ardent, and beautiful youth, a brilliant capital, a disciplined display of music and muscle, and an imperial presentation of the élan of an entire people. D'Ormesson warned his readers to beware of those who, having been "propagandized," would come back as "propagandists," firm in the belief that Hitler and Order with a capital O was the way of the future. It would be a terrible mistake, for while Germany "is a sick country that looks healthy, France is a healthy country with all the appearances of ill health."

Figaro, mainly through André Reichel, looked to Britain as its model in sport. Reichel recognized the problems of professionalism, cabals, doping, and the intrusion of politics, but he hoped that sport would triumph through its educative and health qualities.[51] He was incensed by the exhibitions put on by German youth on orders from above, believing that sport had to be consented to freely and that to subordinate it to a political goal was to rob it of part of its nobility. This was a moral commercialization as bad as any material commercialization: "You don't run 100 meters in jackboots."[52] *Figaro*'s main innovation in response to the Games was to set up an "Inquest" in its issue of August 13, where it canvassed the opinion of France's sporting and political leaders on how the physical and moral health of the nation could be improved. Their replies were published over subsequent issues.

* * *

It was with eyes wide open, then, that the French athletes, reporters and spectators left for Berlin. The German hosts were equally prepared to set them straight on the realities of the "New Order" as they wanted the world to see it. From the moment the French delegation set foot in Germany they were greeted as honored guests, and although they arrived very early on the morning of July 30 they were given an official welcome. Ambassador Poncet made a short speech in which he expressed his hope that France's colors would be hoisted to the mast to show that France was not decadent and that when the athletes returned they would do all they could to spread the "idea that physical education is a great national cause on which depends the future of our country."[53] At the opening ceremony the French delegation was given an ovation as in February because they were believed to have given the Hitler salute, a reception that was surpassed only by that given the host nation and Austria. The following day the athletics got under way, and some journalists claimed that it was with relief that they could get on with the job of reporting athletics instead of describing the forests of flags, columns of marching youths, and the pomposity of officials of various grades in uniforms of many colors.

But the politics could not be wished away. Even when the athletes took over, the press could not overlook the magnificence of the presentation, and once more lead writers ran out of adjectives to describe its sheer grandeur and scale. The very success of the German organization upset some French consciences, but underlying any jealousy was a genuine irritation at the Nazi undertones. Roger Malher of the *Petit Parisien,* a leading skeptic, admitted how on one occasion he was about to be won over by the spectacle of eight thousand German girls dancing in beautiful rhythm, wishing young French women could do the same, when the scene was ruptured by a battalion of swastika-brandishing young boys breaking through the "gentle blonde harvest." He noted that at the Olympic Village the separation of the women from the men left them unjustly on their own, but he took some comfort in the fact that the cuisine was French.[54] He denounced the use of the German national anthem to greet the entry of the Germans at the opening ceremony and declared that the Hellenic beauty of the occasion was spoiled by the sight of the dirigible *Hindenburg,* pride of the German zeppelins, flying overhead.[55]

The first day of athletic competition was a brilliant success, but Malher, excusing himself on the grounds that he had described on the previous day the "magnificent success of the Opening Ceremony," loosed a few barbed criticisms. He commented sarcastically on the Nazi exultation as the swastika was hoisted to the mast, accompanied by "Deutschland über Alles" and the "inevitable" Horst Wessell song, which the National Socialists had made the second official hymn of Germany. He also objected to the howls of joy and thrice-repeated "Heil Hitlers!" that shook the enormous stone stadium. He described as "raucous and symbolic" a speech by von Tschammer und Osten sending the torch on its way to Kiel and concluded in exasperation that at Olympia, a festival of youth, where the first duty of the hosts was to keep themselves discreetly in the background, the Germans inflicted on their guests "constant demonstrations of national fervor."[56] He had a few lighter comments the following day, humorous reflections on whether Owens would find enough earth in his native soil to grow the oak sapling given to all the victors and less humorous comments wondering whether Helen Stephens had yet agreed to the operation that would make her a man, as "this is the fashion right now."[57] All this came under headlines that proclaimed: "The Games of the XIth Olympiad among a People / The German People Who Have a Terrible Love of Winning / The Capital of the Reich Is Buried under Flag-bedecked Colonnades / The Swastikas Have Become an Obsession and the Five Olympic Rings a Haunting Memory."

Jean Routhier, the chief sports writer for the *Echo de Paris,* had two clouds hanging over his reports of the Games. One was the threat of war with Germany, whose proclamations of peaceful intent he could not take seriously, particularly the self-appointed role of Hitler as principle apostle of peace;[58] the other was the clenched fist of the reds in France, so reminiscent of the raised arms of young Nazis. He was well aware of the propaganda value of the Games and claimed that those who thought this a stupid waste of money—and there were many such people in France—did not understand international propaganda.[59] At the end of the first week of the competition he had come to the conclusion that the Olympic Games had become little more than "a Hitlerian demonstration."[60]

Leading the criticism, however, was Gaston Bénac of *Paris-Soir*, who was in charge of one of the most impressive reporting teams at the Games. Sports reporters for France's best-selling evening newspaper had at their disposal one car for radio reports, one for sending back photographs ("bélinographie"), five motorcycles, and one airplane.[61] Bénac's criticisms were often less political than the product of wounded national pique: the faults in organization, the breaches of protocol, the failure to use French, the language of the Games, in official communiqués, the deplorable press services, and the food arrangements, reporters often being forced to stand up and eat sausages with mustard instead of being able to sit down to a leisured lunch.[62] But he was not above making political attacks. In one of Bénac's first articles he compared Berlin to his visit of the previous year, and noted that there were less brownshirts roaming around or yelling their hatred of Jews and Catholics from the backs of trucks. There were even some non-Aryans, people of mixed race, and Negroes walking around undisturbed. But this was the "truce of muscles."[63] The following day *Paris-Soir*'s front page had a spectacular picture of a pole vaulter superimposed over an aerial photo of athletes passing through the Olympic Gates[64] with a lead article emphasizing the masses of young men who "belong to the nation and practice sport as they are commanded. From ten years of age are they not soldiers of the Reich?"[65] The next day appeared his complaints about the military atmosphere, the foul-ups in press communications, with delays, empty information boards, and only "the language of Goethe" being used. And, as always, the journalists were left to starve inside the stadium. Despite the great success of the opening ceremony, he found that there was too much that had nothing to do with sport, a "formidable mobilization of young athletes marching around Berlin in strict regimentation, wishing, it would seem, to give an impression of power. They no doubt succeeded in this, but it should not be forgotten that the purpose of the Games was to clip a tenth of a second off the 100 meters, add half a centimeter in the high jump and win by the length of a hand in swimming."[66]

What French critics found most distasteful about their German hosts, other than their lack of gastronomic sensibility, was their lack of spontaneity, their love of, or need for, discipline. Cartoons depicted spectators marching in step and cheering in time, with one character warning her friend, a visitor, that she had to keep in step or else people would look at them; in another, a German wife scolded her husband (Herr Bitteschön, "Mr. Thank-you-very-much") as a bad German for not appearing at the final of the triple jump. (One cartoon had a husband leaving home with a "Negro" in bed with his wife, muttering that if it was to help France's future medal chances then so it had to be.) As the "Führer weather" (all that was good, even the sunshine, was attributed to Hitler) gave way to cold and rain and thousands caught colds, one reporter rejoiced that at least sneezing was something the Germans could do spontaneously.[67] A favorite French character was the "resquilleur," or the "fly man." This was the type who bluffed his way past the "Schupos" although he did not have a ticket or earned a free meal through his quick wit and ready tongue. These were French traits of which Roger Malher was particularly proud.[68]

* * *

The French athletes performed as poorly as expected, and although Louis Hostin (weightlifting) and Emile Poilvé (wrestling) were France's first gold medal winners, it was the qualification of Robert Goix for the final of the 1,500 meters, the first Frenchman to breast a tape, that most roused the French public. In the final of what was then generally regarded as the greatest event of the Games, the metric mile, Goix recorded his best ever time, one that would have equaled Nurmi's winning time in the 1924 Games, and for this he was feted in the French press as though he had won the race: in fact he came in eighth, six seconds and almost fifty meters behind Jack Lovelock (New Zealand), who set a new world record.

The French were as captivated by Owens as the other visitors. His feline grace, winning smile, and relaxed demeanor were described in a variety of metaphors, mostly without racist overtones. Owens granted several interviews to the press and radio, presumably for a fee, although this was never mentioned.[69] Out of the imagination of the journalists a picture of Owens could be created that did not exactly coincide with the truth, that of the Cleveland-born African American, a friend of Joe Louis, whose favorite recreations included music, painting, cinema, reading, and radio,[70] although his main ambition, despite a gift for music that made of him a "virtuoso" saxophone player,[71] was to become an athletics coach. Among his rewards for all this talent was a house and car given to him by his university. The myth of the Hitler "snub," however, was one of Owens's own inventions.

Only two reports came close to what later became part of the Owens legend.[72] One appeared on the front page of the *Petit Journal* on August 4 and reported that Owens, perhaps to console himself for not having his record of the previous day recognized because of the following wind, had the honor of being presented to the Führer by the chief of German sport: "The onlookers watched with curiosity this meeting between the Negro and the champion of Nordic racism. Before the great black devil, svelte and supple, the German chancellor appeared quite small and strangely gauche." This story was never disavowed. In *Regards*, a Communist newspaper aimed at an audience beyond the party faithful, it was claimed that Hitler had refused to shake Owens's outstretched hand at the "obligatory presentation,"[73] but this was later admitted to have been an oversight. One of *Paris-Soir*'s reporters put the question straight to Owens after his win in the 100 meters and was told that Hitler had not received him, that after his medal he went straight to the cinema cabin to see a film of his performance.[74]

Apart from Owens, the major personality at the Games was Hitler, and none of the visitors could fail to note how rapturously he was greeted by the crowds. It was a reception no French politician could hope for, and unflattering comparisons were made with French politicians who could not be bothered to go to any sporting event, let alone attend virtually every day and follow the events with obvious interest. The Führer was spared the sarcasm the French reporters reserved for their own politicians, even in regard to the exaggerated influence he was said to have in inspiring German athletes to greater efforts. The French reporters reserved their sarcasm for athletes who won medals and were rewarded by the regime with a promotion—and this was announced over the microphone. Hans Woelke, whose gold in the shot put made him the first German to win gold in an athletic event, was the first to be so honored. When the French gold medallist in wrestling, Emile Poilvé, was later promoted to brigadier in the French police, this was seen as no more than he merited.

The sportsmanship of the German crowds in 1936 was generally applauded, but their chauvinism could not be overlooked. It was clear that the German spectators warmed to Owens, and if they did not always applaud non-German victories with the same fervor that greeted their own athletes, this was perhaps a normal failing. In reporting the events of August 8, *Sporting,* for instance, claimed, "The Hitlerian chauvinism surpasses all boundaries and the spectacle of a crowd that was interested only in winning national glory was nauseating."[75] In the same newspaper, however, the former French athletic champion Alfred Spitzer, a regular columnist, said that the French would have been as bad if they had had as many victories to celebrate and that the Germans had every right to manifest their joy. He could never quite accept the French preference for cycling over athletics and commented somewhat sourly that sixty thousand French people would not have turned up to see a French athletic triumph and most of them wouldn't know the words of the Marseillaise.

At the end of the first week and with the end of the track and field events, interest dropped off sharply, and the crowds were noted to be singing the German and Hitler national anthems with less enthusiasm. The French were cheered by medals in boxing and cycling, but these did not carry the same glamor as the blue riband track and field events; true merit in cycling and boxing, after all, was measured by performances in the professional circuits. It was in cycling that one of the inevitable controversies in regard to cheating erupted, as well as the capacity for nationalism to overlook it or exaggerate it, depending on who the culprit was. *Sporting* was so incensed by the cheating by which it believed the German Merkens won a medal at the expense of the Dutchman van Vliet in the 1,000 meter sprint, claiming that this was passed over in the Berlin press and by the "blind, chauvinistic and wild crowd," that it called on French sports people to turn out to abuse him should he ever appear at "a velodrome near you"[76] When Guy Lapébie was held back by his compatriot Robert Charpentier to be robbed of gold in the 100 kilometer road race, the French press was more inclined to give credence to a tear-stained Lapébie's claim that he had been held back by an Italian.

In the final medal count Germany came out on top, but it was a "victory" regarded with some cynicism by its rivals. The French in particular were quick to point out that the medal tally included many new events—several aquatic events that were introduced for the first time—that were given gold along with the blue riband events. Then, as now, these benefited the host nation. This prompted some French writers to suggest that pétanque or some French regional sports be introduced when France next got the Games. In a more tongue-in-cheek spirit, it was suggested that there be races for café waiters, where the French garçons would be sure to sweep the pool.

* * *

Almost as soon as the last lights had gone out in the closing ceremony, the simmering resentment of two of France's leading reporters, Bénac and Jacques Goddet, boiled to the surface in withering attacks on they way the Olympic Games had been hijacked in the interests of a political regime.[77] Much of this was justified, some of it was sour grapes, and all of it was directed at France's rulers, demanding that something be done to improve the physical condition of French youth. On this the entire French sporting press could come together, denouncing the indifference of French politicians and the incompetence of the French National Olympic Committee.

They could rationalize that success in athletics does not indicate any intrinsic moral worth, but the sight of Germany's young men and women, fit, healthy, and proud of the fatherland, had given them a severe jolt, whether it was as athletes or spectators. They could point with justification to the unhealthy willingness of Germany's overdisciplined youth to act under orders, but they knew equally well that France's young people had been let down by an education system that did little to develop sound minds in the population at large or sound bodies among the intellectual elite. The Popular Front government was committed to reversing this, but its hold on power was tenuous, and it would soon be broken by the ill will of its opponents and its own internal contradictions. These were the same factors that had militated against the development of a sound physical education system in French schools, for while all factions from the extreme Left to the extreme Right saw the need for a healthy youth, they could not agree on how this should be brought about. The Right was uncomfortable in calling for reforms that the Left had been advocating for years.[78]

The Nazi Olympics were the first that were truly international and popular, in part because of the way the Nazis seized on their propaganda value and in part because sport was coming to be seen as a force in political life. The farce of amateurism was clearly brought to light in Berlin, with the major share of the medals going to the state amateurs of the Reich and other dictatorships and the college athletes of the United States. Like Britain and the countries of its Commonwealth, France generally adhered to the accepted notions of amateurism in most sports, but sport itself was becoming inevitably more professional, especially in the sheer dedication of the athletes. As *Echo des sports*[79] pointed out: "The Olympic Games no longer inspire poetry, only chronometry and the rule of time."[80] The Berlin Games had been big because sport itself was now big. Sport had become an international concern, and this could not be changed. *Echo des sports* commented sarcastically on complaints that the French had been "too well received" and that the small nations had been passed over. The Games, it claimed in a statement that came uncomfortably close to the reigning views in the conduct of foreign affairs, were not there to draw attention to the small nations but to find out who was the best. Or fittest.

Sport and politics have always mixed, most obviously in international competition, more subtly in domestic. The "era of the dictators" between the wars and the organization of the Olympic Games of 1936 by the Nazis clearly demonstrated this; but so too did the attitudes of those who chose to ignore the importance of sport. For some leaders of opinion in the democracies this blindness was willful, for others it was merely a product of ignorance. For the athletes and the sporting public it was a different matter. Athletes could hardly be blamed for the obsession that put winning medals before every other consideration. For the ordinary folks in the democracies, sport occupied a more important place than it did for those whose wealth gave them more options. For them it was more important that their sport be kept as a haven from the everyday world: the starting whistle at work, the supervision of the boss, the boredom of work if they were employed, or idleness if they were not. Sport for them had a drama, excitement, and even beauty that was within their reach, economically or culturally. The failure to win them over to a boycott of the Nazi Olympics was no great surprise, even to the politically committed who wanted to win them over to the class struggle. The main supporters of a boycott were those on the socialist or communist Left, liberals, broad-minded intellectuals, concerned conservatives, and Jews regardless of class or country. For most of these people, sport was a secondary matter. Not only was it a pleasure they could forgo, they had the compensation of the inner glow of being on the side of justice, if not reality.

The most interesting postscript to the Nazi Olympics came with the accolade bestowed on them by the founder of the modern Games himself when the Swiss journalist, André Lang, published an interview with Coubertin in which he said that the Nazi Olympics had lived up to his highest ideals. Perhaps surprisingly, the Left tended to dismiss this as a statement from someone who was losing touch with reality and who was best remembered for what he had set out to do, but others took him seriously. *L'Auto* sent their own journalist, Fernand Lomazzi, to ask Coubertin if he had been accurately reported and went on to expand on what he had said. It was claimed that Coubertin praised the Nazi Olympics for fulfilling his highest ambitions for the Games. The aging and unwell baron— he would die within a year—still harbored resentments against the French for the way he believed they had failed to honor him as he thought he deserved. This the Nazis had done, cynically and to good effect, publishing some of his works in German, offering to play his favorite movement from Beethoven's Ninth Symphony as part of the Games ceremony, and nominating him, albeit unsuccessfully, for the Nobel Peace Prize for 1936.[81]

If the Nazis seduced Coubertin, however, it was a willing seduction. His vision of a world coming together to compete in honest athletic competition accompanied by a cultural festival graced by the presence of the highest in the ranks of title, wealth, and political power was in line with his original courting of those who helped him revive the Olympic Games back in the 1890s. That the regime organizing the Games dismissed the notion of world brotherhood as sentimental claptrap was a small price to pay; the exclusion of the Jews was inconsequential, and the absence of any liberals, socialists, or communists was an irrelevance. Coubertin, a man whose intellect was limited by his passion for his idée fixe, was far from being alone in a make-believe world that others shared more cynically. The world of Coubertin and the IOC and that of the various national Olympic Committees was shared by the sporting world at large. For those who would be the major victims in the coming conflict there was little compensation in knowing that they had been right before their time.

Notes

It is with deep gratitude that I record my thanks to Françoise Hache, who back in 1990 kindly gave me a microfiche copy of her doctoral thesis, "La place du sport dans le système National-Socialiste," University of Paris VIII.

1. Germany was permitted to participate in all winter sports and those summer sports that had more neutral members on their executive boards (such as Scandinavia and Switzerland) than allies of the First World War (such as the United Kingdom, France, and Belgium). See P. O. Holmäng, "International Sports Organizations, 1919–25: Sweden and the German Question," *International Journal of the History of Sport* 9.2 (1992): 455–66.

2. None of this was kept secret from the French public, and the left-wing newspapers in particular were happy to quote from them.

3. For a general work in English on French sport, see R. Holt, *Sport and Society in Modern France* (London: McMillan Press, 1981). For excellent coverage by a journalist who favors the sport but does not overlook the politics, see Jean-Toussaint Fieschi, *Histoire du sport français, de 1870 à nos jours* (Paris: PAC, 1983). In the early 1990s a host of specialist studies were brought together in a history under the directorship of Ronald Hubscher. Although lacking a central theme, this detailed study should be consulted for its comprehensive bibliography of French sports history. R. Hubscher, J. Durry, and B. Jeu, *L'Histoire en Mouvements: Le sport dans la société française (XIXe-XXe siècle)* (Paris: Armand Colin, 1992). See also *Jeux et sports dans l'histoire*, 2 vols. (Paris: Editions du CTHS, 1992). This is made up of papers presented at the Actes du 116ᵉ Congrès National des Sociétés Savantes, held at Chambéry in 1991. For a more up-to-date bibliography of works on French sport, see C. Vivier and J.-F. Loudcher, eds., *Le Sport dans la ville* (Paris: L'Harmattan, 1998); P. Vassort, *Football et politique: Sociologie historique d'une domination* (Paris: Les Editions de la Passion, 1999); and J.-M. Delaplace, ed., *L'Histoire du sport—l'histoire des sportifs* (Paris: L'Harmattan, 1999). See also P. Arnaud, "French Sport and the Emergence of Authoritarian Regimes, 1919–1939," in *Sport and International Politics: The Impact of Fascism and Communism on Sport*, ed. P. Arnaud

and J. Riordan (London: E. and F. N. Spon, 1998), although this is essentially an article on the important archives of the Service des Oeuvres Françaises à l'Etranger and barely covers the period after the mid-1920s. The best account of reactions in France to the Nazi Olympics is Françoise Hache, "La place du sport dans le système National-Socialiste" (University of Lille microfiche, Doctorat Nouveau régime 87/PA08/0050, 1987), which includes many quotes from the contemporary French press. See also J.-P. Saint-Martin and T. Terret, eds., *Le sport français dans l'entre-deux-guerres* (Paris: L'Harmattan, 2001); and P. Arnaud, T. Terret, J.-P. Saint-Martin, and P. Gros, eds., *Le sport et les français pendant l'occupation, 1940–1944,* 2 vols. (Paris: L'Harmattan, 2002).

4. Borotra later played a role in the profascist government of unoccupied France during the war. See D. Amson, *Borotra: De Wimbledon à Vichy* (Paris: Tallendier, 1999).

5. See A. Little, *S. Lenglen, Tennis Idol of the Twenties* (London: Wimbledon Tennis Museum, 1988); and S. Bandy, "Suzanne Lenglen und das Künstlerische und Heroische im Sport," in *Aus Biographien Sportgeschichte lernen,* ed. A. Krüger and B. Wedemeyer (Hoya: NISH, 2000), 163–76.

6. For athletes from the French African colonies on the French teams, see B. Deville-Danthu, *Le sport en noir et blanc: Du sport colonial au sport africain dans les anciens territoires français d'Afrique occidentale (1920–1965)* (Paris: L'Harmattan, 1997).

7. Ladoumègue continued to enjoy good press in France, and he seemed to be able to keep the favor of newspapers of all political persuasions. For his continuing popularity at the time of his death in 1973, see G. Meyer, *Le grand livre de l'athlétisme français* (Paris: Calmann-Lévy, 1975), 62.

8. See T. Terret, "L'entraîneur et le nageur: Le cas Hermant—Taris," in J.-M. Delaplace, *L'histoire du sport,* 31–38.

9. *Paris-Soir,* July 30, 1936. As a critic of *L'Auto, Sporting* did not share *L'Auto*'s enthusiasm but was in general critical of a paper that favored cycling over athletics (*L'Auto* was the founder and sponsor of the Tour de France).

10. J.-M. Renaitour, *Vive le sport!* (Paris: Fernand Sorlot, 1934). The book is dedicated to Desgrange and opens with the Pajol story.

11. A. Obey, *L'orgue du stade* (Paris: Gallimard, 1924). For the role of the Tour de France, see P. Boury, *La France du Tour, Le Tour de France: Un espace sportif à géographie variable* (Paris: L'Harmattan, 1997).

12. E. Seidler, *Le sport et la presse* (Paris: Armand Colin, 1964); G. Meyer, *Les tribulations d'un journaliste sportif* (Paris: Jean-Claude Simoen, 1978).

13. See the *Communist International* 14 (Apr. 8, 1937): 579–87, for the admission that the Communists had neglected the deep-seated sporting interests of the workers. For workers' sport in general, see A. Krüger and J. Riordan, eds., *The Story of Worker Sport* (Champaign, Ill.: Human Kinetics, 1996).

14. W. J. Murray, "The French Workers' Sports Federation and the Victory of the Popular Front in France," *International Journal of the History of Sport* 4.2 (1987): 203–30. See also W. Murray, "France," in Krüger and Riordan, *Story of Worker Sport,* 27–42; L. Strauss, "Le sport travailliste français pendant l'entre-deux-guerres," in *Les origines du sport ouvrier en Europe,* ed. Pierre Arnaud (Paris: L'Harmattan, 1994), 193–218.

15. See, for instance, *Le Journal,* Aug. 7, 1936, where this rate is advertised. Some newspapers had special arrangements with particular radio stations, to which they gave prominence in photos of athletes being interviewed at the microphone. At the same time a weekly sports journal cost between half a franc and a franc. Wages in France were generally lower at the time than in the United States.

16. *Die Olympiade Berlin, 1936, im Spiegel der ausländischen Presse,* esp. the section entitled "Gesamt-Stimmungsbild der französischen Presse über die Olympiade 1936 in Berlin." Much of this is reproduced in J. Bellers, ed., *Die Olympiade Berlin im Spiegel der auslandischen Presse* (Münster: Lit., 1986). For the Winter Olympics, see *Presseberichte des Aussenpolitischen Amtes der NSDAP: Die Olympischen Winterspiele in der Kritik des Auslandes* (Berlin, March 1936). At the Carl and Liselott Diem Institut of the Deutsche Sporthochschüle in Köln, where the above are held, there

are also the press cuttings from which these reports were made, occasionally with comments on the extracts. All the above documents are marked "Strictly Confidential." I am grateful to the Carl and Liselott Diem Institut for allowing me access to the above works and for their unfailing kindness during my stay there in 1990.

17. For the boycott campaign in France, see J.-M. Brohm, *1936: Jeux Olympiques à Berlin* (Brussels: Editions Complexe, 1983); and B. Kidd, "The Popular Front and the 1936 Olympics," *Canadian Journal of the History of Sport and Physical Education* 11.1 (1980): 1–18.

18. *Sport,* Nov. 20, 1935. The slogan was taken from an earlier resolution by some Socialists at their annual congress at Tours in 1931: "Not a sou, not a man for the military machine of the bourgeoisie." See N. Greene, *Crisis and Decline: The French Socialist Party in the Popular Front Era* (Ithaca, N.Y.: Cornell University Press, 1969), 6.

19. *Sport,* Nov. 20, 1935. In fact, *Sporting* did not favor a boycott but was responding to an article in *L'Auto*, which was said to have given an anti-Semitic twist to a statement by M. Jacob, a prominent Jewish sports official. *Sporting* would later call for his resignation from the French National Olympic Committee (COF) and the French Football Association (FFFA) because he was opposed to the Berlin Olympics for "political or religious reasons" (*Sporting,* May 28, 1936).

20. Brohm, *1936*, 85–95; Kidd, "Popular Front and the 1936 Olympics," 1.

21. Murray, "French Workers' Sports Federation," 219–22.

22. *Presseberichte des Aussenpolitischen Amtes der NSDAP,* "France," 1.

23. *Paris-Soir,* Aug. 9, 1935. Saint-Cyr was the French Military Academy (1808–1940).

24. *L'Auto,* Jan. 17, 1936.

25. *L'Auto,* Feb. 19, 1936.

26. There is as yet no published biography of Desgrange, despite his central importance in French sports history. Although he was clearly involved in sport for the money he could make out of it—he owned important sporting venues and had suspect dealings with some professional sports agents—he was also a fanatical sportsman. See Seidler, *Le sport et la presse;* and Meyer, *Les tribulations d'un journaliste sportif.* Through *L'Auto* he virtually ran a campaign for an "open" Olympics, frequently pointing to the hypocrisy of those who claimed to be amateurs. In this he was supported by other members of the commercial press but also, however indirectly, by *Sport.* See Jean Durry, "Un champion populaire: André Leducq, Vainqueur du Tour de France cycliste," *Sport Histoire* 1.1 (1988): 123–36, for the amount of money to be made by a good amateur cyclist: one thousand francs a month all year for being selected on the French Olympic team, plus two thousand for an Olympic victory and other prize money, at a time when three hundred francs a month in expenses (and no premium for victories) were permitted for no more than six weeks. As a professional in cycling, in 1932 Leducq made fifty-one thousand francs for winning the Tour de France and received five thousand francs in appearance fees for small races after the grueling tour (conversion rates for francs appear on p. 132 of Durry's article). In 1936 only 10 percent of Americans made more than three thousand dollars a year. See E. S. Waytinsky, *Profile of the U.S. Economy: A Survey of Growth and Change* (New York: Praeger, 1967), 142.

27. *Miroir des Sports,* Feb. 18, 1936.

28. *Match,* Feb. 11, 1936.

29. *Flambeau,* Feb. 22, 1936.

30. These are conveniently brought together in the "Sport Vorbereitung Frankreich," held in the DSHS, Köln.

31. *Le Jour,* Mar. 3, 1936.

32. *Match,* Mar. 24, 1936.

33. *Petit Parisien,* Mar. 24, 1936.

34. *Le Jour,* May 15, 1936.

35. *Intransigeant,* Apr. 29, 1936. See T. Terret, "Histoire de la natation," in *Histoire des sports,* ed. T. Terret (Paris: L'Harmattan, 1996), 51–86.

36. *Le Journal,* May 21, 1936.

37. See especially *Marianne,* Feb. 14, 1934. It noted only the second edition, as the first had appeared weeks before Hitler took power. See B. Malitz, *Die Leibesübungen in der nationalsozialistischen Idee,* 2d ed. (München: Eher, 1934).

38. *Marianne,* Mar. 18, 1936.

39. Lewald-Coubertin correspondence held at the DSHS, Köln. For quotes from the Farrère-Coubertin correspondence, see also L. Callebat, *Pierre de Coubertin* (Paris: Fayard, 1988), 213.

40. These can be consulted in what remains of the correspondence between the French embassy in Paris and the minister for foreign affairs at the Quai d' Orsay, "Archives du Ministère des Affaires Etrangères, Série Europe, 1930–40, Allemagne." See in particular carton no. 660 for reports on the nature and purpose of German physical education training. For the letter of June 22, 1936, see carton no. 680, 149. See also F. Poncet, *Souvenirs d'une ambassade à Berlin, septembre 1931–octobre 1938* (Paris: Flammarion, 1946), 262–67. For Poncet's opinion as quoted in the press of the time, see G. Meyer, *Petit Journal,* May 23, 1936, who emphasized that France had to keep its promise to go to Berlin.

41. There have been some fragmentary accounts of the Barcelona Popular Olympics. Although they never took place, they still warrant a serious study for the events leading up to them and the ambitions destroyed by the insurrection against the government. On the experiences of some British participants, see P. K. Martin, "Spain's Other Olympics," *History Today* 42 (Aug. 1992): 6–8. Probably the best account is by X. Pujadas and C. Santacana, "Le mythe des Jeux Populaires de Barcelone," in *Les origines du sport ouvrier en Europe,* ed. Pierre Arnaud (Paris: L'Harmattan, 1994), 267–78.

42. He introduced the "Brevet Sportif Populaire," a fitness badge, following the German lead (but including rope climbing, an activity close to the heart of his friend Georges Hébert). For the performances, see J. Zoro, *150 ans d'EPS* (Clichy: Amicale EPS, 1986), 198.

43. The ill feeling—that the Socialists had campaigned for workers' sport and supported bourgeois sport once in power—lasted into the present day. See F. Hache, "Der Arbeitersport in Frankreich: Zwei Wendepunkte 1936 und 1981," in *Der internationale Arbeitersport,* ed. A. Krüger and J. Riordan (Cologne: Pahl-Rugenstein, 1985), 64–84.

44. *Sporting,* June 18 and 25, 1936.

45. Brohm, *1936,* 90–91.

46. Murray, "The French Workers' Sports Federation," 224.

47. *Le Jour,* Aug. 2, 1936.

48. *Le Jour,* Aug. 3, 1936.

49. Ibid.

50. *Le Jour,* Aug. 7, 1936. In fact, 538,142 tickets had been sold for the 1924 Olympics, amounting to 5,423,184 francs (a little more than one million dollars). See W. Lynberg, *Fabulous 100 Years of the IOC: Facts, Figures, and Much, Much More* (Lausanne: IOC, 1996), 247.

51. *Figaro,* Aug. 1, 1936.

52. *Figaro,* Aug. 3, 1936.

53. *Figaro,* July 31, 1936.

54. *Petit Parisien,* Aug. 1, 1936.

55. *Petit Parisien,* Aug. 2, 1936.

56. *Petit Parisien,* Aug. 3, 1936.

57. This was a major topic of interest in the press, with Helen Stephens, Marie Dollinger, and Stella Walsh usually the center of the stories or insinuations. One article in *Paris-Soir,* Aug. 9, 1936, was headed "Amazons of the Stadium" and asked whether these women who wanted to rival men were in fact still women, while another pointed out that Stella Walsh never allowed herself to be seen naked in the showers. The Polish-born American Stella Walsh actually was a man, a fact discovered upon her death, the innocent victim of a shooting nearly fifty years later.

58. *Echo de Paris,* Aug. 1, 1936.

59. *Echo de Paris,* July 30, 1936.

60. *Echo de Paris,* Aug. 7, 1936.

61. *Paris-Soir* boasted of its reporting team and the resources it was sending to cover the Games in its number of July 8, 1936.

62. On this point the Germans might well have learned from Coubertin himself, who long before 1936 responded in exasperation to the constant criticisms of the organization of the Games and prognostications of their imminent demise with the claim that the origins of the problem were in some journalist or other being given a bad seat, being poorly fed, or in some way not having his sense of self-importance pandered to.

63. *Paris-Soir,* Aug. 1, 1936.

64. This is reproduced in F. Hache, *Jeux Olympiques: La flamme de l'exploit* (Evreux: Gallimard, 1992), 135. Although the 1936 Olympics are only a small part of this short but insightful book, it includes some excellent illustrations.

65. *Paris-Soir,* Aug. 2, 1936.

66. *Paris-Soir,* Aug. 3, 1936.

67. Cartoons were a regular feature of *Paris-Soir,* although most papers included some line drawings.

68. Aspects of French nationalism are discussed in more detail in W. J. Murray, "France, Coubertin, and the Nazi Olympics: The Response," *Olympika* 1 (1992): 46–69.

69. *Paris-Soir* ran especially long interviews. I have no evidence of "check-book journalism," but given Owens's clear-eyed intention to use the Berlin Olympics to make money, and the resources at the disposal of a newspaper like *Paris-Soir,* it is not unreasonable to believe that some money changed hands. This would not have been made public, as it would have been a violation of the amateur rules.

70. See, for instance, the Sunday edition of *Paris-Soir,* Aug. 16, 1936.

71. *Match,* Aug. 11, 1936.

72. On this and other aspects of Owens's career, see the superb biography by W. J. Baker, *Jesse Owens: An American Life* (New York: The Free Press, 1986).

73. *Regards,* Sept. 3, 1936, 20.

74. *Paris-Soir,* Aug. 5, 1936.

75. *Sporting,* Aug. 13, 1936.

76. Ibid.

77. I have discussed this in more detail in "France, de Coubertin, and the Nazi Olympics," 46–49.

78. Fascist Italy, which was praised for its athletic success, having placed second in Los Angeles and third in Berlin, had a primary school physical education system very similar to that in France; the problems were with the later school years and the sport system outside of the schools. See T. Terret and R. Vescovi, "L'éducation physique à l'école primaire de l'entre-deux-guerres: une comparaison des systèmes français et italien," in *The History of Physical Education and Sport from European Perspectives,* ed. A. Krüger and E. Trangbaek (Copenhagen: University Press, 1999), 269–83.

79. *Echo des sports,* Aug. 25, 1936.

80. *Echo des sports,* Oct. 6, 1936.

81. See Murray, "France, de Coubertin, and the Nazi Olympics," where this issue is covered in some detail.

CHAPTER 5

Italy:
Mussolini's Boys
at Hitler's Olympics

Gigliola Gori

Italy came to the Olympic Games in Garmisch-Partenkirchen and Berlin not only to build on the triumph of "Mussolini's Boys" at Los Angeles in 1932 but also as an act of friendship toward its new political ally. It also needed to build up its image at home after the conflict in Ethiopia and the economic sanctions and moral reprobation that resulted from the unwarranted attack on that near-defenseless African country. Since the mid-1920s sports in Italy had been firmly tied to the Fascist regime, with the "fascistization" of sport only one part of the regime's wider aim of gaining total control of the cultural and social life of the country. To achieve this aim the regime created new structures or penetrated existing ones, using the mass media as a constant means of propaganda. All dissent was banned. The Roman spirit of the past was reinvented to give historical depth to the values of the regime. The regime also encouraged activities, like sport, that make life more enjoyable. International successes came in cycling, soccer, and boxing, while Italy's success at the Olympic Games in Los Angeles was unprecedented. More successes followed when Italy became world champion in soccer in 1934 and 1938, while its club teams starred in European competitions. In motor sports and aviation Italy also had some resounding successes. These victories were attributed by the Fascists to the regime's ideals of strength and discipline, demonstrating the superiority of fascism as an efficient system of social organization.

The Organization of Fascist Sport

Sport and fascism went together as a means of directing the aggressiveness of the Italian people in the years after World War I. The regime came to power in 1922 but had to wait a few more years before gaining absolute control. In 1925 the Fascist party (Partito Nazionale Fascista; PNF) took complete control of the different sports associations with the election of a committed Fascist, Lando Ferretti, as president of the Comitato Olimpico Nazionale Italiano (CONI). Faith in fascism became an essential function of sports leaders, who changed statutes as they wished. At the same time, workers' sports and Catholic organizations were banned, while the bourgeois clubs and local associations were undermined by petty party officials, who made them organs subordinate to the regime.[1]

Basic physical education was first reformed in 1923, as young people's physical and moral health was an essential Fascist priority. The Fascist minister Giovanni Gentile took physical education out of the control of the education ministry and transferred it to an independent organ, the Ente Nazionale Educazione Fisica (ENEF). The ENEF proved to be incompetent,[2] and all responsibility for physical education was soon passed on to the Opera Nazionale Balilla (ONB). Founded in 1926 "for the assistance and physical and moral education of young people,"[3] in 1927 the ONB started to take responsibility for the physical education and sport of all primary and secondary school children. In 1929 it was placed under the responsibility of the Ministry of National Education. It had generous financial means at its disposal, and this allowed it to improve considerably the practice of physical education and sports among students of both sexes, even outside school hours. The young people were divided according to their age into Balilla (eight to fourteen years) and Avanguardisti (fourteen to eighteen years); they wore uniforms and were organized into squadrons. From the beginning, the ONB, directed by Renato Ricci and placed at the direct service of Mussolini, also had the task of educating girls, who were divided according to age into Piccole Italiane and Giovani Italiane and adapted names and symbols from the ancient Roman past. The aim was to mold Fascist youth from the earliest age, and in addition to the ONB, other organizations controlled activities in secondary and higher education. All that remained for the regime was to organize the young people who did not go to school, those who had left school, and the working class. Thus in 1925 the Fascists created the Opera Nazionale Dopolavoro (OND) for intellectuals and manual laborers and in 1930 the PNF founded the Fasci Giovanili di Combattimento (FGC) for young people who were not students.

Whatever the success of the Fascists in creating a morally acceptable regime, there could be little doubt about their success in winning major sporting events. Sport was followed passionately in Italy, and in 1936 it was reported that forty million spectators watched thirty thousand sport events in one year.[4] Banti pronounced this a magnificent physical and mental preparation for a "dangerous" but "heroic" life of military service, inflated rhetoric that overlooked the fact that most Italians preferred watching to playing. The leaders were carried away by their slogans, and they left no doubt about their contempt for "sport for sport's sake": sport was to further the cause of fascism, to create dedicated "citi-

zens for peace and heroic soldiers for war."[5] Most Italians were culturally unprepared for the sporting life and, tired of being obliged to do often boring and
monotonous drills, preferred as soon as possible to play the role of spectator.
So despite the massive work of propaganda, in 1930 the CONI had only six
hundred thousand members, a mere 0.75 percent of the population; half of this
figure moreover was formed by hunters.[6] All the other enrollments in the ONB,
OND, Gruppi Universitari Fascisti (GUF), FGC, and Milizia Volontaria per la
Sicurezza Nazionale (MVSN) were compulsory, so it is difficult to evaluate their
membership figures.

The regime showed more interest in creating stars and devoted itself to the
selection and training of champions, who were often professionals or pseudo-
amateurs, in order to shine on the international stage. In this way the regime
itself encouraged the tendency toward a sedentary enjoyment of sport. This
could be overlooked in the 1930s, however, as Italy achieved startling successes
in international competition. Heroes became more important than a healthy
populace.

The Italian government offered financial rewards and special privileges to all
its champions, who were seen as special emissaries of Mussolini. In return they
had to adhere to strict discipline, maintaining the good name of their country,
which, as "soldiers of sport," they were called upon to defend and honor in the
eyes of the world.[7] The Duce himself was built up as a living example of an active sportsman,[8] and he did not fail to encourage competitions himself. Mussolini attended competitions and award ceremonies, sent messages of encour-
agement, and gave medals and diplomas to the winners, celebrating them
officially by posing proudly alongside them.

The Italian Press and the Making of Heroes

Mussolini was a master of propaganda, and the sports press of the 1930s was
given every opportunity to create other Italians in his image. In addition to being
an active sportsman, Mussolini had been a successful journalist and showed a
personal interest in the press. He kept in constant touch with journalists and
with the Ufficio Stampa (the press office), the main instrument of propaganda
and control. The control of the press became legal at the end of 1925, when
opposition papers were forced to close down,[9] while those papers that had been
relatively neutral toward fascism were permitted to continue under the control
of editors, directors, and journalists who were loyal supporters of the regime.[10]

The press office regularly distributed bulletins to the editorial offices of the
news media. These bulletins contained strict advice on how to deal with certain news items. Some were very specific, explaining minute details such as the
space a certain news item should be given, the type and size of the letters of a
headline, or the vocabulary to be used to describe certain events. Therefore, the
press tended toward homogeneity. The Duce was also aware of the power of the

word, having risen to power as an effective speaker as well as a writer. Somewhat enigmatically, he claimed that under his regime the Italian press was the freest in the world since it had to serve only one cause: to control, criticize, and enhance the power of the regime within the boundaries of the law.[11] The role of the Italian press, then, was to speak out for the Fascist ideology and praise il Duce, la Patria, the family, its Roman roots, and also sport, which served as symbol of the discipline and struggle that made of young men citizens and soldiers capable of living and dying for an ideal.[12]

Sports journalism was well established before the arrival of fascism, with twenty-four sports papers of various types in 1919. This figure grew to thirty-four in 1922, but between 1924 and 1934, 129 new papers were started. Some journals closed down in the meantime, and Italian sport was represented by ninety-four journals and daily sports papers in 1935.[13] The sporting press in the 1930s used many new techniques and the most modern layout to satisfy an increasing enthusiasm among Italians for sport. The number of pages was increased, the printing type became bigger, the columns were narrowed, and the articles shortened to make for easier reading. Headlines were underlined in red or blue, and some photos appeared in color, which at that time was still added by hand. It was only later that these techniques were copied by the more traditional daily press.[14]

The language followed the "Fascist style," triumphant and repetitive.[15] International victories were praised in resounding rhetoric, defeats minimized, but all was related to the glories of the nation. Before the Olympic Games weeklies such as *La Domenica Sportiva* (Sport on Sunday)[16] started competitions and previews to raise the general interest in and awareness of the competition. Radio complemented the press, and the Ente Italiano Audizioni Radiofoniche put out radio transmissions at the exact time when the Olympics were to be transmitted to accustom their listeners to the time and location on their dial. This program was conducted with the assistance of the CONI after October 20, 1935.[17]

Even in the nonsporting press the Olympic Games came to take over the front pages, with lengthy reports and commentaries inside. Some of the articles before the Games came from the official propaganda monthly of sport, which dedicated many editions to the Olympics, or from the daily *Gazetta dello Sport,* which had a special Olympics supplement just prior to the opening of the Games.

Italy at Garmisch-Partenkirchen: An Inauspicious Beginning

The year of the Eleventh Olympic Games found Italy struggling on two different fronts: abroad against Ethiopia in a war of conquest and at home against the effects of the economic sanctions imposed by the League of Nations.[18] On both fronts Mussolini's Italy emerged victorious: in May 1936 the Ethiopian conflict ended with the surrender of Addis Ababa, followed by an end to the sanctions a few days later. Despite the difficulties of war and economic sanctions, Italy was determined to take part in the Winter Games. It would show the world that neither sanctions nor wars could weaken the will of young Fascists; at the same time it would also honor the nation that had refused to have anything to do with the sanctions. In Ferretti's words, Germany had not provided "a single link in the chain intended to suffocate the surge of its youth and the already flourishing Italian empire."[19]

Italy, selected as a candidate to organize the 1908 Olympic Games, which it had to forgo because of internal disputes,[20] had hoped to bring the 1936 Olympic Games to Rome.[21] Now, well trained and ready to fight its sports battle, it opened a new "front" on the snow of Bavaria. The athletes had been in training close to Garmisch-Partenkirchen for some time before the Games began. Their final meeting took place in Madonna di Campiglio, a well-known ski resort in the Dolomites, in the presence of Renato Ricci, the secretary of the ONB and a member of the general staff of the Federazione Italiana Sports Invernali (FISI).[22] From there, the first group of athletes reached Bavaria at the end of January, followed by the ice hockey team, the skaters, and the bobsledders, who had been in training at Cortina d'Ampezzo until the last minute.[23]

The Italian press had high hopes for success. If miracles could not be expected of the ski jumpers, the ice hockey team could aim for one of the top places; the bobsledders were favored to do well, and the couple in the figure-skating competition had "the probability of being placed alongside the world's best." The cross-country skiers were "clearly improving," but the greatest hopes were placed in the downhill racing. As to the Italian military patrol, which did not depend on the FISI because it remained under the traditional inspectorship of the Alpine troops, judgments were prudently avoided.[24]

The special interest in the Winter Games rested not only on its military implications: Mussolini himself had often been photographed with his bare torso and with skis on his feet on the steep downhill ski course of Terminillo, near Rome, sometimes alone and sometimes in the company of his relatives.

As a result, winter sports were well provided for. The ONB offered young people basic activities and then entrusted the best athletes to the FISI, where they were coached all year long by specialized trainers, who came in large part from abroad.[25] Ski schools and schools for ski teachers were founded, while the lower middle class was urged to frequent ski resorts, formerly the monopoly of the elite. With this in mind, the mass media, especially magazines, reviews, and sports newspapers, produced numerous articles accompanied by photographs about the best winter resorts and the fashionable clothes to wear there.[26] The result, as far as the diffusion of winter sports is concerned, was that in 1936 there were more than 550,000 winter sports tourists in Italy.[27]

The Italian athletes at the "snow front" of Garmisch-Partenkirchen were highly praised by the press.[28] The connection to Ethiopia was clearly drawn when Achille Starace, the president of the CONI and secretary of the PNF, theatrically resigned to depart as a volunteer for the "real" war front. That sensational piece of news, capable of putting strong psychological pressure on the *azzurri* soldiers of Italian sport, came on the eve of the Winter Olympic Games. The athletes answered with a telegram to congratulate Starace, promising "to intensify their ardor, in the name of the Duce, through the sterling example of that new enthusiastic African legionary."[29]

The opening of the Games, seen as a "wonderful ceremony in its severe austerity," touched the Italians, who thought about "their country in arms."[30] The Italian press did not fail to underline the political aspect of the spectacle, lingering over the hearty welcome by Germany to the *azzurri* delegation: "His Excellency Ricci, newly arrived at Garmisch, was received by the Chancellor of the Reich, who entertained him with a very cordial conversation for a long time."[31] And with regard to the Italians' parade at the ski stadium, their representation had "excited the liveliest admiration for perfect behavior in their stately walk and discipline, and for the elegance of their uniforms, all very well-chosen in color and design." The public had "warmly" applauded the superb team, which clearly won over the spectators.[32]

Nevertheless, the results achieved by the Italian athletes in the competitions were not equal to the expectations, which had also been nourished by the successes obtained by the Italians the preceding year at the international competitions of the German championships, which were also held in Garmisch-Partenkirchen.[33] Despite the rhetoric that infused every journalistic and radio report, disappointment increased day by day.

Large headlines helped to hide modest results, such as "Skiers' Audacity and Style at the Olympic Games / Italian Downhill Racers, Up with the Best,"[34] "The Italian Ice-Hockey Team Defeats the United States by 2 to 1,"[35] "The Exciting Cross-Country Ski Competition / Swedish Victory and the Brilliant New Performance of the Italians,"[36] "The Italians' Great Success in Garmisch in the Relay Race, Won by the Finnish team."[37] The only placing of some importance was obtained in the 4 × 10 kilometer relay race, in which the Italian team came fourth. In the bobsled the Italians had moved back down to the tenth and eleventh place, compared with the fifth and the sixth gained at the 1932 Winter Olympic Games at Lake Placid. Some protests rose from the Italian press about the high starting number, twenty-one, given to the downhill racer Giacinto Sartorelli, who had to start among the mass of "the very cream of the Balkan downhill racers";[38] his time, at the two-thirds mark, was the same as the first two classified racers, but after a while "he had suddenly found himself in front of a stumbling Bulgarian skier, Jordannoff, who blocked his way."[39] Without such an accident, the newspapers observed, he could have surely conquered one of the first places, since Sartorelli had appeared "absolutely at the same level as the most famous first-rate champions."[40]

Even the Italian ice hockey team had suffered an "injustice" during the match against Switzerland, which they lost 1 to 0; the U.S. umpire had unreasonably refused a goal scored by Italy, a decision severely criticized by the foreign newspapers: "They were all unanimous in declaring that the defeat of Italy by the 'Red Cross' squad had been absolutely unmerited."[41] Likewise, criticism was made of the judges who had assigned an inadequate point score to the couple in figure skating, A. and E. Cattaneo, who arrived ninth at the end of a program of difficult but correct figures, accompanied by a synchrony of movements and an agility of action that had conquered the public, so that "when the judges had lifted up the score sign, hissing was heard."[42]

At last, an Italian victory came unexpectedly and providentially with the military patrols competition, the predecessor of the biathlon. Although that competition was not included among the official competitions of the Olympic program, it was immediately brought to the Italian people as "the most beautiful competition and most important victory of the fourth Winter Olympic Games."[43] The occasion to raise spirits again and to redeem bitterness and disappointment had finally arrived; at last, Fascist sport came on the scene and its anthem, "Giovenezza" (Youth), could echo through the air while the Italian flag rose to the highest standard!

Headlines appeared in block letters, and columns were filled with successes here and in Ethiopia: "Clamorous Success of the Italian Patrol at the 4th Winter Olympic Games,"[44] "The Green Streamers of Italy Triumph at Garmisch in the Hard Competition for Military Patrols,"[45] "The Glorious Alpine Soldiers Come Out at Garmisch As Being the Best Soldiers in the World, Proving the Efficiency of the Army in Every Field."[46] In the *Corriere della Sera*, the front-page article, "Alpine Soldiers Win at the Garmisch Olympic Games, Demonstrating Beyond Doubt Their Military and Athletic Virtues," was accompanied by a large photograph of the patrol at the finishing line. This dominated all news items, including one that reported, "Abyssinian Units Taken by Surprise and Defeated on the Gestro and on the Daua."[47] The sports event immediately became a political event. In describing victories in such dramatic tones, it was recalled that the Alpine soldiers had forgone their supplies "to show that they did not care about the sanctions"[48] and that their commander, Captain Silvestri, "had sworn to his superiors that he would have died rather than come back defeated to Italy."[49] It did not matter in this context that Italy had won by only 1 to 0 over the favored Finns—and did not win a medal in hockey.

Since the beginning of the Winter Games the Italian press had exalted with exaggerated patriotism both the athletes and the soldiers involved in fighting bravely for the glory of their country in Africa. In this way, every competition that had some Italians among the competitors was presented to the readers as a war bulletin, with missing soldiers and the fallen, every petty placing seen as a position conquered from the enemy, every defeat as a strategic retreat, another Italian victory. "We are involved in an enterprise, which will weigh heavily on the history of peoples. . . . Each battle, especially in a foreign land, each competition, particularly if of worldwide character, requires from the Italians that they draw on their deepest resources, the most passionate ardor, their most scrupulous seriousness. We are looked on with envy from abroad, we are feared and obstructed from abroad. Therefore sports competitions must also be considered real battles."[50]

Italian newspapers did not fail to underline that the foreign press had the greatest admiration for its soldiers of the Alps. The Germans, on good political terms with the Duce's Italy, publicly praised the Italians because "they had taught everyone how to fight in a foreign land for their own country."[51]

Successes in Ethiopia were proclaimed on the front pages of the Italian press with headlines such as "The Grandiose Extent of the Italian Victory to the South of Makallé / Retreat of the Enemy Army under our Squadrons' Bombardments."[52] Memories of the Alpine soldiers' victory at Garmisch-Partenkirchen remained on the inner pages of the newspapers for a long time. At the end of February, articles could still be read concerning the kind of reception the Italian athletes had received from the king, Prince Umberto, and the Duce himself.[53] The desperate search for medals, achieved at the very end of the Olympic program, had made up for earlier disappointing performances. It also allowed the regime to transform the event into "a national triumph, adding at the same time a political and military prestige for Fascist Italy, and a warning to the whole world."[54] One can only wonder at what the newspapers would have written if Italy, thirteenth among the twenty-eight participating nations,[55] had won the Olympic Games at Garmisch-Partenkirchen.

Italy at the Battle of Berlin

After victory in Africa in May 1936, Italy—an empire at last—could concentrate on the "Battle of Berlin," in which it wanted to show to the world that the strength of its athletes, the soldiers of sport, were not inferior to its real soldiers in Africa and that the heroism of its people, still suffering from what were considered the unjustified sanctions of the League of Nations, endured. After all, some papers had actually admitted that Italy's glory had come at the expense of mere "Negro and Negroid barbarians."[56] Berlin might be a more glorious field of battle.

Italy hoped to at least equal its performance in Los Angeles. The journalists praised the "athletes of the Duce"[57] who had "shown, during and after the war, that Italy is establishing the tradition of winning battles—this time in the world of sport."[58] The more cautious journalists mentioned that some athletes were still in Africa and so the "troops" in Berlin were not up to full strength;[59] others noted that the sanctions were bound to have negative effects on sport.[60] Others expected Italy to come third after the United States and Germany, with Japan emerging as a possible threat.[61] It was of particular importance to defend that third place against the British.[62]

Italy made its debut on the Berlin Olympic scene as an imperial power. There was a certain pride among the Italian public as Italy had inspired many of the

Nazi innovations in sport. In only three years Hitler had revolutionized German physical education and sport as well as its leisure-time activities,[63] and much of these innovations were based on the Fascist model. Germany gave Italy a warm welcome, as the two countries were ideologically very close. Both had suffered from what were considered unjust sanctions: one on the economic field and the other in the field of sport, with the threat of an Olympic boycott. Italy had entered its team early and gave its "enthusiastic and sincere collaboration for the best success of the XIth Olympics."[64] Moreover, Italy had been a "successful mediator to ensure the inclusion of the athletes of a reluctant Austria."[65]

In the weeks leading up to the Games, the Italian journals reported warmly from Berlin on the splendor of the facilities and their ideal location in a green belt,[66] as well as the efficiency of the Olympic Village. Surprisingly, the Italians complained about the somewhat military behavior of the German people,[67] but they were very happy with the hospitality and the festive mood in Berlin.[68]

The Italian delegation was officially welcomed by Theodor Lewald, the president of the Organizing Committee, who addressed them in "good Italian . . . in the name of a nation of good friends."[69] The *Berliner Zeitung* (evening edition) was quoted as saying before the opening of the Games that they were playing an important role in increasing the friendship between the two peoples. Germans could wish success at the Games to no other country so wholeheartedly as to Italy.[70] These Germano-Italian gestures continued until the opening of the Games, with the Italian team paying tribute to the German soldiers who had died in the First World War.[71] Five hundred Italian university students selected by the Fascist University Groups had been selected to watch the Games, and they were warmly welcomed in Berlin.[72] The presence of the Italian Crown Prince Umberto with his two daughters, Mafalda and Maria, raised the tone of the opening ceremony. The Führer underlined his high regard for Italy by asking Umberto to sit next to him while the teams marched in, saluting Hitler as German head of state. For some this was a "marvelous" show that made a "fascinating" impression;[73] others characterized it as "mysterious" or "religious," praising the symbolism of the ringing bell, the choir of eight thousand voices, the doves of peace, and the blond German who lit the Olympic torch.[74]

There were no Italian victories in the first days, and so the weightlifter Terlizzi, an Italian American competing for the United States, received wide coverage instead.[75] The mood changed as journalists complained about German overorganization, the weather,[76] the German press, and the German spectators, "for whom champions of other countries do not seem to exist."[77]

Italian expectations were finally met with the victory of the fencing team, the second place in the men's 800 meter run, and other honorable places. The critical tone disappeared. Italy's Olympic success filled the front pages of the daily press and, of course, the special sporting press.[78] It was now noted that the German postal service provided ladies who could satisfy their customer with answers in any language, "Polish, Chinese, or Italian."[79] At the end of the competition Italy finished third in the official medal count with eight gold, nine silver, and five bronze medals.

Although all Italian triumphs were reported rapturously, the victories in fencing were given the most prominence. Mussolini was an ardent fencer who sometimes performed in public, and Augusto Turati, the secretary general of the Italian Fascist party and an IOC member for Italy, was equally good with the foil. Nine medals in fencing, therefore, had a special significance. Italy even placed one-two-three, so the Italian flag could be raised on all three flag poles.[80]

Italian women took part in the Olympics for the first time, and Ondina Valla brought home a gold medal in the 80 meter hurdles, also placing fourth in the 4 × 100 meter relay.[81] Luigi Beccali, who had won the gold medal in the men's metric mile in Los Angeles, finished third in the 1,500 meters, despite being kicked, suffering deep cuts, and almost falling over. Such "heroism" kept the Italian press happy for some time.[82]

The Italian soccer team also gave cause for rejoicing. Italy had won the World Cup in 1934, but at the Olympic Games they were not permitted to play their professional players. A student team was formed, which went from victory to victory, eventually winning the gold medal, defeating Austria 1 to 0 in extra-time. One thousand fans from Italy had to compete against the home crowd of one hundred thousand who shouted for Austria, a country closer to the German heart.[83] Of special importance was the Italian victory in the 8 meter class in sailing, as it clearly showed that the economic sanctions against Italy had been in vain; the entire yacht consisted of material that had been banned by the League of Nations.[84] In coming third, Italy had to surpass Finland and Sweden, who were ahead at one stage.[85]

The closing ceremony was reported with a "certain sadness, something religious and mystical, with a bit of poetry and a shade of melancholy."[86] The massive German point score of 776¾ against the Italian 237 was considered a victory for the German "masses, of a special school of thought, and of will power."[87] But Germany had won by only one point, and the United States had been best in track and field and Japan had been best in swimming, sports that were considered central to the Olympic Games.[88]

The Italian press was only marginally critical of the situation in Germany once the Italian team did well. The home-town advantage was mentioned, but the near perfect German organization was especially praised. The announcements appearing in German only were shown as a disadvantage,[89] and judges in wrestling were said to have favored German wrestlers. On occasions when Italians were involved this was considered "scandalous."[90]

In the end, it had all turned out to be a glorious triumph for the two great Fascist powers. Germany the host had put on a show to make the world marvel, while Italy had come from the Ethiopian battle front and defied the economic sanctions to take an honorable place among the sporting nations of the world. The Fascist ideology had been well vindicated.[91]

Conclusion

Italy eventually liberated itself from Fascist rule during the war and changed its alliance. This way, Italy was both the first Fascist country and the first to overthrow fascism from within. This created a particular relationship to some of the cultural aspects of fascism, such as physical education and sport. The postwar discussion about the Fascist period in Italy started relatively late and has reached the sports world even later. Although there are now many publications about different aspects of Fascist sport, elite sport is very much excluded from discussion today.[92] There is little contemporary debate about the success of the Italian athletes during the Fascist era, despite this having been Italy's most successful period in sport. The structures that were laid during the Fascist era have been the basis for the success of Italian sport after the war. Although the structures have now been filled with democratic people, the CONI still assumes a leading role, according to a law of 1942. The Unione Italiano di Sport Populare (UISP) as a democratic alternative, based on the workers' sport tradition[93] and active in the "sports for all" field, has reached very little of the population, since the CONI can get to more people with the provision of sporting facilities financed with the help of lottery money. Elite sport was and still is part of the "culture of consent"[94] that keeps a vast country such as Italy together.

Notes

1. F. Fabrizio, *Storia dello sport in Italia: Dalle societa ginnastiche all'associazionismo di massa* (Firenze: Guaraldi, 1977), 118–20.

2. For the administration difficulties of the ENEF, see L. Ferretti, *Il libro dello sport* (Rome: Del Littorio, 1928), 73–95. See also P. Ferrara, *L'Italia in palestra* (Rome: La Meridiana, 1992), 218–22.

3. Article 1 of an Apr. 3, 1926, law entitled "Leggi e Regolamenti dell'Opera Nazionale Balilla" (quoted in full in Ferretti, *Il libro dello sport,* 245–81).

4. A. Banti, "L'importanza dello spettacolo sportivo," *Lo sport fascista* 9.1 (1936): 31.

5. Ferretti, *Il libro dello sport,* 225.

6. G. Cataldo, "Gli sportivi col ma," *Il Littorale,* Apr. 29, 1930.

7. Fabrizio, *Storia dello sport in Italia,* 58–60.

8. An astute communicator, Mussolini loved to be interviewed and portrayed as a skier, aviator, swimmer, motor-boat pilot, fencer, rider, motorist, motorcyclist, and shooter: in short, a superman of sport. See T. Gonzalez Aja and A. Teja, "Mussolini and Franco Sportsmen: Two Contrasting Fascist Conceptions of Sport," in *La Comune Eredità dello Sport in Europa,* ed. A. Krüger and A. Teja (Rome: CONI, 1997), 413–19.

9. At the end of 1926 several important opposition dailies, such as *L'Unità* (Communist), *L'Avanti* (Socialist), *La Voce Repubblicana* (Republican), and *Il Mondo* (Liberal) ceased to exist.

10. On the press in Fascist Italy, see M. Saracinelli and N. Totti, *L'Italia del Duce: L'informazione, la cuola, il costume* (Rimini: Panozzo, 1983), 5–43.

11. See the instructions from Mussolini to the directors of the newspapers for Oct. 10, 1928, cited in P. Facchinetti, *La stampa sportiva in Italia* (Bologna: Patron, 1966), 55.

12. Feretti, *Il libro dello sport,* 147.

13. Faccinetti, *La stampa sportiva in Italia,* 159–82.

14. Faccinetti says that in 1920 this was done for the Antwerp Olympics sports reporting (ibid., 159).

15. Saracinelli and Totti, *L'Italia del Duce.*

16. *La Domenica Sportiva* 13 (1936): 31–32.

17. "La propaganda olimpica in Italia," *Corrispondenza Olimpica* 26 (1935): 5–6.

18. The economic sanctions, signed by fifty-two countries, started on November 18, 1935. Some countries, such as Albania, Austria, Hungary, the United States, Brazil, Japan, and Germany, did not sign the document.

19. L. Ferretti, "Premessa alla XI Olimpiade," *Lo sport fascista* 9.3 (1936): 10.

20. See A. Mosso, "I giochi olimpici a Roma?" *Nuova Antologia* 40 (1905): 401–26.

21. In 1928 Ferretti declared in pompous tones: "And since the Eleventh Olympic Games will celebrate their competitions in 1936—and we hope they will be celebrated in Rome—the sports event will have a greater meaning. That will be, in fact, the eve of the supreme destiny, which the 'Duce' already foresees and prepares in his prophetic mind: the eve of the revision of judgements and of holy revenge, which will give us our peace, protected by the unmutilated Wing of Victory" (*Il libro dello sport,* 228–29). See also L. Ferrario, "Puntare su Roma per i giuochi del 1936," *La Gazzetta dello Sport,* June 12, 1930; and *La Domenica Sportiva* 13.29 (1936): 6.

22. For further details concerning the training of the athletes who were appointed to represent Italy at Garmisch, see R. Giacomini, "Da Madonna di Campiglio a Garmisch-Partenkirchen," *Lo sport fascista* 9.2 (1936): 13–17.

23. See "L'Italia alla IV Olimpiade Invernale—Gli-Azzurri per Garmisch," *La Gazzetta dello Sport,* Jan. 16, 1936. See also "Sciatori e pattinatori azzurri per le olimpiadi di Garmisch," *Il Messagero,* Jan. 16, 1936.

24. The quotes in this paragraph are from Giacomini, "Da Madonna di Campiglio," 14–17.

25. See "40 anni di olimpiadi moderne: Atene 1896 Berlino 1936," *Supplemento speciale della Gazzetta dello Sport,* July 1936, 23–24.

26. See "Signora: ecco la moda; Febbraio sui campi di neve," *Lo sport fascista* 9.2 (1936): 71–77.

27. A. Camisa, "Le vicende delle gare die Anversa e dei Giochi di Chamonix (1924)," *La Gazzetta dello Sport,* Jan. 23, 1936. See also A. P. Caliari: "Il tricolore italiano nel cielo di Garmisch," *Neve e Ghiaccio* 1.6 (1936): 1, who estimates the figure of six hundred thousand participating skiers.

28. See "Garmisch-Partenkirchen, capitale tedesca della neve e del ghiaccio," *Lo sport fascista* 9.1 (1936): 24–28; and R. Nicolini: "Gli impianti sportivi olimpici di Garmisch-Partenkirchen," *Neve e Ghiaccio* 1.1–2 (1936): 5–8.

29. The text of the telegram is quoted by E. de Martino, "Oggi si inaugurano i giochi invernali: Folla e atleti nel quadro della grandiosa organizzazione," *Corriere della Sera,* Feb. 6, 1936.

30. See "I grandi avvenimenti sportivi: Le Olimpiadi invernali a Garmisch sono state inaugurate ieri da Hitler," *Il Messaggero,* Feb. 7, 1936.

31. A. Mignani, "La grandiosa cerimonia inaugurale alla presenza del 'Führer': Il Cancelliere del Reich riceve S.E. Ricci, La pittoresca sfilata degli atleti e le gare di disco su ghiaccio," *Il Popolo d'Italia,* Feb. 7, 1936.

32. E. de Martino, "L'Olimpiade d'Inverno inaugurata da Hitler: La gagliarda squadra italiana sfila ammirata ed applaudita a Garmisch," *Corriere della Sera,* Feb. 7, 1936.

33. See "Il progressivo sviluppo dei ludi olimpici invernali," *Neve e Ghiaccio* 1.4–5 (1936): 3.

34. *Corriere della Sera,* Feb. 8, 1936.

35. *Il Messagero,* Feb. 9, 1936.

36. *Corriere della Sera,* Feb. 13, 1936.

37. *Il Littoriale,* Feb. 13, 1936.

38. See "Olimpiadi 1936," *Neve e Ghiaccio* 1.6 (1936): 4–5.

39. See "Audacia e stile degli sciatori alle olimpiadi: Discesisti italiani in linea con i migliori," *Il Messagero,* Feb. 8, 1936.

40. Ibid.

41. See the front-page article by P. Camisa, *Il Messaggero,* Feb. 14, 1936.

42. See "Il finlandese Valonen primo nel salto," *Il Messaggero,* Feb. 14, 1936.

43. *Neve e Ghiaccio* 1.6 (1936): 12.

44. *Il Popolo d'Italia,* Feb. 15, 1936.

45. *Il Messaggero,* Feb. 15, 1936.

46. *Il Littoriale,* Feb. 15, 1936.

47. *Corriere della sera,* Feb. 15, 1936.

48. A. Mignani, "Clamoroso successo della pattuglia militare italiana alla IV Olimpiade invernale," *Il Popolo d'Italia,* Feb. 15, 1936.

49. Ibid.

50. E. Colombo, "Il tricolore d'Italia sul pennone di Garmisch per la spettacolare vittoria delle Fiamme Verdi nella gara delle pattuglie militari," *Corriere della Sera,* Feb. 15, 1936.

51. These words were pronounced by the minister of war, von Blomberg, during a banquet at which the victorious Alpine soldiers were present, as the commander E. Silvestri recalled. See E. Silvestri, "Come abbiamo vinto a Garmisch," *Neve e Ghiaccio* 1.6 (1936): 15–18.

52. *Il Messaggero,* Feb. 18, 1936.

53. See "Il Duce riceve gli alpini vittoriosi a Garmisch," *Corriere della Sera,* Feb. 26, 1936. See also "Il capitano Silvestri e i suoi alpini festeggiano a Milano," *Corriere della Sera,* Feb. 27, 1936.

54. G. Gerbi, "Superbo trionfo degli alpini d'Italia sulle nevi di Garmisch," *Lo sport fascista* 9.3 (1936): 15–19.

55. According to the unofficial ranking reported in "40 anni die Olimpiadi moderne," Italy placed eleventh, at the same level as Czechoslovakia and Japan (26).

56. "La squadra italiana parte per Garmisch," *Il Popolo d'Italia,* Jan. 18, 1936.

57. P. Rost, "Olimpiadi," *La Domenica Sportiva* 13 (1936): 31–33.

58. E. Colombo, "Maglie azzurre," in "40 anni di Olimpiadi moderne," 14.

59. Gorbo, "Marciatori olimpici," *Lo sport fascista* 9.5 (1936): 77; A. Boitti, "Ginnastica," *Lo sport fascista* 9.7 (1936): 22.

60. L. Ferrario, "224 atleti italiani a Berlino per l'XI Olimpiade," *La Domenica Sportiva* 13.6–7 (1936): 31.

61. V. L. Ferretti, "Premessa alla XI Olimpiade," *Lo sport fascista* 9.3 (1936): 9–13.

62. Ibid., 13.

63. A. Hitler, *Mein Kampf* (Varese-Torino: Ed. La Lucciola, 1991), 40–43.

64. "Le Nazioni comunicano l'entusiastica e sincera collaborazione dell'Italia," *Corrispondenza Olimpica* 4 (1934): 1.

65. Austria threatened not to go to Berlin because of their irritation with the German athletes at the recent international games at Innsbruck. See "Nel fasto rinnovato della Germania sportiva si apriranno domani i ludi dell'XI Olimpiade," *La Gazetta dello Sport,* July 31, 1936.

66. E. Senatra, "Atleti in clausura: Berlino città ideale cinta di verde," *Il Messaggero,* July 23, 1936.

67. "Al villaggio olimpico autentica fiera campionaria dello sport di tutto il mondo," *Il Littoriale,* July 31, 1936.

68. R. Moranzoni, "Gli atleti azzurri festosamente accolti a Berlino," *La Gazzetta dello Sport,* July 21, 1936; "Gli atleti azzurri sono giunti ieri a Berlino, accolti da cordiali dimostrazioni," *Il Messaggero,* July 29, 1936.

69. "Le entusiastiche accoglienze di Berlino agli atleti azzurri dell'XI Olimpiade," *La Gazzetta dello Sport,* July 29, 1936.

70. "Il Principe di Piemonte a colloquio con Hitler," *Il Popolo d'Italia,* Aug. 2, 1936.

71. "Nel fasto rinnovatodella Germania sportiva si apriranno domani i ludi dell'XI Olimpiade," *Gazzetta dello Sport,* July 31, 1936.

72. "Cinquecento goliardi sono giunti a Berlino," *La Gazzetta della Domenica,* Aug. 2, 1936.

73. "Adolfo Hitler presente Umberto di Savoia ha inaugurato ieri la XI Olimpiade," *Il Popolo d'Italia,* Aug. 2, 1936.

74. *La Domenica Sportiva* 13.6–7 (1936): 33.

75. "Folla imponente e valore degli atleti nella prima giornata di gare dell'XI Olimpiade," *La Gazzetta dello Sport,* Aug. 3, 1936.

76. "Il bottino degli americani e le onorevoli prove degli italiani," *La Gazzetta dello Sport,* Aug. 5, 1936.

77. A. Mignani, "L'XI Olimpiade," *Il Popolo d'Italia,* Aug. 4, 1936.

78. "Un brillante secondo posto di Lanzi negli 800m, episodio culminante della terza giornata," *La Gazzetta dello Sport,* Aug. 5, 1936; "L'Italia conquista il primo alloro olimpionico battendo dopo dura lotta la Francia nel fioretto a squadre," *Il Messaggero,* Aug. 5, 1936.

79. "L'Italia vittoriosa nella gara di fioretto a squadre," *Il Popolo d'Italia,* Aug. 5, 1936.

80. Ibid.

81. "Primato olimpionico delle atlete azzurre," *Tutti gli Sports* 33 (1936): 5; "La gara di Ondina Valla: Campione olimpica, Vista e raccontata da lei!" *Lo sport fascista* 9.9 (1936): 17–19.

82. The journalist Vezio Murialdi found him in the changing room, where Beccali showed him his wounds, deep cuts through his torn white leather running shoes and his legs spattered with blood. See *Il Messaggero,* Aug. 7, 1936. See also *Tutti gli Sports,* 34 (1936): 2; and "L'atletismo ha vinto a Berlino le sue piu-belle battaglie," *La Domenica Sportiva* 13.4 (1936): 33.

83. B. Roghi, "Io chiamo la giovinezza del mondo," in P. Wolff, ed., *Olimpiadi 1936* (Milan: Bompiani, 1936), 14. It might also be noted that the Germans had been put off the Italians by their poor sportsmanship in the match against the United States.

84. *Lo sport fascista* 9.7 (1936): 19.

85. "Nuove vittoriose prove degli azzurri nelle eliminatorie di sciabola a squadre," *Il Popolo d' Italia,* Aug. 13, 1936.

86. "La Germania trionfa nell'XI Olimpiade, battendo gli Stati Uniti d'America mentre gli atleti fascisti sono al terzo posto," *La Gazzetta della Domenica,* Aug. 17, 1936.

87. Roghi, "Io chiamo la giovinezza del mondo," 10.

88. Ibid., 11.

89. "Berlino ha rivelato la maturita degli azzurri atleti d'Italia," *La Domenica Sportiva* 13.3 (1936): 34.

90. G. Boriani, "Sergo e Matta," *Lo sport fascista* 9.9 (1936): 34.

91. "E' sceso il velario sul palcoscenio della XI Olimpiade," *La Domenica Sportiva* 13.8 (1936): 33.

92. A notable exception is S. Pivato, "Al servicio dell'ideologia," in *L'era dello sport,* ed. S. Pivato (Florence: Giunti, 1994), 94–119. See also G. Gori, *L'atleta e la nazione: Saggi di storia dello sport* (Rimini: Panozzo, 1996); M. Impiglia, *Campo Testaccio* (Rome: Riccardo Viola, 1996).

93. See S. Pivato, "Socialisme et Antisportisme: Le 'cas' Italien (1900–1925)," in *Les origines du sport ouvrier en Europe,* ed. P. Arnaud (Paris: L'Harmattan, 1994), 129–39; and L. Rossi, "Attilo Maffi e la gimnastica proletaria," in *Coroginnica,* vol. 1, ed. A. Noto and L. Rossi (Rome: La Meridiana, 1992), 136–40.

94. V. de Grazia, *The Culture of Consent: Mass Organization of Leisure in Fascist Italy* (Cambridge: Cambridge University Press, 1981).

CHAPTER 6

Japan:
The Future in the Past

Tetsuo Nakamura

Japan was represented by two athletes in the Fifth Stockholm Olympics in 1912 and has been represented in every Olympiad since. As can be seen in table 6.1, the number of athletes, the participatory events, and the number of medals awarded has been increasing. The Tenth and Eleventh Olympics in Los Angeles and Berlin, respectively, were the turning points in Japanese participation and led to the decision to hold the Twelfth Olympic Games in Tokyo.

In the period between the Tenth and the Eleventh Games, the tone of Japanese society was becoming increasingly militaristic and nationalistic. Japan was also becoming more fascist and increasingly aggressive toward China. The Eleventh Berlin Olympics was therefore a significant Olympiad for Japanese society as well as Japanese sporting circles.[1]

Opinion on the Eleventh Olympics in Japan today is divided. They not only saw the introduction of modern scientific technology in the equipment used but also the introduction of dramatic additions to the opening and closing cer-

Table 6.1. Japan and the Olympic Games

Olympiad	Year	Place	Number of Participants				Events	Medal Won		
			Officials	Males	Females	Total		Gold	Silver	Bronze
Fifth	1912	Stockholm	2	2	0	4	1	0	0	0
Seventh	1920	Antwerp	3	15	0	18	3	0	2	0
Eighth	1924	Paris	9	19	0	28	4	0	0	1
Ninth	1928	Amsterdam	13	42	1	56	6	2	2	1
Tenth	1932	Los Angeles	61	115	16	192	8	7	7	4
Eleventh	1936	Berlin	70	162	17	249	11	6	4	10

Source: Based on the findings in Japan Amateur Sports Association, ed., *The History of 75 Years of the Japan Amateur Sports Association* (Tokyo, 1986).

emonies, the orderly management of the Games, and artistic documentaries. In Japan, the Berlin Olympics have been valued as the Games that showed the best form of the modern Olympics. The Berlin Games have also, however, been labeled as the infamous "Nazi Olympics" because of Hitler's involvement.[2]

Masaji Kiyokawa, who participated in these Games as a swimmer and won a bronze medal, expresses a typical view: "The Olympics were successful in form, management, and planning as well as in the production of many impressive world records. . . . They were, however, labeled critically as the 'Nazi Olympics' due to Hitler's political and military intervention in the Games. It was the case, then, that politics intervened in the Olympics."[3] In Japan the 1936 Olympics in Berlin are said to be the best ever.[4]

The role of Hitler in these Games has been downplayed by Japanese commentators who claim that the IOC, by insisting on the Olympic Charter being respected, caused Hitler a great deal of trouble.[5] Theodor Lewald and Carl Diem have emerged as heroes for the way they stood up to the Führer.[6] These judgments, however, were made after World War II.

The 1936 Games caused great excitement in Japan, particulary since Japan hoped to host the 1940 Games in Tokyo, to coincide with the celebrations of the twenty-six hundredth anniversary of the founding of the empire. This interest increased further when the Tokyo bid was accepted by the IOC on the eve of the opening ceremony of the Berlin Games. In what follows, I will explain why the 1936 Olympics were seen as important by Japan, the way in which this was reported, and the influence these Games had on the way Japan intended to prepare for the next Olympiad.

Interest in the Berlin Games

It was of great interest for Japan that Hitler was inaugurated as German chancellor on January 30, 1933, because already Japan wanted to hold the Twelfth Olympics in Tokyo. It was believed at the time that Hitler was against the Olympics being held in Berlin, and if Berlin relinquished this opportunity, the Eleventh Games would be held in Rome, and Tokyo would have a chance to host the Twelfth Games instead of Rome.

On October 28, 1931, the Tokyo City Assembly decided to propose a bid for the Olympics and began to promote Tokyo as the venue for the Twelfth Olympiad. In the following year, Hidejiro Nagata, Tokyo's mayor, announced Tokyo's candidacy as the site of the Twelfth Games through Jigoro Kano, a member of the IOC. The year 1940, the date for the Twelfth Olympics, was the twenty-six hundredth anniversary of the founding of Japan. For Nagata, who was leading the campaign, the Olympic Games were an important event as a part of the twenty-six-hundredth-year celebration. It was thus vital that they be held in Tokyo in 1940.[7]

On September 29, 1932, Seiichi Kishi, the president of the Japanese Amateur Athletic Association (JAAA), gave a speech to the Tenno (emperor) about the

Tenth Games in Los Angeles. The Tenno had given a grant to the JAAA to send athletes to these Games, and it was a great honor for the JAAA as a private organization to see the Tenno. Usually it was only a few political dignitaries and members of the nobility and royalty who had this honor.

In his speech, Kishi said: "There are nine cities competing to hold the 12th Olympic Games, the likeliest of these being Rome, so it will be difficult for Tokyo's success as matters stand." But, he continued, "the political situation in Germany may help our cause. If Hitler and the Nazis come to power, they have suggested the uselessness of having the 11th Olympiad in Berlin, so secret arrangements were made between Baillet-Latour and Mussolini in order to move the 11th Games to Rome. Should this be the case, we, Japan, may get the chance to stage the 12th Games in Tokyo without difficulty, if we put forward an invitation. If there is not a change of government in Germany, it will be very difficult to bring the 12th Olympiad to Tokyo."[8]

The anticipated political changes did occur, and following Hitler's accession to power, the *Tokyo Asahi* newspaper immediately reported on February 1, 1933: "The emergence of the Hitler government is a good omen for the success of Tokyo City." Its correspondent in Berlin reported on February 14, 1933, on the anti-Olympic campaign by ultra-rightists in Germany, who claimed that "the Olympic idea enervates German military ideas, which are the main spirit of German sport. . . . The future of Germany therefore must be decided in our labor camps, in the farms in our colonies, and by the changing of boundaries; never in a sports stadium." The colored races had to be excluded from the Olympic Games, and if this was refused, the Games should not be held at all. The correspondent quoted E. Neuendorff, the vice president of Die Deutsche Turnerschaft, who said: "How do the blacks, who have thick lips and are ill-cultivated, achieve world records? . . . They will never be allowed into Germany. Should there be objections to this, we will not hold the Olympics in Germany in 1936." The correspondent went on to say that there were a few people against the Olympics, but added that "we have to pay attention to the treatment of the colored races, because it includes the Japanese."[9]

The possibility that Hitler might cancel the Berlin Olympics became of great interest to the Japanese people,[10] but when it became clear that the Berlin Olympics would go ahead, the Japanese had to endeavor to bring the Twelfth Games to Tokyo ahead of Rome and other competitors. Japan sent as many athletes as possible in order to be noticed by the other participating countries and the IOC. A Japanese delegation of 249 participants left for Berlin by train via Siberia.

The second aspect that excited the Japanese was how many medals their athletes would win. As table 6.2 indicates, many sports organizations were founded in Japan in the 1920s by their respective sporting body. The JAAA, which was founded in 1911, was reformed as a union of these organizations in 1925, and the Japanese sports system became gradually more ordered. World standards were aimed at by each of the organizations.

Table 6.2. The Foundation of Individual Governing Bodies and Their Years of Participation at the Olympics

Sport	Year Founded	Beginning of Japanese Championships	Olympic Participation	
Rowing	1920	1920	1928	(Amsterdam)
Soccer	1921	1921	1936	(Berlin)
Table tennis	1921	1922	—	
Lawn tennis	1922	1922	1920	(Antwerp)
Hockey	1923	1923	1932	(Los Angeles)
Lawn tennis	1924	1924	—	
Swimming	1924	1914[a]	1920	(Antwerp)
Track and field	1925	1913[a]	1912	(Stockholm)
Skiing	1925	1923[a]	1928	(Saint Moritz)
Boxing	1926	1926	1928	(Amsterdam)
Volleyball	1927	1921[a]	1964	(Tokyo)
Basketball	1930	1921[a]	1936	(Berlin)
Gymnastics	1930	1930	1932	(Los Angeles)
Yachting	1932	1933	1936	(Berlin)
Wrestling	1932	1934	1924	(Paris)
Cycling	1934	1934	1952	(Helsinki)

Source: Based on the findings in Japan Amateur Sports Association, ed., *The History of 75 Years of the Japan Amateur Sports Association* (Tokyo, 1986).

a. Sponsored by the Japan Amateur Athletic Association.

The most remarkable achievement was in swimming. The Japan Amateur Swimming Federation inspired its members with its motivating slogan, "Olympic victory above all," adopted on August 16, 1926.[11] The result was the unprecedented success by Japanese male swimmers in the 1932 Olympic Games in Los Angeles.

Regarding the track and field events, the Japan Amateur Athletic Federation inaugurated its Eight-Year Plan to Dominate the World on December 11, 1932. According to the plan, in eight years the Japanese team would defeat the United States and Finland, which were strong track and field countries, and gain the world championship.[12] The Eleventh Olympics were targeted as an occasion to show the achievement of the first half of the plan. Success in swimming and track and field by Japan in the Los Angeles Olympics showed that the plan was well on target. The mass media, including the radio and the press, reported all aspects of the Games. The interest of the Japanese people continued to increase, and much more interest surrounded the Berlin Olympics than the Los Angeles Olympics. It was not only the competitors and other sports people who showed great interest but also the general public in Japan. Japanese people were much excited by the possibility of a second world domination in male swimming events and the eventual outcome of the eight-year plan. Not only sports magazines but also popular magazines carried various interviews, reports with athletes, and roundtable talks with representative athletes. The newspapers carried all the relevant stories and forecast every event and fanciful news, awaking the interest of the Japanese people.

Equally important, Japan took a diplomatic interest in the Berlin Olympics. According to Kinoshita, the purpose of the Olympic policy in Japan was two-fold: one goal was to promote international sports in Japan by taking part in internationally recognized competition; the other goal was to exalt Japan's international prestige by winning at the Olympic Games.[13] Taking advantage of the Manchurian Incident in 1931,[14] the Japanese army invaded Manchuria in the northeastern section of China. Thus Manchukuo was founded by Japanese military power on March 1, 1932. As Manchukuo was entirely a puppet state of Japan, the League of Nations did not regard it as independent, placing Japan in a painful position. However, the Los Angeles Olympics in 1932 gave Japan an opportunity to recover its lost national dignity and improve its international relations, especially with Europe and the United States.

The government subsidy for the Eighth Olympics in Paris was ¥60,000, as it was for the Ninth in Amsterdam. This was increased to ¥100,000 for the Tenth Olympics in Los Angeles, however. It was also the first time the Tenno gave a donation (of ¥10,000) to the delegation. The Society for Support of the Olympics, headed by Hidejiro Nagata, the mayor of Tokyo, was first established for the Tenth Games, and it collected contributions from the general public amounting to ¥154,000. This enabled Japan to send 131 athletes, the second largest number behind the Americans. The exploits of the Japanese athletes made a favorable impression in the United States, and many American newspapers reported positively on their sportsmanship. Japan's participation had been a resounding diplomatic success. On August 15, 1932, the day after the closing ceremony of the Tenth Olympiad, Toshihito Sato, who was the Japanese consul at Los Angeles, sent a telegram to Kousai Uchida, who was the minister of foreign affairs: "The 10th Olympic Games held here . . . ended in great success. The largest Japanese delegation next to the United States became the object of foreign attention. Japanese athletes were especially praised by America and other countries for their activities, good records and expression of sportsmanship. . . . These Games may help to sweep away some of the bad feelings toward Japan since the Manchurian Incident and have a favorable influence upon friendly relations between Japan and America. I thought it was the best possible result."[15]

Japan had even more incentive to bring off a diplomatic coup at the 1936 Olympics, as the world frowned on its aggression against China, which continued to simmer until open war was declared in 1937. The Lytton Report on Manchuria criticized Japan's military involvement,[16] and as a result, on March 27, 1933, Japan walked out of the League of Nations. Japan continued its encroachment in northern China, covering its military movements with skillful diplomacy, not least through its prowess as a great sporting nation.

On October 1, 1934, the military service handed out a pamphlet entitled *The*

True Meaning of National Defense and the Reasons for Strengthening It. It suggested that politics, economy, thought, culture, and everything else had to be subordinated to national defense and so proposed to establish a national comprehensive war system. This pamphlet, which opens with the declaration, "Struggle is the father of creation and the mother of culture," sparked a public debate. This angered the military, which was intent on curbing all opposition, and culminated on February 18, 1935, with the emperor-as-an-organ theory.[17] This theory was advocated by Tatsukichi Minobe, who was a constitutional scholar at the Imperial University of Tokyo, and was criticized in the House of Peers. Later, Minobe came under blistering attack from the ultranationalists and extreme right-wingers, who had direct ties to the military. On August 3 and October 5, 1935, the government twice declared Kokutai Meicho Seimei,[18] a statement that officially recognized *Kokutai* ideology. The trend to ultranationalistic thought equated with Tenno intensified and thought control tightened up. The words *Kokuta* and *Nippon Seishin* (Japanese Spirit) were very much in the media, with the aim of indoctrinating the public.

The period between the Los Angeles Games in 1932 and those held in Berlin were of vital importance in Japanese history, from all points of view. Diplomatically it was a time to come to terms with the world of international relations set up by the Versailles Treaty, which tried to recreate a new Europe following the First World War, and the Washington Treaty, which set out to regulate control of the Pacific. Domestically, it was a time to prepare the public for government by the military and a regime in which freedom of speech and thought had little role to play. Sport, on the contrary, had a major role to play. Japan appointed Hiroshi Oshima, who was the military attaché to the embassy in Berlin, as attaché to the Berlin Olympics. In October 1935, Oshima entered negotiations with von Ribbentrop, the Nazi foreign minister, to bring about the Anti-Comintern Pact between Japan and Germany.[19] The pact was concluded on November 25, 1936, against the background of the excitement generated by the Olympic Games.

The headgear for the Japanese athletes in Berlin was of a military style, an innovation thought appropriate for the Nazi Games and the growing JAAA. Matahiko Oshima made a speech over Japanese radio in which he reminded the athletes that they were representatives of the state in the same way as soldiers, whose loyalty was pledged to Tenno, to whom they dedicated their lives and for whom they were prepared to die. He ascribed the improvement in athletics to their adoption of a uniquely Japanese spirit: "Why was the athletic ability of our countrymen improved so early? . . . I think it must have been caused by the Japanese spirit, which tended to fight for the honor of the fatherland and Tenno without fearing death. The athletes who had such a Japanese spirit must be well trained, and if they are sent into battle, they would gladly dedicate their lives for Tenno. . . . I want them to show the Japanese spirit and power to all the world, and display their firm attitude and stern discipline in their sporting events."[20]

The Japanese delegation consisted of 249 athletes and officials. They traveled to Germany by train through Siberia, divided into six parties. The traveling costs were met by a government subsidy of ¥300,000, ¥520,000 in contributions by the Society for Support of the Olympics, and the ¥10,000 gift granted by the Tenno.

The large Japanese delegation was intended to impress other countries and help win their support for Japan's bid for the 1940 Games. The athletes would also show, by their success in competition, the remarkable achievements of the new Japan. In this they differed little from the host nation itself. On February 2, 1934, Herbert von Dirksen, the German ambassador in Japan, had sent a letter to Koki Hirota, the Japanese minister for foreign affairs. "Since the German Government considers the Olympic Games to be one of the most important ways of bringing the youth of all countries to a mutual understanding and to awaken within them a feeling of respect for each other, it has put all its resources into the successful completion of the Games. The German government would therefore be most grateful if the invitation to Japan to take part in the 1936 Games were accepted in the same spirit and in the widest possible sense."[21]

Japan had few reservations about competing in the Nazi Games. It was well aware of the Nazi racial policies and how they might be affected by them, not so much as Japanese but because of the Koreans who were part of the Japanese contingent. The exclusion of Jews did not concern them, and there was little interest in the boycott movements taking place in the United States and Europe. Such matters were usually printed under foreign news and without comment. For example, the following items appeared in the *Tokyo Asahi* newspaper:

> The Jewish tennis players were prohibited from participation in regular matches by the German Tennis Association, regardless of whether matches were at home or abroad. (April 26, 1933; dateline Berlin)

> The IOC demands that the German government obey the IOC Charter. (May 27, 1933; dateline Paris)

> The Amateur Athletic Union decided that the American team would boycott the Games if Jews were prohibited from taking part. (November 22, 1933; dateline Pittsburgh)

> The participation of the American team was decided at the meeting of the AAU. (December 8, 1935; dateline New York)

> The French team may boycott the Games in reaction to entrance of the German army into the Rhineland. (March 10, 1936; dateline Paris)

> The participation in the Games by the French team was confirmed. (June 26, 1936; dateline Paris)

> In France, the government subsidy for the Berlin Olympics, one million francs, and for the Peoples' Olympiad in Barcelona, six hundred thousand francs, was passed in the Cabinet and the Chamber of Deputies. (July 11, 1936; dateline Paris)

These issues were given little prominence, and the Japanese sporting bodies ignored them altogether.[22] One of the reasons for this is that Japan is a "single-race country," not a multiracial country. There are therefore few racial problems, and the Jewish issue is nonexistent. The only problem Japan had with the Nazi regime was whether or not the Japanese would be considered a colored race under Nazi law.[23]

Because Japan governed Korea and Taiwan as domestic regions of Japan, it was not in fact a single-race country. However, Japanese government policy in those days was based upon Kominka, a method of thought control that forced the Korean and Taiwanese to pledge their loyalty to Japanese Tenno in the same way as the Japanese. Hence, the Korean athletes selected as the Japanese contingent were all considered to be Japanese, and the activities of the Korean athletes were reported in newspapers and radio on a grand scale. Incidentally, the first Korean athletes who participated in the Olympic Games for Japan were the two marathoners and one boxer who went to the Los Angeles Olympics in 1932. Seven went to Berlin (two marathoners, one soccer player, three basketball players, and one boxer). In the Garmisch-Partenkirchen Winter Olympics, three Korean skaters were part of the Japanese contingent.

The victory of Son Ki-jong (Kitei Son/Kee Chung Son) in the marathon was given headline treatment in the press when it was announced on August 10: "Japanese Athlete Realizes Our Long-Cherished Hope" (Jijishinpo); "Japanese Marathoner Finally Wins Race" (Houchi); "Japanese Marathoner Conquers the World; Our Heart's Desire over 24 Years Now Realized" (Yomiuri); "Marathon, the Cherished Desire of 24 Years Realized"; "Son Ki-jong: Our Pride before the World" (Tokyo Asahi). Newspapers made no distinction between Son's victory and those of the Japanese. The references to twenty-four years alludes to the fact that Japan sent two athletes to the Fifth Olympics at Stockholm in 1912 for the first time; one was a sprinter, the other a marathoner. Shizou Kanaguri, the marathoner, who showed great promise in the domestic trials, gave up the race halfway. He then took part in the Seventh and Eighth Olympic Games with poor results. Japan sent promising marathoners to the Ninth and Tenth Olympics, but came fourth in Amsterdam and fifth in Los Angeles. Since then, the Japanese had been very enthusiastic about the marathon. Though the Japanese marathoners, judging from their records, could have won a victory, they missed it at the Olympics. So when a Korean marathoner won the race at Berlin, it was seen as Japan's greatest sporting triumph since entering the Olympics in 1912.

Because of the Kominka policy, the Koreans had strong anti-Japanese feelings, and Japan discriminated against the Korean players in many ways, such as in selection.[24] Korean players were fully aware of the contradictions in taking part in tournaments as Japanese, with the national anthem of Japan, "Kimigayo," played and the national flag of Japan, the Rising Sun, hoisted when they won a victory.[25] However, as far as the Japanese media were concerned, the Korean and the Japanese players were the same. For example, two days after the victory of Son Ki-jong, *Tokyo Asahi* ran an editorial titled, "The Victory of a Marathoner from Korea." It read: "This victory is the fruit of toil and cooperation among the people inland and overseas. In this sense, it is significant that the Korean marathoner's strenuous efforts could raise the flag of the Rising Sun." In this way, the Japanese and the Koreans were treated evenly; both were considered Japanese.

The Japanese interest in international sport, like that of the Nazis, represented a reversal of their original ideas. After the Meiji Restoration in 1868, Japan moved rapidly ahead with its program of modernization, based on the advanced countries of the West. In this time various sports were introduced and became part of the education system. This meant that they came under the ultranationalist ethos of Tenno. Fair play and friendliness toward other nations had no place in this, as winning in sport was the same as a victory for the nation. The interest of most Japanese in the Olympics was to win medals, and it was no different with the Berlin Olympics, where attention was focused on how many medals would be won. The athletes therefore participated in the Games with a "death or glory" spirit. For example, Hideko Maehata, who won first place in the 200 meter breaststroke, said after the event: "The Japanese people believed I would be victorious, for I held the world record. I felt I could not lose the race at any cost, even though it was very painful. I decided that if I lost the race, I would not return to Japan."[26] Not exactly the Olympic spirit that promoted international friendship and the search for peace.

The Japanese Media

The Japanese media, essentially newspapers and radio, gave a full coverage of the events in Germany, and when officials and participants returned, their views were sought for further exposure. The decision of the IOC to award the 1940 Games to Tokyo caused great excitement and sparked off renewed interest among the Japanese people. Newspapers reported extensively on the records set by Japanese athletes day after day. An "extra" was issued the day after each victory. Also the radio broadcast, by electronic transcription, from 6:30 A.M. to 7:00 A.M., kept up a running commentary on the Games from 12:00 P.M. until 1:00 P.M.[27] The radio commentary on the women's 200 meter breaststroke was extremely popular. Hideko Maehata was in a dead heat with Martha Genenger of Germany, and the announcer was so excited he exclaimed at the top of his voice, "Come on Maehata! Come on Maehata! . . . She won! She won!"

It was the performances of the Japanese athletes that occupied the attention of the press and radio reporters, and whenever a medal was anticipated they would crowd around the radio to savor it to the full. The medal ceremony itself took on an exaggerated importance and was given a full headline: "EXTREMELY MOVING! / Our National Anthem, 'Kimigayo,' Is Playing for the First-Place Athlete / The Rising Sun Flags Are Four! / God Has Produced His Athletic Japan!" (*Yomiuri* extra on August 7; pole vault and triple jump). "National Anthem Is Resounding All Around, Exchanging Smiles with Hitler" (*Tokyo Asahi* extra, August 10; marathon). "Victory! Japan Has Won the Prize!" (*Tokyo Asahi*, August 16, swimming). "The Swimming Championships, Desperately Defended at the End" (*Houchi*, August 16). Yaso Saijo, a popular poet, was sent to Berlin by the *Yomiuri* newspaper, and he sent back many nationalistic poems to Japan by telephone.

The athletes and their performances were a prime concern to the press, but the social and political aspects were not overlooked. The stadium, stadium equipment, and facilities were large and splendid in scientific, technical, and artistic respects. Hideya Kishida, widely respected as a professor of architecture at the Imperial University of Tokyo, was sent by the Ministry of Education to Germany to inspect the Olympic Stadium, the Olympic Village, and other facilities, and he expressed great admiration for the architectural designs produced by the town planners.[28] Moreover, Katsuyoshi Miyata, a correspondent with *Jijishinpo*, wrote in "The Resolution of the Tokyo Olympics" that the planning of the Tokyo Games had to be begun all over again because those who came to the Berlin Games were so amazed at the splendid facilities; Tokyo would have to compare favorably.[29] This change in policy was confirmed when all the Japanese participants highly praised the equipment and facilities.

Also noted was the German nationalism, which was reflected in the cooperation between the state and people to manage the Games, especially in the participation of the military. Coaches and athletes told of the soldiers' devoted service in the Olympic Village and escorts to and from the training sites. Ryozo Hiranuma, the head of the Japanese delegation and the vice president of the JAAA, praised the management and the organization of the German Games and said that not only the JAAA and those interested in sports but also the government and the military should stand together and follow the German example at the Tokyo Olympics.[30]

They admired the way Nazi Germany portrayed its national power and culture, not only through the Olympics but in other exhibitions held at the same time. Tastuo Hoshino, a correspondent with *Yomiuri* newspaper, reported that many events, such as the Olympic torch relay, the Youth Festival, and the Great Germany Exhibition were held alongside the Games, making the entire city of Berlin part of the Olympic stage.[31] Moreover, Buichi Otani, who was a professor of physical education at the Higher Normal School of Tokyo and was sent to Germany to inspect the Olympic Games by the Ministry of Education, noted that when the Nazis engaged in propaganda, they did such things as put on demonstrations with parades of three thousand people from the Arbeitsdienst, blowing bugles and raising shovels as Hitler passed by, a far more moving spectacle than raising bayonets.[32]

None could overlook the way the German people showed enthusiastic and high regard for Hitler. Fujimura, the principal of the Tokyo Girls Gymnastic Music School, relayed by telephone her observations regarding the enthusiastic support for Hitler when she saw the Games.[33] More cynically, the poet Yaso Saijo wrote on his return to Japan from Germany, "The Berlin Olympics were merely a drama in which Hitler played a leading part and all the athletes played subordinate parts."[34]

All praised the marked improvement in the Germans' sporting ability. It was a wondrous thing to defeat the United States, which until then had always won the Games.[35] The Germans attained eighty-nine medals, as opposed to their twenty in Los Angeles four years earlier. Kohei Yusa, an equestrian coach, considered the reason to be the general strengthening of the nation under a long-term plan.[36] Takeichi Nishi, an equestrian participant, noted that the background to the improvement came from the national physical education program. According to him, "the foundation of the German national policy is the training of the true German character and the implanting of the true German soul into the German people. The way by which this can be achieved, then, is through physical education. All the German people, therefore, attach importance to physical education. Sport becomes the way of physical education. In Germany, sport is the mainstay of the German national policy." In Germany, therefore, the upper classes did not take leading roles, as was the case in Japan.[37]

With regard to German progress, Buichi Otani, in a roundtable talk on the Berlin Olympics, compared Germany and Great Britain. Regarding the poor performances of the British team in the Berlin Games, he gave an ideological appraisal: "In Germany sport is for the development of the discipline of mind and body, that is, for physical education and even more for the fatherland. On the other hand, in England sport is for sport's sake, and it has no higher use. This is the difference between the two countries' sporting ability." Otani suggested that the German ideology presented some problems for the officials. All the participants in the discussion considered that the nation would have to control sports and that Japan would have to change its outlook on sports from the English to the German model.[38]

The general impression conveyed to the Japanese people is reflected in the speech by Ryozo Hiranuma at a homecoming reception that was broadcast all over the country on October 3, 1936: "The 11th Berlin Olympics ended in success as you know, so we offer praise not only to the host country but also the other participating countries whose presence helped generate this success. . . . Germany produced much propaganda about the spirit of the Games and showed the high-spirit of the postwar rehabilitation. So Germany took pride in its great success at the Olympics."[39]

Hachisaburo Hirao, the minister of education, who was also at the reception, praised the splendid achievement of the Japanese athletes, and in preparation for the Twelfth Olympics he said: "At the 12th Tokyo Olympics, which will be held as a part of our 2,600th anniversary festival, Japan should show the Japanese national strength and spirit which have been cultivated based on Japanese Kokutai: that is most important."[40] The 1940 Games would help to promote further friendly relations between Japan and Germany[41] and would be a good opportunity to show other countries Japanese national strength as the Berlin Olympics had done for Germany.

After the Games, in the response to the Japanese press Domei's requests, Hitler gave a message of friendly sporting ties between the two countries. This was reported immediately by the Japanese press on August 27: "The Japanese athletes did their best and displayed their great abilities and spirit during the 11th Games in Berlin. Deep friendships were formed, and we expect the young men from all over the world to gather at Tokyo in 1940 to participate in the next Olympiad. I believe firmly that Japan will give a good display of the Olympic spirit in the 12th Olympics and that the Tokyo Olympics will contribute to world peace."[42]

But there were some who criticized the Berlin Olympics. Kinichi Asano, who participated in the Games as a head official of the delegation, claimed that it was not the German government and national Olympic Committee but Hitler's Nazis who ran the Berlin Olympics. He said: "I did not like the Games because they seemed contrived. It looked as if the sanctity of the Games was being used for the Nazis' own purposes."[43] He added, however: "I was surprised at how well German people were under control; in other words, the national mobilization program worked well." He continued: "I realized fully that Nazi Germany's marvelous development is founded on national mobilization, government control, and the German people's devotion as shown during the Olympics."[44]

It was Count Michimasa Soeshima, a member of the IOC, who looked at the Berlin Olympics most critically. During a roundtable discussion titled "The Guiding Principle of the Tokyo Olympics," sponsored by the *Tokyo Asahi* newspaper, he said that compared with the Los Angeles Games, which were mainly about sport, the Berlin Games were used mainly for national propaganda. At Berlin "there was no Olympic spirit in the Games. They were managed on the basis of Germany's interest. For example, the poverty of the basketball site was unspeakable. The closing ceremony was purely for national propaganda."[45] Regarding the guiding principle of the Toyko Olympics, he declared, "I would not want to make use of the Tokyo Olympics for national propaganda. I want to manage the Games with the same sporting spirit as the Los Angeles Games."[46] Count Soeshima was the only person to criticize the Berlin Olympics so directly, but his opinions carried little weight in regard to the policy of the Tokyo Olympics.

Getting Ready for the Twelfth Olympiad in Tokyo

Count Soeshima did not want the Tokyo Games to be taken over by the government, as in the Berlin Olympics. He planned to form the Olympic Organizing Committee (OOC) under the JAAA as a national Olympic Committee according to the IOC Charter, with himself as leader.[47] He wanted the Twelfth Games to be a pure sports meeting.

Jigoro Kano, another member of the IOC who had attended the Games in

Berlin, however, regarded the Twelfth Olympics as a great national project. He wanted the heads of the government, military, economic circles, Tokyo city, and the JAAA to meet, decide on a fundamental goal, and organize the OOC for this purpose.[48] Kano explained that the Tokyo Olympics was not only a sporting event but also an opportunity to exhibit Japanese culture and national spirit before other countries. He also felt they would help to arouse national spirit.[49] Accordingly, he thought that the Tokyo Olympics should be a national event and so had to be organized at the national level.[50]

Kano, who returned to Japan before Count Soeshima, had a conversation with Hirao, the minister of education, on November 13, 1936, and Hirao completely agreed with Kano. Count Soeshima, coming back to Japan on November 27, was obliged to revise his stance that the OOC should be organized under the leadership of the JAAA after holding two meetings, one with Kano on November 28, another with Hirao on November 30. After the meeting with Hirao, Soeshima announced his conclusions in an informal way: "The national Olympic Committee in the United States controlled all aspects of the Los Angeles Olympics apart from collecting the public loan. . . . It also served to impress on the people the value of sport. Conversely the Berlin Olympics saw an oppressive control of the people mainly through the government's stranglehold on opinion. . . . The problem is: which path shall we take, the American or German? In Japan it is natural and proper that the JAAA as Japan's national Olympic Committee should assume the leadership. However it will be necessary to form the OOC from organized authorities representing various circles so that the Games are held with more credibility. In this sense I don't oppose the OOC even if it is made up of a nationwide committee."[51]

Soeshima made his announcement knowing that his opinion would not be accepted. After the Berlin Olympics, every Japanese newspaper in its editorial column praised the success of the Games and the Japanese athletes' prowess and *Tokyo Asahi* suggested that the Tokyo Olympics should be held under the slogan, "Unity of nation; unity of officials and people,"[52] while *Yomiuri* claimed that this should be "an opportunity to exalt national prestige."[53] Under the circumstances, the Berlin Olympics were regarded as a model for Tokyo, and Count Soeshima's plan did not receive support from the authorities or the public.

After three discussions—between Kano and Hirao, Kano and Soeshima, and Soeshima and Hirao—Hirao held a social gathering concerning the Tokyo Olympics on December 7, 1936. In attendance were Jigoro Kano, Count Michimasa Soeshima, Prince Iesato Tokugawa, the Japanese member of the IOC, Torataro Ushizuka, the mayor of Tokyo city, Ryozo Hiranuma, Matahiko Oshima, and Yoshijiro Umezu, the vice minister of war. In addition, Shunsaku Kawahara, the vice minister of education, and Taku Iwahara, the head of the physical education section, sat with them.

At the beginning of this meeting Hirao explained the intention of the ministry of education: "We would regard the 12th Tokyo Olympics not as a mere sporting competition, but as a good chance to enable other countries to understand our spirit as a nation. We want the Japanese athletes to be fervently motivated in nationalistic tendencies, so winning is not everything. On the basis of this fundamental principle I want to ask all those people present for their support and cooperation with every detail."[54] The basic purpose of the Games was then discussed. Three points were decided, each of them nationalistic and entirely contrary to Soeshima's idea. First, the celebration of the Olympic Games in Tokyo should reflect not only the highest ideals of mankind as manifested in competition in the field of international sports but also an added glory to the Japanese nation, because the year fell on the occasion of the twenty-six hundredth anniversary of the founding Tenno. The celebration should be a tremendous spiritual aid to the people of Japan in working together for the success of these festivities. The Japanese national spirit and the true aspects of Japanese culture, old and new, would be shown to the eyes of the world. Therefore, the organizers were advised to be aware of the fact that careful attention should be given in the preparations to convey the true spirit of Japan to the world. Second, all the parties concerned, whether directly or indirectly, should give wholehearted support and cooperation to ensure the perfect functioning of the preparations for the Twelfth Olympiad. The Tokyo Olympics must be an undertaking supported by the whole nation. Third, the preparations should not be frivolous and for fun but should be carried out constantly and vigorosly. As to the training of the athletes, special care should be taken to foster the cooperative spirit and the training of the mind and body of the youth in general.[55]

The influence of the military could be seen in a number of areas, and after five meetings the OOC was organized with those present as leaders, on December 24, 1936. The nationalistic and militaristic slant was emphasized in the *Japan Advertiser,* an English-language paper in Japan, which reported on the process of the military's intervention in the preparation for the Games with the following headlines: "Show Japan Spirit, Army's Aim in 1940 / Umezu Says Emphasis Should Be on Mass Training, Not Victories,"[56] and "War Vice Minister Stresses Need for National Coordination to Stage Games."[57]

On December 30, 1936, Kimitomo Mushakoji, the Japanese Ambassador to Germany, received a visit from Lewald, who was told about the plans for the Tokyo Olympics. On January 4, 1937, Mushakoji reported the repercussions to the minister of foreign affairs, Hachiro Arita: "On December 30, Lewald said to me that there was some talk that Japan regarded the next Olympics as a thoroughly national event to the exclusion of its international significance, and this made him very angry. . . . I just want to raise the concerned party's attention."[58]

The OOC continued to prepare for the Games according to the prearranged plan. However, after the Lukouchiao incident on July 7, 1937, war between Japan and China was openly declared. When the war became hopelessly mired in a stalemate, on July 15, 1938, the cabinet advised the OOC to call off the Twelfth

Olympiad. The next day, July 16, in obedience to the government's advice, the OOC decided to hand the Tokyo Games back to the IOC. The Japanese people accepted the news calmly, in stark contrast to their reaction when it had been announced that Tokyo would host the Games two years previously. It would not be until the Fifteenth Olympic Games in Helsinki in 1952 that Japan again participated in the Olympics.

Notes

1. Masao Maruyama, the historian of political thought, has divided the Japanese fascist movement into three periods: (1) The term of preparation, from the end of World War I to the Manchuria Incident in 1931; the age of the nongovernmental right-wing movements. (2) The term of maturity, from 1931 to the military coup on Feb. 26, 1936; the age of military fascism, which was combined with the nongovernmental right-wing movements. (3) The term of accomplishment, from 1936 to the end of World War II in 1945; the age of the construction of fascism by the military in concert with the bureaucrats, monopolistic capital, and bourgeois political parties. See M. Maruyama, *Thought and Behavior in Modern Japanese Politics* (Tokyo: Mirai-sha, 1976), 32. The period between the Los Angeles Olympics and the Berlin Olympics roughly corresponds to the period of maturity.

2. Japan Olympic Committee, *The Olympic Encyclopedia* (Tokyo: Press Gymnastica, 1981), 208–9; Japan Amateur Sports Association, *The Newest Sports Encyclopedia* (Tokyo: Taishukan, 1987), 147–48.

3. M. Kiyokawa, *Sports and Politics* (Tokyo: Baseball Magazine-sha, 1987), 28–29.

4. Japan Amateur Sports Association, *Newest Sports Encyclopedia*, 147.

5. N. Kawamoto, "The Olympics and Internationalism," in *Sport Nationalism Series: Thinking of Sport,* vol. 5, ed. K. Kageyama et al. (Tokyo: Taishukan, 1978), 288–90; Y. Suzuki, *Tidbits of the Olympic Information* (Tokyo: Baseball Magazine-sha, 1983), 78–79.

6. Y. Suzuki, *An Olympic Reader* (Tokyo: Obunsha, 1949), 187; Japan Amateur Sports Association, *A Hundred Years of Japanese Sports* (Tokyo: Japan Amateur Sports Association, 1970), 610.

7. As 1940 was the twenty-six hundredth year following the ascension of the Tenno, Jimmu, to the throne as first ruler of Japan, the government was planning grand ceremonies. One of the most momentous events was to be the Olympics and the international exposition. The Jimmu's ascension of twenty-six hundred years had been seen previously not as a historical fact but a mythological story. However, the ceremonies were planned on the basis of the governmental philosophy of those days, which held that Japan has been ruled by an unbroken line of Tennos, who were the god incarnate since the first Tenno, Jimmu. Therefore Japan was a divine land. At that time in primary and secondary school, the myth was taught as a historical fact, and many Japanese people did not doubt Jimmu's existence. Also it was taboo to research the myth scientifically. Soukichi Tuda, the historian, who wrote of Jimmu's nonexistence in scientific books, had a complaint lodged against him because he infringed on the law to maintain the dignity of the Tenno and the imperial household in 1939. He was found guilty, and the sale of his publications was prohibited.

8. JAAA, *Report of the 10th Olympic Games* (Tokyo: JAAA, 1933), 5.

9. *Tokyo Asahi,* Jan. 14, 1933.

10. In some general and sport magazines there were articles on whether or not the Nazi Government would call off the Olympics in Berlin. Kawamoto, for example, introduced Hitler's critical view of the Olympics from two points: one was that the Olympics as an international movement was Jewish; another was that France was the main supporter of the Olympic movement. And he explained the possibilities of the abandonment of the Berlin Olympics and the invitation of the Twelfth Games to Tokyo. See N. Kawamoto, "Fascistic Sport," *Shin Seinen* 14.5 (1933): 248–50. Kitazawa declared that the Nazis would not give up the Olympics because they thought too much

of physical education and sports, and after their accession to power they began to speak of international cooperation. See K. Kitazawa, "Hitler and the Olympics," *Olympics* 11.4 (1933): 32–35.

11. Japan Amateur Swimming Federation, *40 Years of the Japan Amateur Swimming Federation*
(Tokyo: JASF, 1969), 56.

12. *The Monthly Report of the Japan Amateur Athletic Federation,* nos. 21 and 23 (Tokyo: JAAF,
1932, 1933).

13. H. Kinoshita, *A History of Sports in Modern Japan* (Tokyo: Kyorinshoin, 1970), 206–9.

14. The Manchurian Incident was a military operation in which part of the South Manchuria
Railway was blown up by a section of the Japanese army stationed in Manchuria. The Japanese
army blamed the Chinese army and used the incident as a pretext to invade the whole of Manchuria, which they conquered by the beginning of 1932.

15. *Documents Referring to the International Olympic Games,* vol. 2, Diplomatic Records Office,
Tokyo.

16. The report of the investigation committee, the chairman of which was Lord Victor Lytton,
was sent by the League of Nations. The committee investigated the Manchurian Incident and submitted a report to the League of Nations. It found that the Japanese military activities were not
recognized as a legal defense and Manchukuo also was not recognized as a legal independent state.

17. At the time, there were two interpretations of the Meiji Constitution with regard to the sov-
ereign power of the state. One was that the sacrosanct Tenno personally held the power; the other
was that the state held it itself and that the Tenno was nothing but the supreme organ of the state.
After World War I, the latter view was prevalent among learned society as a more democratic theory of the Meiji constitution. Tatsukichi Minobe, the premier scholar of constitutions, supported
the latter theory.

18. It identified the origin and the history of the Japanese state with an unbroken line of Tennos and justified Japanese dignity and superiority over other countries.

19. Japan Society of International Politics, *The Route to the Pacific War,* vol. 5 (Tokyo: Asahi-
shinbun-sha, 1987), 17.

20. Matahiko Oshima, "Sending Off the Japanese Delegates," *Olympics* 14.7 (1936): 3.

21. *Documents Referring to the International Olympic Games,* vol. 3, Diplomatic Records Office,
Tokyo.

22. Shuhei Nishida, the pole-vault silver medalist in the Berlin Games, told me, "In those days,
I did not know that there was a Berlin Olympics boycott movement in Europe and the United States
at all" (personal interview, Feb. 15, 1992).

23. Matsuzo Nagai, the Japanese ambassador to Germany, called on von Neurath, the minister
of foreign affairs, on Oct. 20, 1933. The reason for the meeting was that Nagai wanted to know
whether the Japanese were considered a colored race under the bill for amending the criminal law.
The minister answered that the Japanese were never considered a colored race. *Tokyo Asahi,* Oct.
24, 1933, Oct. 25, 1933 (evening edition). Thereafter Nagai became the general secretary of the Olympic Organizing Committee (OOC) and a member of the IOC from 1939 to 1950.

24. For example, in soccer, the Korean team, Seoul Soccer Club, won an overwhelming victory
at the All Japan Championship in 1935 and again at the Meiji Shrine Athletic Meet, a nationwide
athletic meet of many sports. Strictly speaking, the contingent to the Olympics should have been
chosen from the team that won a championship. But most of the players who were selected were
students from Tokyo, and only two players came from Seoul Soccer Club. One of two Korean players
decided not to participate in the Games, expressing his discontent with the selection. As a result,
only one Korean actually played soccer in the Olympic Games. See T. Kamata, *The Rising-Sun Flag
and Marathon* (Tokyo: Ushio Publishers, 1984), 408.

25. In the autobiography that Son Ki-jong wrote about half a century after the Berlin Olympics, he describes how he felt standing on the victory dais after winning the race: "It was an un-
bearable disgrace for me that I listened to 'Kimigayo' on the honor platform, seeing the flag of the
Rising-Sun on the pole. Unconsciously, I hung my head and wondered whether I was really a Jap-

anese. If I were, what did the Japanese maltreatment against my fellow countrymen mean? In fact, I can never be a Japanese. It's impossible for me. I myself don't think that I ran for the Japanese. In my heart I ran for myself, and for my compatriots who were groaning under oppression. Anyway, what on earth do the sun flag and 'Kimigayo' mean, what do they symbolize? I will never run under the flag of Rising-Sun in the future." See Son Ki-jong, *Autobiography: Tears for the Laurel* (Tokyo: Kodan-sha, 1985), 179.

26. H. Maehata, "Behind the Victory (2)," *Jijishinpou*, Oct. 2, 1936.

27. Hashimoto noted that the Berlin Olympics marked the beginning of a new epoch in the history of Japanese sports journalism. The radio made on-the-spot broadcasts for the first time for simultaneous listening in the homes of the Japanese. Some pictures were printed in the newspapers the next day using radio photography, and news about athletes who set records was reported in the newspapers the next day. At the Los Angeles Olympics, the radio announcer would watch the Games and then go back to the radio station and broadcast the event as if it were taking place live. For example, the 100 meters, which took about ten seconds to complete, took one minute to report. And as the photographic films were transported across the Pacific by ship and plane, they were not reproduced in newspapers until two weeks later. The background to the increasing interest in the Berlin Games could not be explained without the prompt reports due to the technological improvements in communication. See K. Hashimoto, *The History of Sportcasting in Japan* (Tokyo: Taishukan, 1992), 52–55.

28. JAAA, *Report of the 10th Olympic Games*, 402; *Tokyo Nichinichi*, Oct. 7, 1936.

29. *Jijishinpo*, Aug. 18, 1936.

30. JAAA, *Report of the 10th Olympic Games*, 3.

31. *Yomiuri*, Aug. 19, 1936.

32. B. Otani, "The Meeting for Listening to the Report of Otani, Mori and Yoshioka (1)," *Taiiku to Kyogi* 15.11 (1936), 17.

33. *Tokyo Asahi*, Aug. 5, 1936.

34. Y. Saijo, "Memoirs of the Berlin Olympics," *Hinode*, Dec. 1936, 85.

35. This was, of course, not true. In 1912, for example, Sweden was the most successful nation, but Japan was under the impression that the United States had always been victorious.

36. K. Yusa, "Report on the Equestrian Events," *Olympics* 14.12 (1936): 33–34.

37. T. Nishi, "Report on the Equestrian Events in the Berlin Olympics," *Olympics* 14.11 (1936): 27.

38. Otani, "Meeting for Listening to the Report of Otani."

39. JAAA, *Report of the 10th Olympic Games*, 1.

40. H. Hirao, "Welcome to the Olympic Delegation," *Olympics* 14.11 (1936): 3.

41. Hoshino, the sports editor for *Yomiuri* newspaper, reported that the German interest in Japan was so strong that the Japanese athletes were given good coverage in the German newspapers, and even the Japanese press were treated as VIPs. He concluded that it was a great success to send a large Japanese delegation (*Yomiuri*, Aug. 17, 1936). Teru Yamamoto, who, with Sansei Kasai, was in charge of radio announcements at the Games, told me that the Japanese received an ovation in Germany and were popular everywhere they went (personal interview, Dec. 19, 1991). Eiichi Isomura, who had met Hitler as the mayor's personal envoy in order to seek his support for the realization of the invitation of the Twelfth Games to Tokyo, explained to me his conjecture that Hitler's ulterior intentions perhaps made the German people receive the Japanese warmly on the grounds of intimate relations between the two countries (personal interview, Jan. 7, 1992). Isomura later became the person at the Tokyo city administration in charge of the preparation for the Tokyo Olympics.

42. *Tokyo Asahi*, Aug. 27, 1936.

43. K. Asano, "The Nazis and The Olympics," *Bungeishunju* 14.11 (1936): 268.

44. Ibid., 270–71.

45. *Tokyo Asahi*, Dec. 3, 1936. The participants in the roundtable discussion were: Jigoro Kano,

Michimasa Soeshima, Hachisaburo Hirao, Torataro Ushizuka, the mayor of Tokyo, Ryozo Hiranuma, Matahiko Oshima, and Eiji Amou, the head of the Information Bureau in the Ministry of Foreign Affairs. Thereafter they occupied a responsible position in the OOC.

46. *Tokyo Asahi,* Dec. 3, 1936.

47. *Tokyo Asahi,* Nov. 6, 1936. *Yomiuri,* Nov. 28, 1936; evening edition.

48. *Yomiuri,* Nov. 13, 1936.

49. *Tokyo Ninchininchi,* Nov. 14, 1936.

50. Yotaro Sugimura, the Japanese ambassador to Italy and a member of the IOC, suggested before the Berlin Games, on May 17, 1936, what he thought the basic purpose of the Tokyo Olympics should be: "The 11th Games, properly speaking, should be sponsored by Berlin City, but in fact the government is preparing for them. The Twelfth Games will be held at Tokyo in 1940. It will be a great undertaking, not only for Tokyo city and the Japanese Amateur Athletic Association but also for the government and the military. It will give rise to an increase in youthful spirit and overall morale. This undertaking therefore needs the requisite help of the latter." He suggested that they needed the support of the government and the military, as in Germany. See "Documents Referring to the International Olympic Games from June 1932 to Dec. 1935," 91120–3, microfilm 20–25, in the Diet Library, Tokyo. Sugimura, who was Kano's pupil in Kodokan Judo, was a man with a long diplomatic career. He had served, for example, as the assistant director general in the League of Nations. His proposal had a great influence in Japanese sporting circles.

51. *Yomiuri,* Dec. 1, 1936.

52. *Tokyo Asahi,* Aug. 17, 1936.

53. *Yomiuri,* Aug. 18, 1936.

54. *Tokyo Asahi,* Dec. 8, 1936.

55. M. Nagai, ed., *The Report of the Organizing Committee of the 12th Olympiad Tokyo 1940* (in Japanese) (Tokyo: OOC, 1939), 46. The report written in English is different in places from the original report written in Japanese.

56. Quoted in *Olympics* 15.1 (1937): 79.

57. *Japan Advertiser,* Dec. 9, 1936.

58. Letter to Arita, Jan. 4, 1937, "Documents Referring to the International Olympic Games," vol. 4, in Diplomatic Records Office, Tokyo.

CHAPTER 7

Finland: The Promised Land of Olympic Sports

Leena Laine

Translated by Hannu Tervaharju

Along with the rest of the Western world, Finland experienced a deep depression at the end of the 1920s during which it was confronted with a political crisis as well, as the unrest among the extreme right culminated in an attempted rebellion in 1932. The sports movement was also in a state of crisis: the bourgeois sports movement and its credibility were seriously undermined by the question of so-called covert professionalism, which culminated around the expulsion of Paavo Nurmi on the eve of the Los Angeles Olympics in 1932. The Worker Sports Federation (TUL) broke up in 1929–30, and its left-wing sports clubs were suppressed as "communist organizations." Several top athletes chose to defect into bourgeois clubs that offered them money or jobs, making the problem of covert professionalism even more difficult. "To Berlin!" was a call that was alluring to the Finnish sports movement for several reasons: revenge for the Nurmi defeat at Los Angeles, reassurance concerning the strength and ability of Finnish sports, and as a basis for entering the queue of applicants for the Olympic Games of 1940.[1]

During the first decade of the twentieth century, Finland, boasting three million inhabitants, had developed into a significant sports country. The Stockholm Olympics of 1912 had been a turning point as the "culture of the flesh" so loathed by the national cultural circles became an accepted means of unifying the people and spreading the concept of "Finnish Finland" abroad—both before the independence gained in 1917 as well as after it, especially in the 1920s and 1930s.[2] The central competitive sports organization in Finland was the Finnish Gymnastics and Sports Federation (SVUL, founded in 1906), its main sports being of the "layman variety": track and field, wrestling, gymnastics, and, later, cross-country skiing. Outside the federation there were several specialist associations for ball games, skating, and sailing. The Swedish-speaking population (10 percent of the total population) had their own sports organizations. The TUL and two associations of women's gymnastics had stayed outside Olympic sports.

The basic work in physical exercise, which proved useful for the SVUL, was being carried out by a military defense organization, the Civil Guards, whose network covered the entire country. The bourgeois sports movement had connections with the "ardent Finnish" and "kindred ideal" organizations. The extreme right, which had a hand in the supreme leadership of the educational system, the Parliament, and the Association of Gymnastics Teachers also exerted pressure on the Parliament, especially regarding decisions on sports funding. It secured control over the TUL's political activity and eventually brought about the abolition of the TUL's state subsidies in 1932–33.[3]

The state favored the sports movement because of its "public relations value abroad" and the unifying effect of "sports fanaticism"; the voluntary sports movement was also regarded as a necessary part of national defense. The state granted generous funding for international representative sports and especially the Olympic Games, but also for teams taking part in the Workers' Olympics. State subsidies were necessary because the major part of the representative athletes came from the ranks of workers, the indigent rural population, and the lower middle classes.[4] Olympic success became the central athletic objective, and this dictated the major sports of the country: track and field, wrestling, and, as in the Winter Games of the 1920s, cross-country skiing.

In the Olympic medal statistics, Finland, despite its small population, had reached fourth position among the nations by 1932 with 172 medals, after the United States (498 medals), Great Britain (293), and Sweden (242). Since the Paris Olympic Games the results, however, had gone steadily downhill.[5]

Finland, the Finnish Press, and Germany

According to Britta Hiedanniemi, who has studied Nazi Germany's cultural propaganda in Finland, the Finns' general attitude toward the "new Germany" was similar to the attitudes toward Finland's own extreme-right movement. According to Hiedanniemi, Finland's social democrat, liberal, and Swedish press were all part of the international criticism directed toward Germany after 1933.[6] The social democratic trade union movement boycotted imported German goods. The conservative Coalition party and its newspapers, however, assumed a matter-of-fact, even friendly attitude toward Germany, while the papers of the extreme right defended the Third Reich and National Socialism.

Nazi Germany was worried about the possibility that Germany's political change would bring Finland and Great Britain, Finland's most important trading partner, closer to each other and lead Finland's sympathies toward the democracies.[7] Because even the extreme Right in Finland seemed to be critical of Nazi Germany, the Finns themselves being "non-Aryan," while the Swedish minority in Finland could rightfully claim to be even more Aryan than the average German, the German embassy in Finland stressed that National Socialism was an internal German matter while also emphasizing that Germany did not support any Nazi groups acting abroad.

Germany's cultural position in Finland was supported by deliberate German policy and propaganda, which exploited cultural ties dating to the nineteenth century as well as the military aid white Finland had received from Germany to quell the "Red Rebellion" in 1918. In the summer of 1933 festivities were arranged in Finland to commemorate the so-called liberation war and the fifteenth anniversary of Helsinki's deliverance. A German delegation was in attendance, led by General von der Golz. The conservative newspaper *Uusi Suomi* told its readership how the people of Germany put their faith in Hitler. It considered Germany's national integration and rise to be important for the disunified and humiliated country. It additionally stressed that National Socialist Germany and Fascist Italy formed an essential part of the front against communism.[8]

Germany's propaganda in Finland was intensified after 1933, especially through the embassy, the German Chamber of Commerce in Helsinki, and also a local branch of the NSDAP. In the autumn of 1933 a Finnish journalist's delegation was invited to get acquainted with National Socialism, with the German Automobile Club acting as the formal host. The guests were also introduced to the headquarters of the NSDAP and a labor camp of the work front.[9]

The German Chamber of Commerce in Helsinki transmitted to Finland material from the information department acting under the rule of Germany's Ministry of Propaganda, and this material was published in various papers as articles, reports, and news as follows:[10] 372 in 1933; 578 in 1935; 240 in 1934; and 407 in 1936.

In addition to this, the information department sent material directly to the foreign branches of the NSDAP. Germany's representatives in Finland edited the received material with a view to Finnish circumstances. The material distributed to the papers dealt mainly with Germany's industrial life, trade policy, and technical achievements—the most blatant propaganda material was omitted. In 1935 and 1936 the main issue of foreign information from the Germany Ministry of Propaganda related to the Olympic Games.[11]

The Debate on the "Nazi Olympics," 1933–35

The central organization of Finland's Olympic sports, the SVUL, did not react at all to the change of power in Germany. The Finnish Olympic Committee observed the change equally quietly: both organizations made enthusiastic preparations for sending teams to the Winter Games in Garmisch-Partenkirchen and to the main event in Berlin. Because the decision to name the host nation for the 1940 Olympics was to be made in Berlin, many connections were established with the hosts of the German sports movement: in 1934 the Finnish Federation of Athletics signed agreements for engaging in track and field internationals; the Ball Games Federation also had a treaty for international competition with Germany. The Boxing Federation had a German Olympics coach, and the Ball Games Federation also employed one in the spring of 1936.[12] In 1934 a delegation of the excursions board of the Ministry of Education and the Office of School Travel went to Germany, also escorted by a representative of the Finnish Women's Federation of Physical Education (SNLL), which had decided to send a gymnastics team to Berlin with hundreds of women. The training of the team was described in several radio broadcasts in 1935 and 1936.[13] Representatives of the Skiing Federation visited Central Europe and Germany in the spring of 1935 and gave the SVUL's honorary certificate to J. Maier, the chairman of Germany's Skiing Federation.[14] The only time the leadership of the SVUL appeared to take note of the political nature of the German Olympics was toward the end of 1935. According to a note in the minutes of the federation's Executive Committee meeting on December 21: "A decision was made concerning a letter from journalist Bernard Heimann from Copenhagen received on November 7 in which he opposes participation in the Berlin Olympics because of the so-called Jewish question. It was decided that the letter be transferred to the Federation's archives."[15]

The hands of the TUL were tied regarding political questions since the state subsidies previously denied due to the federation's political activity were restored in 1934, after it had agreed not to engage in party politics.[16] The newspaper of the TUL did, however, enter the political debate around the Olympics of 1936, and the newspaper *Suomen Sosialidemokraatti* acted even more aggressively as the critical mouthpiece of the Left in regard to the Nazi Olympics. While the bourgeois sports organizations remained silent on the controversy concerning the Games, the sports magazines talked politics and took note, even if only casually, of the movements against the Olympics.

Soon after the Nazi accession to power, the Swedish-language sports journal *Idrottsbladet* published several articles presenting and supporting Nazi policy, some of them copied directly from German propaganda sources. The article that was published on April 20 under the heading "Olympic Dissonances" attacked the criticism of Nazi Germany by Swedish papers: "It is not our business, nor the business of the world at large, if Germany wants to carry out a spring-cleaning within its own borders. . . . The Germans' only desire is to keep their country for themselves."

In May of the same year the paper quoted the statement of Mr. Trossbach, a representative of the organization Reichsausschuss der Leibesübungen, according to whom the Jewish question was Germany's internal affair: if foreign Jews were to participate in the Olympics, they would be treated with respect. In

Trossbach's statement a new sports system, called Wehrsport, was presented, as was the reform of German sports based on this system. The *Idrottsbladet* also published a report on "Contemporary Germany," because again "the Swedish papers had published malicious propaganda against Germany." "For a long time the sacred fire had flamed in German hearts, only the leader was missing. He came—and he has won the heart of his people," proclaimed the story, which was decorated with a picture of Hitler, doubtless donated by the propaganda office.[17]

Later the paper described the sports of Fascist Italy with equal thoroughness—there were also four Finnish track and field coaches working in that country's universities. The major bourgeois sports paper, *Suomen Urheilulehti*, which was independent of any organization, had also written articles on sport in Fascist Italy, on the organization Opera Nazionale Dopolavoro, among others.[18]

In May 1933, *Urheilulehti* presented "the future of the new Germany's sports" by publishing a statement by von Tschammer und Osten, the sports commissar of the Reich, in which the "assimilationist program" of the new sports was described. Von Tschammer und Osten assured that freedom of action was guaranteed for the former athletic federations, although there might be some slight "limitations." Reorganization required cooperation and the finding of the right leaders for the right posts. The most important task for the near future was working on behalf of the Olympic Games. The chancellor of the Reich was doing all he could to create good foreign relations in the field of sports.[19]

International criticism of the Nazi Olympics came mainly from the leftist papers. When the United States cast doubt in the autumn of 1933 on its participation unless there were some guarantees concerning the safety of Jewish athletes, *Suomen Sosialidemokraatti* reported the issue and predicted that the Berlin Olympics would turn into a fiasco. In the autumn of 1933 the TUL paper accused the SVUL of collaboration with the Nazis.[20]

Suomen Urheilulehti paid attention first and foremost to the development of the German preparations for the Games, in terms of which it appeared that everything possible was being done to make the Games a success—even in the field of women's sports, which in Finland were undervalued. *Urheilulehti* encouraged the Finns to work industriously for the benefit of the Olympic participants, as it was after all a fact that "sports have had an invaluable impact on our position among other nations." The paper also took note of the political events in terms of the Olympics, first and foremost of the U.S. development, about which the paper was able, in the autumn of 1935, to state jubilantly: "Others are also for participation!"[21]

Early in 1935 information began to arrive from Germany on the results of the practical preparations. Finland's representative on the IOC, the director Lars Krogius, and the chairman of the Finnish Olympic Committee, K. Levälahti, had visited Germany to prepare the ground for Finland's application to host the Olympics of 1940. They used the occasion to acquaint themselves with the German preparations for the Olympics and found that they were "magnificent."[22]

For its part, the TUL paper published a derogatory article in the autumn of 1935 on Germany, claiming that "all of the ideals of humanity, freedom, and peace were trodden" underfoot. The holding of the Games in Germany was the "Trojan horse of political ideas." The Chairman of the SVUL had encouraged working-class athletes to enter the Games as well—at the same time that their own costumes, flags, and songs were forbidden in Finland.[23]

Prior to the Winter Games *Sosialidemokraatti* and the left-wing cultural political publication *Tulenkantajat* presented a booklet, made famous by Reuter's news agency, that had been written for German sports organizations for political education. According to the booklet, sports were a school for political will, and it explained the Nazi doctrines of blood, race, Jews, and Catholics. "Apolitical, that is to say impartial athletes, are an impossibility in Hitler's Reich," the booklet proclaimed. It also denounced the booklet of the U.S. Fair-Play Committee, in which it was pointed out that the Germans had severely breached the Olympic peace.[24] *Tulenkantajat* also reflected on the racial question in the coming Games and discussed boycott plans. *Sosialidemokraatti* emphasized first and foremost the debates and expressions of opinion in Sweden, particularly among the Swedish workers' movement.[25]

No serious movements were created in Finland to oppose the Olympics: the left wing and its few newspapers were the only ones to protest or to criticize the Finns' enthusiasm to take part.

The Winter Games

Finland sent sixteen cross-country skiers, a military patrol team of seven men, and six skaters to the Winter Games. They left on January 29, "January Sunday," the anniversary of the beginning of the Liberation War in Finland in 1918, as *Suomen Urheilulehti* wrote. The advance information boasted handsome preparations and quality premises for sports and accommodation. *Suomen Urheilulehti* used a great deal of space to describe them, as well as the other preparations. *Helsingin Sanomat*—a publication of the Progressive party—also reported extensively on the preparations for the Games, at the same time advertising its own future reporting during the Olympic year. The paper also published the greetings for the Olympic year signed by Theodor Lewald and the president of the German Olympic Committee, Hans von Tschammer und Osten.[26]

In Garmisch-Partenkirchen the Finnish leaders had several meetings with Germany's sports leaders and during the competitions informed themselves about the interests of the German audience. As the national anthem sounded, the audience made the Hitler salute, with Hitler and his staff in attendance at the opening ceremonies: Hitler declared the Games opened and during the parade the German team, with its hundred competitors, was led by von Tschammer und Osten, to the cheers of the spectators. The most enthusiastic receptions were for those who gave the so-called Olympic salute, which was a slightly modified Nazi salute. The Finnish team was not cheered very much because they did not make the salute, unlike the French team, who followed Finland and received a resounding ovation from the crowd. *Helsingin Sanomat,* which devoted a lot of space to the occasion, mentioned only "a salute."[27] Willy Bogner, who swore the Olympic oath, did so only after having saluted the swastika flag, which he held with his left hand. *Helsingin Sanomat* published the oath in full, describing how the Olympic flame burned "to promulgate the holy Olympic peace for the world." According to the paper the audience rushed to the tribune of honor after the ceremonies, demanding that Hitler appear; joy and applause followed him wherever he appeared in the festive city. Critical comments in the paper were relegated to short stories and in some cartoons by "Tiger," who published a series of "Olympic letters to my cur," where, for example, he made fun of the saluting at the opening ceremony.[28]

The reports from the Games themselves were widely carried in *Helsingin Sanomat,* and Finnish success in the skiing sports was well publicized. The highest German military leadership attended the military patrol skiing event, and they greeted the members of the Finnish team, who came in second, with handshakes. The closing ceremonies of the Games were attended by Hitler, Göring, and Goebbels—in other words, the German state and political leadership took part in the organization and in the events in a greater capacity than had been customary at any preceding Games. *Suomen Sosialidemokraatti* commented on this: "The German Olympic Committee, as well as the organizers, represent the powers who also vanquished democracy."[29]

After the Winter Games *Soihtu,* published by left-wing students, demanded that the athletes, not merely the worker athletes but also those bourgeois athletes who were against fascism, form a strong movement in Finland against the Nazi Olympics. This demand was written before the German army reoccupied the Rhineland. At the same time, *Sosialidemokraatti* began to inform its readership about the boycott movements and later about the "anti-Olympics" to be arranged in Madrid (in fact, Barcelona) in July. The paper stated that the Social Democrat Society in Stockholm was boycotting the Berlin Olympics due to the gigantic trial in Wuppertal against over six hundred organized workers, and that the Socialist Worker Sport International was boycotting both the Olympic Games and the congresses arranged in connection with them. The paper also reported on the boycott movements in France, Holland, Denmark, and other countries.[30]

Courting the Hosts

Finland was anxious to secure the position of host for the Olympic Games of 1940. Japan, the closest competitor, had launched a massive propaganda operation to get the Olympics, and the Finns got to work straight after the Winter Games: a constitutive meeting of a propaganda committee was held on February 16, 1936. The principle adopted was to have as large a representation in Berlin as possible.

Secondly, the Finns agreed to do all that was in their power to create good relations with Germany and its aims for the Berlin Games. The committee arranged a meeting with Finnish journalists on April 3, urging them to act "as regards the Olympics, in a proper manner and to avoid making headlines of any news that could endanger Finland's prospects of having the Olympics."[31]

In June 1936 Baillet-Latour and Lewald were invited to Finland to inspect the planned Games premises as well as to lay the foundation stone of Helsinki's future stadium. The president of the IOC considered Finland's chances to be good, but Lewald talked only about the Berlin Olympics.[32]

It was typical of the situation that the propaganda committee called an emergency meeting when it turned out that there was not going to be a Finnish football team in Berlin—it was, after all, intended to have as large a representation in the Games as possible; besides, the team had had a German coach for four months! The chairman of the Finnish Olympic Committee had already stressed the importance of "even the most minute things" to do with public relations, such as the Finnish success at the Finnish-German track and field international in the autumn of 1935.[33]

As if on command, *Suomen Urheilulehti* published an article of obviously German origin on April 16, entitled "How the Capital of Berlin Receives the Olympic Guests." The article concluded: "It is our sincere wish that our foreign friends take back with them a favourable impression of the new Germany and the capital of the 'Third Reich' when they return to their own countries." In July the Coalition party's *Aamulehti* published a report by the secretary of the German Organizing Committee, Carl Diem, on the cultural side of the Berlin Games, involving among other things a youth convention, a sports pedagogic convention, theater, music, and science; Diem compared the Berlin Olympics to those held in ancient Greece. The paper also familiarized its readership with Berlin's economic life, architecture, and even Frederick the Great.[34] The papers blamed criticism of the Games on the Communists and attacked the TUL and the left-wing papers, accusing them of isolationism and slander against the Olympics.[35]

Nevertheless, Martti Jukola, the chief editor of *Urheilulehti* as well as a radio commentator, reflected in his newspaper report prior to the Games that "all of the advance fuss about the preparations in Berlin is motivated by plain marketing and underlined the German advertising skill." He also said that the Third Reich had worked hard to get along with the press, which was snowed under with invitations to dinners, concerts, and excursions hosted by Göring, Hitler, and others. Herr Stortz, a journalist representing the *Völkischer Beobachter*, who visited Finland in July, acknowledged that the Berlin Olympics went beyond merely Olympic matters so that the world at large would receive the correct picture of the circumstances in Germany. The poster of the Olympic torch relay of late July 1936—which the Coalition party's paper *Uusi Suomi* commented on daily—was condemned by *Suomen Sosialidemokraatti* because the borders in the poster had been changed.[36]

Finnish organizations sent observers before the Games to inspect the general arrangements, particularly in regard to publicity, gymnastics, swimming, and football. In their reports attention was directed to the excellent organization, impressive technical preparedness, and equipment. Expenditure on publicity was estimated to break all records, but in Finland such expenses would not be called for. The military forces were in charge of information and transportation during the Games. The representative of the Gymnastics Federation was guided by W. Dick, the head of the National Socialist newspaper office; he had agreed on a Finnish-German gymnastics international in 1937 with Martin Schneider, the Reichsturnwart, and visited a National Socialist gymnasium for boys, among others. At the Düsseldorf Stadium he had noticed a sign: "No admittance for Jews." The representative of the Swimming Federation reported on the excellent preparations and the huge size of the swimming stadium (during the last day of the competitions, when Hitler was in the audience, there were twenty-five thousand spectators).[37]

The Summer Games

The main event, the Summer Olympics, was reported extensively by the Finnish press. Several papers sent correspondents, some as many as five, to Berlin.[38] The most enthusiastic papers devoted three to four pages to the Olympics every day during the week of track and field competition, which was of greatest importance for the Finns; much space was given to accurate reports, results, interviews, descriptions of competitions, commentaries, news, and descriptions of "the American Negroes."

The largest paper, *Helsingin Sanomat*, sent five commentators to Berlin, some as early as mid-July. The services, premises, and decorations were described, as was the ultramodern technology and the awe-inspiring magnificence of the stadium: Berlin surpassed all the previous Olympics in terms of internal order and external splendor. The paper's most critical comment was made by a writer with the pseudonym Clever; his article pondered what was going to happen after the magnificence of the Games. After the successful Winter Games, he mused, Germany demanded the Rhineland back—it was interesting to think what would be happening in two months' time: "Can the Olympic ideal of peace pacify the hosts, who keep saluting themselves, crying 'Heil!' all the time?"[39]

The home press and radio accompanied the Finnish team to the harbor, but the German afternoon papers took no notice of the Finnish team's arrival in Germany; nevertheless, the reception was hearty. The Olympic Village had already been described in the papers; the radio described it once more in its own report. It was described as pleasant, the rooms were nice, and even a Finnish sauna, complete with a Finnish sauna oven, had been situated by the Village pond. Every athlete was given a "Hitler Jugend" messenger. Göring, the minister of the Reich, conducted a "bunk inspection." The women's Olympic Village, which somewhat overawed the women gymnasts, was described with its beauty parlors and gymnasia.[40]

Before the opening ceremonies, however, the Finns suffered a bitter defeat: the Olympic Games of 1940, which they had expected to win as recognition of "the sporting people of Finland," were voted by a narrow majority (32 to 27) to be held in Tokyo. All of the papers considered this a political decision. "Power goes before justice," proclaimed the Coalition party's *Aamulehti. Uusi Suomi,* another Coalition paper, published an editorial under the heading "The XI Olympic Games": "Germany had done all it can in arranging the Olympics. However, the magnificence of the Games does not bring joy to those who 'cherish sporting values.' For this reason it would have been fitting that a country appreciating the athletic values of the Games would have been chosen as the next host."

The paper also criticized the fact that the Games had been given to a great power for the third time in a row. It assumed that Tokyo had won because of the many proxies it had received; however, a large number of nations had supported Finland. The transfer of the Olympics to Tokyo could spell the end for the Olympic Games, concluded the paper.[41]

Finland's defeat by Tokyo signified a turn in its attitude toward the Games and their host country. The decision was seen as political play of the great powers, in which the sporting merits of small countries did not amount to much. The disappointment was especially bitter as regards Germany, which was supposed to have supported the Finns. When the Games were lost and there was no further need for self-censorship in this sense, even the bourgeois papers began to observe the events in a more critical vein.

As the competition proceeded, the representatives of the "sporting people" were shocked by the large German audience's lack of sporting knowledge, looking after the pennies and giving applause according to political sympathies. The first disappointment was experienced during the opening ceremonies. When the competitors marched into the stadium, as at the Winter Games, the most enthusiastic applause was given to those teams that made the so-called Olympic salute. Finland's team did not consent to make it and was applauded only mildly, whereas the French team, which followed Finland, received an uproarious welcome, appearing to have made the Hitler salute. All the bourgeois papers reacted irritably to the events, as they did to the chauvinist behaviour of the audience and the propaganda ceremonies and talks arranged in the middle of competitions.[42]

The local Coalition paper, *Karjala,* published an article under the heading "Athletic Disappointment," of which *Suomen Sosialidemokraatti* made a summary: "The Hitler salute decided even the athletic value of nations in the eyes of hundreds of thousands of German spectators." *Sosialidemokraatti* itself stated that the Games had begun with a universal cry of "'Heil Hitler!' and the raising of arms to the skies."[43]

Also *Maakansa,* of the Agrarian party, expressed its disappointment by stating that the German propaganda offices provided the foreign papers with a lot of material under the pretense of "Olympic advertising," material that in fact had nothing to do with the Olympics—they were blatant advertisements about the circumstances and achievements of the Third Reich. According to the paper, this "Nazi advertising" had been just as glaringly obvious during the Winter Games. "It must unfortunately be stated that the Nazis have subjected even sports to a propaganda instrument of their ideals." The paper considered Tokyo to be a political choice. *Helsingin Sanomat*, which quoted the *Maakansa* article, seemed to act somewhat hypocritically: while it claimed to maintain a neutral attitude, it perpetually criticized the left wing for their criticism of the Games.

According to *Helsingin Sanomat*, Germany aroused justified indignation in choosing Tokyo as Germany had "obviously been acting on behalf of Japan all along"; great power politics had to be the explanation. "This German action has hardened the Finns in regard to German propaganda in Finland."[44]

The Competition

Like other countries, the Finns were most interested in the success of their own competitors at the Games: the country had, after all, performed exceptionally well ever since Stockholm. The first week into the Games proved to be the most important, as it was then that the track and field events were held. The first day of the Games brought Finland a triple victory in the 10,000 meter run and a silver medal in shot put—*Sosialidemokraatti* reminded those who were impressed by the rise of "new talents" from the bourgeois sport circles that both Askola (silver medal), Iso-Hollo (bronze), and the silver medalist in the shot put (Bärlund) were bought from the TUL.[45]

The expected gold medal in javelin went in the end to the German Stöck; *Suomen Urheilulehti* announced: "The Finns Best in Javelin—Stöck Won!" According to Finnish papers this was due to the presence of the Führer, who seemed to have a magical effect on German athletes; he "reigned over his army of athletes through some mysterious power from his seat in the tribune of honor." Hitler made his presence felt in many other ways: "Hitler, Göring, and Goebbels congratulated Iso-Hollo," *Aamulehti* wrote on August 9. Hitler had invited Volmari Iso-Hollo, the champion of 3,000 meter steeple chase, and Alfred Dompert, the German athlete who came in third, to the VIP room, "where he offered his guests coffee and beer and kept saying 'Wunderschön, wunderschön.'"[46]

The most jubilant reports from Berlin were provided by the women of the Finnish Women's Physical Education Association, which boasted a team of two hundred members. They had prepared gymnastic and folk-dance programs; they also had a ten-member hiking team. In Berlin they had the opportunity to perform in the folk gymnastics and dances, which the Games program included. Also performing were the teams from the Nazi cultural organization Kraft durch Freude, as well as the unemployed people of the Arbeitsdienst organization.[47]

The Finnish women's trip was funded by the Ministry of Education and their own Olympic fundraising. The association's paper, *Kisakenttä,* reported their travel experiences in the form of a diary and reports. On August 6 the women successfully performed their gymnastics program in the stadium. Their team was invited on August 13 to meet Goebbels, the minister of propaganda, and, later during the same day, Hitler. Goebbels made a big impression on the women, but they were even more stunned by the magical personality of Hitler. On meeting Hitler the women made the Hitler salute, which the Finns had refused to do in the opening ceremony. Hitler and Goebbels had their pictures taken, surrounded by the women, and served them coffee. The journalist from *Kisakenttä,* using the pseudonym Pikkutohtori, wrote about the occasion: "In our country there is much talk about the ridiculous Hitler worship. But let me tell you, once you have spent half an hour under the same roof as this man, you can clearly sense that his genius has created something unified, big, and powerful, which you cannot but respect."[48] The experiences of the women were also described in a book for girls published a couple of years later, *The Olympic Girl,* a somewhat more critical story about a gymnast girl's trip to the Olympic city.[49]

In 1937 the association was invited to appear in a folk dance festival arranged by the organization Kraft durch Freude through June 9 to 13. The trip by the group of forty dancers became in the end a tour of nearly two weeks.[50]

In its editorial on August 11, 1936, *Helsingin Sanomat* assessed the Berlin Olympics as the most enormous in the history of sports in terms of the wide range of the programs, their balance, and the level of results. The Finns had done their best in all senses. An immense machinery underpinned the organization, and it was natural that the host country should utilize its position to advertise its achievements: "Those who have criticized the circumstances in Germany have also been against the Games, similarly some extremist circles have tried to make use of the situation. Needless to say, the Finns were never interested in any of the above; their main interest has been the sport." Koukku, the columnist of the paper, wrote about the overorganization of the Games and noted that Germany would have received enough attention even with less propaganda. Koukku remembered a time when propaganda praising the host country had been a secondary matter at the Olympics.[51] The *Helsingin Sanomat* article also attacked *Sosialidemokraatti,* which had accused the paper of taking to heart the defense of Nazi Germany and being "saturated with repugnant scribbles about Berlin and defense of the criticism of Nazi Germany."[52]

The extreme-right newspaper *Ajan Suunta* praised the excellent order that was characteristic of the Berlin Games but criticized the German audience's lack of sports knowledge. It also encouraged the vigorous "popularization" of Finnish sports along the lines of the German model. The extreme elements, Reds and Jews, had attempted to make the Games into stump games, fortunately to no avail.[53]

Even Martti Jukola of *Suomen Urheilulehti* wrote some words of criticism: "Never before have the Games been carried out with such enthusiasm, ecstasy, and mass hysteria—the perpetual Hitler salutes are beginning to strain the arm."

Jukola remarked, too, that the Olympic Games in Los Angeles had also been well organized, large, and handsome; but Los Angeles was far away, and the European papers went over the top in regard to the German Olympics. He also said that if he were a political propagandist, he would write with even greater joy if and when the Germans pushed the Bolshevik borders far into the East, but he was just a sports journalist and had to stick to sports.[54] The commentator for *TUL* regarded the Games as "a tragicomic farce, and not even the symphony of Finnish enthusiasm had resounded without dissonant voices. Even Mr. Jukola had so much fun among the swastika flags, *Horst Wessel* hymns, and Fascist salutes that he was unable not to reveal his true colors, proclaiming in his paper: 'We have never experienced the new and stirring national spirit of today's Germany. This spirit has lifted Germany to a new high.'"[55]

TUL called the Olympics "the Potemkin villages" that were used to cover up Germany's economic problems, to which the military-industrial complex brought temporary aid. The paper claimed that the Berlin display windows would be emptied of goods after the Games. The left-wing *Tulenkantajat* was happy to comment that the Finnish athletes had refused to be exploited by Nazi propaganda. The paper was also satisfied with the final statement of Urho Kekkonen, the chairman of Finland's Track and Field Federation, when he judged the Games to have been unsportsmanlike. The paper also stated that the Olympic fire had been used to kindle the new smelting furnace of Krupp's gun factory in Essen.[56]

The summary made by the German propaganda office of the Finnish press during the Berlin Games[57] is correct on some points, while on others it is selective and/or decorative. The space given to the Games was not "the major portion of the pages" (with the exception of the small right-wing paper *Uusimaa*); the papers did write a lot about the Games, but this had been the case with previous Olympic Games as well. What was exceptional was the amount of space used to describe the circumstances of the host country, the material for which was provided by the host country itself, and which was obviously affected by Finland's willingness to influence Germany's stand in terms of the choice of the future host of the 1940 Olympic Games.

The representative of the liberal tradition, *Helsingin Sanomat*, was acknowledged for its positive attitude toward the German Olympics—as was the Swedish-language major paper *Hufvudstadsbladet*—although it had shared the view that there was too much Nazi propaganda in the Games.

Criticism, writing about the darker side of the Games, was left to the left-wing papers before the Olympics. According to the German press report, "the Marxist press utilized the occasion to disparage the Games and to attack Germany." The report acknowledged that there had been other criticism as well: the press had criticized the unsportsmanlike attitude of the German public, picking out as an example the German javelin thrower Stöck, whom "the Germans had cheered more than the Finns, who had not thrown the javelin as well as him."

The turning point in the reporting was the loss of the 1940 Olympics to Tokyo. The difference between reporting the Winter Games and the Summer Games is clearly discernible. During the Winter Games even the most blatant propaganda was swallowed, but during the Summer Games the equally obvious Nazi intrusions were criticized when they were mixed with "pure sports." The German report stated that the choice of Tokyo had had a *verstimmend* (dissonant) effect on the Finns' writing—it stated with indignation that, despite the secret ballot, the Finnish papers had been told that Germany had supported Japan. According to the report, the other reason for dissatisfaction was Finland's moderate success in the Games—even the country's hostility toward women's sports is mentioned, because in this regard the German women were quite successful.

Conclusion

The Finns were (and are) a sporting people, and already in the 1920s and 1930s there was a very large and expert sports public in the country. It is likely that the self-esteem of the geographically small but sport-savvy country was strained on the European fields while the "Great Powers" were taking care of their reputations and solving their riddles at the expense of "pure sport." The nearsighted political maneuvering and naiveté also bore bitter fruit.

Vesa Vares shows in his research about the leading Finnish newspapers' relationship to Nazi Germany that the political attitudes of the Finnish press toward Germany were most critical and confrontational at the end of 1934; after that, and especially after 1936, Germany's position as a foreign-policy reality became the most important factor, and Germany's internal issues were left aside. It was mainly the leftist papers that went on with criticism of the internal developments in the country.[58]

This is not borne out by the attitude of the press to the Nazi Olympics: the political Right and the liberal press wrote positively about the host of the 1936 Olympics—the borderline runs exactly between right and left. The leftist papers are, in this as elsewhere, the only critics. Thus in the frame of "pure sport" the Nazi Olympics with their huge Third Reich propaganda backing made a clear exception compared with other writing about Germany in the Finnish press. The turning point is June 1936; Germany's vote for Japan was an early landmark of the imminent pact between the two states. The Nazis, in many ways, had been successful in using sport and the Olympic Games as "The Trojan horse of political ideas."

Notes

I am grateful to proseminar students in the Department of History at the University of Tampere who contributed to this chapter: Jari Aronen, Sinikka Aura, Sari Heiskanen, Markus Henriksson, Nina Ignatius, Mikko Hetemaa, and Kristiina Vanhala. The papers they wrote as well as the newspaper articles, radio recordings, and archive material they collected were invaluable in writing this chapter. I also wish to express my thanks to the Department of History for providing funds for a research trip and for the translation.

The following newspapers and sports journals were examined during research for this chapter: *Suomen Urheilulehti* (Finland's sports journal, independent); *TUL* (Workers' Sports Federation); *Kisakenttä* (Finnish Women's Physical Education Association); *Idrottsbladet* (independent Swedish-language sports journal); *Ajan Suunta* (IKL, Patriotic Popular Movement party); *Uusimaa* (IKL, local); *Uusi Suomi* (the Coalition party); *Aamulehti* (the Coalition party, local); *Helsingin Sanomat* (National Progressive party/liberal); *Suomen Sosialidemokraatti* (the Social Democratic party); *Tulenkantajat* (left-wing culture and politics); and *Soihtu* (leftist students).

1. See R. Häyrinen and L. Laine, "Suomi urheilun suurvaltana" (Finland as a great power of sport), *Liikuntatieteellisen Seuran julkaisuja* 115 (1989): 305–24. For the Nurmi issue, see U. Hamilton, "The Paavo Nurmi Issue: A Matter of Class and Nationality," in *Transformations: Continuity and Change II*, ed. A. Krüger and W. Buss (Hoya: NISH, 2002), 188–94.

2. See L. Laine, "Vapaaehtoisten järjestöjen kehitys ruumiinkulttuurin alueella Suomessa v. 1856–1917 II" (The development of voluntary organizations in the area of physical culture in Finland, 1856–1917 II), *Liikuntatieteellisen Seuran julkaisuja* 93.B (1984): 365–67.

3. R. Häyrinen and L. Laine, "Suomi urheilun suurvaltana," 84–116; S. Hentilä, *Työväen urheiluliikkeen hi I: Työväen Urheiluliitto, 1919–1944,* vol. 1 (The history of the Finnish worker sports movement: The Worker Sports Federation, 1919–1944) (Hämeenlinna: Karisto, 1982), 311–47. See also L. Laine, "TUL: The Finnish Worker Sports Movement," in *The Story of Worker Sport*, ed. A. Krüger and J. Riordan (Champaign, Ill.: Human Kinetics, 1996), 67–80.

4. R. Häyrinen and L. Laine, "Suomi urheilun suurvaltana," 150–54, 233–55.

5. Ibid., 26–29.

6. Britta Hiedanniemi, *Kulttuuriin verhottua politiikkaa: Kansallissosialistisen Saksan kulttuuripropaganda Suomessa, 1933–1940* (Politics wrapped in culture: The culture propaganda of National Socialist Germany in Finland, 1933–1940) (Helsingissä: Otava, 1980), 42.

7. Ibid., 43.

8. Ibid., 45.

9. Ibid., 45.

10. Ibid., 103.

11. Ibid., 104–6.

12. A. Halila and P. Sirmeikkö, *Suomen Voimistelu: ja Urheiluliitto (SVUL), 1900–1960* (The Finnish Gymnastics and Sports Federation, 1900–1960) (Helsinki: SVUL, 1960), 377; *The Finnish Ball Games Federation, Executive Committee, Minutes* (Helsinki: Finnish Sports Archives, Apr. 9, 1935, spring 1936, esp. Feb. 8, 1936); *Suomen Urheilulehti,* Jan. 2, 1936. The major part of the archives of the Finnish Olympic Committee from the 1930s was destroyed by a fire.

13. *The Annual Report of the Finnish Women's Physical Education Association, 1934* (Helsinki: Finnish Sports Archives, 1935), 10; *The Annual Report of the Finnish Women's Physical Education Association, 1935* (Helsinki: Finnish Sports Archives, 1936), 4–8; *The Annual Report of the Finnish Women's Physical Education Association, 1936* (Helsinki: Finnish Sports Archives, 1937), 9.

14. *Finnish Sports and Gymnastics Federation, Executive Committee of the Council, Minutes* (Helsinki: Finnish Sports Archives, Apr. 17, 1935).

15. *The Finnish Gymnastics and Sports Federation, Executive Committee of the Council, Minutes* (Helsinki: Finnish Sports Archives, Dec. 21, 1935).

16. S. Hentilä, *Suomen työläisurheiluliikkeen historia*, vol. 1 (Hämeen Linna: Karisto, 1982), 351.

17. *Idrottsbladet,* Apr. 20, 1933, by the columnist Teutonia; *Idrottsbladet,* (May 4 and 11, 1933), under the pseudonym "Resenär."

18. *Idrottsbladet,* May 15, May 31, and June 14, 1934; *Suomen Urheilulehti,* Apr. 2, 1930.

19. *Suomen Urheilulehti,* May 18, 1933.

20. *Suomen Sosialidemokraatti,* Nov. 24, 1933; *TUL,* Dec. 31, 1933. See also *TUL,* Jan. 12, 1934.

21. *Suomen Urheilulehti*, Jan. 21, Mar. 21, June 25, and Apr. 29, 1935. On the political debate, see *Suomen Urheilulehti*, Nov. 25, 1935. See also *Suomen Urheilulehti*, Jan. 31, Sept. 19, and Dec. 30, 1935.

22. *Helsingin Sanomat*, Feb. 15, 1935.

23. *TUL*, Sept. 10, 1935, written by the former TUL secretary W. J. Kostiainen. The writer refers to the 1934 laws that denied political agitation and the use of political symbols and clothing in public in order to hamper possible clashes between the extremist groups; the political situation in the country was still unsteady after the right-wing extremists' rebellion attempt in 1932. See also Hentilä, *Suomen työläisurheiluliikkeen historia*, vol. 1, 322–25.

24. *Suomen Sosialidemokraatti*, Jan. 8, 1936; "Don't Go to the Berlin Olympics!" *Tulenkantajat*, May 23, 1936

25. "Germany Favors Blonds," *Tulenkantajat*, Mar. 12, 1935, 49; *Tulenkantajat*, Jan. 13, 1936, 21; *Suomen Sosialidemokraatti*, Jan. 16, 1936.

26. *Suomen Urheilulehti*, Jan. 9, 13, 20, 24, 27, 30, and Feb. 6, 1936. Some writers were Germans, like Lisa Gross (Feb. 6), who wrote about women's skating in the Garmisch-Partenkirchen Olympic program and demanded that a successful young Finnish girl, Verne Lesche (second at the First Women's World Championships in skating in January 1936), be sent to the Olympics (*Helsingin Sanomat* also published her article on Jan. 24, 1936). Käte Brauchel-Essen described the Olympic town and surroundings in "Olympic Guests: Welcome!" *Suomen Urheilulehti*, Jan. 27, 1936. See also *Helsingin Sanomat*, Jan. 1, 3, 8, 9, 28, and 29, 1936. On Jan. 30, 1936, *Helsingin Sanomat* described the site for the Summer Games under the title "Olympic Fields in Berlin Will Soon Be Ready."

27. See *Helsingin Sanomat*, Feb. 1, 1936, for the Finnish team leaders visiting von Halt and for von Tschammer und Osten's speech and *Helsingin Sanomat*, Feb. 2, 3, and 4, 1936, for von Tschammer und Osten's invitation to Finnish leaders to a beer and sausage evening. See also *Helsingin Sanomat*, Feb. 6, 1936.

28. See *Helsingin Sanomat*, Feb. 7, 1936, for the opening day report. *Helsingin Sanomat* published a photo of Hitler opening the Games (Feb. 10, 1936). The "Tiger" cartoon is in *Helsingin Sanomat*, Feb. 11, 1936. The conservative paper *Aamulehti* also described the opening ceremony (Feb. 7, 1936), and in later articles the presence of the Führer was carefully reported.

29. *Helsingin Sanomat*, Feb. 10, 11, and 12, 1936 ("the best Winter Games ever organized"); ibid., Feb. 15 and 17, 1936 (closing day report); *Suomen Urheilulehti* (issued every day during the Games), Feb. 10, 1936 ("Letter of Olympic Travel" and Hitler congratulating the winners in the alpine combined); ibid., Feb. 11, 1936 (Finns' day); ibid., Feb. 12, 13, and 14, 1936 (a bitter comment on the audience, which was more attracted by the Führer than by sport); ibid., Feb. 15, 1936 (report on patrol skiing, in which Finland lost to Italy by .14 seconds and German military leaders were present to congratulate the best patrols); ibid., Feb. 16, 1936 (the day of the Swedes); ibid., Feb. 17, 1936 (closing ceremonies, at which the presence of political and military Nazi elite is described in detail; *Suomen Sosialidemokraatti*, Febr. 7, 1936 (Hitler saluting the state flags by "raising his hand").

30. *Soihtu*, Mar. 2, 1936; *Suomen Sosialidemokraatti*, Jan. 1 and May 27, 1936. For boycott attempts in other countries, see *Suomen Sosialidemokraatti*, Mar. 11 and 21 (France), Mar. 22 (Denmark), Mar. 31 (Sweden, France), May 18 (Holland), May 27 (Denmark), and June 27, 1936 (Holland).

31. *The Committee of Olympic Propaganda, Minutes* (Helsinki: Finnish Sports Archives, Mar. 31, 1936), the Collection of J. W. Rangell, Olympic Museum, Helsinki.

32. Ibid.; *Helsingin Sanomat*, June 4, 9, and 10, 1936.

33. *Committee of Olympic Propaganda, Minutes* (Helsinki: Finnish Sports Archives, July 9, 1936); *The Finnish Football Federation, Minutes* (Helsinki: Finnish Sports Archives, spring 1936); *Helsingin Sanomat*, Sept. 28, 1935.

34. *Suomen Urheilulehti*, Apr. 16, 1936; *Aamulehti*, July 15, 1936: Carl Diem; *Aamulehti*, July 19 and 25, 1936. The paper published some long reports during the Games—e.g., Aug. 6, 9, and 16, 1936.

35. For examples of critics in leftist papers, see *Aamulehti*, July 10 and Aug. 5, 1936. See also the local Coalition party paper *Karjala*, May 27, 1936.

36. *Suomen Urheilulehti,* July 30, 1936; *Suomen Sosialidemokraatti,* July 9 and 30, 1936.

37. The Archives of the Finnish Gymnastics and Sports Federation, *Papers Related to Olympic Games: Berlin, 1936* (Helsinki: Finnish Sports Archives, 1936). The reports were written after the Games.

38. See the list of papers consulted. See also V. Vares, *Hakaristin kuva: Kansallissosialistinen Saksa Suomen johtavassa puoluelehdistössä sisä-ja ulkopoliittisena tekijänä, 1933–1939* (The symbol of the swastika: National-Socialist Germany in the leading Finnish party press as an internal policy and a foreign-policy factor in 1933–1939) (Turku: Turun yliopisto, 1986).

39. *Helsingin Sanomat,* July 18, 1936.

40. *Aamulehti,* July 29, 1936; *Uusimaa,* July 30, 1936. The tape recording is in the Archives of the Finnish Broadcasting Corporation, tape rec. nos. 217–218 (July 28, 1936).

41. *Aamulehti,* Aug. 1, 1936; *Uusi Suomi,* Aug. 1, 1936.

42. *Aamulehti,* Aug. 2, 1936; *Uusi Suomi,* Aug. 14, 1936; *Suomen Urheilulehti,* Aug. 2, 1936.

43. *Suomen Sosialidemokraatti,* Aug. 4, 1936.

44. *Helsingin Sanomat,* Aug. 5, 1936 (the *Maakansa* article). For comments about *Helsingin Sanomat*'s attitude, see *Suomen Sosialidemokraatti,* Aug. 9, 1936. The minor criticism by *Helsingin Sanomat* was hidden in "chatty lines," as was done during the Winter Games (Aug. 11, 1936).

45. *Suomen Sosialidemokraatti,* Aug. 4, 1936.

46. *Suomen Urheilulehti,* Aug. 7, 1936; *Aamulehti,* Aug. 7, 1936.

47. *The Annual Report of The Finnish Women's Physical Education Association, 1936* (Helsinki: Finnish Sports Archives, 1937), 9–10.

48. Ibid., 8, 16.; *Kisakenttä,* Aug. 11, 1936 ("A Sports Letter from Berlin," written in May 1936); *Kisakenttä,* Aug. 11, 1936 ("With the Women's Olympic Team in Berlin" and "Once upon a Time There Were Olympic Games").

49. A. Kivi, *Olympialaistyttö* (The Olympic girl) (Helsinki: Kivi, 1948).

50. *The Annual Report of the Finnish Women's Physical Education Association, 1937* (Helsinki: Finnish Sport Archives, 1938), 10–11.

51. *Helsingin Sanomat,* Aug. 6, 1936.

52. *Helsingin Sanomat,* Aug. 11, 1936; reply to *Suomen Sosialidemokraatti,* Aug. 9, 1936.

53. *Ajan Suunta,* Aug. 10 and 17, 1936.

54. *Suomen Urheilulehti,* Aug. 12 and 15, 1936.

55. *TUL,* Sept. 15, 1936.

56. *Tulenkantajat,* Aug. 15, 1936.

57. "Die Berliner Olympiade in der Finnischen Presse," in *Die Olympiade Berlin 1936 im Spiegel der ausländischen Press,* ed. J. Bellers (Münster: Lit, 1986), 45–50.

58. Vares, "Hakaristin kuva."

CHAPTER 8

Sweden:
Business as Usual

Lars-Olof Welander

During the first decades of the twentieth century Sweden was rapidly transformed from a mainly rural country to a modern industrialized society based on a considerable export trade.[1] As a result, Sweden, like other industrialized nations, was hit hard by the depression of the early 1930s, but unlike most of them it came out of the crisis in the mid-1930s and progressed steadily, through its expanding social democratic government. Unlike the other Scandinavian countries Sweden was not a belligerent in the Second World War, and as a result it has in some ways continued to replay the debates concerning its association with Nazi Germany that had characterized its attitude to taking part in the 1936 Olympics.

Sport in Sweden

The dominant influence in the early development of Swedish sport was the interest in gymnastics initiated by Per Henrik Ling. Between the wars there was a rapid growth in the number of active members in the various athletic clubs, particularly in the 1930s.[2] In 1934 there were 3,677 clubs with 270,000 members, but only five years later, in 1939, these figures had increased to 5,790 and 390,000, respectively. This increase represented a growing popular interest in sport,[3] which continued in an essentially amateur way. This was a genuine amateurism, which bore little resemblance to the control of sport in Nazi Germany, but sport in Sweden did receive much help from the state. The year after its successful organization of the 1912 Olympics, a permanent Olympic Committee was set up to organize Sweden's participation in future Games. Annual grants were given to sports clubs by the government after 1914, and by 1939 the Swedish

Sports Federation (RF), which governed sport throughout most of the country, was responsible for distributing the state grants to its various members.

In spite of their dependence on government grants, sports clubs retained their independence. The attitude toward sports among the political parties fluctuated during the twentieth century, but by the mid-1930s the dominant political power —the Social Democratic party—had accepted sport as one of the essential factors in Swedish popular movements. The broader social basis of sports was an important factor in this process. Traditionally, Sweden has been strong in winter sports. The 1912 Olympic Games in Stockholm, where Sweden was the most successful nation, resulted in an international breakthrough that was followed by further success thereafter. During the interwar period the Anglo-Saxon influence on Swedish sports was considerable, adding to the variety of Swedish sports, which has always been one of its strengths. Traditionally, Sweden had had great success in track and field, wrestling, riding, modern pentathlon, and other "military" sports, but also in canoeing, swimming, sailing, and boxing. At the time of the 1936 Olympic Games a well-organized Swedish sports movement was prepared to send the strongest possible teams to Garmisch-Partenkirchen and Berlin.

The Swedish government showed a benevolent attitude and granted S.Kr 338,000 for the Olympic preparations. The public interest in sports and the Olympic Games was supported by a relatively developed sports journalism, especially in the big-city papers. When Hitler came to power, Swedish sporting contacts with the new Reich actually increased, and this led to opposition from the political Left and the trade union movement. Boycott actions against German goods were instigated and became a lively issue at the time of the Olympic Games.

Enter Politics

After World War I, Germany and its allies were banned from international competition in most sports. Germany was not allowed to take part in Olympic competition again until 1928, as the French and British influence in the IOC was sufficiently strong to exclude Germany until the signing of the Locarno Treaty in 1925, which accepted Germany back into the international community. Some countries, however, above all Sweden, refused to take part in the ban and engaged with Germany in many sporting competitions. All leading administrators of the RF accepted the notion that sport should be free from political influences, but the nature of "politics" was never precisely defined. It did include party politics, and many members of the RF belonged to the Social Democratic party. Had they wanted to mix sports and politics, they would have had to join the workers' sports movement, which was much closer to them politically.

Many of the Swedish sport administrators that were active in Olympic matters between 1933 and 1936 had a long-standing relationship with their German counterparts, especially J. Sigfrid Edström (1870–1952). He had been president of the International Amateur Athletics Federation (IAAF) since its initiation in

1912. He was also president of the Swedish Athletics Federation. Edström had met Avery Brundage, Karl Ritter von Halt, and Carl Diem at the 1912 Olympics and had stayed on close terms ever since. As a member of the IOC executive board he kept close ties with his long-time friend von Halt, who had been president of the German track and field organization since the mid-1920s. As president of the IAAF he also maintained close ties with Brundage, who represented U.S. track and field. Diem, who had been on the IAAF executive board since 1913, knew that he could entirely trust Edström, as he had steered the IAAF around a boycott of German track and field after the World War I. For German track and field athletes it was a pity that they could not take part in the Olympic Games, but they were not excluded from any international track and field meets, and their German federation was able to hold international dual meets against their neighbors without endangering their status as amateur athletes. After the Paris Olympics in 1924, from which Germany was banned, the American winners in track and field were able to tour Germany and compete in international track and field meets against the best Germans in front of huge crowds.

This was the work of J. Sigfrid Edström and Carl Diem. Edström, who can be called the greatest leader Swedish sport has produced, tried to avoid putting the German question onto the agenda of the IAAF conventions. In early 1920 he contacted Diem and asked him to stay away from the Executive Committee's meetings to avoid the German question being raised. The IAAF held a convention during the Antwerp Olympics in 1920. It did not exclude Germany but rather asked Germany to refrain from international competitions. This did not, however, ban individual athletes from taking part in international track and field meets in Germany, which was part of the European circuit of high-profile track meets.

At the IAAF convention in Geneva in 1921, the German question was discussed at great length. As Austria was already a member of the League of Nations and Hungary was about to become one, the IAAF did not find it necessary to take action against its German members. Edström had formally invited the Germans to participate and had written an unofficial letter to Diem the same day, urging him to make sure that no Germans would show up in Geneva, as he was sure that this was the best way to keep competitions open. As Italy, Yugoslavia, and Czechoslovakia wanted to compete against Germany anyway, the Executive Committee recommended to the full convention that the German matter should not be discussed. Only the French abstained, and so German track and field was effectively only banned in 1919, when feelings still ran high in the aftermath of the First World War. Edström made sure that the German delegates would not show up at the IAAF conventions in France in 1923 and 1924, thus ensuring that the German question would not be on the agenda. With his tact he kept the IAAF together, assuring that track and field competitions would take place as freely as possible.[4] Under such circumstances it is understandable that Diem had full confidence that their Swedish friend would also help to keep sports and politics apart in 1936.

Edström studied engineering in Göteborg and in Zürich, Switzerland. He started his professional career in the United States, where he worked for several electrical companies between 1893 and 1897 before becoming the technical director of the Zürich Tram Company from 1897 to 1900. In that year he moved to the Göteborg Electrical Company, before he moved on to the Swedish Electrical Company in Vesteras. When he retired as director of that firm in 1934, he stayed on as the chairman of the company's Supervisory Board until 1949. Apart from the Scandinavian languages, he was fluent in speaking and writing in English, German, and French, and he also spoke some Russian.

Edström had been a gifted athlete. He was an 11.0 second 100 meter sprinter who also ran a 16.4 second 150 meter, which was a world record for a short time. He was also active in rowing and did some wrestling. In 1901, at the age of thirty-one, he became president of the Swedish Athletics Federation, his first major office in sports administration. Two years later he also became president of the RF, which was the result of a merger of Swedish sports and gymnastics that he had arranged with Victor Balck, a Swedish IOC member and a friend of Coubertin. When he was elected as the founding president of the IAAF, he continued as vice president of the RF, an office he held until 1940.[5]

Edström's contacts with Victor Balck brought him into contact with the IOC very early. He attended the Olympic Games in St. Louis in 1904, the Intermediate Games in Athens in 1906 and the Olympic Games in London in 1908. In 1912 he was Balck's vice chairman of the Organizing Committee, attending all the IOC sessions in that function. At the IOC Convention in 1914 he represented the IAAF and took a leading role in running the technical side of the Olympic program. He was also active in the international employers association, helping to organize their international conference in Washington, D.C., in 1919, and he was elected president of the International Chamber of Commerce in 1920.[6] After the war, in 1921, he became a member of the IOC and was immediately elected to the newly founded executive board, on which he served until his death in 1952. The IOC president, Baillet-Latour, made him vice president of the IOC in 1937. After the death of Baillet-Latour, Edström became acting president of the IOC (1942–46). He was then elected president, and he served from 1946 to 1952. Edström was a keen team worker, who continued until old age to help facilitate athletics meets. He knew how to lead but also how to be a member of a team.

Edström's record in regard to anti-Semitism is more clouded, but it certainly posed no threat to the boycott. In a letter to Brundage in the midst of the boycott discussion he wrote: "'As regards the persecution of Jews in Germany I am not at all in favor of said action, but I fully understand that an alteration had to take place. As it was in Germany, a great part of the German nation was led by the Jews and not by the Germans themselves. Even in the USA the day may come when you will have to stop the activities of the Jews. They are intelligent and unscrupulous. Many of my friends are Jews, so you must not think that I am against them, but they must be kept within certain limits.'"[7]

Swedish soccer had many contacts with German clubs, and again Sweden helped prevent Germany from being banned by the world body governing soccer, the Fédération Internationale de Football Association (FIFA). The four British associations, although latecomers to FIFA, still dominated it, but during the war it was sustained by the Dutch general secretary, C. A. W. Hirschmann, and after the war he and the Swedish vice president of FIFA, C. L. Kornerup, along with the "hard man" of Swedish soccer, Anton Johanson, prevented the British from imposing their will on countries that had been neutral during the war. When the four British football associations supported by Belgium and France tried to exclude Germany, along with Hungary and Austria, Johanson and Kornerup stoutly resisted. A majority, led by Sweden and German-speaking Switzerland, defended the right of the members to stay in FIFA and argued that there was no reason to exclude its German members. The English Football Association (FA), together with the other British associations, tried to blackmail FIFA by threatening its own boycott and the formation of a separate association with those nations that also did not want to have contacts with Germany. The FA soon realized that it was isolated. Although it left FIFA, it could not prevent German teams as well as its national team from playing in all major European matches. A working agreement was reached with FIFA that permitted the British to play with whom it wanted. This split in the football movement showed that the Swedish position and that of the other neutral countries won the day.[8]

Football was good business, and there was no reason to stop the football business as long as no other business ventures with Germany had stopped. Johanson had represented the Swedish position well. There should be no interference with Swedish sport. Others could exclude themselves, as long as it did not interfere with Swedish interests. When Germany was excluded from the Olympic Games in 1920 and 1924, Sweden did not protest or threaten a boycott—but neither did it participate in any of the boycott actions. This position was a major influence on all of the subsequent decisions of Swedish sports administrators, which emerged out of the First World War, as it would out of the Second, with an enhanced sporting and business position. But the nonboycott decisions after the First World War had been so traumatic for the Swedish sports movement, as it was forced to define its own position in the world of sports, that the discussion of a boycott of the 1936 Olympics was strongly influenced by the previous antiboycott position.

Edström had learned many things in international sports from the senior Swedish IOC member Victor Balck (1844–1928), who was a founding member of the IOC. Balck also served as president of the International Ice Skating Federation (ISF) from 1895 onward. He delayed holding a congress of his federation after the war and then made it clear that he insisted on German participation in the congress and in any competition. In Amsterdam on October 20–22, 1921, the first sporting congress took place in which former allies, Central Powers, and neutral countries all attended, and German and French delegates sat side by side.

The atmosphere was described as cordial. From 1922 onward, international championships could take place again without any "political" discrimination.

Balck's partner in the IOC was Clarence Count Rosen (1867–1955), an IOC member from 1900 through 1948. In his correspondence with Brundage in conjunction with the boycott threat of the 1936 Olympics it is obvious that he was a rabid anti-Semite: on Brundage's success in beating the boycott movement in the United States, he congratulated him for the way in which he had "'conquered the dirty Jews and politicians.'" Even after the end of the Second World War, with German atrocities in the death camps made known to the world, Rosen still insisted: "'Do everything possible to stamp out this mad expression of Jewish fanatism! The Jews are at the bottom of all disturbances in the civilized world. Their 'Talmud' bids them to despise and destroy the Christians and all others— not Jews. Communism is their political creed and a weapon whereby they hope to destroy all organized civilization.'"[9]

Rosen's was not a lone voice; there also was an "Aryan" movement in Sweden, which produced many pamphlets as vile as those produced by the Nazis at their worst. Racial stereotypes were frequent.[10] In Sweden, however, in contrast to many other countries, equally obnoxious propaganda from the other end of the political spectrum was tolerated. In such a climate it is perhaps possible to insist without hypocrisy upon the notion that "sport and politics should not mix"; certainly it helped preserve the unity of the sports movement in Sweden.

Sweden and Nazi Germany

The establishment of the Nazi regime in Germany led to many tensions in German relations with Sweden. The excesses against Jews, trade-union members, and political opponents led to a demand in Sweden to start boycott actions and break off connections with German sports, including a boycott of the Olympic Games.[11] Nevertheless, the number of sporting encounters against Germany increased considerably between 1933 and 1939, and Germany became Sweden's most important partner in international competition at both the international and club level. This was partly because Germany was the "logical" opponent in many branches of sports, and the economic profit was good. No political considerations within the sports movement seem to have been discussed.[12] The opposition to sporting relations with Germany was restricted to the AIF (the Swedish labor sports organization), the Swedish Communist party, parts of the trade-union movement, and the rest of the political Left. At some international matches, club matches, and other Swedish-German sports contests in Sweden between 1933 and 1936, unsuccessful attempts were made to start a boycott.[13]

As the Olympic Games approached, efforts were intensified and were linked to the cause of some Swedish citizens who had been interned in Germany for distributing "anti-German" propaganda. A committee working for their liberation became a focus for those favoring a boycott, which culminated during the spring of 1936. The main argument was that participation in the Olympic Games amounted to the recognition of a brutal dictatorship, but in the end only about a dozen sportsmen stayed at home out of conviction or out of fear of reprisals from trade-union organizations.[14] The government party, the Social Democrats, and the leaders of the trade-union movement were in a dilemma before the 1936 Olympics. On the whole, the principle of the RF was that sports should be kept free from politics. However, many party members and about 150,000 out of 700,000 members of the Swedish Confederation of Trade Unions were against participation in the Olympic Games.[15] In April 1936 the leaders of the Confederation of Trade Unions decided not to boycott the Olympics in Berlin and declared that the federations should not take measures against participating members. The government party came to the same opinion after the question was dealt with by the party congress in April 1936.[16] Thus the question of Sweden's participation was left to the sports organizations themselves to decide. The political Right opposed a boycott.

These decisions were dictated by foreign, especially trade reasons, Germany being Sweden's most important trade partner. Sweden was also the object of heavy German propaganda in which the Games were portrayed as an arm in the service of peace. German sports leaders within or outside the Olympic Committee made frequent visits to Stockholm.[17] Finally, even the government probably estimated that the majority of the people were in favor of participation in the Games.[18] This decision implied an acceptance of the opinion of the sports movement and the political Right that sports and politics should and could be kept apart, in spite of the general brutality of the Nazi regime and its expected propaganda gains in connection with the Games. But—as the situation after the First World War had shown—major Swedish sports leaders succeeded in keeping all of their contacts with Germany open.

The leading bodies, the RF and the specialized sport associations, consistently rejected all attempts to boycott Swedish-German sports contacts after 1933.[19] On the few occasions when the question of participation in the 1936 Olympic Games was brought up, the board of the sports federation and the Swedish Olympic Committee favored participation, claiming that Jews were not prevented from participating, according to the German promises given to Sigfrid Edström, and that sports had a reconciling mission among people and nations—the usual clichés.[20] In the press the debate was conducted more fulsomely and with more fiery criticism.

Press Debate

The Olympic Games in Berlin were well reported in the Swedish press, especially the big-city nonsocialist press.[21] During the Games, four to five pages were spent on the competitions, which included news and front pages. Special editions on the Olympic Games were printed by some papers just before the opening. Even the Social Democratic press devoted one to two pages each day, mainly concentrated in the sports section. Newspapers on the extreme left tended to restrict their coverage to reporting results, while at the same time their campaign against the German regime and its political use of the Games continued. The left-wing press was more concerned to mold political opinion than the bourgeois or nonsocialist papers, which were more concerned with circulation and hence took a lower political profile. Ever since Hitler's takeover in Germany, every measure of the Nazi regime was discussed in the Swedish press. The left-wing and one or two nonsocialist papers strongly criticized its excesses, and this resulted in tense relations between Sweden and Germany. For their part, the Nazis launched a massive cultural propaganda campaign through radio, daily press, magazines, and lectures, conducted by their propaganda agency Nordische Gesellschaft.[22]

The question of participation in the 1936 Olympic Games was frequently raised in editorials in the big newspapers.[23] The socialist press as well as the *Göteborgs Handels-och Sjöfartstidning* took a clear position against participation in the Olympics. They regarded sports in Germany as heavily politicized and claimed that to participate in the Olympic Games would legitimize the Hitler regime, with its excesses and racist politics. They heavily criticized the Swedish sports movement, so that the Social Democratic newspapers took a different position from the party itself.

The nonsocialist press dissociated itself from all boycott plans, stressing the significance of the Olympic Games as a reconciling and peacekeeping power that stood above local and temporary regimes. They looked upon the Games as a final proof of the acceptance of Germany as an equal among nations. The nonsocialist press criticized the boycott movement in other countries, especially in the United States, and said that a unilateral decision to boycott would only damage the United States itself.[24] The socialist press followed the debate in the United States with sympathy and urged that Sweden should follow the example of America in its decision not to take part.[25]

The Competition

The Swedish press showed particular interest in the Winter Games, which was natural, considering the strong position of winter sports in Scandinavia. A large team of journalists went to Garmisch-Partenkirchen, mainly representing the bigger nonsocialist newspapers in Stockholm, most of which had a well-developed sport section,[26] although the news pages also gave sports news.[27] They concentrated on the sports and spoke favorably of the way the Games were organized and performed. The Social Democratic and Communist press were more critical and used every opportunity to stress the politics and propaganda.

The nonsocialist papers were impressed by the opening ceremony, with a few reservations over the salute,[28] while the left-wing press mocked its military overtones, which it claimed to be typically "German." The Communists took a more legalistic line and pointed out how the organizers ignored the rules governing amateur status and how on the whole they did not abide by the Olympic rules.[29] Praise with few reservations came from the pro-Nazi papers, *Aftonbladet* and *Nya Dagligt Allehanda*,[30] although even they noted the shortcomings regarding the press service and suggested that things were "overorganized" in the typical German way.[31] The extreme-left newspapers printed nothing more than the results.[32] The entire press criticized the poor sportsmanship of the Germans in the ice hockey match between Germany and Canada, which they considered a *skandalmatch*,[33] and overall ascribed German success to the advantages they were careful to assure to themselves on home territory.[34]

During the spring and summer of 1936 the Swedish press devoted much space to detailed reports on the German preparations and the sports grounds in Berlin,[35] claiming that Germany would keep to the rules and organize an Olympic Games devoted to peace and reconciliation among people.[36] The left-wing press kept the boycott issue alive and had no illusions about the true intentions of the Nazi regime: sport served dictatorship; Germany kept or ignored treaties when convenient; while overall the Games would give the impression of "a happy and satisfied National-Socialist Germany."[37]

The Swedish delegation was welcomed in a spirit of great friendship, first at Sassnitz upon arriving by ship from Sweden, and then in Berlin itself. The boycott committee had tried to distribute leaflets detailing the realities of life in Germany to the delegation, but this only aroused indignation in the press. Other matters for discussion in the media were the cancelled official reception in the Berlin Town Hall and the failure to supply music when entering the Olympic Village.[38] The Left preferred to ignore the reception and treated ironically the exaggerated politeness and excessive hospitality.[39] The Communist press dismissed the opening ceremony as a coarse piece of propaganda, and Hitler's acceptance of the Olympic laurel-wreath was looked upon as a particularly bad joke that profaned the Olympic idea.[40] They had to admit that the opening ceremony was well presented but made a point of remarking on the frenetic response of the spectators, whose piercing *Heils* terrified even the peace doves.[41] They also denounced the playing of the German national anthem as the German team entered the arena, pointing out that this was a severe break with tradition, and found offensive the adulation accorded the "Brown Idol." The nonsocialist press, however, portrayed a happy atmosphere in which the enormous audience provided a suitable backdrop for the greatest spectacle ever seen in the history of sport to that time.[42] The liberal press was irritated at the overly nationalistic atmosphere, which was not only provocative but overshadowed the Games themselves.[43]

The success of the black Americans captured the interest of the Swedish press. The conservatives reported their performances in racist language, referring to them as "darkies" and even comparing the high jumpers to monkeys,[44] but even they had to admit that Jesse Owens was the best sportsman at the Olympics.[45]

The Left enjoyed the success of the "non-Aryan" athletes and used it in an ironical way to show up Nazi racial theories.[46] Only the socialist press criticized Hitler's disappearance before the black athletes won the high-jump medals,[47] but by and large this was not seen as a significant issue by most reporters.

Germany's success was explained in large measure by its being the host nation,[48] and when there was a setback, as in the defeat by Norway in football, the socialist press liked to show the bad reaction.[49] German successes were also attributed to the wildly partisan attitude of the spectators, who created a "national storm" that put terrible pressure on the judges.[50] In more objective terms, the large German medal tally could be measured against the way in which Germany was represented in every event, of which there were perhaps too many.[51]

Even the nonsocialist press was forced to comment on the chauvinism, which affected the judges and the competitors from other nations.[52] In addition, they pointed to the questionable degree of state support,[53] which included career promotion for medals won in the field, as rank-and-file members of the police force became officers overnight.[54] The way in which athletes were coached by fully paid trainers and coaches in the service of the state was denounced as straight-out professionalism[55] and totally different from the system that operated in Sweden with its "clean" amateurism, where athletes engaged in regular jobs and whose leaders were all in nonprofit roles.[56] These accusations of cheating, bias, and chauvinism took some of the luster off otherwise bright-eyed admiration, but it was with an eye to the future of sport in smaller countries that the Swedish press criticized the way such a powerful nation devoted so much of its resources to achieve athletic success: smaller nations could not compete in this way, and the very idea of amateurism was under threat.

* * *

The closing ceremony was seen to bring the Games to a dignified and suitable conclusion, even if it lacked the enthusiasm of the opening day. There was a certain tiredness in the speeches, and the long delays evoked several complaints.[57] In their final comments, journalists were inclined to find fault in the very perfection of the organization. There were many comments on German Gründlichkeit (thoroughness), but the press arrangements came in for frequent criticism, and other complaints were reiterated, such as the poor arrangements in events that involved Sweden, such as sailing, wrestling, and the modern pentathlon,[58] and the overchauvinistic spectators.[59] Overall, the combination of a military atmosphere and the extreme nationalism, the constant playing of the national anthem, and the endless number of ceremonies and speeches that had nothing to do with the Games and which interfered with them, were matters that had to be considered.[60] In a confidential report submitted after the Games, the Nazi organizers were virtually condemned for having done their job too well; the Swedish Olympic Committee said that the Games had been given such a splendid framework that it overshadowed the competition. It advocated that future ceremonies be kept to a minimum and that the times as set out on the official program for the distribution of prizes be adhered to. It also recommended that the number of events be limited, as there had been too many in Berlin.[61]

As in other countries, few newspapers changed their opinions as a result of the Games. All agreed on the success of the propaganda and the order that had reigned throughout, although they disagreed over whether this was good or bad. Sport had served the regime well.[62] For the nonsocialist press, Germany had gained in international standing as a result of its "organizing genius,"[63] despite the nationalism and militarism.[64] From a purely sporting point of view there were many complaints about the Games becoming too big and fears expressed about the threat posed by the state amateurs.[65]

The possibility of Sweden boycotting the Games in Germany was never very likely, as Swedish life was dominated by its links with its powerful neighbor as a major trading partner. Even the Social Democrats had to live with this when the Second World War broke out. Bourgeois complacency about sport and politics being separate areas of activity was severely shaken but not upset by the events in Berlin. It was clear that behind the mass involvement and ordered leadership was something more than just sport. The socialist press simply saw this as leaving a bad taste in the mouth. Some left Berlin with their illusions lost, others with misgivings about the future, and at least in some small way this reduced the political gains for the German hosts: "Man merkt die Absicht" (The future was there to be seen).

Notes

1. This section is mainly based on S. Hadenius, H. Wieslander, and B. Molin, *Sverige efter 1900* (Stockholm: Aldus/Bonnier, 1969), 127.

2. J. Lindroth, *Idrott mellan krigen* (Stockholm: HLS, 1987), 22.

3. J. Lindroth, *Från sportfaneri till massidrott* (Stockholm: KLS, 1987), 29.

4. P. O. Holmäng, "International Sports Organizations, 1919–25: Sweden and the German Question," *International Journal of the History of Sport* 9.3 (1992): 455–66.

5. K. Lennartz, "The Presidency of Sigfrid Edström (1942–1952)," in *The International Olympic Committee: One Hundred Years,* vol. 2, ed. R. Gafner (Lausanne: IOC, 1995), 15–76.

6. P. Cholley, *Pierre de Coubertin: La deuxième croisade* (Lausanne: IOC Museum, 1996), 138.

7. Quoted in A. Krüger, "'Fair Play for American Athletes': A Study in Anti-Semitism," *Canadian Journal of the History of Sport and Physical Education* 9.1 (1978): 43–57.

8. See Holmäng, "International Sports Organizations." See also B. Murray, *The World's Game: A History of Soccer* (Urbana: University of Illinois Press, 1996), 42–43; B. Murray, "FIFA," in *The International Politics of Sport in the 20th Century,* ed. J. Riordan and A. Krüger (London: Spon, 1999), 28–47.

9. Quoted in Krüger, "'Fair Play for American Athletes.'"

10. T. Stark, "'Stortysk fuga och negerjazz': Ras-stereotyper och rastänkande i svensk massmediabevakning av Berlinspelen 1936," *Idrott Historia och Samhälle,* SVIF-Nytt 18.4 (1998): 103–29.

11. P. O. Holmäng, *Idrott och utrikespolitik* (Kungälv: Goterna, 1988), 122.

12. Ibid., 126.

13. Ibid., 138.

14. R. Pålbrant, *Arbetarrörelsen och idrotten 1919–1939*, Studia Historica Upsaliensia, vol. 91 (Uppsala: University, 1977), 220; see also R. Pålbrant, "A Vital Period in Swedish Worker Sport: 1919–1936," in *The Story of Worker Sport*, ed. A. Krüger and J. Riordan (Champaign, Ill.: Human Kinetics, 1996), 117–30.

15. Holmäng, *Idrott och utrikespolitik*, 136.

16. Pålbrant, *Arbetarrörelsen och idrotten 1919–1939*, 213.

17. Ibid., 221.

18. Holmäng, *Idrott och utrikespolitik*, 154.

19. Ibid., 147.

20. Ibid.

21. L. O. Welander, "Sverige och Olympiaden 1936," in *Studier i idrott, historia och samhälle*, ed. J. R. Norberg (Stockholm: HLS, 2000), 280–92.

22. A. Thulstrup, *Med lock och pock, Tyska försök att påverka svensk opinion, 1933–45* (Stockholm: Bonnier, 1962), 16, 21, 31, 34.

23. See L. O. Welander, "The View on Democracies and Dictatorships in Swedish Newspapers 1936" (Licentiate diss., Lund University, 1971).

24. See, for instance, *Nya Dagligt Allehanda*, Sept. 16 and Oct. 22, 1935; and *ST*, Nov. 7 and Dec. 16, 1935.

25. *Social-Demokraten*, Oct. 27 and Dec. 3, 1935.

26. See, for instance, *Dagens Nyheter, ST, Aftonbladet, Nya Dagligt Allehanda*, and *Svenska Dagbadet*.

27. *Nya Dagligt Allehanda*, Jan. 8, 1935; *Aftonbladet*, Jan. 22, 1936, and May 10, 1935; *Dagens Nytheter*, Feb. 6, 1936.

28. *Dagens Nytheter*, Feb. 8, 1936; *Nya Dagligt Allehanda*, Feb. 7, 1936; *ST*, Feb. 7, 1936.

29. *Dagens Nytheter*, Jan. 10, 1936; *Nya Dagligt Allehanda*, Feb. 7, 1936.

30. *Social-Demokraten*, Feb. 7, 1936; *Arbetet*, Feb. 6, 1936; *Ny Dag*, Feb. 7, 1936; *Folkets Dagblad*, Feb. 7, 1936.

31. *Dagens Nytheter*, Feb. 6, 1936; *Nya Dagligt Allehanda*, Feb. 11, 1936; *Aftonbladet*, Feb. 17, 1936.

32. *Nya Dagligt Allehanda*, Feb. 17, 1936.

33. *Aftonbladet*, Feb. 7, 1936; *Nya Dagligt Allehanda*, Feb. 11, 1936; *ST*, Feb. 13, 1936.

34. *Ny Dag*, Feb. 11, 13, and 17, 1936; *Folkets Dagblad*, Feb. 8–17, 1936; *ST*, Feb. 14, 1936; *Aftonbladet*, Feb. 15, 1936; *Svenska Dagbladet*, Feb. 10, 1936.

35. *ST*, Jan. 19 and May 6, 1936; *Nya Dagligt Allehanda*, May 30, 1936; *Aftonbladet*, June 2 and 4, 1936.

36. *ST*, Apr. 30, 1936; *Nya Dagligt Allehanda*, Mar. 29 and July 31, 1936.

37. *Social-Demokraten*, Jan. 31 and June 4, 1936; *Göteborgs Handels- och Sjöfartstidning*, June 30, 1936; *Ny Dag*, May 9, 1936.

38. *Dagens Nyheter*, July 30 and 31, 1936; Aug. 1, 1936; *Svenska Dagbadet*, July 30, 1936; *Aftonbladet*, July 31, 1936; *Nya Dagligt Allehanda*, July 31, 1936.

39. *Arbetet*, July 31, 1936.

40. *Ny Dag*, July 31, 1936; *Folkets Dagblad*, Aug. 3, 1936.

41. *Arbetet*, Aug. 1, 1936.

42. *Social-Demokraten*, Aug. 2, 1936.

43. *Dagens Nyheter*, Aug. 2, 1936; *Svenska Dagbadet*, Aug. 2, 1936; *ST*, Aug. 2, 1936.

44. *Dagens Nyheter*, Aug. 2, 1936; *ST*, Aug. 2, 1936.

45. *Dagens Nyheter*, Aug. 2, 1936.

46. *Dagens Nyheter*, Aug. 2, 1936; *Arbetet*, Aug. 3, 1936; *ST*, Aug. 2, 1936; *Svenska Dagbadet*, Aug. 4, 1936.

47. *Ny Dag*, Aug. 18, 1936.

48. *Ny Dag*, Aug. 5, 1936; *Nya Dagligt Allehanda*, Aug. 3, 1936; *Folkets Dagblad*, Aug. 4, 1936. Swe-

den won the medal count in the Olympics only once, in the 1912 Stockholm Games, and so it was natural to assume that the success in Germany was due to the hometown factor.

49. *Dagens Nytheter,* Aug. 2, 1936; *Svenska Dagbadet,* Aug. 4, 1936; *ST,* Aug. 3 and 14, 1936; *Nya Dagligt Allehanda,* Aug. 14, 1936.

50. *Social-Demokraten,* Aug. 7, 1936.

51. *Arbetet,* Aug. 8, 1936; *Social-Demokraten,* Aug. 7, 1936.

52. *Ny Dag,* Aug. 4, 1936; *Social-Demokraten,* Aug. 7, 1936.

53. *Social-Demokraten,* Aug. 14, 1936.

54. *Dagens Nytheter,* Aug. 9 and 14, 1936; *Nya Dagligt Allehanda,* Aug. 15, 1936.

55. *ST,* Aug. 4, 1936.

56. *Nya Dagligt Allehanda,* Aug. 7 and 11, 1936; *ST,* Aug. 14, 1936.

57. *Dagens Nytheter,* Aug. 15, 1936; *Social-Demokraten,* Aug. 13, 1936.

58. *Nya Dagligt Allehanda,* Aug. 14, 1936; *Arbetet,* Aug. 14, 1936.

59. *Dagens Nytheter,* Aug. 17, 1936; *ST,* Aug. 17, 1936; *Svenska Dagbadet,* Aug. 17, 1936; *Nya Dagligt Allehanda,* Aug. 17, 1936.

60. *ST,* Aug. 7, 1936; *Aftonbladet,* Aug. 7, 1936; *Nya Dagligt Allehanda,* Aug. 6, 1936; *Svenska Dagbadet,* Aug. 3, 1936; *Dagens Nytheter,* Aug. 15, 1936; *Social-Demokraten,* Aug. 6, 1936; *Arbetet,* Aug. 11, 1936.

61. *Dagens Nytheter,* Aug. 9, 1936; *Folkets Dagblad,* Aug. 6, 1936. The medalists' podium had only been used for the first time in Lake Placid in 1932, on the insistence of the IOC president, Baillet-Latour, who had seen such a procedure at the First Empire Games in Hamilton, Ontario, Canada. In Garmisch and Berlin the full-length version of the national anthem was played. In the 1912 Stockholm Olympics there were no anthems for the winners, who received their medals from the Swedish Crown Prince Charles at the closing ceremony. Here it was the Crown Prince standing elevated on a podium while the athletes stepped forward to receive their medals. See R. K. Barney, "The Great Transition: Olympic Victory Ceremonies and the Medal Podium," *Olympika* 7 (1998): 89–112.

62. *Social-Demokraten,* Aug. 7, 1936; *Arbetet,* Aug. 4, 1936; *Dagens Nytheter,* Aug. 12, 1936.

63. Sveriges olympiska kommittes arkiv, Stockholm, vol. EI:12.

64. *Göteborges Handels-och Sifärtsridning,* Aug. 13, 1936; *Ny dag,* Aug. 13, 1936.

65. *ST,* Aug. 17, 1936; *Aftonbladet,* Aug. 10, 1936; *Nya Dagligt Allehanda,* Aug. 18, 1936; *Dagens Nytheter,* Aug. 10, 1936.

CHAPTER 9

Norway:
Neighborly Neutrality

Matti Goksøyr

In Norwegian history the Olympic Games of 1936 have always evoked mixed feelings: on the one hand, the success of Birger Ruud, Ivar Ballangrud, Sonja Henie, and football's "bronze team" evokes pride, while on the other hand, the inevitable reality of the Nazi presence generates a certain ambivalence. In terms of sporting success, the performances at the Winter Games in Garmisch-Partenkirchen were not matched until the Albertville Games in 1992. Although the term "Nazi Olympics"[1] has not been commonly used in Norwegian history books, this does not mean that general attitudes to the 1936 Olympics in Germany have been milder here than in most other countries. Rather, the denomination "The Olympics of 1936" and especially "The Berlin Olympics" have been marked with a historical stigma. In Norway there has been an unspoken tendency to associate the "real" Nazi Olympics with the Summer Games, while the Winter Games have more or less been left in peace. This has helped to prevent a retrorationalization, in which the many Norwegian triumphs in the Winter Games are overshadowed by political affairs.[2] However, the main focus of this chapter will be a discussion of the specific Norwegian background that made the question of participation into a controversial political question. Public attitudes and political opinion underline the perspective toward the Olympics as seen from a little nation, both a "winter nation" and a supposedly "Germanic" Nordic nation.

In short, the political climate of the 1930s made the forthcoming Olympics in Germany into a major political and moral issue in Norway. The events became a matter of conflict at the highest political level. Indirectly, the Olympics were part of the beginning of the unification of Norwegian sports. Paradoxically, perhaps, it was the Socialist Labor party's takeover of governmental power in 1935 that ensured Norwegian participation in the Games. This is ironic, because it was their socialist comrades in the trade unions and in the workers' sports movement who were in the forefront of a substantial boycott campaign. This was not only a matter of some people holding one position when in opposition and another when in power. To explain the case, one needs to investigate political, social, and cultural factors.

The Norwegian Background: Politics and Society

The Norwegian interwar period consisted of two distinct political phases.[3] The political issues and cleavages during this period were of such an importance that they had effects on most fields of society, including sport. The first phase, which includes the years from the end of World War I to the middle of the 1930s, was distinguished by strong and outspoken sociopolitical dichotomies. Echoes of the Russian Revolution reached Norwegian shores, contributing to a radicalization of the workers' movement. Problems in the economy and the labor market made strikes, lockouts, and a growing unemployment dominating factors on the social scene, which created a social and political atmosphere in which terms like "revolution" and "class struggle" were applied with sincerity, especially in the early 1920s.

In parliamentary politics this phase was characterized by instability. From 1920 to 1935 Norway experienced no less than eleven minority governments—one of them from the Labor party[4]—while the others were led by Liberals or Conservatives. These were kept in power through changing support from the Farmers' party[5] and other "bourgeois"[6] parties. At the same time, as in other Scandinavian nations, the workers' movement grew strong and gained substantial political momentum, so that the attitudes and political decisions in the various workers' organizations (political parties, trade unions, and the workers' sport organizations) became essential for any understanding of general developments.

The originally revolutionary Labor party in 1923 experienced a split between Social Democrats and Communists, leading to it adopting a somewhat milder political rhetoric. The mainstream of the Norwegian workers' movement thereafter adhered to a more moderate road to socialism. Although this did not ease the "bourgeois" propaganda against the "communist threat," by 1927 Labor had become the largest political party in Norway. In the 1930s it also became a more influential party in its ambition to strive for government office. The workers' movement as a whole in this decade grew to become a powerful factor in Norwegian politics. Between the Labor party (DNA), the Trade Unions (LO), and the workers' sport organization (AIF), there were close political and personal connections among workers.[7]

Toward the middle of the 1930s classical sociopolitical antagonisms were becoming less absolute, introducing the second phase of the interwar period.[8] On the political scene this change was dramatically visible by 1935. In March, what was then considered as one of a number of consecutive Liberal minority governments was forced to resign. This led to more than a change of governments—it led to a change of regime.[9] A parliamentary agreement between Labor and the Farmers' party set the terms and paved the way for what was to become a stable era of Labor governments for thirty years. The new alliance changed the nation's politics, as it did those of the Labor party.[10]

The revolutionary rhetoric of the first half of the 1930s was replaced by a more moderate parliamentary reform policy. This was evident in the debate over Norwegian participation in the 1936 Olympics. The "ministerial socialism," which left-wing skeptics had feared when the issue was government power, proved to be a very responsible kind of socialism. Foreign politics was pursued in accordance with "correct diplomatic" procedures. Particular care was taken not to offend other nations.

On the labor market and on the social scene in general a parallel development took place. While the social dichotomies of the 1920s were prevalent and could be seen in a series of strikes and lockouts, social relations took on other expressions in the 1930s. In professional life an agreement between the trade unions and the employers association in 1935 to sign a general treaty on solutions to trade disagreement was another mark of the change from what in Marxist terms could be called "class struggle" to "class cooperation." The aim of the treaty— with minor revisions it has stood to the present day—was to codify all labor slogans into legal or illegal terms of industrial action and in general to regulate the relations between employers and employees. The former antagonists were to become partners.[11]

Sports Politics: Confrontation or Collaboration?

Naturally, the sharp political antagonisms of the 1920s and early 1930s were reflected and nurtured in sport. The most obvious result of this was an organizational cleavage between the state-authorized—or, in the workers' terms, "bourgeois"—sports federation, the Norges Landsforbund for Idrett (NLFI),[12] and the new workers' sports organization, the Arbeidernes Idrettsforbund (AIF), founded in 1924.

The workers' sports movement rose to become a considerable factor in the sports life of the nation, and the AIF developed into a major sports organization, with a following and influence far beyond those of workers' sport organizations in neighboring countries like Sweden and Denmark.[13] By the end of the 1930s the AIF had over a hundred thousand members—approximately half the membership of the official federation and equal to the number of members reached by the NLFI at the beginning of the decade. This meant that Norwegian sport in most of the interwar period was split in two opposite blocs, based on social and political antagonisms.

Because it was so tightly connected to political conjunctures, the workers'

sport movement suffered internal splits. Rivalry between Communists and
Social Democrats continued until the Labor party gained political hegemony
and full control in 1929. Two years later, in 1931, cleavages divided organized
workers' sport. For the next three years Norway had three separate sports federations, as the Communists formed the Kampforbundet for Rod Sportsenhet,
of foreign, mostly German inspiration.[14] Directives from the Comintern ("the
Strasbourg theses") on "social fascism" had a direct impact on sport in a small
country like Norway. The growing threat from real fascism likewise led to a re-
union in workers' sport in 1934.[15]

The changing political conjunctures of the 1930s affected sport. Harsh revolutionary rhetoric was gradually replaced by increasing collaboration. A "sports
reconciliation" or a softening of former antagonisms between the NLFI and AIF
in 1936 was a natural part of a larger societal development. This sports reconciliation was a product of active official intervention. It was one of the last official
acts of the Liberal government in 1935 to appoint a committee consigned to find
a solution to the cleavage in Norwegian sports politics. The long-term goal of
the authorities was to return to the old structure of Norwegian sport, with a
monolithic and almost centralized sports federation that harbored all Norwegian sport. This organization established close relations with the authorities
concerning consultations and distribution of state grants to sport.[16] The government action led to a consolidation of official relations between state and sport
shortly before the Olympic year 1936.

The Boycott Debate

The discontent that led to official intervention in sports was created by unrest
over the situation in Germany.[17] The political battle over the position to adopt
took place in the two years preceding the Games and was decided before the
Winter Games started. This struggle mirrored various political attitudes concerning sport and politics.

Up to 1933 the AIF had extensive contacts with the German workers' sport
movement.[18] After the Nazi takeover in Germany, the workers' sport movement
and the labor movement in general were swift to oppose what was happening
there. In the following years there was a growing consciousness of what nazism
really was. Resistance was nurtured by reports of imprisoned comrades and the
banning of all organized workers' sport.[19] The AIF took a stand to show solidarity with their German comrades by fighting nazism in any way possible. That
meant resisting anything that resembled fascism at home, or it could mean breaking formal relations with Germany. As in Norway's struggle for separation from
Sweden in 1905, sport had become an appropriate arena of international struggle.

The AIF broke off formal relations with Germany and called for other sportsmen to do the same. The "official" sports federation, the NLFI, however, would
not consider a boycott. They claimed "neutrality" and agitated to maintain re-

lations with Germany. It was this federation and their affiliated national associations that kept the international cooperation going, hence it was against them that the battle had to be fought. However, despite appeals, the Football Association continued to send national teams to Germany, as did the Ski Association and others. Before the change of government in 1935 these different attitudes were reflected also in parliamentary politics. A debate in 1934 after the Norwegian national team played football in Germany was of particular interest.

To answer heavy attacks from Labor speakers who criticized the Norwegian team's appearance in Germany, the representative Trygve Sverdrup from the Conservatives (Høire) stated that this action had prevented sports and politics from being mingled. As a representative of the side who preached sport's non-political purity, he claimed that the very fact that Norway took part in the match meant that "there was no mixing of sports and politics."[20] The Conservative legislator here pointed to a central issue in a growing debate. It is perhaps a historical irony that similar principal conclusions had been made in earlier debates and would be made again in future debates, usually to suit the argument of a particular group.[21] The Labor counterparts in the debate applied "bourgeois" rhetoric when they accused Nazi sport of being outspokenly political. It did not help that Hans von Tschammer und Osten, on his visit to Oslo in 1935, tried to convince Norwegians that the new German sport was totally unpolitical.[22]

The anti-German position of the AIF had strong support in the Trade Unions. A formal connection between the AIF and LO had been put into force from 1929. From then on the AIF received financial support from the unionized workers. The workers' sport organization responded with a resolution that all workers holding membership in the AIF should be members of the union. The relations made possible another strategy to replace the previously fruitless efforts to prevent the "bourgeois" federation from competing in Germany. A joint "nonsocialist" majority in Parliament made it impossible to oppose relations with Germany. But the powerful Trade Unions could be used to prevent individuals from participating in Germany. On December 7, 1934, the LO congress voted to prohibit all organized workers from playing sport in Germany. This was not so much directed toward the coming Olympic Games as it was a signal of international solidarity and a political blow against internal political enemies. Although the AIF largely recruited from the working class, the NLFI also had a substantial number of organized workers among their members.[23] Thus the official "bourgeois" sport felt the decision as a real threat.

The resolution by the Trade Unions forced the "bourgeois" side, which until the beginning of 1935 had tried to avoid the problems of Nazi Germany, to get involved. Mere suggestions and agitation for a boycott decision had met with little interest outside the workers' movement.[24] When the boycott became a concrete decision, however, things changed. The resolution made no specific reference to the Olympic Games. However, it met with fierce counterattacks. "Bourgeois" newspapers called it a "provocation," with papers like the influential *Aftenposten* leading the campaign.[25] They were supported by the main sports periodical, *Sportsmanden,* edited by the former track and field hero Charles Hoff, who at this stage already had distinct Nazi sympathies. The NLFI justified its stance on the grounds of "international obligations." Then the German authorities entered the debate. Hans von Tschammer und Osten warned of the "consequences" if the resolution was put into action and advocated visa denials against members of the Norwegian organizations involved.[26]

The workers' movement was soon to find out that their decision was perhaps too hot to handle. Their faith was based on the existence of "the class enemy," which provided the ammunition for their arguments, but this roused the hostility of those who believed that this interfered with the freedom of individuals to decide their own lives. Liberal newspapers like *Dagbladet* made similar arguments.[27] The conservative media went on to say that this revealed the dictatorial tendencies of the Bolsheviks.[28] Since the unions had the power of "freezing" employees out of their jobs, they were accused of driving people into unemployment. Efforts to implement the boycott were unsuccessful. Threats to expel organized athletes who went to Germany were not popular and did not have great visible effects. The Norwegian skiers who were invited to compete in Garmisch-Partenkirchen in February 1936 left as a complete group and returned in triumph.[29]

All these arguments met with some response. The political leadership in the Labor party—to a large part synonymous with the leadership in the AIF—tried to tread water without committing themselves too much. One of the reasons for this was that government office was no longer such a distant dream. The "responsible" socialists did not wish to be placed in a situation in which they would have their hands tied by resolutions from the LO and the AIF. Statements from two leading politicians from the Labor party revealed some limitations on their former "class solidarity" stand when it came to practical politics. The foreign minister in the new Labor government that was instituted in spring 1935, Halvdan Koht (a historian by profession), later asserted that it had never been his intention to support a boycott of Germany. In fact, the only precondition he had made for entering his post was that the cabinet should commit itself to ending all boycotts against Germany, "for example in sport."[30] With the politician responsible for Norway's relations with Germany holding such opinions and at the same time being a Labor spokesman, a boycott campaign stood little chance in the long run. The prospects were not enhanced by the entry of AIF delegates into the debate.[31] One of the representatives of workers' sport was the chairman of the AIF, Trygve Lie (1931–35), who became home secretary (minister of justice) and who received a cabinet post soon after the start of the negotiations. He also adjusted his official viewpoints to support his colleague, Halvdan Koht. The other delegates from the AIF were politicians as well, with a strong loyalty to their new government. As a result, the strength went out of the workers' boycott movement.[32]

However, the issue had not faded from the public agenda. Liberal and radical intellectuals continued to campaign against what was happening in Germany. While the treatment of Jews and to a certain extent the element of paganism in the Nazi ceremonies most worried foreign observers and critics, other matters were also emphasized in Norway.[33] Here the repressive and antidemocratic politics of nazism were focused on. Since it was the workers' movement that was among the principal critics of nazism—while the non-Socialists, the "bourgeois parties," tried to avoid the problem, preferring to criticise the Soviet Union—the focus lay on the prosecutions against workers' leaders, left-wing politicians, civil rights spokesmen, and pacifists, Jewish and non-Jewish. The repression and assaults on German Jews were an essential part of this overall antidemocratic, fascist picture. It was the Left in Norway that first raised the question of the Nazi treatment of Jews as a principal point of criticism. "Official Norway" had no wish to castigate a nation with which they had formal relations. One consequence of this was that Norway, in line with several other Western European countries, was reluctant to receive and provide shelter for Jewish refugees.

Much of the pre-Olympic debate in Norway centered on matters of principle. It dealt with questions of how to handle the sports relations between Norway and Germany: participation, boycott, or other measures. However, the coming of the Olympics led to a sharpening of the situation and to a more rapid solution of the boycott question. So when the Olympics took place, sportsmen and -women from the NLFI were able to go to Germany without risking their jobs or facing other repercussions. It should also be pointed out, however, that the AIF set out for the Workers' Olympics in Barcelona with a substantial delegation of thirty-three members.[34]

With the boycott question solved, did this mean that what was left during the Olympics in Garmisch-Partenkirchen and Berlin was sport itself? Did it mean that Germany already had won the propaganda war? Not entirely, and not even to a considerable degree. Participants and observers from Norway would not or could not refrain from reflecting and reporting.

The Winter Olympic Games

It has been pointed out that the Olympics came at a convenient time for Hitler.[35] Norwegians shared the doubts and uncertainties about what Hitler would do, but he also had many admirers. Influential newspapers like the best-selling *Aftenposten* and *Tidens Tegn* showed a remarkable degree of tolerance and sympathy for the new Germany, and they promoted the Olympics as best they could. *Aftenposten,* for example, organized group travel to Garmisch-Partenkirchen.[36]

Still, the overall Norwegian attitude was hesitant. Reports on Nazi propaganda from the Winter Games made their impact.[37] In Garmisch-Partenkirchen the journalists and some Norwegian athletes could not help noticing that Hitler and Göring got more attention and greetings than the athletes. *Aftenposten* blamed the "inhibited mood" on the strong pre-Olympic agitation against Germany, because on site their journalists could not detect any "political misbehavior."[38] It was not until the Games were under way and the medals started to roll in that public interest took off in Norway.

The Winter Olympics in Garmisch-Partenkirchen have gone into Norwegian sports history as one of the most successful of all time. The speed skaters swept the gold medal table clean, with Ivar Ballangrud's three gold medals the outstanding accomplishment.[39] While the Norwegian cross-country skiers were not as successful as they had been in the two previous Winter Games on European snow, their teammates in the Nordic combined and in ski jumping defended the national sport with success. Birger Ruud—one of the three Ruud brothers from Kongsberg who each won international competitions in the 1930s—won his second Olympic gold medal and made a name for himself in Germany.[40]

A special case was Sonja Henie, who won her third consecutive Olympic gold medal to cap an incredible career. Henie was the only Norwegian gold-medal winner who became an international star.[41] In fact, she already was a star before the Games. Adolf Hitler knew how to take advantage of this, and the "ice queen" herself did not seem to mind. The two posed willingly as a popular and frequent photo opportunity. The interesting question of why Sonja Henie became more of an international star than a national sports hero are not the main goals of this essay to investigate. However, her willingness to pose with Hitler was surely not the only reason for this. Other factors, such as her choice of sport—figure skating is not exactly the national sport of Norway—her social status and identity, her emigration to the United States, and her ambivalent behavior during World War II, diminished her popularity in the eyes of Norwegians. The winners in the national sports, skiing and skating, Ruud and Ballangrud, did become national heroes, but not, at least in Ballangrud's case, international stars.[42]

In the media and in politics Norwegian successes soon swept away initial doubts. The Labor government, which included some who had once supported the boycott, even sent congratulatory telegrams to Garmisch. The irony of this was quickly pointed out by opposition newspapers. The sports periodical *Sportsmanden* called the telegram a "divine comedy" that had wiped out all former protests.[43] However, this internal quarrel was soon drowned in national enchantment over new victories. Contributing to this was the fact that the media coverage of the Games was implemented to a degree previously unheard of during Olympic Games. The newspapers had increased their reporting staffs considerably, and the Norwegian Broadcasting Corporation contributed for the first time with radio reports, stirring public interest to new heights.

After the Winter Games, the "nonpolitical" view on sport remained dominant. The national victories outweighed the obvious German political propaganda. The national self-image of an enduring winter nation with capacities surpassing most had been consolidated. Ties of personal friendship were established, giving the pictures of admiring German skiers making friends with Birger Ruud a certain legitimating function. The portraits of Hitler and Sonja Henie naturally did not have the same effect, and they were downplayed in some newspapers. Nevertheless, the general attitude toward Germany stemming from the Winter Games seems to have been like a "postponement of the verdict" until after the Games in Berlin.

For the ruling politicians the Winter Games calmed things down, and the neutrality policy worked to the government's satisfaction. It also helped revise the impression made by an embarrassing incident before the Winter Games, when Norway was invited to participate in "military patrol racing" at Garmisch-Partenkirchen. Although Norway had previously won this skiing event, the Ministry of Defense declined the invitation, saying that such races were neither organized nor practiced in Norway.[44] The conservative press did not accept this reason and was eager to portray the negative answer as an intentional offense to Germany. They ascribed political incentives to the decision, claiming that it harmed national and commercial interests. The Norwegian Olympic Committee (NOC) followed this up, and their envoy at the Winter Games, Colonel Fougner, threatened to leave his chair if the decision was not changed. After several fruitless initiatives, he kept his word and left the post in Garmisch-Partenkirchen— but not in the NOC.

The underlying motives for the government's sudden tough stand in regard to German desires in this case are not easy to trace.[45] There is, however, reason to believe that the response to the German invitation would have been different if it had gone through the Foreign Ministry, and not the Ministry of Defense. While Koht was determined to go through with his peacekeeping neutrality line, however, he did not always understand sport. He had a rather academic, distant attitude to sport and the importance that was given to the whole Olympic arrangement. This disposition almost created a diplomatic incident during the Games in Berlin.[46]

The Rhineland affair in the spring of 1936 had no effect on the Norwegian government. Norwegian internal political demands outweighed the effects of Hitler's spring adventure. For the Berlin Olympics this meant participation.

The Olympic Games in Berlin

In Berlin, Norway had no Sonja Henie, nor a Birger Ruud or Ivar Ballagrud, for that matter. The participants in the traditionally successful events, sailing and marksmanship, performed well without causing any major rapture in the home country. However, the nation's football team took many, including the German hosts, by surprise. The achievements of the "bronze team," and especially their victory over Germany, have gone into Norwegian history, often interpreted as a symbolic precursor to the Second World War, and at least as a blow by a small nation against the mightier Germany. Other small countries also saw it this way, and the symbolic effect was strengthened since the Führer himself was at the game.[47]

The Norwegian media coverage of the Berlin spectacle was even greater than that for the Winter Games. The radio coverage of the matches of the bronze team have become classics in Norwegian radio history. From a larger Scandinavian perspective, however, the Norwegian presentation was small compared to that of Sweden. This probably says more of general German-friendliness in the two countries than of the general sports interest. The German press reports of the Norwegian coverage of the Games were sober, and the agents did not try to make the picture brighter than reality.[48] They had little reason to do so. The largest and most influential paper, *Aftenposten*, supported Germany and Hitler in its editorials and also in its sports pages. When it came to German-friendliness, however, *Aftenposten* was outdone by the smaller but still influential *Tidens Tegn*, whose sympathies for the new Germany were notorious. Neither of these papers, however, was in any way related to the Nazi party.[49]

There were other Norwegian newspapers with more antagonistic views. The liberal *Dagbladet* stood out as a central organ for the anti-Nazi intelligentsia, and also in editorials marked a clear stand against the German regime. *Dagbladet* would not, however, support a boycott of the Games. The liberal paper instead preached the right of the individual to make his or her own decisions. But the strongest and most uncompromising critique of the German Olympics came from the press connected to the workers' movement. Although the government's policy had taken the wind out of the sails of the boycott movement, the attitudes in the workers' press was still antagonistic. *Klassekampen*—a youth organ—in February 1936 still urged a boycott or removal of the "Hitler Olympics" and made their own version of the Winter Games poster, where the silhouette of the saluting skier was accompanied with the shadow of a figure with gun, gas mask, and swastika.[50] Even these papers, however, could not subdue their pleasure as successful Norwegian results from Garmisch-Partenkirchen and Berlin started to come through on the teleprinters. The workers' press was part of the national press, and their readers were as interested as others in being informed of Norwegian representatives doing well in Germany.

The opening ceremony and the other ceremonies of the Berlin Games called for different commentaries in the press. Whereas papers like *Aftenposten* and *Tidens Tegn* had reported a marvelous and impressive "demonstration of brotherhood and will for peace,"[51] *Arbeiterbladet* saw a "pompous exaltation of splendor" and ceremonies for mass suggestion "in which the Nazis are experts." The workers' organ from Oslo also noticed the "typical military and sanctimonious religious character" of the opening ceremony and worried about its effect on young "blue-eyed Norwegian sportsmen."[52] Among the Norwegian journalists there were substantial differences of opinion. *Arbeiterbladet* attacked the bourgeois press for having swallowed the whole bait of the "swastika theater," meant to impress foreign correspondents.[53] The truth was exactly the opposite, according to *Arbeiterbladet;* Germany cultivated not peace and harmony but war and hatred. The goal of German sport was education for war.

Other newspapers did not see or did not wish to see that far. But even *Tidens Tegn* could not help noticing that Hitler's popularity among the crowd was "terrifying."[54] *Aftenposten* preferred to underline the warm welcome that was given to the French during the opening ceremony; "never was the danger of war on the Rhine smaller than in this moment."[55] Thoughts of war, even on this brotherly opening day of the Olympic Games, were still on people's minds.

An important part of the press picture was presented by the less happy reporters of the nonworkers' press. Even though *Tidens Tegn* in principle was impressed, some voices of reflection and doubt were heard from its own staff. Their sports editor, Jørgen Juve, also captained the successful Norwegian football team in Berlin. His reflections after the Games are therefore noteworthy from more than one perspective. Juve agreed on the technical success of the Games but could not refrain from wondering where the "Olympic spirit" had gone. Thus he confessed to have been "moved, but not touched." The sports editor and team captain delivered harsh criticisms of the Germany of 1936; to him Germany was a nation that "has thrown overboard her old precious culture" and thus "completely lacks the tradition necessary to give the Olympic Games a spiritual frame." "Order, uniforms, and armored vehicles" were not what Juve wanted to find at the Olympics.[56]

The notoriously critical *Dagbladet* was banned for sale in Germany in 1936. It still maintained a broad coverage of sports and like everybody else took part in the national joy when Germany was knocked out of the football tournament. *Dagbladet* sent one of its editors, Gunnar Larsen, to write cultural and political comments. In his closing commentary he reflected upon what the Olympic sports success would do to the German self-image. It was Larsen's impression that since the Germans had taken their success "to a seriousness without limits"—lacking even the "smallest piece of self-irony"—he feared a further "confusion in the German mentality" that would materialize in a "forced-patriotic muscle-exaltation of the worst sort." The sports victories were probably the "last missing link in the building of national self-glorification in Germany. Now the circle of heroic glory and greatness was closed."[57] Hitler would soon prove Larsen correct, when he used the Olympic success as a proof of "Aryan" supremacy and launched his new four-year plan for a military buildup.[58]

So, while the workers' press and *Dagbladet* before the Games had depicted war preparations and assaults on Jews and Communists, newspapers like *Aftenposten* and *Tidens Tegn* repeatedly stated that it was not "the mayor of Philadelphia" who decided the fate of the Olympics.[59] The most influential of them went as far as to characterize the pre-Olympic arguments against Germany as untrue, collected by "the fabricators of lies in Copenhagen, Paris, and Philadelphia."[60] Undeniably there were examples of race bigotry in the papers. While Jesse Owens during and after his outstanding performances received massive appreciation, he was not presented in the same respectful way before his victories. For instance, *Aftenposten* reported on Owens almost being denied the right to go to Berlin by his university because he was falling behind in his studies: "The Negro Jesse Owens" has it "all in his legs." The paper could not hide an underlying contentment that he was "not quite as good in his studies."[61]

Other Results of the Olympics

The Games caused some significant changes of attitudes in Norway. They became an important stage in the unification of Norwegian sport, a reconciliation that reached a further stage in 1940 and culminated in the merging of the two sports federations (the AIF and NLFI) into one (Norges Idrettsforbund) in 1946. The 1936 Olympics represent the introduction of a new stage in the cultivation of national sports heroes. They also forced intellectuals to deal with sports and the politics of sport and made sports into a topic for artistic expression. An important episode related to the Olympic discussion was the nomination of candidates and the awarding of the Nobel Peace Prize in 1936. All these were related to general attitudes and impressions of Germany in Norway, which reached a special acuteness during the Olympics.

Those who claimed to be apolitical, of course, were never as apolitical as they claimed to be, especially when this attitude was adopted in the middle of a tense political struggle. The cultivation of national sports stars, taken to an unprecedented degree in Norway, naturally had political implications in a period in which class antagonisms gave way to cooperation. The national unity and joint interest in "our" common heroes—Birger Ruud, Ivar Ballangrud, and the Bronze Team—fit well into the dominant ways of thinking in the second half of the 1930s. In these same years, the Labor party changed its ambitions from being the party of the working class to become the whole Norwegian people's party, and earlier social dichotomies were overlooked. There were changed attitudes, too, among the workers, in the celebration of national festive days, such as Constitution Day, May 17. In the first phase of the interwar period this holiday was considered a "bourgeois" affair, not worthy of celebration, while May 1 was the day to be observed, preferably with red flags. After 1936 the workers' organizations started to celebrate May 17 and to use the national flag as well.[62] To paraphrase Eugen Weber, the development could well be called "from workers into Norwegians."[63] So, while the Olympic Games and the German system did not get much credit, one outcome of the Olympics went straight into domestic Norwegian development and supported a growing tendency to cultivate common national symbols, which Birger Ruud and the Bronze Team had become.

Another significant change came in the reactions from intellectuals and artists. One of these was the author, playwright, war journalist, and poet Nordahl Grieg. Undoubtedly an intellectual spitfire, he had a clear eye for international developments. He reported from various hot spots, including Spain, the Soviet

Union, and China. During World War II his nationalism led to him leaving Norway to join the Royal Air Force. He was killed in an air raid over Germany in 1943.

In the years between 1936 and 1939 Grieg dealt with political, cultural, and moral issues in his own journal, *Veien frem*. In 1936 he published an open letter to the Swedish explorer Sven Hedin, who had been chosen by the Germans to speak on behalf of Europe at the opening of the Games in Berlin. Hedin previously had not been known as a critic of the Nazi regime and he was not distinguished. However, Grieg wanted to confront "the spokesman of Europe" with the obvious treason of the Olympic idea, "the brotherhood of all peoples and races." He did so by pointing to the poster from Garmisch-Partenkirchen published in the *Manchester Guardian,* which read "Juden Zutritt verboten," and in general by referring to the treatment of a people "who have created many of the deepest treasures in German culture, as unclean animals." At the same time Grieg suggested that Hedin's experiences as an explorer might have led him to the conclusion that "human values do not depend on race or people." He therefore urged the "voice of Europe" to speak against racial hatred. "If a betrayed idea is saluted, then Europe speaks with a cancerous tumor in her throat."[64]

Hedin seemed to have taken little notice of Grieg's appeal.[65] Grieg's opinions are interesting as expressions of the concerns of a broad alliance of the Norwegian Left—he was on his way to becoming an idealistic communist—over the persecution of Jews. He was followed by other intellectuals, especially liberals in the newspaper *Dagbladet*. Grieg was also the most expressive of the artists who used materials from the Olympics to create poetry. His poem "The Sprinters" brings together in a compelling way the Berlin experience of the all-conquering black athlete Jesse Owens, Nazi ideology, and the treatment of Jews. The poet suggests in a bitterly sarcastic tone, after having witnessed Jesse Owens humiliate German race theories, that they:

> Take consolation then
> that the Jews who
> ran for their lives
> in your streets
> men and women
> you did catch up with them.[66]

Coubertin and the Nobel Peace Prize

Norwegian intellectuals also involved themselves in the Nobel Peace Prize discussion in 1936. This became one of the most heated moral and political debates in Norway in the 1930s. In a way it took over as the "real" German debate in Norway, since the boycott question already had been decided at the highest political level. The dispute was related to the politics of sport and the Olympics in 1936, since Pierre de Coubertin's nomination for the prize was based on his role in the Olympic Games. The debate achieved a certain notoriety, since one of the other nominees was Carl von Ossietzky, who was imprisoned by the Germans, while it was (as it still is) the Norwegian Parliament's Nobel Committee that awards the prize. The debate also involved the most esteemed author, the Nobel laureate Knud Hamsun, who was opposed by younger opponents like Nordahl Grieg.

The relationship between the Olympic Games and the Nobel Peace Prize has received much more attention in recent times than it did in the 1930s.[67] Those books that refer to the issue in 1936 usually claim that Coubertin was nominated by the Nazi government out of gratitude for supporting the Berlin Olympics.[68] However, the files of the Nobel Committee in Oslo give a slightly different picture of the process leading up to the actual awarding of the Peace Prize of 1936. The prize was bestowed on an enemy of nazism, the concentration-camp prisoner Carl von Ossietzky.[69] From several sources it seems that the idea of nominating Coubertin had been present for a number of years.[70] However, the prescripts of the Nobel Committee demand a certain procedure for nominating candidates. Only persons holding positions in a nation's governing assemblies or former prize winners have the right to nominate a candidate. To an assembly like the IOC, these demands should not have caused much of a problem. So the initiative for the Coubertin nomination came from IOC circles.

The initiative for the nomination of Coubertin was raised by the German representative Theodor Lewald at the IOC session in Oslo in February 1935. What his motives or instructions were other than the ones he gives in a letter to the organizers of the session is a matter of speculation.[71] Lewald acknowledged that "for years" he had been pondering the idea of a Nobel Prize for Coubertin, whom he saw as "one of the last great humanists" holding high the idea of reconciliation. The true proof of this was Coubertin's determination to keep Germany inside the Olympic movement after the outbreak of World War I, and he was one of the first to seek its reentry afterward. Lewald naturally stressed the Games' great importance, not only for sports, but their "national and political importance" as well.

Lewald had petitioned the IOC for some time to get support. At the same time he held official positions in Germany and could have been considered a spokesman of the regime. But he was not in a position himself to nominate candidates. Whether it was a deliberate tactic to choose the IOC road to nomination and not the more compromising German political way, we do not know. However, it took some time to make a proper formal nomination through IOC channels. In the meantime, the Norwegian Olympic Committee, in a letter to the Nobel Committee, tried to "draw the Committee's attention" to the Baron. The NOC were "familiar with plans—seconded by the French government—to nominate Coubertin for the Nobel Peace Prize."[72]

The IOC strategy, according to the president, Henri Baillet-Latour, was to mobilize every IOC member with a nomination right to sign a petition for

Coubertin but to let the French representative—a cabinet minister for naval affairs—make the proposal, since Coubertin was a Frenchman. So the official nomination letter of January 15, 1936, was signed by François Pietri of France, Paolo Thaon di Revel of Italy, and Geza Andrassy and Jules de Muzsa of Hungary. The nomination was later cosigned by Lord Burghley of Great Britain, Jigoro Kano of Japan, and Ignacy Matusewski of Poland.[73]

Coubertin could perhaps have stood a better chance in other circumstances. As it was, the political reality of the time worked against him. The way the Olympic "peacefighters" followed up their case, by continually addressing the Nobel Committee with proofs of Coubertin's greatness, may not have served their cause. German propaganda for the Berlin Games, put out by Coubertin and Baillet-Latour, probably worked in the opposite direction, all the more so since Coubertin's infamous statement after the Games was enclosed in the correspondence to the Nobel Committee. Here he praised the German people "und seinem Führer" for their marvelous achievements in cultivating the Olympic spirit during the Olympics.[74] Baillet-Latour followed up by asserting that the Berlin Olympics had created "the deepest happiness" among all true Olympic and peace friends. Germany had, according to the IOC president, "understood the real value of peace . . . in the spirit of Coubertin." Baillet-Latour's judgment of the steps toward peace in Berlin was no accident; it was also stressed in interviews during the Games.[75]

During the first eight months of 1936 there was frequent coverage of Coubertin's nomination, especially in *Aftenposten* and *Tiden Tegn*. It was hardly mere coincidence that these papers also were among the most germanophilic. Speculation, as always, ran high. One headline in *Tiden Tegn* read, "Nobel Peace Prize Probably to Coubertin."[76] *Sportsmanden,* run by an editor with outspoken Nazi sympathies, supported Coubertin as a true representative of "sport." *Fritt Folk,* an openly Nazi periodical, backed Coubertin's nomination, saying, "a more worthy candidate is not to be found."[77]

The liberal press was relatively uninterested in Coubertin's candidature and concentrated more on the fate of his rival nominee, Carl von Ossietzky. So did the workers' press. They preferred a resolution passed at an RSI meeting in Prague that declared it "completely ridiculous to award the Peace Prize to Coubertin" in light of the Olympics in 1936.[78] The entire labor movement supported Ossietzky.[79]

After the Berlin Olympics, most of the interest in Coubertin as a candidate seems to have gone. This can be interpreted as an indication of where the winds were blowing after the Games. In Norway, Coubertin's nomination was too clearly connected to the Olympics of 1936 to make any serious impact. Interest instead centered around Ossietzky, whose nomination was a direct blow to the German regime and as such destroyed much of what had been achieved in Berlin. While Coubertin was associated with the current Olympics, and therefore also to a certain extent with the German organizers, Ossietzky was embraced by all shades of opposition to the Nazis and to the German Olympics. The outcome of the debate showed perhaps that sport as a social and cultural institution was not treated seriously.

For the Nobel Committee this meant that the social and political role of sport was not worth considering. Like most of the forty-six nominees, Coubertin did not make it to the final heat. Eight people (and three organizations) were considered and evaluated more closely for the final decision, which ended with the Peace Prize to Ossietzky.[80] This was both a controversial and a courageous award by the committee. It certainly angered the German regime. It also provoked Knud Hamsun to publish a counterattack on the rather defenseless concentration-camp prisoner, while the "voice of Europe" from the opening ceremony in Berlin, the Swede Sven Hedin, denounced the decision as a "scandal."[81]

* * *

The observation of the German press agents in Norway that the Olympic Games of 1936 rapidly ceased to be a vital political issue in the public debate was to the point.[82] What this overlooks, however, is the extent to which it was taken over by the Nobel Peace Prize discussion. Moreover, there were other ways in which the Olympic debate left some lasting impressions on the Norwegian political and cultural landscape. The Olympic Games of 1936 must be seen in a total perspective, including all the other sides of Nazi politics. Hence, the Olympics, along with much more crucial episodes such as the remilitarization of the Rhineland, contributed to a change in the German image in Norway. In Scandinavia, Germany had long held a reputation as a cultured nation, although this was somewhat altered by World War I, in which Norway remained officially neutral. Germany was still a nation of poets, philosophers, and artists who had created extraordinary things for humanity. German was the first foreign language taught at schools and was frequently applied as a scientific language among Norwegian scientists. The sports movement had received most of its inspiration from the Anglo-Saxon world, but the German Turnen had been an important source of influence to the whole Norwegian "idretts" (sports) movement. Moreover the workers' sports movement had frequent and stable contacts with their brother organizations in Germany until 1933. It took some drastic measures to change all this within a couple of years.

So when popular attitudes toward Germany were turning in a negative direction, it was only partially because of the experiences in Garmisch-Partenkirchen and Berlin. One can, however, detect slight changes in attitude among several of the observers in Germany during the Olympics. Even if they came with an open, unbiased mind, the Nazi Olympic experience seems to have been a bit too much. The Norwegian footballer Jørgen Juve was one example of this. In spite of working for a germanophilic newspaper, it became hard for him to defend the seriousness, the "preussen" discipline, and the military emphasis that dominated the sports meetings. The culture clash between blue-eyed Norwegian visitors brought up to believe in democracy for all and the Nazi reality of 1936 seems to have been considerable, even though this was concealed as much as possible.

Sport can sometimes act as a gloss. However, the Nazi way of organizing the Olympic Games left Norwegian visitors and general public opinion not less suspicious and reluctant than before but either more confused regarding their previous sympathies or strengthened in their views that something ugly was going on in Germany.

Notes

1. R. Mandell, *The Nazi Olympics* (Rpt., Urbana: University of Illinois Press, 1987).

2. Mandell claims that nazism's brutal side was more prevalent in Garmisch-Partenkirchen than in Berlin (ibid., 139).

3. This is a rather uncontroversial statement. See, for example, B. Furre, *Vårt hundreår: Norsk historie, 1905–1945* (Oslo: Samlaget, 1991).

4. When the Norwegian king, Haakon VII, responded to the crisis of 1928 by calling for a government from the Labor party for the first time, this did not create more than minor complaints from bourgeois politicians. Labor rule, led by Christopher Hornsrud, however, did not last longer than three weeks.

5. The Farmer's party was called the Bondepartiet in 1920, after a split from the old Liberal party (Venstre). Today it is known as the Senterpartiet.

6. The term, much applied in Norwegian politics, is "borgerlig," which has a more accurate translation to German: "bürgerlich."

7. The later general secretary of the United Nations, Trygve Lie, is a prominent example of this. Lie, one of the few tennis players in the AIF, rose to become leader of the organization (1931–35) before he was appointed home secretary (minister of justice) in the new Labor government. Lie was, of course, a member of the union.

8. For a general historical treatment of this development, see Furre, *Vårt hundreår*. See also E. Bull, *Norges historie, 1920–1945*, vol. 13 of *Norges historie*, ed. K. Mykland (Oslo: Cappelen, 1979).

9. J. Arup Seip, *Fra embetsmennsstat til ettpartistat* (Oslo: Universitetsforlaget, 1974).

10. Det Norske Arbeiderparti (Labor) officially followed revolutionary ideas, supported the Russian Revolution, and was a member of the Communist International, the Comintern, since 1919. In 1921, a fraction to the right of the mainstream broke away, forming the Social Democratic Labor party. In 1923 the Norwegian Communist party, committed to the Twenty-one conditions of the Comintern, was founded. In 1927 the two other tendencies, Social Democrats and Labor, merged again to form one big Labor party. There has been some debate among Norwegian historians over when the change in Labor policies took place. E. Bull and H. Koht have put their marks on this debate, while others, like Odd Bjørn Fure, have questioned their statements. They all seem to agree, however, that the change occurred before the government takeover in 1935.

11. Furre, *Vårt hundreår*.

12. The NLFI was founded out of the remains of the former official sports federation, Norges Riksforbund for Idraet, in 1919, after ministerial intervention. See M. Goksøyr, *Staten og idretten, 1861–1991* (Oslo: Kulturdepartementet, 1992).

13. See A. Krüger and J. Riordan, eds., *Der internationale Arbeitersport* (Köln: Pahl-Rugenstein, 1985).

14. Directly translated into English, it means "Federation to fight for red unity in sport."

15. For an English-language account of the history of Norwegian workers' sport, see G. v. d. Lippe, "Landmarks in the History of Norwegian Worker Sport, in *The Story of Worker Sport*, ed. A. Krüger and J. Riordan (Champaign, Ill.: Human Kinetics, 1996), 131–42.

16. It should be noted, however, that state authorities had taken similar steps three times before: in 1893, 1910, and between 1917 and 1919. See Goksøyr, *Staten og idretten.*

17. B. Sveen's "Idrett og politikk: Hitler-Tyskland og Norge: Samarbeid eller Boikott" (Hovedoppgave i historie, Universitetet i Trondheim, 1976) is a useful study. Sveen emphasizes the boycott campaign as the main cause for government action. Another useful investigation is F. Olstad's *Norsk idrettshistorie,* vol. 1, *1861–1939* (Oslo: Aschehoug, 1987).

18. The AIF had joined the Communist Red Sports International (RSI) at its foundation in 1924. After the social-fascism schism in 1931, the AIF again joined the RSI in 1934.

19. The resistance movement was supported by German refugees in Norway such as Willy Brandt, who became a Norwegian citizen. See E. Lorenz, ed., *Willy Brandt: Skrifter fra eksilra i Norge* (Oslo: Universitetsforlaget, 1993).

20. *Stortingstidende* 80 (1934): 963.

21. The first Norwegian boycott of an international sports encounter was at the Nordic Games in 1905; it was a result of the "ill-feeling caused by Swedish attitudes in the struggle over the union between the two nations." See J. Lindroth, *Unionsuppløsningen 1905 och idrotten* (Stockholm: Archivsamf., 1979); and Goksøyr, *Staten og idretten.*

22. *Aftenposten,* Feb. 28, 1934.

23. The Labor chairman Oscar Torp's calculation of 80 percent probably is much too high. See F. Olstad, "Historien om arbeidernes idrettsforbund: keiserens nye klaer," *Norsk idrettshistorisk årbok* 1 (1989), 7–17.

24. Sveen, "Idrett og politikk, Hitler-Tyskland og Norge," 35.

25. Ibid., 42. *Aftenposten* was by far the largest newspaper in the country.

26. *Aftenposten,* Dec. 12, 1934. See also Sveen, "Idrett og politikk, Hitler-Tyskland og Norge," 117.

27. *Dagbladet,* Feb. 7, 1935.

28. *Aftenposten,* Jan. 31 and Feb. 8, 1935.

29. See Sveen, "Idrett og politikk, Hitler-Tyskland og Norge," 46.

30. Koht, *For fred og fridom, 1939–40* (Oslo: Tiden, 1957).

31. This became part of the negotiations leading up to the "sports reconciliation" in 1936.

32. Trygve Lie's personal preference had, according to his memoirs, always been for nonpolitical sport. See T. Lie, *Oslo-Moskva-London* (Oslo: Tiden, 1968), 82. Lie's role in workers' sport has been studied by Olstad, *Norsk idrettshistorie,* vol. 1 ("Historien om arbeidernes idrettsforbund"). See also Sveen, "Idrett og politikk, Hitler-Tyskland og Norge," 116.

33. See, for example, Mandell's description of the American discussion, with its heavy emphasis on the treatment of Jews (*Nazi Olympics,* 66–67).

34. Frode Rinnan has on several occasions (radio, TV, and personal meetings) given evidence of the Norwegian delegation's experiences.

35. See, for example, works by Mandell and Krüger.

36. *Aftenposten,* Jan. 2, 1936.

37. This was mostly reported in the workers' press and in the *Dagbladet.*

38. *Aftenposten,* Feb. 7, 1936. See also Mandell, *Nazi Olympics,* 93.

39. Mandell claims that this accomplishment was not given proper recognition, however (*Nazi Olympics,* 99).

40. German occupation forces would try to exploit this fact during World War II.

41. Mandell, *Nazi Olympics,* 105.

42. Contributing to Ruud's image as a national hero was his versatility. In the 1936 Olympics he also placed first in the downhill event of the men's alpine combined. The same thing made Laila Schou-Nielsen a female national idol. She won a bronze medal in the women's alpine combined and was also a national top-level athlete in handball, speed skating, and tennis, but far from a diva like Henie.

43. *Sportsmanden,* Feb. 24, 1936. See also Sveen, "Idrett og politikk, Hitler-Tyskland og Norge," 112.

44. Statement of Defense Secretary Fredrik Monsen (Archive of the Foreign Ministry, Oslo, Mappe G 31, C 2/33). See also Sveen, "Idrett og politikk, Hitler-Tyskland og Norge," 117–19.

45. Sveen, "Idrett og politikk, Hitler-Tyskland og Norge," 118, suggests a protest against the obvious militarization of sport as a possible motive.

46. The Norwegian minister at the legation in Berlin, Scheel, was called to Oslo for a meeting at the same time as the opening ceremony of the Berlin Games. The rather careful and germanophilic Scheel had to point out to the foreign secretary that it would not look good if he stayed away on this occasion, "it would (also) presumably be attributed to political motives" (Archives of the Foreign Ministry, Mappe G 31, C 2/33). See also Sveen, "Idrett og politikk, Hitler-Tyskland og Norge," 118.

47. J.-C. Bussard, "Les Jeux de 1936 dans la presse suisse de langue française," in *The Olympic Games through the Ages: Thirteen HISPA Conference Proceedings,* ed. Renson, Laemmer, Riordan, and Chassiotis (Athens: Hellenic Sports Research Institute, 1991), 357–70.

48. J. Bellers, ed., *Die Olympiade Berlin 1936 im Spiegel der ausländischen Presse* (Münster: Lit, 1986), 177–78, refers to forty-one columns devoted to the Olympics in "a Stockholm paper," compared to *Tidens Tegn,* which had seven columns (while the *Daily Mail* had two and *The Times* one column).

49. During World War II the media situation was altered, leading to a trial after the war. See G. Hjeltnes, *Avisoppgjøret etter 1945* (Oslo: Aschehoug, 1990). The Nazi party (National Samling), led by Vidkun Quisling, was a minor party at all democratic elections.

50. *Klassekampen,* Feb. 2, 1936.

51. *Aftenposten,* Aug. 3, 1936.

52. *Arbeiterbladet,* Aug. 1, 1936.

53. See J. Bellers, "Nachwort: Presse-Berichterstattung, Aussenpolitische Konstellation und die Olympischen Spiele 1936," in *Die Olympiade Berlin 1936 im Spiegel der ausländischen Presse,* ed. J. Bellers (Münster: Lit, 1986), 267–87. See also R. Beduhn, "Berlin 1936: Olympia im Potemkinschen Dorf," in ibid., 250–66; and Mandell, *Nazi Olympics,* 96.

54. In Norwegian, "forskrekkelig," which is not exactly the same. See *Tidens Tegn,* Aug. 4, 1936.

55. *Aftenposten,* Aug. 3, 1936.

56. *Tidens Tegn,* Aug. 22, 1936.

57. *Dagbladet,* Aug. 18, 1936.

58. H.-J. Teichler, "Berlin 1936: ein Sieg der NS-Propaganda?" *Stadion* 2.2 (1976): 299–300.

59. *Aftenposten,* Mar. 13, 1936.

60. *Aftenposten,* Mar. 19, 1936.

61. *Aftenposten,* Jan. 8, 1936.

62. T. Pryser, *Klassen of nasjonen, 1935–1946: Arbeiderbevegelsens historie i Norge,* vol. 4 (Oslo: Tiden, 1988).

63. E. Weber, *Peasants into Frenchmen: The Modernization of Rural France, 1870–1914* (London: Chatto and Windus, 1977). For the Norwegian development, see M. Goksøyr, "Phases and Functions of Nationalism: Norway's Utilization of International Sport in the Late Nineteenth and Early Twentieth Century," *International Journal of the History of Sport* 12:1–2 (1995) 125–46; and M. Goksøyr, "The Popular Sounding Board: Nationalism, 'The People,' and Sport in Norway in the Inter-war Years," *International Journal of the History of Sport* 14.3 (1997): 100–114.

64. *Veien frem* 1.1 (Feb. 1936), reprinted in *Veien frem: Artikler i utvalg, v/Odd Hølaas* (Oslo: Gyldendal, 1974).

65. See Hedin's statements where he glorifies "die Kämpfer" and "die Unsterblichkeit" as the highest ideals for youths of the world in a "Kurzbericht" intended to function as pure propaganda for the German regime after the Olympics (n.73 below). See also his reaction toward the Nobel Peace Prize award in 1936 (n.80 below).

66. Nordahl Grieg, "Sprinterne" (my translation), first published in *Veien frem,* Sept. 1936; reprinted posthumously in 1945. The poem is now part of the national literature curriculum. See J. Havnevik, ed., *Lyrikkboken* (Oslo: Bokklubben, 1977).

67. There were negative reactions in Norway when it was revealed that the IOC had hired a PR agency to promote their chances of a Peace Prize for their candidate.

68. A. Guttmann, *The Olympics: A History of the Modern Games,* 2d ed. (Urbana: University of Illinois Press, 2002), 59.

69. A thorough study of the case is G. Hestness, "Ossietzky-saken" (Hovedoppgave i historie, Universitetet i Bergen, 1973).

70. See P. Foss, letter to the editor, *Tidens Tegn,* Feb. 4, 1936, on a suggestion involving the former Peace Prize laureate.

71. Letter to "Insp. der Königlich Norwegischer Kavallerie Herrn Oberst Fougner, Oslo," Mar. 31, 1935, signed "Dr. Lewald, Staatssekretär a.D. Wirchlicher Geheimrat," on letterhead from "Der Präsident des Organisationskomittees für die XI Olympiade Berlin. E.V.," *Nobel Institute Archives: Correspondence Journal* (Sept. 23, 1935–Dec. 7, 1936), enclosed materials.

72. Letter from the NOC, Nov. 11, 1935, *Nobel Institute Archives: Correspondence Journal* (Sept. 23, 1935–Dec. 7, 1936). In this letter, "Geheimrat Lewald" is referred to as a neutral observer who "gives a touching picture."

73. Letter, Jan. 15, 1936, *Nobel Institute Archives: Correspondence Journal* (Sept. 23, 1935–Dec. 7, 1936). See also *Nomination Journal, 1933–1953.*

74. Coubertin's and Baillet-Latour's statements are in *Kurzbericht des Deutschen Akademischen Austauschdienstes e.V.,* nos. 15–16, Aug. 25, 1936, 219–20.

75. *Aftenposten,* Aug. 10, 1936.

76. *Tidens Tegn,* Jan. 31, 1936.

77. *Fritt Folk,* Aug. 1, 1936.

78. *Hardanger Arbeiderblad,* Mar. 21, 1936.

79. The Labor foreign minister Halvdan Koht's role in this process falls outside the frame of this article, but briefly it is worth noting that while the workers' movement as a whole, including the entire Parliament group from Labor, strongly supported Ossietzky's nomination, Koht delivered a private proposal on two other candidates who were not so controversial: the Nansen Bureau in Geneva and the high commissioner for refugees in London (*Nobel Institute Archives: Fredsprisen, Forslagsjournal 1933–1953,* Jan. 31, 1936).

80. "Redegjørelse for Nobels Fredspris XXXVI 1936," Det Norske Stortings Nobelkomite (konf.) 5 (*Nobel Institute Archives*).

81. Hestness, "Ossietzky-saken," 91.

82. Bellers, *Die Olympiade Berlin 1936 im Spiegel der ausländischen Presse.*

(

CHAPTER 10

Denmark:
Living with Reality

Jørn Hansen

The picture of "charming little Inge" from Skovshoved, the twelve-year-old Danish bronze medalist, remains a classic reminder of Danish Olympic participation in Berlin in 1936. Strange as it may seem, however, Denmark's part in the 1936 Olympic Games has not been studied in any depth. And yet discussion in Denmark about playing games with the Nazis was as intense as elsewhere, in some senses even more so, as it took place against the background of a mighty neighbor whose history warned the Danes that they had to treat it with care. Such issues were never far from the surface in the debates surrounding the boycott movement and the reception of the Games by Danes as reported in the press and radio.

The main core of support for Danish participation in Berlin was found within the athletic movement in the Danish Sports Federation and in the Danish Olympic Committee (DOC), whereas the Danish Workers' Sports Federation and the Jewish Athletic Association, Hakoah, which at the time had nearly 160 members, including wrestlers of an international class, opposed Danish participation in Berlin.[1] The strongest public opposition came from the so-called intellectual liberals in the circle surrounding the Liberal Fight for Cultural Freedom (Frisindet Kulturkamp) and its periodical, *Kulturkampen* (Cultural fight). There was also opposition from the Communist and the Social Democratic wings of the labor movement. It was the Communist newspaper *Arbejderbladet* and the Social Democratic paper *Social-Demokraten* that were in the forefront of the opposition to the Games. The rest of the press was generally in favor of participation, supported by the bourgeoisie at large, but with one notable exception: the politician Christmas Møller.

Opposition to Nazism

The Danish Workers' Sports Federation (Dansk Arbejder Idraetsforbund; DAI), which had broken away from the Danish Sports Federation in 1931, naturally regarded the development in Germany with great concern and discouraged any cooperation with Nazi Germany in sporting events immediately after 1933. In 1934 the organization published an informative periodical called *Arbejder Idraet*, which in a regular column entitled "The Struggle against Nazism" informed its readers of the developments in Germany. The editor, N. Spelmann, of whom we will hear more later, was also the secretary of the DAI. A resolution from the Workers' Games Union was published in the first issue, urging Danish athletes to boycott any Nazi athletic meetings. The desire of Danish athletes to participate in the Olympics in Berlin was first mentioned in the form of a caricature depicting athletes from the bourgeois athletic associations on a pilgrimage to Hitler.[2]

This matter became a part of the DAI's criticism of developments in Nazi Germany and widened the rift between the DAI and the Danish Sports Federation. Already in the second issue of *Arbejder Idraet*, the DAI posed the question: "What is the opinion of the Jewish athletes?" Goebbels was reported to have said in the Sports Palace in Berlin that Jews in Germany would not be molested as long as they did not expect to be regarded as being of equal importance with the German athletes.[3] It soon became clear that the Danish Sports Federation and the Danish Olympic Committee would be the target for the labor movement's criticism of Nazi Germany and the events in Berlin in 1936. Another obvious target was Niels Bukh, who had been labeled as a Nazi sympathizer in the DAI's cartoons, a favorite method of criticizing nazism at that time. The ideological differences between the DAI and the Sports Federation were most noticeable in the period between 1931 and the occupation of Denmark in 1940.[4] The fact that the Danish Sports Federation did not repudiate the Nazi regime to a great extent certainly strengthened the DAI's image. After a football match against Germany at Idraetsparken (the football stadium) in Copenhagen in 1934, where a number of spectators gave the Nazi salute, the president of the DAI released the following statement: "Workers' sports should be a mass movement which uses the benefits of physical education as a step forward in the emancipation of the working classes. This recent football match between Denmark and Germany, including the Nazi salutes and *Horst Wessel* song, has revealed the so-called neutrality of bourgeois sports for what it really is. The events which working men and women with an interest in sport were subjected to has clearly unmasked the true character and ultimate aim of bourgeois athletics in Denmark."[5]

The Germans had demanded that the *Horst Wessel* song be played as well as the German national anthem before the match and had sent a score of music for a twenty-piece orchestra to the Danish Football Federation (DBU). According to the papers *Social-Demokraten* and *Arbejder Idraet*, the protests that followed only reached a few outside the circle of the labor movement.[6] The DAI's periodical, *Arbejder Idraet,* was having financial difficulties, and it ceased publication in 1935 after only three issues. In its place, *Social-Demokraten* had a regular column on the sporting pages next to the general sporting news entitled "Workers' Sports."[7] *Arbejder Idraet* managed to express its opposition to nazism and bourgeois sports in Denmark in its last issue in 1935: "There is a growing opposition among athletes to act as an advertising medium for Nazism by participating in the Olympic Games in Berlin, and those Brownshirts who are spattered with the workers' blood realize that something must be done. Even the Third Reich's sports Führer has been sent abroad to gather advice from his 'kindred spirits.' He has even paid a visit to a 'neutral' general of sports in Denmark, and was photographed from every possible angle. Since then the sport führer [von Tschammer und Osten] has visited Ollerup, where he, according to the Randers Social Democratic party, had a conversation lasting seven hours with the Danish super-Nazi Niels Bukh."[8]

The "neutral" sports leader mentioned was General Castenschiold, the secretary of the Danish Sports Federation. The membership of the DAI was predominantly Social Democrat. Apart from N. Spelmann and Chr. Bruun, two future prime ministers also had a seat on the Executive Committee, H. Hedtoft Hansen and H. C. Hansen. At the time of Hitler's accession to power there already existed opposition to cooperating with Nazi Germany in sporting events. It was therefore not surprising that the DAI soon disassociated itself from Danish participation in the Olympics in Berlin. The Social Democratic working-class movement was known to be the largest and most dominant movement within the labor movement as a whole. By comparison, the Communist wing was small. Nevertheless the Communist party still managed to have an ideological impact, causing a rift in the relationship between the two movements, but as far as cooperation with Nazi Germany went, the two parties had only a few differences of opinion. The Communist newspaper *Arbejderbladet* was simply more radical in its refusal to have sporting contacts with the Nazis. The Communist party and the Social Democratic party had a covert ideological struggle within the cultural-political sphere. According to the Social Democratic party, the Communists were having too much influence among artists and intellectuals. This was especially true of the association named the Liberal Fight for Cultural Freedom. In the autumn of 1935 these intellectual liberals became prominent opponents of Germany hosting the Olympic Games.

A Protest from Artists and Intellectuals

The Liberal Fight for Cultural Freedom was founded in 1935 as a protest against nazism and was intended from the beginning to be an anti-Nazi front. The committee was made up of many prominent citizens, including Professor Jørgen Jørgensen (chairman), the illustrator Hans Bendix, Elias Bredsdorf, an undergraduate, Professor H. M. Hansen, Dr. Svend Hofmeyer, the economist Niels

Lindberg, Professor Albert Olsen, and a school principal, Anna Westergaard. The editor of the periodical *Kulturkampen* was Jørgen Jørgensen.[9] The Liberal Fight for Cultural Freedom emphasized from the start that it was a strictly nonpartisan organization. Since the start of the modern Olympic Games, from 1912 competitions for arts and crafts accompanied the sporting events, as they did in Berlin in 1936. It was made known in the national press in September 1935 that an arts and crafts competition would be held at the same time as the Olympics in Berlin and would embrace music, poetry, art, sculpture, and architecture. The Danish Selection Committee was made up of the following members: the sculptor Johannes Bjerg, the artist Axel Jørgensen, the professor of architecture Edvard Thomsen, and the composer Louis Glass. The works of poetry were to be selected by a committee appointed by the Danish Society of Authors.[10] Professor Axel Jørgensen was also a member of the Danish Olympic Committee. When the news of the formation and composition of this committee was released to the press, the Liberal Fight for Cultural Freedom took the initiative to write a letter of protest. This was sent to several artists on September 25, after which it was published in the daily newspaper. The protest ran as follows:

> Due to the establishment of a Danish Selection Committee for the arts and crafts competition which is to be held in Berlin in connection with the 1936 Olympics, we would like to present the following statement: "It is the inflexible aim of Nazism to oppose international opinion in favor of an extreme nationalism and an unscientific and hateful racial theory. That is why we feel it scandalous that the Nazis should now appeal to an organization which it daily opposes, and act as the host country for a sporting event that epitomizes the spirit of equality and peaceful competition between all races and all nations. Therefore, we express our deep regret that Danish artists have of their own free will joined a selection committee involved in these Games, and we urge writers, artists, sculptors, architects, and musicians alike to support this letter of protest."[11]

In order to gather as much support as possible for their protest, the Liberal Fight for Cultural Freedom called a "large public meeting" at the Commercial and Clerical Society's large hall.[12] At the meeting several artists elaborated their reasons for signing the protest letter against participation in the arts and crafts competition. The first speaker of the evening was the artist Albert Naur, who attacked his fellow artist Axel Jørgensen and the sculptor Johannes Bjerg for their participation in the Olympic Committee. By doing so they were, he said, guilty of kicking their Jewish counterparts in the face. Kjeld Abell and Otto Gelsted, who continued in the same vein, discouraging people from taking part in Berlin, were among the other speakers.[13]

The meeting sought support from Denmark's athletes. A representative of the Danish Workers' Sports Association, Svend Møller Rasmussen, said that preparations were in progress for a protest movement within workers' sports. A member of the committee from the Jewish athletics association Hakoah, Emil Wassermann, said that they would also support a protest movement, but did not have the mandate to do so, as Hakoah was a member of the Danish Sports Federation, which supported the Olympic Games in Berlin.[14] The resolution that was put forward was essentially identical to the resolution of September, the only difference being that there was now talk of urging artists and athletes alike to oppose participation in Berlin. They also called for a change in the Games venue.[15] The "artists' protest" did not pass unnoticed. Even before the meeting in November the Danish Olympic Committee had responded to the growing dissatisfaction with the Danish participation in the Arts and Crafts Olympics, as had been expressed at the meeting in September and in the publication *Kulturkampen*. The DOC responded with a statement "in answer to the attacks made on the Danish participation in the Olympic Games in Berlin," which emphasized that the character of the Games would remain unchanged even if the venue chosen was Germany: "It has never been the policy of Danish athletes and sports organizations to interfere in what artists, political societies, or any other single gathering may decide to undertake in this country or abroad, and furthermore we ask that the rights of the individual are respected as they should."[16]

At first the DOC tried to dismiss "the artists' protest" as the reaction of a rather odd set of people, but the November meeting had obviously caused the committee to feel enough doubt to direct an inquiry to the president of the Organizing Committee in Berlin. The inquiry came from Prince Axel, who was the Danish delegate of the International Olympic Committee. In his answer Lewald assured him: "Naturally there is no question that the right of foreign artists, musicians, and authors to participate on equal terms in the Arts and Crafts Olympics, regardless of race or color, has ever been in doubt. . . . I would also like to express the hope that Your Royal Highness will be able to persuade the Danish artists to regard the situation in this light, as the Organizing Committee would greatly regret the absence of Danish arts and crafts at the Olympics."[17]

The initiators of the protest letter were unconvinced by Lewald's assurances to Prince Axel. The ideological basis for the Liberal Fight for Cultural Freedom was its anti-Nazi views, and therefore it kept a close watch on what was happening in Germany and seemed to have a good understanding of the Nazi ideology. The petition for signatures continued, and in the Easter issue of *Kulturkampen* the protest was published once again, this time with 216 signatures from recognized artists.[18] It is not always easy to measure the effect of a protest, and certainly the artists' protest did not result in a complete Danish boycott of the Arts and Crafts Olympics. Several Danish artists did take part in it: Poul Bille-Holst entered a painting of a football match; Thomas Hagedorn entered a painting of a female swimmer; Anna Marie Carl-Nielsen entered a sculpture of a Nordic legendary hero; Aage Nielsen-Edwin entered a painting of a man and a woman bather on the beach; and Knud Gleerup entered a sculpture entitled "Ready, Steady, Go."[19] None of the contestants received a medal for their efforts. The artists' protest had, however, induced a previous Olympic medal winner to boycott the Games in Berlin. Josef Petersen, who had twice received silver medals for poetry, justified his refusal with the following statement: "But how can my answer be anything other than a No? What if Denmark had invited poets to an international competition after first having banished a number of Danish poets into exile, just because they happened to be from, for example, Jutland [in Denmark]? Would we not despise our counterparts in other countries who allowed themselves to be conferred with medals by corporals who had burnt the works of Johs. V. Jensen in a town square and would then socialize with the executioners of literature? Apart from what I have already said, I personally find the arguments put forward by the anti-Semites idiotic and the thumbscrew methods they use against political opponents shameful, and Hitler will always remain Hitler."[20]

Mr. Smile and the Danish Politicians

Even though the artists' protest received wide support because of its origins in the Liberal Fight for Cultural Freedom, it suffered from being regarded as a left-wing project. In the Christmas issue of *Christmas for Sportsmen* in December 1935, there was a cartoon of a sculptor receiving a punch on the nose from his statue under the heading: "The Artist's Risk." The caption read: "Ouch! That's the third time I've run into his left hook."[21]

Christmas for Sportsmen was also called "Mr. Smile's Christmas Issue." Mr. Smile was the pen name of Emil Andersen, who had previously been sports editor for the newspaper *BT* and was at that time working as sports editor for *Politiken*. Andersen had for many years edited *Idraetsbladet* and was therefore an influential figure in the world of sport. He was unequivocal regarding Danish participation in the Olympic Games, and this explains why *Politiken*, despite its intellectually liberal background, also supported participation. Andersen thus stood in direct contrast to the journalists of *Social-Demokraten* and *Arbejderbladet*. Although at the beginning of 1936 it was still not officially decided that the Danish Workers' Sports Association would encourage its members to boycott the Olympic Games in Berlin, its views on this matter were already known. As a part of his campaign for Danish participation in Berlin, Mr. Smile published an article from Sweden's Social Democratic Youth Association, Frihet, in *Idraetsbladet* in 1936. The article was headed "A Word in Time: The Labor Movement and the Olympic Games in Berlin." The message in the article was that Sweden's Social Democratic Youth Association would not support a boycott of the Olympics in Berlin. It believed that "the cause of Socialism is best served by keeping neutral."[22] Although Denmark did not participate in the Winter Olympics in Garmisch-Partenkirchen, Mr. Smile still covered the events in great detail in *Idraetsbladet* and to a lesser degree in *Politiken*. Andersen was enthusiastic about the way the Germans had organized the Games, and he even took the opportunity to visit Berlin to observe the preparations for the Summer Olympics.[23]

Mr. Smile had edited the Christmas issue of *Idraetsbladet* for a number of years, and it was published as an independent publication. However, due to publishing difficulties, the job was given to someone else. Mr. Smile therefore edited *Christmas for Sportsmen* instead. The editor of *Idraetsbladet* was Harry Bendixen, a strong advocate of Danish participation in Berlin. He asked several Danish politicians for their opinion of the relationship between sport and the state. The journalist Tage Taaning posed the following questions: 1. What is your opinion of government grants to sport and athletics? 2. Should the government offer financial support for representation at the Olympic Games in Berlin in 1936? 3. Has sport any social significance? If so, in what way do you think it is significant?[24]

The answers given to the second question caused the most public interest. Christmas Møller, a Conservative member of Parliament, gave a clear and concise answer to the second question. He thought government grants beneficial but added: "I have no sympathy for Danish participation in the Olympic Games in Berlin. The position Germany has taken in many matters has automatically placed itself outside the realm of fair play and the spirit of sporting competitions."[25]

Another Conservative member of Parliament, Victor Pürschel, clearly said "yes" to the question of government support for Danish participation in Berlin. If Pürschel's answer together with the positive opinion of *Berlingske Tidende* were at that time representative of Conservative opinion, then Christmas Møller must have been quite isolated within the Conservative party with his negative opinion of the Olympics in Berlin. A new member of Parliament, the Social Democrat party secretary and committee member of the Danish Workers Sports Association Hans Hedtoft Hansen, was in favor of government grants for sport and athletics: "I fully support the idea of government grants to sports and athletics, providing that the original idea behind the Olympics is strictly adhered to. The ruling idea is that free competition between all nations of the world prevails and so the prerequisite for grants must depend on the willingness of the host country to adhere to these principles."[26]

This was a much more diplomatic opinion than that of Christmas Møller, due perhaps to the fact that the DAI had not yet made its final decision on the matter. Hedtoft's reluctance to express himself more forcefully could also have been out of consideration for his party's role as a coalition party.

Arthur Jensen, a Liberal MP, agreed with government grants to sport and Danish participation in Berlin. The founder of the Free Popular party (Det Frie Folkeparti), MP, and gentleman farmer Vald. Thomsen also supported Danish participation in Berlin, while the chairman of the Single-Tax party, Dr. Axel Dam, rejected the idea of government grants on principle as "matters that have no bearing upon the state."[27] The chairman of the Parliamentary Group and minister of education Jørgen Jørgens held a positive view of government grants and avoided the question of Berlin altogether. Whether this was out of consideration for the minister of foreign affairs, P. Munch, and the delicate nature of Danish foreign politics is difficult to determine. The politicians' answers were

published in most of the large newspapers. The workers' press especially welcomed the opinion of Christmas Møller.[28] *Arbejderbladet* did not refrain from
commenting on Hedtoft's diplomatic answer on Berlin.[29]

Hakoah Says "No!"

The decision of the Danish Sports Federation to participate in Berlin posed a
problem: one of its member bodies could hardly be expected to welcome sporting relations with a nation that oppressed its coreligionists. This was the Jewish
Athletics Association, best known as Hakoah, among whose 160 members were
some of Olympic standards. Hakoah was duty-bound to obey the dictates of the
larger federation, and so it was in the workers' associations that the case of
Hakoah was taken up most earnestly. In August 1935 *Social-Demokraten* raised
the problems faced by Hakoah, where a majority of mainly younger athletes favored participation by Jewish athletes, while others regarded participation as
morally repugnant. The Hakoah committee was at first tentative in its treatment
of the issue, and, as reported by *Social-Demokraten,* its chairman, Schwartzmann,
expressed his views at a meeting in the Jewish community: "I regard the existing
problems between Nazis and Jews in Germany as a purely internal problem, in
which Denmark and Danish Jews should not become involved. Jews in Denmark
are Danish and should feel Danish; that is why Danish Jewish athletes should be
allowed to take part in the Games in Berlin if they are called upon to do so, but
note, only if Jews from other countries also decide to participate."[30]

Emil Wassermann expressed himself in more concrete terms. He felt that it
should be a condition of Danish participation that German Jews be allowed to
participate in the Games in Berlin.[31] It was the same Wassermann who later
appeared at the protest meeting of the Liberal Fight for Cultural Freedom in
November. However, it became clear during the spring of 1936 that
Schwartzmann along with Wassermann was working for a boycott of the Olympics. At the spring general meeting a resolution was passed forbidding anyone
to take part in Berlin if they were selected by the Olympic Committee. This resolution was described by *Social-Demokraten* as a great triumph for Schwartzmann.[32] Hakoah was the only association within the membership of the Danish Sports Federation that boycotted the Games in Berlin. The Danish Workers'
Sports Association, the most important association to oppose the Berlin Olympics, was at that time not a member of the Danish Sports Federation. The Danish Workers' Sports Association, however, was far from embracing all workers'
associations and clubs.[33]

The Workers' Sports Clubs

The largest workers' athletics club in Copenhagen, the Arbejder Idraetsclub
København (AIK), was not a member of the Danish Workers' Sports Association, as it was already a member of the Danish Sports Federation when the DAI

was founded. At the AIK jubilee in 1935 the Danish Sports Federation presented honors to the chairman, Einar Faxøe, in the presence of the editor of *Social-Demokraten,* H. Å. Sørensen, one of the special guests. The AIK acknowledged its position in the labor movement but chose to remain a member of the Danish Sports Federation.[34] One of its reasons for staying was undoubtedly due to the fact that the club had several of Denmark's best athletes. This could also explain why the AIK did not support the labor movement's boycott of the Games in Berlin, even though the AIK was critical and contributed to the exposure of the conditions in Nazi Germany.

At the AIK's Maundy Thursday celebration in 1936 a play entitled *A Vicar Goes Over,* by Alfred Bertold, was shown. The play, about the church conflict in Germany in which the methods of the Gestapo play a major role, was banned from public presentation because of its probable effects on foreign relations. In the end, four AIK members went to Berlin, all athletes, as track and field was its strongest area. One of its younger members was so good that he was specially invited to Germany to "observe and learn."[35] The boycott by the DAI was not mentioned in the members' magazine of the Workers' Athletic Club.

The ramifications of the Socialist/Communist splits in the international world[36] did not make much impact in Denmark, but when the Comintern abandoned its "social-fascist" policies in favor of the United Front, the Communist paper *Arbejderbladet* benefited from the more liberal attitude. When the Socialist Workers' Sports International agreed to cooperate with the Communist Red Sport International at its conference in Prague on November 30 and December 1, 1935, one of the main points of agreement was the opposition to the Nazi Olympics. It was already clear by then that the DAI would boycott the Games, but the final decision was not made until May 1936 when the following resolution was passed: "The Central Committee of the Danish Workers' Sports Association reiterates its earlier appeal to the freedom-loving people of Denmark not to participate in the Olympics in Berlin. The Nazi system, which categorizes people according to race and belief, does not deserve to act as host for the Olympic Games, which in themselves symbolize all the beliefs not recognized by the 'Third Reich' in Germany. The Danish Workers' Sports Association joins in supporting the protest made by the organizations of the international labor movement against the Olympic Games in Berlin. We therefore appeal to all sportsmen not to participate in the Olympics, which has been constructed and planned as part of a large-scale propaganda campaign for Nazi Germany."[37]

Among the members of the Central Committee were Chr. Bruun (the chairman), the politicians H. Hedtoft Hansen and H. C. Hansen, as well as the secretary of the DAI, N. Spelmann.

The Opening Ceremony and the Reaction in the Danish Press

Denmark sent 135 competitors to Berlin, the largest Danish representation to that time. The German Olympic Committee had been obliged to restrict the number of journalists covering the Olympics, as each country was issued a limited number of press passes: Denmark received fifteen, which were distributed by a committee under the Danish Council of Journalists.[38] The labor movement's press did not receive any official press pass. Despite this, *Arbejderbladet* and *Social-Demokraten* published articles on the sporting events throughout the two weeks of the Games. The arrival of the Olympic torch at the Olympic Stadium in Berlin on August 1 made a great impression on all those present,[39] especially Mr. Smile, who praised the opening ceremony to the skies in both *Politiken* and *Idraetsbladet*. In the latter paper he enthused: "The opening was truly an experience, a fairy tale. None of us Danes dare hope for gold medals, perhaps our athletes will not even be placed. Even so we are happy with all our hearts that they will have experienced these days in Berlin. If only the rest of the world was like it is here: the competitive spirit aroused, just waiting to be let loose; people from all over the world ready to give their all in order to win, but without blood and hate."[40]

Berlingske Tidende published a long article on the warm welcome the Danish Olympic team had received in festive Berlin: "On arrival at the Town Hall, the Danish competitors were guided to the main hall, where they assembled under a bust of Hitler. The Danish Team was made especially welcome as a friend and close neighbor of Germany. After the Danish secretary general Peter Jaeger's thank-you speech, Niels Bukh stepped forward and started to sing the Danish national anthem *Der er et yndigt land* [There is a country so green and bright] in which everyone else joined with him in singing while the banners were slowly lowered."[41]

Ejnar Blach chose to focus on the French and Hitler in his article. One subheading read: "When Hitler Arrived at the Stadium It Stopped Raining." The headline of the article proclaimed: "The French Olympic Team Greeted Hitler with the Nazi Salute." This was described in the article under festive moments as a demonstration of friendship.[42]

The large newspapers with conservative views in Copenhagen were very positive in their coverage of the opening ceremony. Only the *Nationaltidendes Kronika* felt that it had been overdone from a Danish point of view. He added that the ceremony resembled a political manifestation more than a sporting event. *Kronika* also disliked the fact that the competitors who gave the Nazi salute received the loudest applause.[43] This point of view was followed by an interview with an Austrian competitor, who was asked why the Austrians had given the Nazi salute. The competitor answered that it was a natural action on their part. When asked whether this indicated that most Austrians were also National Socialists, the competitor answered convincingly and spontaneously: "Yes, without a doubt, everyone."[44] Compared to *Politiken, Idraetsbladet,* and *Berlingske Tidende, Social-Demokraten* and *Arbejderbladet* were less enthusiastic. Even before the opening *Arbejderbladet* had described the Danish team under the headline, "A Disgraceful List,"[45] and later commented through an eyewitness that "Dr. Diem had said that the eleventh Olympics were to be held in the spirit of Nazism, and after having seen the opening ceremony, I am left in no doubt that this has been realized. Hysteria, as was displayed at the stadium would indeed be hard to find anywhere else."[46]

Social-Demokraten was more moderate in its criticism of the Games. On August 1 it noted that the issue of race had fallen into the background, as the aim of the opening ceremony was to impress the world. It compared it, however, to the empty show of Potemkin villages[47] and took consolation in the fact that while most teams gave the Nazi salute, "the Danes just politely lifted their caps." In conclusion it said: "The enthusiasm of the crowds together with the thump of the orchestra in the background, playing military marches, sounded throughout the opening ceremony. Time after time hands were raised in the Nazi salute, and voices raised in the *Horst Wessel* song. Despite all of this, it is still the Olympic banners that flutter highest over Berlin and the 'Third Reich,' and the words of an ancient Greek which will count for most during the next two weeks."[48]

* * *

As well as being a member of the Danish Olympic team, Niels Bukh, as a member of the Danish Rifle, Gymnastic, and Sport Association, participated in Berlin with an exhibition team, representing popular Danish sports as a member of his club. Several others within gymnastic circles were similarly impressed with the way Nazi Germany combined physical training with the education of young people. One article on the exhibition events by Kr. Kristensen, published in *Højskolebladet* (in which the boycott had not been debated), read: "The Germans had 4,000 gymnasts in the stadium at one time. They regard athletics and gymnastics as a necessary link in the combined work of national regeneration. This must give the Danish high school teacher faced with this fact food for thought. It is almost 100 years since the death of P. H. Ling, but we are still a long way from realizing his dream."[49]

The gymnastic exhibition given by Niels Bukh was a great success in the eyes of the public and was much praised in *Politiken* and *Berlingske Tidende*.[50] However, *Arbejderbladet* once more took the opportunity to attack Buhk, who had often sympathized with developments in Germany. Under the headline "Niels Bukh Would Like to See a Fascist Dictatorship in Denmark," *Arbejderbladet* demanded that the government grant to Bukh's Ollerup Gymnastic High School be stopped.[51]

Bukh's sympathies for what was happening in Nazi Germany raised some public debate. In an interview with *Flensborg Avis* he told of how he admired a society that encouraged order, efficiency, and a feeling of solidarity. And while he stressed that the German model was not necessarily suitable to the Danish lifestyle, he insisted that young Danes could learn a lot from the Germans in terms of community spirit, order, discipline, and training.[52]

A number of international youth camps were held at the same time as the Nazi Olympics. Erik Aggerholm took part in one of these international student camps as an undergraduate. He reported to the *Hejmdal* (a newspaper in South

Jutland) how the sports Führer had given a lecture on the military connection to sports training in Germany, a lecture that the student regarded as being completely nonpartisan.[53] The man in charge of the thirty Danish participants in the international youth camp, H. Muller-Christiansen, expressed pleasure at having been able to take part in an event of such size and importance.[54]

The opinion of the Danish press was exactly the same at the finish of the Olympic Games as it was at the opening ceremony and before the Games had even started. However, a few of the journalists covering the events moderated their enthusiasm. Many felt that the theatrical staging of the opening and closing ceremonies had been far too overpowering. The most direct criticism came from Axel Lundquist in his article headed "Sport's Fateful Hour," published in *Idraetsbladet* in September 1936. His criticism was that the "sporting spirit" and the enjoyment of participating in the events had been lost in the spectacle. There was a clear lack of appreciation of the "sporting spirit," as brilliant achievements by the German athletes were given second billing to the Führer. As Lundquist noted, "the headlines did not mention the athletic achievements first, but the Führer in whose presence they were achieved. In the presence of Blomberg. . . . In the Führer's presence, etc."[55]

There was rarely direct criticism of nazism, however, and when *Idraetsbladet* urged its readers to write about their most interesting athletic experience in 1936, the Olympic Games was chosen as the event that had made the most favorable impression. Memorable events ranged from medals won by female swimmers to the theatrical staging of the opening ceremony.[56] The prizes won by the female swimmers was the only subject that came under discussion after the Games. "Charming little Inge" was only twelve when she won her first medal, which prompted a discussion in the Danish Sports Federation and *Højskolebladet* as to whether it was wise to allow children to participate in international competitions.[57]

In the Shadow of Germany: Wishes and Reality

The boycott movement in Denmark had only a limited success. A few artists refused to participate in the Arts and Crafts competition, and Hakoah's boycott resulted in the loss of only one or two wrestlers to the Games. *Idraetsbladet* wrote a few articles on the problem of raising money for the athletes, which it put down to the boycott campaigns and constant criticism of Nazi Germany in the press, but when it came to the crunch the money had been found to send the various teams to Berlin: reality had won out over troubled consciences.

The Danish Olympic Committee was aware of the reality of Nazi Germany, of the concentration camps, the anti-Semitism, and the persecution of the labor movement, all of which were reported in the press. But it still supported the Games wholeheartedly. Even *Politiken* reported the dark side of the Nazi regime. The DOC, however, preferred to believe Lewald's assurance that the Olympic rules would be observed at the Olympic Games in Berlin. With the knowledge we have today, the decision to participate can appear naive, reactionary, or, when seen in the light of the crimes committed by the Nazis, simply grotesque. However, the attitude of the DOC was anything but unique. In fact, most of the other countries that participated did so in accordance with their government's wishes. If there were governments that were critical of Nazi Germany, the criticism in 1936 had not as yet been officially worded.

As a close neighbor to Germany, Denmark had to take special considerations into account. In 1864 Denmark lost Schleswig-Holstein to Prussia, and after the Prussian victory over Napoleon III in 1871, Danish foreign affairs were guided by its dread of the newly united Second Reich. This dread disappeared with the German defeat in 1918 but returned with Hitler's assumption of power in Germany. It was said that the German emissary wore out the steps of the Danish Foreign Ministry, complaining over the slightest anti-German comments, and responsible Danish politicians had once again to ensure that Germany did not find an excuse to interfere in Danish affairs.[58]

Even a left-wing government had to be aware of these realities, and since 1929 Denmark had had a Liberal–Social Democratic coalition government. The prime minister, Thorvald Stauning, was a Social Democrat, and the minister of foreign affairs, P. Munch, was a Liberal. The Social Democratic party had close connections to the German Social Democratic party, which Hitler suppressed. We have seen how the Social Democratic press criticized nazism in Germany and the Danish participation in the Olympic Games. Although the Social Democratic press criticized German domestic affairs and the Danish participation in the Olympic Games, the newspaper *Social-Demokraten* was less radical in its criticism compared to the Communist *Arbejderbladet*. This could have been due to the dilemma the Social Democratic party found itself in. It was decidedly anti-Nazi, but it was also part of the coalition government in Denmark, which had to consider the close proximity of Germany. It was the foreign minister's job to deal with the threat of Germany at the time of Hitler's rise to power and subsequent occupation of Denmark. Munch was aware that another conflict between the great powers could occur and that if it did, Denmark could not expect to receive any assistance from "outside." It was said of him that although deeply discouraged, he worked to keep Denmark out of any conflict.[59] After Hitler came to power in Germany, Munch held a press conference in which he asked journalists to take a conciliatory tone toward Hitler and the Nazis. "It never pays," he said, "to be unpleasant to people you might have to sit down with at a later date."[60] The press, however, were not all prepared to take notice of Munch's appeal to preserve a conciliatory tone. As a result, Munch received countless representations and complaints from the German emissary, through the Danish emissary in Berlin and the Danish Consul in Flensborg. The Germans were informed confidentially that the Danish government had done everything in its power to guide the press, and that Stauning personally had ordered his party's own newspaper to use a conciliatory tone in its dealings with Nazi Germany. It was impossible for the Danish government to admit publicly that it had tried to restrain the Danish press, and other countries would just have to understand that Danish Socialists could not cooperate with Nazis. It was Munch's opinion in general that Denmark should not become involved in the internal affairs of other countries. This was probably also the position of the Danish government concerning the Olympic Games in Berlin, which were seen as harmless to sensible people. In March 1936 Munch said of German propaganda: "It is not a form that would have any effect on the Nordic mentality."[61]

The financing of the Danish team for Berlin came entirely from private funds, and this limited the pressure that could be brought to bear on the government. Unlike the Swedish government, which gave direct grants to its federations and thereby to its athletes, the DOC received nothing; discussion of grants for such purposes was still in its early stages in Denmark.[62]

Denmark's official position was a solution in the true liberal sense. No active financial support was given, while Danish participation was not disapproved. The 1936 Olympics were even regarded as being beneficial for Denmark despite their unpleasant theatrical staging. In turn, the Social Democratic party more or less openly and actively supported the labor movement's attempt through general opinion to establish a boycott of the Olympic Games. The boycott movement never amounted to much, but still it was an attempt that did credit to those involved at the time of "The Pest over Europe."

Notes

1. A. L. Andersen, J. Budtz-Jørgensen, V. Gay, eds., *Dansk Sportleksikon* (Copenhagen, 1945), 488.
2. *Arbejder Idraet* 1 (1934).
3. *Arbejder Idraet* 2 (1934).
4. J. Hansen, "Fagenes Fest—Arbejderkultur og Idraet," *Idraetshistorisk Årbog* 7 (1991): 113–34; and E. Hansen, "Arbejderidraetten i Danmark 1929–1943," *Sporthistorie: Den Jyske Historiker* 19–20 (1981).
5. *Arbejder Idraet* 6 (1934): 3.
6. Ibid., 11.
7. In 1937 the DAI again put out a magazine.
8. *Arbejder Idraet* 3 (1935): 11. For the most recent interpretation of Bukh, see H. Bonde, *Niels Bukh—En politisk-ideologisk biografi*, 2 vols. (Copenhagen: Museum Tusculanums Forlag, 2001).
9. *Kulturkampen* 2 (1935).
10. *Kulturkampen* 4 (1935).
11. Ibid.; *Social-Demokraten*, Sept. 25, 1935.
12. *Social-Demokraten*, Nov. 21, 1935; *Politiken*, Nov. 21, 1935; *Berlingske Tidende*, Nov. 21, 1935.
13. *Politiken*, Nov. 22, 1935.
14. *Social-Demokraten*, Nov. 22, 1935.
15. *Kulturkampen* 5 (1935); *Social-Demokraten*, Nov. 24, 1935.
16. *Meddelelser fra Danmarks Olympiske Komité* 25 (Nov. 1935): 3.
17. *Meddelelser fra Danmarks Olympiske Komité* 26 (Dec. 1935): 1.
18. *Kulturkampen* 2 (1936): 2.
19. *Social-Demokraten*, Aug. 1, 1936.
20. *Kulturkampen* 3 (1936): 28.

21. E. Andersen, ed., *Jul for Sportsmaend* (Copenhagen: Idraetsbladet, 1935), 38.

22. *Idraetsbladet* 2 (Jan. 9, 1936): 5.

23. *Idraetsbladet* 7 (Feb. 19, 1936): 12–13.

24. *Idraetsbladet*, Christmas issue (1935): 29.

25. Ibid.

26. Ibid., 30.

27. Ibid.

28. *Social-Demokraten*, Dec. 11 and 13, 1935.

29. *Arbejderbladet*, Dec. 12, 1935.

30. *Social-Demokraten*, Dec. 12, 1935.

31. *Arbejderbladet*, Dec. 12, 1935.

32. *Social-Demokraten*, Apr. 3, 1936.

33. Hansen, "Arbejderidraetten i Danmark 1929–1943."

34. *Arbejdernes Idraetsklub Medlemsbladet* 9 (1935): 2.

35. See Hansen, "Fagenes Fest."

36. *Arbejdernes Idraetsklub Medlemsbladet* 6 (1936): 1, and 11 (1936): 2.

37. *Social-Demokraten*, May 27, 1936; and *Arbejderbladet*, May 27, 1936.

38. *Meddelelser fra Danmarks Olympiske Komité* 26 (Dec. 1935): 2.

39. J. Bellers, ed., *Die Olympiade in Berlin 1936 im Spiegel der ausländische Presse* (Münster: Lit, 1986), says little about the view of the Danish press during the Games.

40. *Idraetsbladet* 32 (June 8, 1936).

41. *Berlingske Tidende*, Aug. 1, 1936.

42. *Berlingske Tidende*, Aug. 2, 1936.

43. *Nationaltidende*, Aug. 2, 1936, in Bellers, *Die Olympiade in Berlin 1936 im Spiegel der ausländische Presse*, 7–18.

44. *Nationaltidende*, Aug. 4, 1936.

45. *Arbejderbladet*, July 19, 1936.

46. *Arbejderbladet*, Aug. 4, 1936.

47. *Social-Demokraten*, Aug. 1, 1936.

48. *Social-Demokraten*, Aug. 2, 1936.

49. *Højskolebladet*, Sept. 4, 1936, 570.

50. *Politiken og Berlingske Tidende*, Aug. 5, 1936.

51. *Arbejderbladet*, Aug. 3, 1936.

52. *Flensborg Avis*, Aug. 8, 1936, in Bellers, *Die Olympiade in Berlin 1936 im Spiegel der ausländische Presse*, 14.

53. *Hejmdal*, Aug. 14, 1936, in Bellers, *Die Olympiade in Berlin 1936 im Spiegel der ausländische Presse*, 14.

54. *Hejmdal*, Aug. 18, 1936.

55. *Idraetsbladet*, Sept. 17, 1936, 10.

56. *Idraetsbladet*, Feb. 4, 1937.

57. See, for example, *Højskolebladet*, Dec. 4, 1936.

58. R. Andersen, *Danmark i 30'erne: En historisk mosaik* (Copenhagen: Gyldendal, 1986), 355.

59. See ibid.; V. Sjøquist, *Danmarks udenrigspolitik 1933–40* (Copenhagen: Gyldendal, 1966); and O. Krarup Pedersen, *Udenrigsminister P. Munchs opfattelse af Danmarks stilling i international politik* (Copenhagen: Fermad, 1970).

60. Quoted in Pedersen, *Udenrigsminister P. Munchs opfattelse af Danmarks stilling i international politik,* 281.

61. Quoted in ibid., 282.

62. See P. O. Holmäng, *Idrott och utenrigspolitik: Den svenska idrottsrörelsens internationella förbindelser 1919–1945* (Goterna: Kungälv, 1988), 154–55.

CHAPTER 11

The Netherlands:
In the Shadow of Big Brother

André Swijtink

The swastika, the Nazi salute, and the *Horst Wessel* song were seen and heard for the first time in the Netherlands during the women's international dual meet in track and field against Germany in September 1933. Dutch sports organizations, then, were the first to be faced by the issue of how to deal with the coordinated sports under Nazi influence. A small minority, mainly consisting of Jews and socialists, was against such sports contacts, while the large majority insisted upon the so-called political neutrality of sport. The Olympic Games of 1936 in Berlin stood at the center of this dispute.

Dutch Sport in the 1930s

In the spring of 1933 a regional international track and field meet took place between North Netherlands and North Germany in the German coastal town of Wilhelmshaven. The Northern German federation demanded that the Dutch team not include Jews and that "Marxists" on the Dutch team not use the opportunity to establish contacts with their German comrades. The Dutch Track and Field Federation informed their German counterpart that they would not compete under such conditions and denounced this interference in internal Dutch affairs.[1] This reaction was somewhat typical for much of the Dutch sports world in the 1930s. German interference in internal Dutch affairs was not tolerated, but neither did long-standing relations with German sports organizations permit interference in German internal affairs. Most of the Dutch sports federations took the position that sport and politics should be kept separate. The Netherlands Swimming Association distributed a communiqué in June 1933 in which it explained to its members and the public that the actions of the German Swimming Association (for example, when it excluded all Jewish swimmers and gave up its democratic structure) was an internal German question and should not concern the Dutch. Dutch swimming clubs should not get involved in politics and the external affairs of the country—which of course maintained diplomatic relations with Germany.[2] The Swimming Association then entered a large team in the European Swimming Championships in Magdeburg in August 1934. The Dutch Bicycle Association took the same stand and sent a team to the World Championships in Leipzig in August 1934. There were also many other, lower-profile sports competitions—as there had been before January 1933—between the two countries.

The position held by most sport federations was identical to that held by the wide spectrum of the nonleftist press. Despite all the political changes that had taken place in Germany after Hitler's takeover, which the sport movement in Germany could not and would not counteract, the Dutch bourgeois press (such as *De Telegraaf, Algemeen Handelsblad, De Tijd*) stressed the pure sporting nature of the ties between Germany and the Netherlands. The consequences of the Nazi revolution on the sports movement were not generally mentioned. Only the specific sporting press, *Sport in Beeld/De Revue der Sporten,* contained regular articles about the consequences of the nazification of German sport.[3] *Sport in Beeld/De Revue der Sporten* not only reported on the changing situation in Germany and particularly in German sport, it also commented on the consequences the Nazi takeover should have for Dutch-German sporting relations. The journal was critical of the new situation in Germany, particularly in 1933 and 1934, and regarded Hitler as personally responsible for the complete change in the German sport system, since he took away all its autonomy.[4] In spite of its criticism of nazism in sport, the journal did not advocate a break in sporting relations between the Netherlands and Germany. It believed that everybody should be aware of the political character sport had taken in Germany and should not be fooled by the Nazis—but a boycott of German sport meets was of a different order and was not advocated by the journal.[5] Although Germany brought politics into sports, this was no reason for the Netherlands to do likewise. On the contrary, the Dutch should maintain their position and present a picture of clean, "impulsive" sport.[6] *Sport in Beeld/De Revue der Sporten* recognized that the German political system had taken over sports, but it accepted this as unavoidable.

Opposition

In some Dutch sports federations the situation was different: they did prohibit some bilateral sport contacts with Germany. These were particularly those sports organizations that traditionally had a large proportion of Jewish leaders.[7] The Amsterdam Gymnastics Association (Turnbond), a member of the Royal Netherlands Gymnastics Federation, voted in March 1933 that competitions with the "coordinated" Deutsche Turnerschaft (the German Gymnastics Federation)

were out of the question. The freedom of speech and religious belief as practiced in the Netherlands were incompatible with the political system in Nazi
Germany. As the Deutsche Turnerschaft had officially offered to be part of this
Nazi system, all established contacts should come to a complete standstill.[8] The
Twentse Atletiekbond, a small track and field association independent of the
national one, decided in May 1933 to cut off relations with Germany until further notice.[9] The Dutch Korfball Federation (korfball is a game similar to basketball) declined the invitation to the German Turnerfestival in Stuttgart in July
1933, the large festival of the Deutsche Turnerschaft in which Hitler made his
first statements relating to physical education and sport.[10] The Netherlands
Bowling Association got into turmoil over the question of taking part in international matches in Frankfurt. In spite of a letter by the leader of the German
Bowling Association stating that every foreigner would be welcome—Jew or
non-Jew—the council of Dutch bowlers decided not to participate. The Jewish
lobby in this association had been successful in prohibiting participation in
Germany, and they used their numbers to stay away from sports in Nazi Germany throughout the 1930s.[11] Within the Netherlands Billiards Association the
"German question" resulted in a crisis that almost split the association. When
the International Billiards Federation refused to exclude the German federation
for having thrown out its Jewish and Marxist members, the majority of the
Dutch Billiards Association accepted and followed this decision. As a result, the
Jewish president of the Dutch Billiards Association resigned.[12] The Dutch Billiards Association was one of five national sports organizations—mostly smaller
ones—that openly discussed sporting ties with Hitler's Germany in the first half
of 1933. In most cases the ban on Jewish sportsmen and -women from German
sport was the main point of contention.

The sports people who favored breaking sporting ties with Germany were
backed by the daily papers on the Left. They were well informed about the situation in Germany, including German sport, and they took their arguments from
the Social Democratic *Het Volk* and the Communist *De Tribune*. These dailies
took a firm stand against Hitler's Germany. For them, National Socialism was
a perverted system that should be opposed wherever anyone had any influence,
including sports.[13] The editors of the sport sections of these two papers did not
differ from their political editors: German sport, in their view, was infected by
Nazi ideology. A differentiation between sport and politics was therefore impossible, as the German Nazi government had taken over sports. Both journals
continuously advocated an end to sporting contacts between the two countries.
Het Volk argued that no sportsman—of any religion or political conviction—
could reasonably compete against a sports organization that had made the exclusion of Jews their rule.[14] The boycott was followed by very few sports organizations, but those that did were applauded by the two left-wing papers. *De
Tribune* even published an "honor's list" of the sports organizations that had
decided to boycott Nazi Germany.[15]

The Soccer Federation

For most of the Dutch sports organizations the German revolution and the consequences this has had for the German sports system was of no concern and did not hinder sporting relations with their German neighbors. The largest of all Dutch sports organization, the Royal Dutch Football Federation (KNVB), did not behave differently. In September 1933 the executive board of the KNVB held a discussion about sporting contacts with Germany. The Jewish member of the executive board, M. Sajet, raised the question about competitions with teams from Nazi Germany. His plea to cut off sporting contacts with Nazi Germany, as it had excluded Jews and Marxists from the sporting scene, did not convince the other members of the board. The most prominent member of the board, Karel Lotsy,[16] belittled the problem (claiming "that this revolution has not been any different from the one in Italy") and idealized the possibilities of sport ("sport should be above politics and have an ennobling effect"). The board sided with Lotsy and not with Sajet.[17]

These opinions were not shared by all in the Football Federation. Some of the Amsterdam clubs—as in many other areas of public life, the capital city was the center of the opposition to Hitler's Germany—tried in vain to have the KNVB review their decision and prohibit matches with Germany.[18] The German question was again taken up by the executive board of the KNVB in autumn 1934. The preparation for the clash between the two national teams on February 17, 1935, set the scene for the discussion. Sajet motioned that German supporters should not sing political songs in the stadium. At the occasion of the friendly match between Poland and Germany, German fans had sung the Nazi hymn. The executive board of the KNVB decided that the Dutch ambassador in Warsaw and Copenhagen should be asked about incidents in the German football matches against Poland and Denmark. The ambassadors reported that no irregularities had taken place.[19] Afraid of public turmoil, the executive board discussed whether the match with Germany should be cancelled. The majority decided, however, that they should not give in to such pressure but that all preparations should be made to have a most agreeable and friendly match. The Amsterdam local football association, HEDW, appealed the decision and demanded that no matches be played with Germany as long as the "current situation in Germany hinders free exchange."[20] In January 1935, about eighty football clubs (nearly one fifth of all KNVB clubs) passed a resolution forcing the executive board to take the matter up again.[21]

These clubs were supported in their efforts by the Communist daily *De Tribune.* In the last months of 1934, this journal put the question of the international football match at the center of its antifascist agitation. It claimed that the neutral KNVB was converting into a propaganda institute for fascism—the organization of the international match was considered one of the more obvious proofs of this.[22]

The executive board discussed the matter again—and obviously did not agree with the protesters—but it would not permit political interference from either side. Dr. D. J. van Prooye, the president of the KNVB, insisted that the executive board act according to its statutes and not be influenced by a direct vote of the membership.[23] But the board agreed that the match against Germany should receive special security measures to avoid too much fan interference. Extra police were to guard the stadium, and the number of tickets sold in Germany was strictly limited. The German swastika flag and the *Horst Wessel* song remained the center of a heated debate. The majority of the board recognized that Germany had two flags and two anthems and that this fact should be recognized appropriately. But the board was afraid that this might provoke some Dutch fans and so held discussions with the Reichssportführer, von Tschammer, and with the leading member of the German Football Federation, Dr. Peco Bauwens. As representative of a Cologne Club in the German Rhineland and a member of the World Football Federation (FIFA) executive board, Bauwens had close ties of long standing to all Benelux countries. The Germans insisted that—if national anthems were played—the two German anthems had to be played, as the *Horst Wessel* song had become the second official national anthem of Hitler's Germany. They accepted, however, the compromise that no music be played and that no anthems be sung at all. On the flag question, the delegates also reached a compromise: the swastika was less conspicuously hung in the Amsterdam Olympic Stadium.[24] The international friendly competition (which Germany won, 2 to 1) led to the first widespread discussion among sports people and officials about the situation in German sport. Afterward, the Dutch sportsworld started to prepare for the 1936 Olympics, an event in which the political influence of the Nazis would be even more obvious.

Pure Sport

Although the term "Nazi Games" was used in those years, for the majority of the Dutch people and functionaries in the sports movement, the term was irrelevant. Participating in the Olympics was considered by the athletes—who were only concerned with athletic performances—the highest aim one could have. In the sports world, the chances for medals were discussed, but the political question was scarcely raised. Possible doubts about the political wisdom of participation in the Games were downplayed by that part of the press that discussed Dutch medal prospects. The cyclist Arie van Vliet, a former Olympic gold medalist, argued that he was only interested in competition of the highest caliber and that this was his last chance to defend his Olympic crown.[25] The sprinter Wil van Beveren, an Olympic finalist in the 200 meters at the Los Angeles games, was quoted as saying that he had never considered boycotting the Games. Many were not really aware of the situation in Germany in the years between 1933 and

1936. As far as the athletes were concerned, there was no doubt that a strong Dutch team should participate in the Olympic Games in Nazi Germany.[26]

The members of the boards of the various sports federations did not discuss a boycott of the Olympic Games in either Garmisch-Partenkirchen or Berlin. They wanted medals from the Olympics to advertise their sport at home. National sentiments were also strong prior to the Games. The Netherlands needed a strong team to do well at the Games; this was considered a question of national honor. Just before the Games the president of the Dutch Swimming Federation declared: "It is our holy duty to bring our flag at least four times to the top of the victory pole and have our national anthem heard in the Olympic Stadium and bring it to the lips of all our proud supporters."[27]

This nationalist pathos was also typical of the bourgeois press. The *Algemeen Handelsblad* considered the Games a question of national reputation and honor. The honor of the Netherlands was at stake, but it was also considered a chance for the individual sportsmen and -women to reach the highest athletic crown possible. To take part in the Olympic Games was no dead notion of the past for *De Telegraaf* but a living ideal that every red-blooded boy was facing whether he was a swimmer, a rider, or a football player.[28] Prestige for the Dutch fatherland was the foremost argument of all public speeches. Opposition was disdained, as it supposedly weakened Dutch representation in Berlin.

There were very few—if any—questions asked about Berlin hosting the Games. The Netherlands Olympic Committee (NOC) set the tone for this point of view. Its president, Alphert Baron of Schimmelpenninck van der Oye, spoke of honor and duty toward the IOC during the NOC congress of 1935. He was sure that the Olympic Games would take place in an Olympic atmosphere and with due respect to the Olympic ideals.[29] This was also the position of the vast majority of the sporting press. The *Revue der Sporten* pointed out the "permanent untruth" in May 1934 that German Jews would be permitted to be part of the German Olympic squad on equal terms[30] and in July 1934 published a picture of three athletes with the Star of David on their chests on its title page. It claimed that these three had been selected to participate in the Games but did not differentiate between preselection and final selection. This gave the false impression that German Jewish athletes had a fair chance to qualify for the German Olympic team. Such reports influenced the editorial policy of the journal to give up their original skeptical view toward the Games in Germany. As of August 1934 the journal took and maintained a clear pro-Berlin stance.[31]

De Telegraaf was the only non-Left paper that was really concerned about the possibility that Jewish athletes might be barred from participating in the Games. The paper undertook a thorough investigation of the situation in Germany in the second half of 1935 and came to the conclusion that, although Jewish sport in Germany was completely isolated, nothing stood in the way of Jewish athletes preparing and qualifying for the German Olympics team. Therefore, the formal conditions of the IOC seemed to be fulfilled.[32] The other bourgeois papers were interested in Dutch participation and nothing else. Appeals for a boycott of the Games were resented with the standard argument that sport and politics should be kept separate. In most of the Olympic sports federations doubts about participation in Berlin were not permitted to develop.

Of course, the members of the sport boards knew about the situation in Germany, but the general opinion was that sport in general and the Olympic Games in particular should not get too excited about all this. For instance, *Athletiekwereld,* the periodical of the Dutch Track and Field Federation, wrote: "We can safely assume that all the important gentlemen in Berlin are smart enough to assure that the Olympic celebration shall not be blemished by incidents that are inspired by National-Socialist racial theory. . . . The Germans have always had a reputation as good organizers. I am convinced that the pure Aryan point of view of organization will not ruin that reputation."[33] The Bicycle Racing Federation acknowledged that the integrity of the German organization should not be questioned at all and argued that the Dutch sportsworld should not interfere with the internal affairs of a foreign country.[34]

Other sports federations did not deal at all with the political aspects of the Games in Berlin. Politics in relation to the Berlin Olympics was for many bourgeois sports federations simply irrelevant, a matter for "Jews and Socialists." *Hockeysport* wrote, in a way typical of field hockey people: "We understand why Jews and Socialists don't want to go to Berlin, but we get angry when Jews and Socialists want to stop others from going to Berlin."[35] "Jews and Socialists" were considered quite odd from the point of view of the well-to-do hockey people. To be against Berlin was identified with people who knew nothing about their beloved sport of hockey.

The situation was similar in other sports where the more prosperous members of society had a majority, such as riding and yachting. It should not be overlooked that these bourgeois elitist federations did contain a certain amount of latent anti-Semitism themselves. Among rowers, for example, it was an open secret that Jews were not welcome in the Amsterdam Rowing and Sailing Club, De Hoop.[36] As late as 1947 De Hoop had considerable problems when a Jewish girl was refused admission to a club social event.[37] Anti-Semitism, not always in a hidden way, was also apparent in the middle-class clubs: the prominent position of Swaab de Beer, a Jewish member on the executive board of the Dutch Bicycle Union, provided a reason for an anti-Semitic campaign of the other national cycling federation, De Wielerbond. Their journal, *De Wielrijder,* wrote in the summer of 1936 "that it was not against the Jews, but Swaab happens to be a Jew and he made sure that the Jewish lawyers Belinfante and Kokosky have an extraordinary amount of functions, introducing a true terrorism on our healthy sport of cycling. No less than 24 different functions have gotten into the hands of Jews."[38]

The Debate

For the vast majority of Dutch sports people and functionaries the Olympic Games of 1936 were nothing but a pure sporting event. A minority had a different opinion, and two sports organizations refused to go to Berlin. In addition, several individual athletes from federations that on the whole were in favor of going to Berlin decided individually not to go. They claimed that "the athletes who will participate in the Games will not be the guests of the IOC, nor of the Dutch NOC, but of the German state, that is, by the National-Socialist state."[39] *Krachtsport*, the journal of the Royal Dutch Strength Sport Federation (KNKB; i.e. weightlifting, wrestling, and artistic strength exercises), was one of the two federations that refused to go to Berlin. The other was the Gymnastic Federation, citing political reasons. In September 1935 the executive board of the KNKB issued a referendum among its membership on the question of participation: 308 wrestlers and weightlifters said "No"; 167 favored participation, while 30 abstained. I assume that it is due to the relative smallness of this organization—no more than five hundred members voting—that their boycott went almost unnoticed.[40]

The Gymnastics Federation was much bigger and was much more in the general public interest. The developments in this federation were less obvious than those in the strength sports. Members in favor of and against participation in Berlin opposed each other so violently that for some time they even discussed splitting up their federation. Both factions maintained respect for the "neutral" character of the Gymnastics Federation. Members of their board in favor of going, including their president, J. H. O. Reys, argued that the nonpolitical nature of their sport prohibited a boycott of the Games for political and/or religious reasons. Those against going, in particular the Jewish members of the Amsterdam Turnbond, argued that the Berlin Olympics were anything but politically neutral and that they should stay home to avoid participating in a propaganda show.[41]

The decision of the federation was taken at an extraordinary annual assembly meeting. President Reys took a last stand to convince the representatives to send a team to Berlin and condemn the Amsterdam Turnbond: "They are driven by motives that have nothing to do with our federation, and which should not have any place within our ranks. They break up the brotherhood of Jews, Catholics, Christians, Socialists, and Fascists [*sic*] which we always have had and which we want to continue to have."[42] That Reys mentioned Jews and Fascists with equal emphasis in the same sentence shows that the position of him and his followers was completely incompatible with those who favored a boycott.

The "sentimentalists," as the people in favor of the boycott were termed by their opponents, gained a majority, however. A motion against participation in Berlin was carried with 153 votes against 107, with 7 abstaining. It has been argued that the large majority was because many wanted (opportunistically) to maintain the unity of their federation, which would have been more endangered by going than by not going. Many gave priority to the unity of their organization over the question of the actual boycott.[43]

In addition to the Strength Sport Federation and the Gymnastics Federation, the Football Federation also stayed home in 1936. The largest Dutch sports federation abstained for a different reason, however: the amateur rules of the IOC were so different from what the KNVB was practicing that participation was not feasible. The stricter IOC rules would have excluded two of the most prominent Dutch players. They had received payment from the KNVB for "broken time." Because of this rule, the KNVB feared that it could not send their strongest squad and preferred to stay home. The basis for the decision of the KNVB does not seem to have been political at all. There were many resentments in the KNVB against the political conditions in Germany, but it did not refuse to go to Berlin as a form of boycott or for any political reasons. As a pro-Berlin decision would have most likely caused public protests, the football board postponed the decision as long as possible, "to make the time for counteractions as short as possible."[44] De Volewijckers from Amsterdam, the most prominent of the football activists against Berlin, did not wait for the decision of the board in January 1936. This football club, which was particularly popular with workers, tried to force the KNVB board to have a referendum of the membership. The board refused this attempt on formal grounds—the KNVB statutes did not allow a referendum. The league boards of the Second, Third, and Fourth Dutch Leagues appealed to the KNVB board to reconsider their decision. But that, too, was brushed aside.[45]

As much as the "broken time" question of the KNVB was always given as the official reason for not going to Berlin, it seemed to cover up the inconsistencies in the decisions of the football board. Maybe it offers an explanation as to why the KNVB board did not appeal the IOC decisions. A vote in favor of Berlin might have encouraged a number of clubs to break away from the KNVB. The discussions within the gymnastics federations were certainly closely watched. Such a split would have been too high a price for participation in a tournament that was already devalued by the fact that the best team, the United Kingdom, was represented by its purely amateur players. By overruling Sajet, the football board had already done what it could without breaking up the organization. One man on the board had, however, no problems at all with the decision one way or the other: Karel Lotsy, the chairman of the KNVB. He acted as head of the Dutch Olympic team in Berlin.

There were also some individual athletes who decided for themselves not to go to Berlin. Many of these were boxers. The Boxing Federation had decided—after long discussions—to participate in Berlin.[46] Ben Bril, the Dutch welterweight champion in 1936, had already decided in 1934 that he would not go to the Olympic Games in Berlin. In that year, he had been with his club, Maccabi, in Berlin. He had the chance to box against Jewish athletes and witnessed the anti-Semitic conditions under which they were living. This made him decide not to box in Germany so long as Hitler was in power.[47] Bril was the best known but not the only Dutch boxer to boycott Berlin. Batterman, De Gooyer, Kneppers, Termeulen, and De Vries expressed their personal decisions not to participate in Berlin to their executive board. Reports in the leftist press about the conditions in Germany had convinced them that taking part in sport in Hitler's Germany was undesirable. The "coordinated" character of German sport and solidarity with the suppressed athletes there made Olympic sport in Germany impossible for them.[48]

From track and field, the triple jumper Wim Peters and the sprinter Tollien Schuurman renounced participation. Their protest was directed against the conditions in Nazi Germany in general and the discrimination against Jewish athletes in particular. The board of the Track and Field Federation tried to convince Schuurman to take part in the Games, but he stayed with his decision, leaving the board members to explain to the press that their sprint star was injured. The Track and Field Federation also refused to reveal Peters's political reasons for refusing to participate in Berlin. In an interview with *Sport in Beeld/ De Revue der Sporten*, they claimed that Peters had not been selected because of lack of form—despite his having just become Dutch national champion.[49]

Peters and Schuurman had received much of the information that convinced them to boycott the Games from the Social Democratic daily *Het Volk. Het Volk* and also *De Tribune* concentrated particularly on the situation of Jewish sport in Germany. Reports that Jews had been present in selection competitions for the German team were put into question.[50] *Het Volk* and *De Tribune* also reported the prohibition of *Der Stürmer* and the SA order to leave Jews in peace until September 1, 1936.[51] After the reports about Jewish sport, the dailies published material that demonstrated the extent to which the Nazis were using the Games for propaganda—sport was only a secondary matter in these Olympics.[52] Much attention was given to the Dutch athletes who were not going to Berlin. The two dailies also tried to convince possible spectators that they should stay home. *Het Volk* appealed to the conscience of its readers, claiming that "conscience cannot be thrown overboard."[53] Federations and athletes that nevertheless went to Berlin were blamed for their self-centered behavior. Athletes and cyclists could do whatever they wanted, they nevertheless would receive bad reports in the leftist press. The president of the Bicycle Federation, Swaab de Beer, was the personification of the mentality of these federations for *De Tribune*: "The Jew Swaab de Beer is giving an Olympic salute to the murderers of his brothers."[54]

Het Volk and *De Tribune* did not send their own journalists to Berlin but did their duty as newspapers by taking the ANP news service information and supplementing it with their own commentary.[55]

There were also organizations outside the sports world that took action against Berlin, in particular the Committee to Protect the Olympic Idea (BOG) and the Federation of Artists to Protect Cultural Rights (BKVK). The BOG was founded in 1935 to explain the Olympic idea and the conditions in Nazi Germany; it consisted of athletes and artists as well as the general public. According to them, the mentality of the Hitler regime was such that neither the holding of the Olympic Games nor of the artistic competitions within the Games was justified.[56] On November 20, 1935, the Committee of Art Lovers organized a protest in the Amsterdam Concert Hall at which men and women from the sports world and the art world, including the president of the Dutch Billiard Federation, spoke out against nazism. He and many of the other speakers pointed out that the demonstration was not directed against the German people nor against the IOC: the holding of the Olympic Games in Hitler's Germany was an attack upon the Olympic idea itself.[57] That was the major activity the BOG had organized, but it had little impact.

Some of the leaders of the BOG were also active in the organizing committee of De Olympiade Onder Dictatuur (Olympics under a dictatorship; DOOD). This initiative was presented by the artists' organization Bond van Kunstenaars, the BKVK, and the BOG. The BKVK was started in 1935 as a united front of the cultural workers against nazism.[58] It had many Communist members and developed into the center of the protest of artists against the suppression of cultural values in Hitler's Germany. In the years 1935 and 1936, the organization concentrated on the artistic competitions that were to take place parallel to the regular Olympic Games in Berlin. The BKVK refused to participate in Berlin itself: "We know that there is no beauty, no civilization, and no chivalry which is not based on goodness. We know that the Olympic idea in Germany is not above the politics of the state—but a part thereof. It is therefore impossible for us to participate in the Olympic art competition."[59]

In the exhibition, DOOD showed why they were against the Nazi Games. It was not only Dutch but also foreign artists and scientists who presented their work at this exhibit, which took place in Amsterdam from August 1 to September 17. The DOOD exhibition achieved more prominence than the actual artistic competition in Berlin itself—which suffered from lack of foreign participation. The exhibition, organized by artists and scientists, was for some time closer to the center of public interest than even the athletic Olympic Games. This was one of the reasons why bourgeois sporting groups neglected or condemned the exhibition. Another reason for the bourgeois disinterest in the work of DOOD was the large percentage of Communists involved in it. The dominating opinion in the Netherlands about the Olympic Games in Berlin was therefore barely influenced by the exhibition on the Olympics under Dictatorship nor the Committee to Protect the Olympic Idea.

The Winter Games and Summer Games

The Netherlands was mainly interested in the Summer Games in Berlin and had very little interest in the Winter Games in Garmisch-Partenkirchen. For many Dutch people the Winter Games were but a prologue to the Summer Games.

This can partially be explained by the small number of Dutch athletes who took part in the Winter Games: one speed skater, one skier, and one bobsledder, none of whom was considered a medal prospect. The bourgeois press included these sportsmen in their arguments about how Germany was organizing the Olympic Games. The president of the Dutch Olympic Committee, baron A. Schimmelpenninck van der Oye, was quoted as saying that the most important aspects of these Games were to take part and that the youth of the world had a chance to meet and understand each other. The Winter Games were considered by him nothing but a good omen for Berlin.[60] Even C. Groothof, a sports journalist working for *Sport in Beeld,* found nothing but praise. He pointed out that Rudi Ball, a German Jew, had been a member of the German ice hockey squad and that some of the German newspapers had even praised him. He expected that the reservations against Berlin should stop now.[61]

Opposition to the Winter Games was particularly visible in *De Tribune* and *Het Volk,* but the two papers had different strategies. While *Het Volk* ignored these Games almost completely, *De Tribune* used the Winter Games as a means to start their offensive against Germany. Under the pretext of covering the Games, reference was made to the people who had been deported to concentration camps.[62] Results from the Games seemed to be used exclusively to bring across the Communist ideas about Nazi Germany. The Canadian defeat of Germany in ice hockey was used to describe the chauvinistic behavior of the German spectators. This was a country where the spectators could not take national defeat, since they were used to competition in which the best of the opposition was either in jail or had been shot, the paper claimed, and so it should not be allowed to stage the Games.[63]

The Dutch team had a number of very good performances in Berlin. In particular the swimmers were very successful. There were gold medals for Rie Mastenbroek, Nida Senff, and the 4 × 100 meter freestyle relay team. Daan Kagchelland in yachting and Arie van Vliet in cycling came home with gold medals. The two bronze medals by the sprinter Tinus Osendarp were a good example of the improvement in Dutch sports. He was third in the 100 meter and the 200 meter, placing as the best European in the races that were won by Jesse Owens ahead of other African Americans. Upon his return, Osendarp was therefore called "the best white sprinter" by the Dutch press.[64]

Sports fans, sports officials, and the Dutch sporting press were enthusiastic about the way the Olympic Games had been celebrated in Berlin. It was certainly the case with Tinus Osendarp, who joined the SS during the Second World War. The basis for his future involvement in National Socialism was laid in Berlin. It was here that he first came under the influence of National Socialist propaganda and here, too, that he saw the privileged positions of sport and athletes in the Third Reich.

Dutch sports officials, too, were deeply impressed. The chef d'équipe Karel Lotsy called the organization "perfect." The journals of the sports federations were full of favorable reports and admiration after the Games.[65] The bourgeois press all agreed that Germany had received a tremendous boost in prestige. *De Tijd* called the Berlin Games the high point in the Olympic Games since 1896.[66]

The leftist press, *De Tribune* and *Het Volk,* took up the points it had criticized about the Games beforehand and saw their reasons for a boycott strengthened. In the opening ceremony *De Tribune* heard many "Sieg Heils" and the shooting of cannons, and in the rest they saw mainly a propaganda show for Hitler.[67] The press argued that the Social Democrats and Communists had rightfully asked for a boycott of the Games. *De Tribune* closed its report on the Olympic Games with a short poem that was supposed to have been circulated in Berlin:

> Ist erst Olympia vorbei
> dann kommt die Reinemacherei
> dann packen wir den Judenmann
> noch einmal ganz gehörig an
> Nimm dich in Acht, o Israel
> und mach Dich aus dem Staube schnell.[68]

> [As soon as the Olympics are over
> we will get on with the clean-up
> Then the Jew will again be given his deserts
> Take heed, oh Israel
> and clear out as fast as you can.]

After the Games

After the 1936 Games, the football match between the Netherlands and Germany in December 1938, to be played in Rotterdam, was again the focal point of the discussion about the conditions in German sport in the Dutch press. Following the Reichs Crystal Night from November 9 to 10, in which many Jewish shops and synagogues went up in flames in Germany, mayor Oud of Rotterdam prohibited the international match. The decision made the front page in all the Dutch papers. The bourgeois papers even accepted the prohibition. Normally politics had to stay outside the realm of sports, but this time it was different. *De Telegraaf* called Oud's decision in its editorial the "smallest possible evil." Otherwise there would have been the danger that "inconsiderate elements" would take the opportunity to use the football match for a protest demonstration that would have caused more problems than simply calling it off.[69] The leftist press was also content that the match would not take place, but they had different arguments from *De Telegraaf. Het Volk* and *Het Volksdagblad (De Tribune* had closed down) would have preferred the Football Federation to have cancelled the match, as it would be impossible to play against a country that had placed itself outside the pale.[70]

Even the Second House of the National Parliament discussed Oud's decision. Some members close to the NSB (Dutch Fascists) used the prohibition of the international match to raise the question of the "Jewish Peril" in general and its role in the relationship between Holland and Germany in particular. Rost van Tonningen, MP, included in his opening statement in the economic debate the remark that systematic provocation against Nazi Germany was frequent not only in economic matters but also in the field of sport. The Dutch actions were supposed to have negative consequences for the port of Rotterdam. The foreman of the Historic Christian Union, D. J. de Geer, reacted immediately and called this a statement unworthy of a Dutch Member of Parliament. This was followed by the applause of almost the whole House. Rost van Tonningen was called a traitor to the Dutch cause.[71]

Oud's decision had a mixed reaction abroad. He took away the opportunity from the opponents of Nazi Germany to have a powerful demonstration and so provoke Germany. The Germans themselves, however, considered the cancellation a provocation. In December 1938 Germany suspended all sporting contacts with the Netherlands, "a German answer to Jewish terror," according to *Der Angriff*.[72] Several international meets between Germany and the Netherlands were called off,[73] but on the whole the disruption of the sporting contacts did not last for long. In March 1939 the Dutch ambassador in Berlin and the Reichssportführer discussed the continuation of sporting contacts between the two countries, which were soon taken up again.[74] The official restarting of sporting ties did not come to much, though. The matches that were cancelled were not put on the agenda again, and the German invasion of Poland in September 1939 made all sporting contacts impossible. Only after the German occupation of the Netherlands were sporting ties reopened, but by force—as in the case of other occupied countries.

Conclusion

The beginning of the Second World War was a temporary end to sports contacts between Germany and the Netherlands; the Nazi rise to power in 1933 was not. On the contrary, the sports contacts between the countries were considerably intensified.[75] In the period between 1920 and 1931, there were twenty-one official dual meets between Germany and the Netherlands. Between 1933 and 1938, however, there had been twenty-five international A-matches between the two neighboring countries. France, Hungary, Switzerland, and Poland were even more active against Germany.[76] Many Dutch sports federations had historic ties with their German counterpart. Hitler's revolution did not—on the whole—make any difference in that. The German sports federations often contained the same personnel despite their "coordinated" character. What was more, they were geographically easily accessible, and by that financially interesting, and they were on the whole a guarantee of an attractive high-class competition.

As most Dutch sports federations were convinced of the dogma that sport and politics should not mix, they ignored as much as they could the Nazi infiltration of sport. The differentiation between sport and politics has for many sport functionaries served a sort of alibi function, as otherwise they would have had to end the competitions with an attractive opponent. Some functionaries put the sport question into a broader context to justify sporting contacts with Nazi Germany. They argued that sporting ties could have a positive effect on the political situation. In the discussions about competition with Germany, chairman Lotsy of the KNVB argued: "Sport can put itself above politics and have a civilizing effect . . . it can serve the spirit of friendship and brotherhood. In that sense the maintenance of contacts with Germany and the Germans is better than their isolation."[77] The sporting contacts with Germany were considered by some a crime against Dutch dignity. But for the sports federation the question was discussed differently: as long as the Germans did not interfere in the composition and selection of Dutch teams, which could include Jews, the Dutch federations would also not interfere in the interior matters of the German federations. The hierarchical interior structure of most Dutch sports federations also hindered any boycott against Germany. Even if some organizations voted for a boycott, that would not influence the federation as a whole. From this situation it cannot, however, be construed that there was an explicit sympathy for what was taking place in Germany. The power of the sports organizations should not be overestimated. The sports movement had its responsibility for good neighborliness with Germany, but it was only one responsibility among many others.

People who were mainly interested in sports had a considerable sympathy for the situation of sports in Germany after 1933, an appreciation that for many became the basis for full approval of the situation in Germany in general. The most famous Dutch sports journalist of the time, Joris van den Bergh, the author of some of the classics of Dutch sports literature,[78] wrote in May 1933 after the "coordination" of German sports: "As concerns sport, there is much good [in this coordination]. Mind you, in my reasoning sport always has first priority. What the Germans have achieved with their Gleichschaltung [coordination], I have demanded for Dutch sports all along when nobody was speaking about Hitler and the Nazis."[79] Sport first, then the rest, was the typical attitude of many sports authorities. In the years of the German occupation in 1940 through 1945, this fixation on sport was one of the reasons why many Dutch sports authorities went in step with the German occupation forces.[80] A considerable percentage of the Dutch sports world, however, resented the nazification of German sports. Some considered the political situation in Germany so evil that sporting contacts were automatically out. Others argued on the sporting grounds of Germany's racially unified sport, the symbolism of the Olympic flame, and the outbreak of Olympic fever. In other areas of civic life in the Netherlands such positions were most likely to be taken by leftist Jews, Social Democrats, and Communists. These groups tried to achieve a sports boycott against Nazi Germany, and they expressed their disdain for the situation in Germany, including German sport.

Notes

1. *Het Volk,* May 17, 1933.
2. *De Revue der Sporten,* Sept. 11 and 18, 1933.
3. *De Revue der Sporten,* Apr. 24 and May 1, 1933.
4. *Sport in Beeld/ De Revue der Sporten,* Dec. 11, 1934.
5. *De Revue der Sporten,* Sept. 25, 1933.
6. *De Revue der Sporten,* Oct., 9, 1933.
7. For the situation of Jewish sports in the Netherlands, see A. Krüger and A. Sanders, "Jewish Sports in the Netherlands and the Problems of Selective Memory," *Journal of Sport History* 26.2 (1999): 271–86.
8. *Het Volk,* Apr. 24, 1933.
9. *De Sport,* May 30, 1933.
10. *Het Korfbalblad,* May 23, 1933.
11. *Het Kegelblad,* Mar. 30 and Apr. 27, 1933; Notes of the Executive Board (Bestuur) of the Kegel Bond (Archives of the *Koninklijke Nederlandse Kegel Bond,* Haaksbergen, July 9, 1933).
12. *De Revue der Sporten,* Sept. 11, 1933.
13. *Het Volk,* July 13, 1933.
14. *Het Volk,* Apr. 24, 1933.
15. *De Tribune,* May 18, 1933.
16. See *Documentaire Nederland en de Tweede Wereldoorlog,* vol. 27 (Zwolle 1990), 640.
17. *Notes of the Executive Board (Bestuur) of the Football Federation* (Archives of the KNVB, Zeist, Sept. 23, 1933; hereafter cited as *Notes of the Executive Board*).
18. *Het Volk,* June 20, 1933.
19. *Notes of the Executive Board* (Sept. 15, Oct. 27, and Dec. 8, 1934).
20. Ibid. (Oct. 27, 1934).
21. *Het Volk,* Jan. 14, 1935.
22. *De Tribune,* Dec. 12, 1934.
23. *Notes of the Executive Board* (Dec. 8, 1934).
24. Ibid. (Dec. 8, 1934, and Jan. 19, 1935). For Bauwens's role, see A. Heinrich, " 'Rücksichtslos deutsch': Peco Bauwens, das Fachamt Fußball und die FIFA," *Sportzeiten* 2 (2002): 39–52.
25. *N.R.C. Handelsblad,* Feb. 2, 1980.
26. Author's interview with W. van Beveren, Amsterdam, Aug. 8, 1985.
27. *De Zwemkroniek,* Jan. 3, 1935.
28. *Algemeen Handelsblad,* Mar. 8, 1936; *De Telegraaf,* May 17, 1936.
29. *De Tijd,* Oct. 28, 1935; *De Telegraaf,* Oct. 27, 1935.
30. *De Revue der Sporten,* May 28, 1934.
31. *De Revue der Sporten,* July 16 and Aug. 6, 1934.
32. *De Telegraaf,* Aug. 6, 17, and 21, Oct. 8 and 10, 1935.
33. *De Athletiekwereld,* Jan. 22, 1935.
34. *Sport in Beeld/De Revue der Sporten,* Nov. 25, 1935.
35. *Hockeysport,* July 28, 1936.
36. As other Amsterdam rowing clubs were also anti-Semitic, the Jewish rowers set up their own club, "Poseidon."
37. See A. Swijtink, *In de pas: Sport en lichamelijke opvoeding in Nederland tijdens de Tweede Wereldoorlog* (Haarlem: De Vriesbosch, 1992), 328–32.

38. Quoted in *De Tribune*, Aug. 6, 1936.

39. *Krachtsport* 15 (Aug. 1934).

40. A. Krüger, *Die Olympischen Spiele 1936 und die Weltmeinung: Ihre außenpolitische Bedeutung unter besonderer Berücksichtigung der U.S.A* (Berlin: Bartels and Wernitz, 1972), 189; H.-J. Teichler, "Die internationalen Sportbeziehungen des Deutschen Reiches im Spannungsfeld von Frieden und Krieg," in *Sportler für den Frieden: Argumente und Dokumente für eine sportpolitische Bewußtseinsbildung,* ed. S. Güldenpfennig and H. Meyer (Cologne: Pahl-Rugenstein, 1983), 172–73.

41. *Het Turnblad,* Nov. 1, 1935; *Sport in Beeld/De Revue der Sporten,* Mar. 19, 1935.

42. *Het Turnblad,* Nov. 15, 1935.

43. *Algemeen Handelsblad,* Nov. 11, 1935; *Arbeidersport,* Nov. 23, 1935.

44. A. van Emmenes, ed., *Jubileumsboek KNVB, 1889–1939* (Amsterdam: KNVB, 1939), 88.; *Notes of the Executive Board* (Jan. 25 and Apr. 4, 1936).

45. *Notes of the Executive Board* (Jan. 25, 1936); *De Tribune,* Apr. 27, 1936.

46. *Bokssport,* Mar. 31, 1936.

47. Author's interview with B. Bril, Amsterdam, Aug. 6, 1985.

48. *De Tribune,* Apr. 20 and 27, 1936; author's interview with B. Kneppers, Amsterdam, Aug. 6, 1985.

49. Author's interview with W. Peters, Amsterdam, July 16, 1985; T. Schuurman to the author, July 30, 1985; *Sport in Beeld/De Revue der Sporten,* Nov. 4, 1935.

50. *Het Volk,* Jan. 16 and Nov. 18, 1935.

51. *Het Volk,* Dec. 5, 1935; *De Tribune,* May 25, 1935.

52. *Het Volk,* Jan. 21, 1936; *De Tribune,* Sept. 13, 1935.

53. *Het Volk,* Jan. 21, 1936.

54. *De Tribune,* Apr. 15, 1936.

55. *Het Volk,* July 8, 1936; *De Tribune,* Aug. 3, 1936.

56. *BKVK-Bulletin* no. 12.

57. *De Tribune,* Nov. 21, 1935.

58. *De Tribune,* July 8, 1936; F. Gribling, "'Tendenzkunst': De politisering van Nederlandse kunstenaars tussen twee werelddoorlogen," in *Berlijn—Amsterdam 1920–1940: Wissewerkingen,* ed. K. Dittrich, P. Blom, and F. Bool (Amsterdam: Querido, 1982), 324–31 (quote on 330).

59. *BKVK-Bulletin* no. 6.

60. *Algemeen Handelsblad,* Feb. 17, 1936; *De Tijd,* Feb. 11, 1936.

61. *Sport in Beeld/De Revue van de Sporten,* Feb. 24, 1936.

62. *De Tribune,* Feb. 6, 1936.

63. *De Tribune,* Feb. 15, 1936.

64. *Algemeen Handelsblad,* Aug. 6, 1936.

65. *De Waterkampioen,* Aug. 21, 1936; *De Sportkroniek* no. 62 (1936).

66. *De Tijd,* Aug. 3, 1936.

67. *De Tribune,* Aug. 3, 1936.

68. *De Tribune,* Aug. 17, 1936.

69. *De Telegraaf,* Nov. 30, 1938.

70. *Het Volk,* Nov. 26, 1938; *Het Volksdagblad,* Nov. 23, 1938.

71. *Handelingen en bijlagen van de Tweede Kamer der Staten-Generaal* (1938–39), 848, 889; *De Tijd,* Dec. 10, 1938.

72. Quoted in *De Telegraaf,* Dec. 12, 1938.

73. *De Telegraaf,* Dec. 9, 1938.

74. *Sport in Beeld/De Revue der Sporten,* Mar. 27, 1939.

75. The German data are taken from H.-J. Teichler, *Die internationalen Sportbeziehungen,* 165–172; and H.-J. Teichler, "Sport und NS-Außenpolitik: Zur Rolle des Sports in der Macht- und Herrschaftspolitik des Dritten Reiches," in *Die Entwicklung des Sports in Nordwestdeutschland,* ed. W. Buss (Duderstadt: Mecke, 1984), 227–54.

76. H.-J. Teichler, *Die internationalen Sportbeziehungen*, 171.

77. *Notes of the Executive Board* (Sept. 23, 1933).

78. His most famous books are *Mysterieuze krachten in de sport* and *Temidden der kampioenen*.

79. *Sport-Echo*, May 24, 1933.

80. See Swijtink, *In de pas*, 79.

Epilogue

Arnd Krüger

By focusing on the major countries involved in the 1936 Olympics, some questions concerning issues of general importance warrant further study. The Olympic boycotts of 1976, 1980, and 1984 taught us a great deal about how boycotts of the Olympic Games work, about the amount of government and parliamentary involvement, and the resistance of the sports culture against such influences.[1] Considering that the Nazis were a masculine brotherhood (Männerbund), many of their actions in such highly symbolic spheres as the Olympic Games could also be regarded from a gender perspective. The question of female participation was still on the agenda of the IOC, so when the Executive Committee met on April 24, 1931, a vote decided that women could take part in track and field (16 to 3), fencing (17 to 2), swimming, gymnastics, and figure skating.[2] Also overlooked here are fuller discussions of such activities as the three scientific Olympic congresses, the Olympic Youth Camp, the international reaction to and artistic merit of Leni Riefenstahl's movie, *Olympia,* the cultic plays performed in the Olympic arena during the Games, the 1936 Barcelona Popular Olympics, and many more. Here, then, we will concentrate on some remaining gaps and suggest directions for future research into hitherto underdeveloped areas.

Participation

We have shown why the major countries of the world attended the Nazi Olympics. While only thirty-eight countries were represented at the Los Angeles Games in 1932 (forty-six had been present in Amsterdam in 1928), forty-nine made it to Berlin, a new Olympic record. In 1933, fifty-two national Olympic

Committees were recognized by the IOC, and by 1936 the number had risen to fifty-nine. Of those, fifty-three accepted the invitation to come to the Berlin Games, and forty-nine actually came. Spain, for instance, accepted but was unable to participate due to the Civil War. Among the invited and acknowledged national Olympic Committees, Cuba, Haïti, Panama, and Lithuania did not answer the German call and had previously only been represented by very small teams. The Irish Free State and the newly founded Palestinian Olympic Committee were not represented and explained in letters to the IOC why they did not participate.[3]

The IAAF had ruled in August 1934 that a member federation is limited by the political boundaries of the country or nation it represents. Since 1914, the international sports federations were also in charge of the rules for their sport in the Olympic Games. As the national sports federations of Ireland claimed jurisdiction over all of the thirty-two counties of Ireland and not only the twenty-six counties of the south, the Irish Free State, its National Athletics and Cycling Association had to decide whether to accept the split of the nation—partitioned in 1921 and all remaining ties with Great Britain to be removed with the Constitution of 1937—and compete in Berlin with a southern team or to stay home. It preferred to stay away from Berlin in spite of having won two gold medals in Los Angeles.[4]

The Palestinian Olympic Committee, which had been acknowledged by the IOC only in 1934,[5] contained Jewish and non-Jewish members and simply was not yet ready to appear internationally and was having numerous internal differences. In 1936 Palestine was close to a civil war and was unable to muster a strong team.[6]

Not even the Maccabi World Union, the international Zionist sport organization, asked the IOC to refrain from having the Olympics in Nazi Germany. In two letters following the decisions of its 1935 world congress,[7] its president, Selig Brodetzky, demanded from the IOC and the international sports federations only that their Jewish members be permitted individually to refrain from participating in the Games without reprisal from their sports governing bodies: "The Maccabi Movement has never attempted to question the decision of the Comité International Olympique as to the venue of the Olympic Games, but we certainly do wish to urge all Jewish sportsmen, for their own self-respect, to refrain from competing in a country where they are discriminated against as a race, and our Jewish brethren treated with unexampled brutality."[8] Baillet-Latour fully agreed, particularly since the percentage of Jewish athletes was relatively low and so a "quiet" boycott on the part of a few would suit the purpose.[9] He therefore replied that, according to the position of the IOC, no athletes should be hindered from taking part in the Games, nor should anyone be forced to go to Germany if they did not want to.[10]

Notably, the German Maccabi Federation had not voted in favor of a boycott of the Nazi Olympics; instead, it abstained from the crucial vote at this international Maccabi congress. It is open to speculation why this was the case.[11] There were still twenty-one Jewish sportsmen and -women in the Nazi training camps,[12] and the Maccabi Federation did not want to jeopardize their chances, small as they were.[13] Perhaps more important, although the Maccabi world congress took place in Czechoslovakia, so the delegates themselves were safe, the German Jewish representatives still had to consider the fate of their families at home. It should also be noted, however, that in 1935 Germany still favored the aims of the Maccabi, which was for the emigration of German Jews to Israel. Nobody was thinking about a holocaust then.[14]

Press Reaction

The press reaction to the Nazi Games in South America was passed over by the German propaganda minister, and we have overlooked it here. In the Nazi party press reports on the impact of the Olympic Winter Games, South American countries are not mentioned at all—hardly surprising as they did not take part.[15] But in the official press reports for the Olympic Summer Games, which were put together by the German embassies abroad and evaluated by the German Foreign Office, only eleven out of the 248 pages of the report deal with all of Spanish-speaking South and Central America.[16] German radio propaganda geared toward South America began only when the Games were officially opened. The transmissions on short wave to South America required some fine tuning on the side of the receivers. The Olympic radio transmissions made use of the enthusiasm of the ethnic Germans, particularly in southern Brazil and Chile, to search for the new German radio stations and thus develop a new radio connection to the fatherland. South America did not yet play a role in Hitler's plans.

The press (with the exception of Cuba) was on the whole friendly toward the Olympic Games in Nazi Germany, being much concerned with German precision in running the Games and the genuine enthusiasm of the population to have all the world as guests. For reporters from countries where mass rallies were the rule and where dictators have a long political tradition, Hitler's continuous presence at the Games and the massive support of the German spectators for their Führer were most impressive. By South American standards, Hitler made a positive impression as he appeared in his brown uniform with just his Iron Cross and a swastika on an armband and not in the grandiose operetta-like uniform so typical of the South American caudillos. Other than that, the papers seemed to have been mostly concerned with the modest chances of their own athletes. Human rights issues were not discussed in the press reports that were circulated inside the German government.

There are still many interesting issues to consider in the countries we have overlooked. What was the role of the national teams in the young Baltic republics that used their sport teams for national identification? What role did the 1936 Olympics play in Poland, where internal divisions were so strong that the Hitler-Stalin Pact resulted in its new division and the beginning of World War II? How did the German success in the Berlin Olympics influence the Austrians to favor the Anschluss to come? Why did India participate in the Olympics, although Hitler had insulted them in claiming that the British had taught them to walk?[17] The desire to be internationally present, to show one's flag, as demonstrated in the decolonization following the Second World War, was particularly strong in young nations. Many more events surrounding the 1936 Games would make a good story that has still to be told.

Socialist Internationals

The only major country that did not go to Berlin—and was not invited—was the Soviet Union.[18] At that time there were three international sport systems with three separate international championships: the bourgeois world had the IOC and the Olympic Games, the Socialists had the Socialist Workers' Sport International with the Workers' Olympics (Frankfurt 1925, Vienna 1931, Antwerp 1937), and the Communists had the Red Sport International with the Spartakiad (Prague 1921, Moscow 1928, Berlin/Moscow 1931, Antwerp 1937).[19] Members of one organization were banned from participating in the events of another, and the three organizations were constantly at loggerheads. Only through the pressure of fascism did they eventually combine forces. Coubertin had acknowledged the split, tried to overcome it after 1920, and regretted it, but his successors in the leadership of the IOC were much more involved in the day-to-day operation of sports and resented any rapprochement.[20] It was as late as May 1934 that the first thaws in the war between the rival Communist and Socialist bodies appeared, when Stalin sent out orders for a Popular Front against fascism—the first example of this new policy in practice came with the unification of the French Communist (FST) and Socialist (USSGT) sports organizations into the FSGT at the end of 1934.[21] The international bodies became more friendly but never overcame their differences enough to unify, although they did compete against each other at the combined Workers' Olympics in Antwerp, Belgium, in 1937.[22] Their joint struggle against the Berlin Olympics helped them come to terms with each other. The Soviet Union was the only country with a Communist government at the time. The Red Sport International therefore represented the official sport authority in the USSR. It was not invited to the Olympics and started to participate on an international bourgeois field only in 1946 with the European Track and Field Championships in Oslo and in 1952 in the Helsinki Olympics.

The Barcelona Popular Olympics

The "Olimpiada Popular" of Barcelona in July 1936 is a different story. While the French and other journals put it into the context of the Olympic boycott, the Catalan press insisted on its independent character.[23] Catalonia, in north-east Spain with Barcelona as its capital, fiercely defended its Catalan national-ity: industrially strong, with its own language (a mixture of Spanish and French) and its own history (having been part of Aragon, rather than Castille), it never accepted the Madrid-based Spanish centralism. Coubertin's idea of Olympic geography seemed to give them the chance for national representation—as with the Czechs or the Finns, who had their own team prior to World War I inside the Austrian or the Russian teams. But Coubertin's friends were all from Madrid, and he never visited the Catalan capital while in office as IOC president.[24] The Catalan Sport Federation (CCEP) was not recognized internationally.

When it proposed to stage the Popular Olympics of July 1936 it did not have any backing by any international sports federation, yet in the context of the Berlin boycott and the openness of the situation, six thousand athletes and twenty-thousand foreign visitors in twenty-three delegations were expected. Considering that the CCEP prepared this on three months' notice, it is a signifi-cant success that forty-five hundred athletes actually made it to Barcelona. If you look closer as to who had entered teams, it becomes obvious that this was the whole antibourgeois, anticolonial counterculture: Algeria, Spanish Morocco, and French Morocco had separate teams, while internationally the athletes of the colonial powers competed for their colonial masters. Jewish emigrants and Palestine entered as two teams. Galicia, the Basque Country, and Catalonia— three Spanish areas that claimed to be independent nations—entered as three separate teams. The French Popular Front government and the government of Catalonia supported the Popular Olympics financially. On July 18, one day be-fore the Games were supposed to start, General Franco started the Spanish Civil War with his troops stationed in Morocco. The bitter war (1936–39) had many fronts: conservatism versus socialism (in Spain there were also many indepen-dent anarchists), ruralism versus urbanism, independent "states" like Catalonia or Euskadi (the Basque country) versus the central government, and royalism (two kinds, to make things more complicated) versus republicanism.

Spain had been the cradle of guerilla warfare in its struggle against Napoleon; now all sides asked for foreign intervention. Nazi Germany and Fascist Italy in-tervened on the side of Franco, while some of the athletes and fans who had come to the Popular Olympics stayed on in Spain to fight on the democratic side. It took until 1992 for Barcelona to get its Olympics and stage its show of Catalan sovereignty, albeit much diluted.[25] Due to the Civil War, Spain could not partici-pate in the Berlin Olympics. Otherwise, the Popular Front government in Madrid was about to act in the same way as the French Popular Front government, pay-ing to send teams to both, and paying for the staging of the Barcelona Games.

The IOC

In all of the Olympic boycotts and boycott threats in 1936 and since, much has depended on the moral authority embodied in the IOC. The Olympic Games held high prestige, but in contrast to the situation today, neither the archival sources nor the newspapers reveal any evidence of naked bribery of the IOC members to get or maintain the Games. IOC members were fêted and treated as though they were full-fledged ambassadors for their country, but no further favors seem to have been passed on. As shown throughout this book, the Olympics were governed more by pragmatism than moralism.

There was, however, one significant exception: the Nazis' courting of Coubertin himself. Coubertin had spent much of his personal fortune on the Olympics but was financially ruined by the Soviet Revolution as a consequence of his speculation in high-yielding Czarist bonds, which were not honored by the revolutionary Soviet government. He had to give up his previous lifestyle and lived in semiretreat at Lake Geneva. The Nazis made use of this situation, and in addition to the measures detailed in previous chapters provided him with RM 50,000 (£2,500, or about $12,000).[26] This was roughly the income of an English professional football player for ten years of play, the amount fifty thousand spectators would pay to watch a soccer match, and enough to buy about 250,000 copies of a daily newspaper. Some would say that this was a bribe to buy the goodwill of the IOC members and of the founder of the IOC. Other countries, however, also paid into a fund to assure a dignified lifestyle for Coubertin, but the Nazis paid the largest sum. Considering that Coubertin did not go to Berlin despite several invitations, that he spoke only in his own words and on his own ideas, and not those of the Nazi ideologues, the more likely explanation is that he did not need to be bribed as he had always been in many ways sufficiently profascist. At times he had been involved with the early French Fascists, and many of his ideas went along fine with the Nazis: a white male brotherhood of the strong, armed and well-prepared to fight, the praise of the icon of the warrior athlete, elitism, and anticommunism.[27] Coubertin's humanitarianism would not have gone the road to Auschwitz—but nothing of that was demanded anywhere by 1936.

In terms of propaganda, Coubertin's newspaper interview with André Lang after the Olympics is still puzzling. The founder of the Olympics praised the success of the Berlin Olympics and asked back: "What is the difference whether you advertise Southern Californian weather or the political regime in Berlin? The Olympic Games benefit through the advertisements of the Organizing Committees—and that is what counts."[28] Is it really that simple? But Coubertin also entrusted Diem and the Reichssportführer to continue doing his Olympic research in an Olympic Institute to be founded in Berlin.[29]

Coubertin had always made the point that women—just as in antiquity—should crown the victors but should not take part in the Olympics. As of 1914 the IOC decided against his will that a woman's medal should have the same value as a man's,[30] yet for many the Olympic Games are still considered part of the rites of men and not women.[31] The Nazis themselves were quite ambiguous about their position regarding women's sports. On the one hand, women were biologically needed for breeding;[32] and on the other hand, medals were counted and a woman's medal had the same weight as a man's. German women had already achieved high international acclaim in the Weimar period, and the Nazis profited from that internationally by the first German Fräuleinwunder:[33] twelve medals were won by German women in 1936. The Nazis were not a homogeneous group. Particularly in sport and in other forms of cultural policy, the various factions clashed and were often only kept together by the will of Hitler.[34] The discus gold medalist of 1936, Gisela Mauermayer—childless, unmarried, with an advanced university degree in biology—later referred to herself as *geburtenpolitischer Blindgänger* (a dud in terms of population policy): this was forty-five years after her Olympic victory and thirty-six years after the end of the Nazi reign, thus showing how deep this split went.[35]

Olympic Congress

The Olympic Games in Berlin were surrounded by other Olympic activities that have not been mentioned in this book. Immediately prior to the Games, the Nazi Kraft durch Freude organization staged a major scientific congress in Hamburg for which it would receive the Olympic Cup, a rare IOC honor, in 1939. The extent to which participation in this scientific congress was disputed among the scientific community has never been fully looked into. The British Nobel Prize–winner A. V. Hill, a leading physiologist whose work is still used as a basis for sports medicine today and who had published in German,[36] refused to go: "I am sorry for I have many German friends, but so long as the German government and people maintain their persecution of our Jewish and other colleagues, it will be altogether distasteful to me as to most English scientists to take part in any public scientific function in Germany."[37] Many participants from around the world were less reserved, including American physical educators, some of whom received a free trip as keynote speakers.

Much of the conference would have disappeared into oblivion had there not been a massive amount of printed material and the parliamentary protest of Luxembourg. The tiny Archdukedom of Luxembourg, neighboring Germany, Belgium, and France, was and still is a politically independent constitutional monarchy. The country is basically bilingual, German and French. At the time it had a conservative majority that favored close cooperation with Germany and a strong socialist parliamentary opposition based in the trade unionism of the steel industry. Luxembourg participated with forty-four male (and no female) athletes in Berlin.

The German organizers of the scientific congress offered free transportation inside Germany and free participation plus room and board for those foreign participants who would show by their dress, customs, name tag, and language that they were Germans living outside the Reich as Auslandsdeutsche. This was geared toward the Germans in Denmark and Poland, the Sudetendeutsche in

Czechoslovakia, the Austrians, the German minority in Northern Italian South Tyrol, in Switzerland, in French Alsace and Lorraine, the Moselle Francs in Luxembourg, the German minority in eastern Belgium, and it would also address the Flemish and the Dutch. North and South Americans of German descent could claim these reductions as well.[38] I have not been able to find out how many physical educators and sport scientists made use of these reductions. Obviously all of the Sudetendeutsche did so.

Nobody outside the field of physical education seemed to care—except Luxembourg. Considering that all of Luxembourg had less than one tenth of the population of the city of Berlin and that it had been easily overrun by German forces at the beginning of World War I, the sensitivity seems understandable. The parliamentary debate in the Luxembourg Chamber of Deputies took the conservative majority by surprise, as it did not have all of its unpaid Members of Parliament present. The opposition mustered a slim majority, and Parliament censored the Luxembourg participants of the Hamburg congress for "un-Luxembourgeois behavior" that endangered the sovereignty of the state and the government for not stepping in.[39]

The government lost the vote for letting the physical educators participate in the Kraft durch Freude Conference. That also broke the rules of the International Labor Bureau, a subsection of the League of Nations, of which Luxembourg but not Germany was a member at the time and which prohibited participation in actions of "wild" unions. The government was sufficiently embarrassed by the local papers to continue the debate the next day after having mustered its majority. So, the next day a new parliamentary resolution was passed expressing deep respect for the good neighbor Germany and their efforts, which were worthwhile to learn from, in the field of leisure activities, physical education, and sport.[40]

Were the Nazi Olympics Successful?

There is still some debate over whether or not the Nazi Olympics were a success, and, if so, in what ways. This question has been raised in all of the chapters in this book, with various responses, participants and participating nations each entering for their own reasons. German propaganda was very efficient, so efficient that as late as the 1972 Olympics many commentators would still not recognize that the Berlin Games had, in fact, been the Nazi Games.[41] Even as late as 1996 the city of Garmisch-Partenkirchen celebrated the sixtieth anniversary of their Olympics, as if this had been nothing but a big happy sports meet.[42] So much for the long-term effect of efficient propaganda.

Inside the Nazi system it was apparently quite different from outside. When Albrecht von Kessel testified in the Nuremberg trials for war criminals in 1946, he said: "In 1936 there was an episode that was very depressing for us as it seemed to be so symptomatic of the reaction of the foreign countries in relation to the

Jewish question. . . . I refer to the Olympic Games, which were the biggest international triumph of the National-Socialist regime. . . . The International Olympic Committee had demanded as its condition to maintain the Olympic Games in Berlin that Germany give up its discrimination against the German Jewish athletes. . . . The Nazis did not keep their pledge. In the very last moment they excluded the German Jews." Attorney Dr. Becker: "Is it true that this was interpreted by the Nazis as a reinforcement of their position?" Kessel: "Oh yes. They said to themselves and also to us: you see, you can do anything, you just have to know how."[43]

The IOC and the integrity of international sports may have suffered a moral blow, but in monetary terms it was essential for the IOC to avoid an Olympic boycott. If the Games could take place under a Nazi regime—provided the rules of the sport were respected, if nothing else—any organizer in the future could be sure that it could stage and keep the Games no matter what its political regime, its involvement in warfare, in human rights violations, or even in contravention of the rules of the IOC itself. In this respect the immense Nazi propaganda helped the IOC as it made the Olympic Games even more visible as a top-class international sports event.[44] It showed that there is an international sports culture that disregards much of the political culture—in spite of being financed by the political sphere. In 1980—and, for the other half of the world, 1984—many of the same questions were raised. In this respect, the modern Olympics may even be similar to the ancient, when the quadrennial Olympic truce helped keep the ancient world together. The Greeks fought their wars, but every four years they paused for a month in respect for the rules of the game, honoring their gods.

In each country the context for the propaganda was different, and it therefore had a different effect for the Nazi regime. The discussion of human rights issues on the sports pages in many countries helped raise the level of awareness of the situation in Germany. The American consul, George Messersmith, claimed that holding or not holding the Olympic Games would make a big difference for the future development of Europe and the world. He was probably right. There was no world leader, no moral authority, trying to stop the Nazis in 1935 or 1936. All of the countries were looking after their own affairs, the League of Nations did not function well, nor did the leadership of any other organization. Arthur Morse has argued that the world looked the other way while six million died—and that Berlin was the beginning of all this.[45]

In 1936 there was still hope that the Nazi Olympics were not only a propaganda show but that they were really a step in the right direction. From hindsight and looking into the archival sources we know that they were not. Nazi propaganda and the goodwill and genuine enthusiasm for international understanding of much of the German population at the time were sufficiently impressive to give Germany the benefit of the doubt for the following three years.

The only German group that was permitted to stress their point that they were unjustly treated and staged large and violent demonstrations were the Sudetendeutsche (they still demonstrate today, now as refugees inside Germany, trying to get their property back from the Czech Republic). This German minority at the rim of Czechoslovakia had to wait for another two years before they were "liberated" from the Czech "yoke." They had been quite happy until 1919, when Czechoslovakia became an independent state and was no longer part of the Austro-Hungarian Empire. Although they have always identified more with Bavaria and Germany than with Austria, they resented that they had to learn Czech, as many of the old institutions changed hands after Czech independence. It should not be overlooked that Prague had the oldest German university, and that long-standing cultural ties were cut after 1918. Turnen was one of their main traditional cultural activities. Their Turnen differed from the Sokol kind of gymnastics of the Czechs and other Slavic people. Konrad Henlein, the president of the Sudetendeutsche Turner Federation, was also the leader of their Nazi party, and thus the Olympic Games were used as an international stage for agitation. After the peaceful inclusion of the Saar after a plebiscite (1935), the march into the demilitarized Rhineland (1936), the Anschluss of Austria (1938), and the occupation of the Sudetendeutsche rim of Czechoslovakia (1938, as agreed at the Munich conference with Chamberlain and Daladier) were the next steps toward the Second World War. Only after the invasion of the rump of Czechoslovakia in March 1939 did the Western world muster enough strength to call for a halt to the Nazi expansionism.

Research is an ongoing process. We have looked mainly at the political history of the Nazi Olympics. There remain many opportunities for future researchers to look more closely into the cultural side of the Games.[46] What made the Olympic Games so susceptible to the Nazis that the Riefenstahl film *Olympia* has been regarded by some as a work of art that best represents the Olympic spirit, while for others it is a piece of Nazi propaganda?[47] For athletes taking part in the Olympic Games there is no higher pinnacle of achievement, for some it matters not how this is achieved. If the Nazi contempt for weakness[48] had not been so close to the internal code of athleticism, the Olympic Games of 1936 would not have become such a perfect vehicle for Nazi propaganda.

Notes

1. The best overview in German is still R. Pfeiffer's *Sport und Politik: Die Boykottdiskussion um die Olympischen Spiele von Mexico City bis Moskau 1980 (Mit einem Exkurs zu den Spielen von Los Angeles 1984)* (Frankfurt: Lang, 1987).

2. J. Fauria Garcia, "Spain: Barcelona and the Popular Olympics," *Annual of CESH* 2 (2001): 119–29. The original vote that women's medals would carry the same weight as men's had been taken (against the vote of Coubertin) in 1914. See A. Krüger, "Forgotten Decisions: The IOC on the Eve of World War I," *Olympika* 6 (1997): 85–98.

3. Organisationskomitee für die XI. Olympischen Sommerspiele, ed., *Amtlicher Bericht*, vol. 1 (Berlin: Limpert, 1937), 56.

4. See P. Griffin, *The Politics of Irish Athletics, 1850–1990* (Ballinamore: Marathon, 1990), 116–

49. Similar decisions had to be taken by the German and Chinese Olympic Committees after World War II. See also R. Espy, *The Politics of the Olympic Games* (Berkeley: University of California Press, 1981).

5. "Palästina in das Olympische Komitee aufgenommen," *Jüdische Rundschau: Sportrundschau* 39.41–42 (May 25, 1934).

6. U. Simri, "Hapoel: Israel's Worker Sport Organization," in *The Story of Worker Sport,* ed. A. Krüger and J. Riordan (Champaign, Ill.: Human Kinetics, 1996), 157–66. If they had really wanted to participate they could have left their athletes in Berlin, which held international Jewish meets in June 1936. See also "Palästinensische Sportler in Berlin," *Jüdische Rundschau: Sportrundschau* 41.51 (June 26, 1936).

7. Letter of the Maccabi World Union to Baillet-Latour (Sept. 26, 1935), IOC Archives, Lausanne, Jeux Olympiques 1936, Question juive.

8. Ibid. (Nov. 20, 1935).

9. The exact number of Jewish athletes in the Games is disputed, as it depends upon one's definition of being "Jewish." The racial definition of the Nazis was broader than that of Jews themselves, while the religious and cultural definition is often too narrow. See P. Y. Meyer, *Jüdische Olympiasieger—Sport: Ein Sprungbrett für Minoritäten* (Kassel: Agon, 2000).

10. Baillet-Latour to S. Brodetzky (Nov. 20, 1935), IOC Archives, Lausanne, Jeux Olympiques 1936, Question juive (partially reprinted in O. Meyer, *A travers les anneaux olympiques* [Geneva: Caillet, 1960], 149). Baillet-Latour used "il," the male form, only.

11. J. Lichter, *Die Diskriminierung jüdischer Sportler in der Zeit des Nationalsozialismus* (Köln: Forschungsinstitut für Sozial- und Wirtschaftsgeschichte, 1992).

12. B. Postal, J. Silver, and R. Silver, eds., *Encyclopedia of Jews in Sport* (New York: Bloch, 1965), 339.

13. Twenty-one in four thousand had received special training privileges and had pledged the German Olympic oath to be in serious training for the fatherland. See H. Bernett, *Nationalsozialistische Leibeserziehung* (Schorndorf: Hofmann, 1971), 204ff.

14. A. Krüger, "'Wenn die Olympiade vorbei, schlagen wir die Juden zu Brei': Das Verhältnis der Juden zu den Olympischen Spielen von 1936," in *Menora 5: Jahrbuch für deutsch-jüdische Geschichte* (Munich: Piper, 1994), 331–48.

15. See *Presseberichte des Aussenpolitischen Amtes der NSDAP: Die Olympischen Winterspiele in der Kritik des Auslandes,* no. 13 (March 1936).

16. "Latein-Amerika," in *Die Olympiade Berlin 1936 im Spiegel des ausländichen Presse,* ed. J. Bellers (Münster: Lit, 1986), 127–38.

17. "India's Reply to Hitler's Insults: Bombay Students Demand Withdrawal from Berlin Olympic Games," *Bombay Chronicle,* Feb. 17, 1936.

18. J. Riordan, "Worker Sport within a Worker State: The Soviet Union," in Krüger and Riordan, *The Story of Worker Sport,* 43–66.

19. A. Gounot, "Die Rote Sportinternationale zwischen Komintern-Politik und den Ansprüchen des europäischen Arbeitersports" (Ph.D. diss., Freie Universität Berlin, 1998).

20. A. Krüger, "Neo-Olympismus zwischen Nationalismus und Internationalismus," in *Geschichte der Leibesübungen,* vol. 3, pt. 1, ed. H. Ueberhorst (Berlin: Bartels and Wernitz, 1980), 522–68; P. Cholley, *Pierre de Coubertin: La deuxième croisade* (Lausanne: IOC Museum, 1996).

21. See W. J. Murray, "The French Workers' Sports Federation and the Victory of the Popular Front in France," *International Journal of the History of Sport* 4.2 (1987): 203–30; and chapter 4 in this volume.

22. E. Box and J. Tolleneer, "'Hinter unserer Olympiade steckt ein anderer Gedanke': Die III. ArbeiterOlympiade 1937 in Antwerpen," *Sozial- und Zeitgeschichte des Sports* 2.1 (1988): 2842; K. Huhn, "Arbeiter Olympiade der Einheitsfront: Vor 50 Jahren trafen sich Arbeitersportler in Antwerpen," *Theorie und Praxis der Körperkultur* 36.3 (1987): 204–7; F. Nitsch, "Die III. Arbeiter Olympiade 1937 in Antwerpen: Problemaufriß. Literaturübersicht. Quellenstand," *Sozial- und Zeitgeschichte des Sports* 2.1 (1988): 1027.

23. X. Pujadas and C. Santacana, "Le mythe des Jeux Populaires de Barcelone," in *Les origines du sport ouvrier en Europe*, ed. P. Arnaud (Paris: L'Harmattan, 1994), 267–77.

24. See A. Mercé Varela, *Pierre de Coubertin* (Barcelona: Edition 62, 1992), 137–48.

25. A. Krüger, "Strength through Joy: The Culture of Consent under Fascism, Nazism, and Francoism," in *The International Politics of Sport in the Twentieth Century*, eds. J. Riordan and A. Krüger (London: Spon, 1999), 67–89; T. Gonzalez Aja, "Spanish Sports Policy in Republican and Fascist Spain," in *Sport and International Politics: The Impact of Fascism and Communism on Sport*, ed. P. Arnaud and J. Riordan (London: Spon, 1998), 97–113; J. Hargreaves, *Freedom for Catalonia? Catalan Nationalism, Spanish Identity, and the Barcelona Olympic Games* (Cambridge: Cambridge University Press, 2000).

26. H. J. Teichler, "Coubertin und das Dritte Reich," *Sportwissenschaft* 12.1 (1982): 18–55.

27. A. Krüger, "The Unfinished Symphony: A History of the Olympic Games from Coubertin to Samaranch," in Riordan and Krüger, *The International Politics of Sport in the Twentieth Century*, 3–27; J. M. Brohm, "Les idées réactionnaires du Baron Pierre de Coubertin," in J. M. Brohm, *Le mythe olympique* (Paris: Bourgois, 1981), 323–471. For the question of the Fascist potential in elite sports, see T. Tannsjö, "Is It Fascistoid to Admire Sports Heroes?" in T. Tannsjö and C. Tamburrini, eds., *Values in Sport: Elitism, Nationalism, Gender Equality, and the Scientific Manufacture of Winners* (London: Spon, 2000), 9–23.

28. *Le Journal*, Aug. 27, 1936.

29. Diem thus started to publish the *Olympische Rundschau* (Olympic review) from Berlin and received many of Coubertin's Olympic papers (which were destroyed in an air raid on Berlin in the night of September 3–4, 1943). See *Olympische Rundschau* 6.22 (1943): 18.

30. A. Krüger, "Forgotten Decisions: The IOC on the Eve of World War I," *Olympika* 6 (1997): 85–98.

31. See V. Burstyn, *The Rites of Men: Manhood, Politics, and the Culture of Sport* (Toronto: Toronto University Press, 1999).

32. See M. Czech, *Frauen und Sport: Eine Untersuchung zur Weiblichen Sportrealität in einem patriarchalischen Herrschaftssystem* (Berlin: Tischler, 1994).

33. See A. Fenner, "The First German 'Fräuleinwunder': Early Development of Women's Athletics in Germany," in *Gender and Sports from European Perspectives*, ed. E. Trangbaek and A. Krüger (Copenhagen: University Press, 1999), 97–114.

34. A. Krüger, "Breeding, Rearing, and Preparing the Aryan Body: Creating the Complete Superman the Nazi Way," *International Journal of the History of Sport* 16.2 (1999): 42–68.

35. A full biography of Mauermeyer has never been written. I spent a week in Greece together with her as part of a traveling symposium organized by the International Olympiade Union in the summer of 1981. Somebody (she would not say who) must have told her that I was a wild muckraking beast, as at first she was very reluctant to talk about her experiences until we found a common denominator in our common Olympic athletic experiences, though thirty-two years apart. For the situation in the United States, see S. E. Cayleff, *Babe: The Life and Legend of Babe Didrikson Zaharias* (Urbana: University of Illinois Press, 1995).

36. He published, for example, "Physiologie der Athletik," in *Athletik: Ein Handbuch der lebenswichtigen Leibesübungen*, ed. C. Krümmel (Munich: Lehmann, 1930), 71–83. This was a groundbreaking book in general coaching theory; however, it was edited by a confessed Nazi who later became head of all Nazi university physical education and sport in the Ministry of Education.

37. Hill to the Olympic Organizing Committee (Nov. 26, 1935), in Political Archive of the German Foreign Office [Auswärtiges Amt], Bonn, Ref. Deutschland, Olympiade 1936, Boykott, Az. 86–26, vol. 3.

38. The information comes from the parliamentary debate. See *Compte-rendu des séances de l'Assemblée d'états du Grand-Duché de Luxembourg* (Luxembourg: Imprimerie d'état, 1936–37), 745–49.

39. Ibid., 748.

40. Ibid., 755.

41. K. A. Scherer, *75 Olympische Jahre* (Munich: ProSport, 1971). This was the official publication of the West German Olympic Committee.

42. G. Sudholt, *60 Jahre Olympiaort Garmisch-Partenkirchen* (Berg am See: VGB, 1996).

43. "Die Olympiade 1936 und die Juden: Aus den Nürnberger Akten," *Die Neue Demokratie im Bild* 3.16 (1948): 6. For the creation of the culture of consent in sports, see A. Krüger, "Strength through Joy."

44. A. Krüger, "Hundert Jahre und kein Ende? Postmoderne Anmerkungen zu den Olympischen Spielen," in *Körper, Kultur, und Ideologie: Sport und Zeitgeist im 19. und 20. Jahrhundert*, ed. I. Diekmann and J. H. Teichler (Bodenheim: Philo, 1997), 277–300; H. Preuss, *Ökonomische Implikationen der Ausrichtung Olympischer Spiele von München 1972 bis Atlanta 1996* (Kassel: Agon, 1999).

45. A. D. Morse, *While Six Million Died: A Chronicle of American Apathy* (London: Secker and Warburg, 1968), 172–86.

46. W. Buss, S. Güldenpfennig, and A. Krüger, "Geschichts-, kultur-, sport(politik)- und wissenschaftstheoretische Grundannahmen—sowie daraus resultierende Leitfragen für die Forschung," *Sozial- und Zeitgeschichte des Sports* 13.1 (1999): 65–74.

47. G. McFee and A. Tomlinson, "Riefenstahl's *Olympia*: Ideology and Aesthetics in the Shaping of the Aryan Athletic Body," *International Journal of the History of Sport* 16.2 (1999): 86–106.

48. H. Ofstad, *Our Contempt for Weakness: Nazi Norms and Values—And Our Own* (Gotheburg: Almquist and Wiksell, 1989).

Appendix

Olympic Summer Games, August 1–16, 1936

Participating Nations[a]	Participants[b]			Medals Won		
	Male	Female		Gold	Silver	Bronze
Afghanistan	13	—		—	—	—
Argentina	50	—		2	1	2
Australia	28	4		—	—	1
Austria	166	17		3	7	3
Belgium	116	5		—	—	2
Bermuda	5	—		—	—	—
Bolivia	1	—		—	—	—
Brazil	66	6		—	—	—
Bulgaria	24	—		—	—	—
Canada	78	17		1	3	5
Chile	39	1		—	—	—
China	52	2		—	—	—
Colombia	6	—		—	—	—
Costa Rica	1	—		—	—	—
Czechoslovakia	150	13		3	5	—
Denmark	101	15		—	2	3
Egypt	53	—		2	2	3
Estonia	33	—		2	2	3
Finland	102	5		7	6	6
France	189	11		7	6	6
Germany	364	42		33	26	30
Great Britain	168	37		4	7	3
Greece	40	1		—	—	—
Hungary	193	18		10	1	5
Iceland	12	—		—	—	—
India	27	—		1	—	—
Indonesia	27	—		—	—	—
Italy	184	13		8	9	5
Japan	138	16		6	4	8

Participating Nations[a]	Participants[b]		Medals Won		
	Male	Female	Gold	Silver	Bronze
Latvia	24	—	—	1	1
Liechtenstein	6	—	—	—	—
Luxembourg	44	—	—	—	—
Malta	11	—	—	—	—
Mexico	32	—	—	—	3
Monaco	6	—	—	—	—
Netherlands	110	19	6	4	7
New Zealand	7	—	1	—	—
Norway	69	2	1	3	2
Peru	40	—	—	—	—
Philippines	28	—	—	—	1
Poland	100	11	—	3	3
Portugal	19	—	—	—	1
Romania	50	2	—	1	—
South Africa	25	—	—	1	—
Sweden	143	8	6	5	9
Switzerland	174	5	1	9	5
Turkey	47	2	1	—	1
United States	290	40	24	20	12
Uruguay	37	—	—	—	—
Yugoslavia	77	10	—	—	—
	3,738	328			

Sources: Based on statistics reported in E. Kamper's *Enzyklopädie des Olympischen Spiele* (Dortmund: Harenberg, 1972) and W. Lyberg's *Fabulous One Hundred Years of the IOC: Facts, Figures, and Much, Much More* (Lausanne: International Olympic Committee, 1996).

Notes: Other figures of interest include: spectators = 3,770,000; foreign journalists = 700 (representing 593 foreign media outlets, including 55 German speakers); German journalists = 1,000 (from 225 different media outlets); wire services = 15; wire service journalists = 150; foreign radio stations = 41 (from 41 countries); radio technicians = 450; official photographs taken by German photographers = 15,950.

a. Participating nations = 49.

b. Total participants = 4,166.

Olympic Winter Games, February 6–16, 1936

Participating Nations[a]	Number of Athletes	Medals Won		
		Gold	Silver	Bronze
Australia	1	—	—	—
Austria	87	1	1	2
Belgium	27	—	—	—
Bulgaria	7	—	—	—
Canada	29	—	1	—
Czechoslovakia	58	—	—	—
Estonia	5	—	—	—
Finland	23	1	2	3
France	32	—	—	1
Germany	77	3	3	—
Great Britain	38	1	1	1
Greece	1	—	—	—
Hungary	25	—	—	1
Italy	44	—	—	—
Japan	31	—	—	—
Latvia	26	—	—	—
Liechtenstein	4	—	—	—
Luxemburg	4	—	—	—
Netherlands	8	—	—	—
Norway	31	7	5	3
Poland	24	—	—	—
Romania	15	—	—	—
Spain	6	—	—	—
Sweden	36	2	2	3
Switzerland	38	1	2	—
Turkey	6	—	—	—
United States	55	1	—	3
Yugoslavia	17	—	—	—
	755[b]			

Sources: Based on statistics reported in V. Kluge's *Winter Olympia Kompakt: Daten, Fakten, Hintergründe der Olympischen Winterspiele von 1924–1992* (Berlin: Sportverlag, 1992) and W. Lyberg's *Fabulous One Hundred Years of the IOC: Facts, Figures, and Much, Much More* (Lausanne: International Olympic Committee, 1996).

Notes: Other figures of interest include: spectators = 543,156; journalists = 498 (from 29 countries); members of the press = 403; radio personnel = 49; photographers = 46 (Germans only).

a. Participating nations = 28.

b. Males = 675; females = 80.

Bibliographic Essay

Arnd Krüger and William Murray

The endnotes to the various chapters in this book give a detailed summary of works in particular countries in regard to the 1936 Olympic Games. What follows is a more general guide.

In contrast to books on Hitler and the Third Reich, where publications in English dwarf those in German, the vast amount of works on Nazi sport and the 1936 Olympic Games in particular have been published in German. This flow of constant research had been started and was strongly influenced by the late Hajo Bernett. His publications began only when all of the major actors of the 1936 Games had died, with the lengthy documentation *Nationalsozialistische Leibeserziehung: Eine Dokumentation ihrer Theorie und Organisation* (Schorndorf: Hofmann, 1966). He followed this up by looking at the archives of Hitler and his Chancellery in *Sportpolitik im 3. Reich* (Schorndorf: Hofmann, 1971). Later he was more concerned with different topics, which included *Der Weg des Sports in die nationalsozialistische Diktatur* (Schorndorf: Hofmann, 1983) and such things as sport journalism: "Sportpublizistik im totalitären Staat, 1933–1945," *Stadion* 11 (1985): 263–95.

Richard Mandell's *The Nazi Olympics* (Rpt., Urbana: University of Illinois Press, 1987) was a landmark in English when it first appeared in 1971; since then there have been many books and articles in English and other languages exploring the topic. Arnd Krüger's *Die Olympischen Spiele 1936 und die Weltmeinung* (Berlin: Bartels and Wernitz, 1972) was the first to cover world public opinion and what the Nazis did to orchestrate it. This book was based on the archival sources of the German Foreign Office and made extensive use of the IOC archives. The same author also presented a biography of *Dr. Theodor Lewald: Sportführer ins Dritte Reich* (Berlin: Bartels and Wernitz, 1975), the president of the Berlin Organizing Committee, while Allen Guttmann explored the personality of Avery Brundage in *The Games Must Go On: Avery Brundage and the Olympic Movement* (New York: Columbia University Press, 1984) and Bill Baker that of *Jesse Owens: An American Life* (New York: Free Press, 1986), the two major American actors on the Olympic stage. George Eisen, in "The Voices of Sanity: American Diplomatic Reports from the 1936 Berlin Olympiad," *Journal of Sport History* 11.3 (1984): 56–78, and Stephen R. Wenn, in "A Tale of Two Diplomats: George S. Messersmith and Charles H. Sherrill on Proposed American Participation in the 1936 Olympics," *Journal of Sport History* 16.1 (1989): 27–43, and "A Suitable Policy of Neutrality? FDR and the Question of American Participation in the 1936 Olympics," *International Journal of the History of Sport* 8.3 (1991): 319–35, demonstrates the opposing political options in the American administration and the public. The role of the German-American community is analyzed by W. Gray and R. K. Barney in "Devotion to Whom? German-American Loyalty on the Issue of Participation in the 1936 Olympic Games," *Journal of Sport History* 17.2 (1990): 214–31.

David K. Wiggins, "The 1936 Olympic Games in Berlin: The Response of America's Black Press," *Research Quarterly for Exercise and Sport* 54.3 (1983): 279–82, gives a brief account of the ambiguous situation of the African American community as regards the Nazi Olympics, which gave them a chance to show their rightful place in the world of sport—although they sometimes had to travel far and leave the South to qualify for the U.S. team in the first place. This was one of the arguments that Brundage employed to convince the American sporting public to send a team to Nazi Germany. His campaign is highlighted in Krüger's "'Fair Play for American Athletes': A Study in Anti-Semitism," *Canadian Journal of the History of Sport and Physical Education* 9.1 (1978): 42–57, which makes use for the first time of the Avery Brundage archives. These archives are now housed in the University of Illinois at Urbana-Champaign and are masterfully maintained by Maynard Brichford. See Brichford's *Avery Brundage Collection, 1908–1975* (Schorndorf: Hofmann, 1977); Brichford has also published a long series of articles dealing with Brundage and many aspects of American and international sports. He has ensured that Brundage's will is strictly adhered to, and thus a microfilm version of much of the Avery Brundage Collection has received a free and liberal distribution and is now available in a number of centers around the world.

The question of anti-Semitism is at the forefront of the American Jewish position, which is examined in Moshe Gottlieb's "The American Controversy over the Olympic Games," *American Jewish Historical Quarterly* 61 (1972): 181–213, and Allen Guttmann's "The 'Nazi Olympics' and the American Boycott Controversy," in *Sport and International Politics: The Impact of Fascism and Communism on Sport,* ed. P. Arnaud and J. Riordan (London: Spon, 1998), 31–50. For a well-composed history of Jewish sport in the United States, refer to S. A. Riess, ed., *Sports and the American Jew* (Syracuse, N.Y.: Syracuse University Press, 1998), and P. Levine, *Ellis Island to Ebbets Field: Sport and the American Jewish Experience* (Oxford: Oxford University Press, 1992). The German Jewish side is highlighted in Krüger, "'Once the Olympics Are Through, We'll Beat Up the Jew': German Jewish Sport 1898–1938 and the Anti-Semitic Discourse," *Journal of Sport History* 26.2 (1999): 353–75. Krüger's "'Sieg Heil' to the Most Glorious Era of German Sport: Continuity and Change in the Modern German Sports Movement," *International Journal of the History of Sport* 4.1 (1987): 5–20, and "The Role of Sport in German International Politics, 1918–1945," in *Sport and International Politics: The Impact of Fascism and Communism on Sport,* ed. P. Arnaud and J. Riordan (London: Spon, 1998), 79–96, put Nazi sport in the wider perspective of sport and politics in Germany. The context of the breeding of the Nazi "superman" is emphasized in Krüger's "Breeding, Rearing, and Preparing the Aryan Body: Creating the Complete Superman the Nazi Way," *International Journal of the History of Sport* 16.2 (1999): 42–68.

For a comparative analysis of race relations in the United States and Germany (including sport), consult N. Finzsch and D. Schirmer, eds., *Identity and Intolerance: Nationalism, Racism, and Xenophobia in Germany and the United States* (Cambridge: Cambridge University Press, 1998). Other good background material can be found in Duff Hart-Davis, *Hitler's Games: The 1936 Olympics* (London: Century, 1986), which takes the British perspective, while

Françoise Hache, "La place du sport dans le système national-socialiste" (Doctorat nouveau régime, 87/PA08/0050), J.-M. Brohm, *Jeux olympiques à Berlin* (Brussels: Ed. Complexe, 1983), and Josef Schmidt, "Evénement fasciste et spectacle moderne: Les Jeux Olympiques de Berlin en 1936," in *Masses et Culture de Masse dans les années trente,* ed. Régine Robin (Paris: Ed. Ouvrières, 1983), 163–79, take the French perspective.

The best overview of the ideological background of Nazi sport as an Aryan cult can be found in a special edition of the *International Journal of the History of Sport* 16.2 (1999). H. J. Teichler has analyzed the Nazi Olympics as a part of internal Nazi propaganda in "Berlin 1936—Ein Sieg der NS Propaganda?" *Stadion* 2 (1976): 265–306, and as part of Nazi foreign policy in *Internationale Sportpolitik im Dritten Reich* (Schorndorf: Hofmann, 1991). John M. Hoberman has put elite sport and the Olympic Games in a number of important contexts that are a useful setting in which to understand the Olympic crisis of 1936; see *The Olympic Crisis: Sports, Politics, and the Moral Order* (New Rochelle, N.Y.: Caratzas, 1986), *Sport and Political Ideology* (Austin: University of Texas Press, 1984), *Mortal Engines: The Science of Performance and the Dehumanization of Sport* (New York: Free Press, 1992), and *Darwin's Athletes: How Sport Has Damaged Black America and Preserved the Myth of Race* (Boston: Houghton Mifflin, 1997).

Two overviews of literature on the 1936 Games came out some years ago. For works mainly in German, see Arnd Krüger's "Puzzle Solving: German Sport Historiography of the Eighties," *Journal of Sport History* 17.2 (1990): 261–77, and in English, Bill Murray, "Berlin 1936: Old and New Works on the Nazi Olympics," *International Journal of the History of Sport* 9.1 (1992): 29–49.

Anniversaries of the Nazi Olympics have noticeably resulted in publications dealing with the Games, and on the occasion of the sixtieth anniversary in 1996 two superb exhibitions were held: one by the Holocaust Museum in Washington, D.C., and another by the Stiftung Topographie des Terrors in Berlin. These provided further insights into the Games and the international interest in them. They show that with international cooperation and sufficient budgets it is still possible to have a better understanding of what was planned at the time and how the international public reacted. The best publication that has come out of this is the bilingual catalogue of the exhibition, *The Olympic Games and National Socialism,* ed. Reinhard Rürup (Berlin: Argon, 1996), which, like the exhibition it was prepared for, also contains many previously unseen photographs and a useful bibliography. This was the result of two years of extensive research by Helga Woggon. Unfortunately, no catalogue was published for the exhibit in the Holocaust Museum, but a review of it can be found in Patrick B. Miller, "The Nazi Olympics, Berlin, 1936: Exhibition at the U.S. Holocaust Memorial Museum, Washington, D.C.," *Olympika* 5 (1996): 127–40. For the political background in the field of sport and politics in the 1930s in Europe, with special reference to the workers' side and for a full bibliography of such works, see Arnd Krüger and James Riordan, eds., *The Story of Worker Sport* (Champaign, Ill.: Human Kinetics, 1996).

In the three decades since 1971, ways of looking at the Nazi Olympics have been modified significantly. While originally there was much more concern for the political meaning of the event, for its social and political context, emphasis has changed toward the interpretation of images, to methods for achieving hegemony and a "culture of consent." The best book that puts the imagery of the 1936 Olympic Games into the proper context is Thomas Alkemeyer, *Körper, Kult und Politik: Von der "Muskelreligion" Pierre de Coubertins zur Inszenierung der Macht in den Olympischen Spielen von 1936* (Frankfurt/M.: Campus, 1996). Hans Bonde has put some of this in a Nordic context in "The Nordic Body: The Vision of an Aryan-Germanic

Body Culture, 1933–1939," *Sozial- und Zeitgeschichte des Sports* 13.2 (1999): 41–58. Cooper C. Graham, in *Leni Riefenstahl and Olympia* (Metuchen, N.J.: Scarecrow, 1986), explores the production and images in the Riefenstahl movie. This in itself has become an icon of the Nazi cult of the body and the shrewd utilization of such images. Riefenstahl, who turned one hundred in 2002, is still active in defending her artistic work during the Nazi period. For a recent critical review, see L. Kinkel, *Die Scheinwerferin: Leni Riefenstahl und das 3. Reich* (München: Europa, 2002). Her own account is in L. Riefenstahl, *Memoiren* (München: Knaus, 1987).

At the other end of the research spectrum there have been several biographies of particular individuals who played a role in the Games or just happened to be there. These publications will eventually also help us to better understand not only what messages the Nazis encoded within their Games but how these were understood by sport leaders and the media as well as individuals. Most of this new generation of literature still comes out of Germany and is in most cases written in German. On the female competitors, see Michaela Czech, *Frauen und Sport im Nationalsozialistischen Deutschland: Eine Untersuchung zur weiblichen Sportrealität in einem patriarchalen Herrschaftssystem* (Berlin: Tischler, 1994); Czech interviewed twelve women participants in the 1936 Games. The story of the flag bearer of the German team in 1936 shows the context of the German state amateur: Arnd Krüger, "Der Fahnenträger: Hans Fritsch (1911–1987)," in *Aus Biographien Sportgeschichte lernen*, ed. A. Krüger and B. Wedemeyer (Hoya: NISH, 2000), 252–71. Although he did not participate in the 1936 Games, the story of Dr. Otto Peltzer, a world record holder and the best German half-miler of the 1920s and 1930s, shows the normative pressure of the sports system—Nazi or otherwise—on this allegedly homosexual athlete: Volker Kluge, *Otto der Seltsame: Die Einsamkeit eines Mittelstreckenläufers, 1900–1970* (Berlin: Parthas, 2000). The international connections of the Nazi sports leaders and their path from imperial Germany, via democratic Weimar, through the Nazi period into the Federal Republic becomes most obvious in the life of Karl Ritter von Halt, which has been published recently by Peter Heimerzheim, *Karl Ritter von Halt—Leben zwischen Sport und Politik* (St. Augustin: Academia, 1999). Whereas in German there have been several biographies of Nazi sports administrators, this is still a wide open field in English. Biographies of administrators like Carl Diem and athletes like Gretel Bergmann and Helene Mayer are yet to be written. A. Laude and W. Bausch, *Der Sport-Führer: Die Legende um Carl Diem* (Göttingen: Werkstatt, 2000), and Paul Yogi Meyer, *Jüdische Olympiasieger—Sport: Ein Sprungbrett für Minoritäten* (Kassel: Agon, 2000), are a modest beginning in German. For a fascinating account of the importance of the Berlin Olympics as seen by a young Jewish boy who would emigrate and become one of the world's great intellectual historians, see Peter Gay (Peter Frohlich), *My German Question: Growing Up in Nazi Berlin* (New Haven, Conn.: Yale University Press, 1998).

For the reactions to the Nazi Olympics in countries not covered in this book, see Bruce Kidd, "Canadian Opposition to the 1936 Olympics in Germany," *Canadian Journal of the History of Sport* 9.2 (1978): 20–40; Ian Jobling, "Australia at the 1936 Olympics: Issues and Controversies," *Canadian Journal of the History of Sport* 13.1 (1982): 18–27; Jean-Claude Bussard, "Les jeux de 1936 dans la presse suisse de langue française," in *The Olympic Games through the Ages: Greek Antiquity and Its Impact on Modern Sport*, ed. Roland Renson et al. (Athens: Hellenic Sports Research Institute, 1991), 357–70; Janusz Slusarcyk and Piotr Halemba, "Press Reaction to the 1936 Olympic Summer Games in the Polish and Upper Silesian Press," Juan Fauria Garcia, "Spain, Barcelona, and the Popular Olympics," Marek Waic, "Czechoslovakia and the Sudeten German Question," Erwin Niedermann, "Austria," and translations from the press reports of the German Foreign Office about Hungary, Poland,

and Czechoslovakia, all in the *Annual of CESH* 2 (2001): 77–129. These give quite extensive coverage. See also V. Zonkov, "Sport und Politik am Beispiel der Spiele an der XI. Olympiade in Deutschland 1936, nach Materialien von der bulgarischen Presse," in *Sport und Politik, 1918–39/40,* ed. Morgan Olsen (Oslo: Universitetsforlaget, 1986), 126–34; and J. Janaušek, "Boj proti usporadani olympijskych her Berline v roce 1936," in *Teorie a Praxe Telesne Vychovy* 24.8 (1976): 451–56. These articles are rather rigidly ideological and suffer as a consequence. On Belgium, see the short account by Roland Renson and Paul Janssens, "The 1936 Berlin Olympic Games and Their Reception in the Belgian Press," in *Proceedings of the XI HISPA International Congress,* ed. J. A. Mangan (Glasgow: Jordanhill College, 1987), 315–19.

The stories behind the Games are as colorful as the countries marching into the Olympic Stadium at the opening and closing ceremonies of the Games. As such, they present opportunities for further works, which we hope this modest bibliography will encourage.

Contributors

MATTI GOKSØYR, Ph.D., is a professor of sport history at the Norwegian University of Sport and Physical Education in Oslo. He has published extensively on Scandinavian sports and politics in the twentieth century and is a fellow of the European Committee for the History of Sports.

GIGLIOLA GORI, Ph.D., is a professor of the history of sport in the Department of Sport Studies at the University of Urbino, Italy. She has published on physical education and sport mainly on twentieth-century Italy and is a member of the executive board of the International Society for the History of Physical Education and Sport and a fellow of the European Committee for the History of Sports.

JØRN HANSEN, Ph.D., is an associate professor in the sport department at the University of Odense, Denmark. He specializes in the history of sport, particularly on Scandinavia in the nineteenth and twentieth centuries.

RICHARD HOLT, Ph.D., is a professor of sport history at De Monfort University in Leicester, England. He has also taught at the University of Stirling and the Catholic University of Leuven, Belgium. He is a distinguished writer on French and British sport history and a fellow of the European Committee for the History of Sports.

ARND KRÜGER, Ph.D., is a professor of sport science and head of the Sport and Society Section at Georg-August Universität in Göttingen, Germany. He has published extensively on various aspects of international sport and has served as president of the European Committee for the History of Sports.

LEENA LAINE, lic. phil., is a researcher with the Finnish Society of Sport History. She was a teacher of sport history at the University of Tampere, is a member of the executive board of the International Society for the History of Physical Education and Sport, and has published widely on Scandinavian sport history and women's studies.

WILLIAM MURRAY, Ph.D., is a reader in history at La Trobe University, Victoria, Australia. He specializes in French history and has published several books on association football and articles on the politics of sport and society in the twentieth century. He is a fellow of the European Committee for the History of Sports.

TETSUO NAKAMURA, Ph.D., is a professor of education at Mie University, Japan. He specializes in modern sport history.

ANDRÉ SWIJTINK, Ph.D., teaches history at a Dutch high school. He wrote his doctoral dissertation on physical education and sport in the Netherlands between the two world wars, which was also the subject of his book *In de Pas*.

LARS-OLOF WELANDER, Ph.D., is an archivist with the Riksarkivet of Sweden in Stockholm. He specializes in twentieth-century Sweden.

Index

Sport and Society

The University of Illinois Press
is a founding member of the
Association of American University Presses.

Composed in 10.5/12.5 Adobe Minion
with Fenice display
by Jim Proefrock
at the University of Illinois Press
Manufactured by The Maple-Vail
Book Manufacturing Group

University of Illinois Press
1325 South Oak Street
Champaign, IL 61820-6903
www.press.uillinois.edu